WHEN
PARIS WENT
DARK

WHEN PARIS WENT DARK

THE CITY OF LIGHT
UNDER GERMAN OCCUPATION,
1940–1944

RONALD C. ROSBOTTOM

LITTLE, BROWN AND COMPANY

New York   Boston   London

Little, Brown and Company
Hachette Book Group
237 Park Avenue
New York, NY 10017
littlebrown.com

First Edition: August 2014

Maps by Lu Yi

Little, Brown and Company is a division of Hachette Book Group, Inc. The Little, Brown name and logo are trademarks of Hachette Book Group, Inc.

The publisher is not responsible for websites (or their content) that are not owned by the publisher.

The Hachette Speakers Bureau provides a wide range of authors for speaking events. To find out more, go to hachettespeakersbureau.com or call (866) 376-6591.

ISBN 978-0-316-21744-6
LCCN 2014938425

10 9 8 7 6 5 4 3 2

RRD-C

Printed in the United States of America

*For my wife, Betty, whose love and wisdom have
sheltered and nurtured me since we first met at
Mont Saint-Michel many years ago;*

and

*For my dear son, Michael, and his loving wife,
Heidi, who gave us Edith and Griffin, truly grand children,
with gratitude for their love and laughter;*

and

For my brother Tim, and in memory of our brother Steedy

Contents

Contents

Chronology of the Occupation
of Paris

1939

September 3: France and Great Britain declare war on Germany

September 5: United States announces its neutrality

Winter 1939–40: "Phony war" (*drôle de guerre*); Russo-Finnish War

1940

April: Anglo-Russian expedition to Norway; Germany occupies Norway

April 3: Prison sentences for former French Communist deputies

May 10: Beginning of German western offensive; Winston Churchill named prime minister of Great Britain

May 15: French prime minister Paul Reynaud informs Churchill by phone: "We've lost the battle"

May 18: Reynaud announces appointment of Maréchal Philippe Pétain as vice president of Council of Ministers

May 25: Charles de Gaulle given battlefield promotion to brigadier general

May 28: Belgium capitulates, to surprise of Allies

June 4: End of evacuation of Allied troops begun on May 24 from Dunkirk

June 5: Retreating French soldiers begin to appear in Paris; Reynaud names de Gaulle undersecretary for war and national defense

June 10: French government leaves Paris; Italy declares war on France and Great Britain

June 12: Paris officially declared "open"; US ambassador William Bullitt essentially "mayor" of Paris with prefect of police Roger Langeron

June 14: First German troops enter Paris

June 16: Reynaud resigns as prime minister

June 17: Pétain named president of Council of Ministers; requests an armistice

June 18: First radio speech to France by de Gaulle from London

June 22: Armistice signed at Compiègne

June 25: Armistice officially begins

June 28: Hitler's only visit to Paris; British government recognizes de Gaulle as head of the "Free French"

June 1940–November 1942: Göring will visit Paris and the Jeu de Paume museum twenty-five times during this period

July 3: Great Britain attacks and devastates French fleet at Mers-el-Kébir in Algeria

July 11–12: Third Republic votes itself out of existence; a new État français is established, with Pétain as its chief executive and Pierre Laval as vice president of the Council of Ministers and his designated successor

July 17: Vichy passes law that forbids employment for those not born of French parents

July 22: Vichy examines post-1927 naturalizations of five hundred thousand French citizens

August 7: Alsace-Lorraine officially annexed to Germany

August 8: Beginning of Battle of Britain

August 13: Vichy abolishes anti-Semitism laws, dissolves "secret societies," aimed principally at Freemasonry; Germans forbid Jews to reenter Occupied Zone

September 12: First German announcement of hostage policy (hostages will be imprisoned or executed if violent actions are taken against German personnel)

September 17: First rationing of essential food products in Paris announced; appearance of *cartes de rationnement*

September 27: Jewish-owned shops must carry yellow signs bearing the words ENTREPRISE JUIVE (eleven thousand complied by late November); census of Jews by French police (under German orders) begins

October 3: First German edict against Jews in occupied France; first Gaullist tags discovered on Parisian walls

October 5: First roundup of French Communists in Paris, by Vichy police

October 12: Hitler postpones indefinitely the invasion of England

October 18: Publication of Vichy edict of October 3–4 forbidding Jewish ownership and management of enterprises and excluding Jews from the army and professions

October 22: Hitler and Pierre Laval meet for first time at Montoire, in France

October 24: Pétain and Hitler meet at Montoire, their only meeting

October 30: Pétain's "path of collaboration" speech

November 5: Roosevelt reelected for a third term

November 11 *Lycéens* **demonstrate in Paris**

December 13: Pétain fires Pierre Laval; Admiral François Darlan will be his successor

December 15: Ashes of Duke of Reichstadt (the King of Rome, a.k.a. Napoleon II) brought to Paris from Vienna

1941

February: Arrest of members of first important resistance group, known as the Musée de l'Homme network because most members worked at that institution; six would be executed in early 1942

February 14: Veit Harlan's strongly anti-Semitic film, *Le Juif Süss*, opens in Paris cinemas

March 29: Creation by Vichy government of the Commissariat Général aux Questions Juives, aimed at coordinating repression of Jews in France

April 26: Third Vichy law regarding Jews forbids them from trading their possessions with Aryans; Jewish bank accounts frozen

May 8: Ordinance listing professions forbidden to Jews is enacted

May 14: First *rafle* (roundup) of Parisian Jews (ca. 3,700, mostly Polish) is conducted

June 21: Exclusion of Jewish students from universities and other professional schools

June 22: Operation Barbarossa: German invasion of USSR

July 16: Jews excluded from legal profession

July 22: All Jewish bank accounts seized; vaults, safe-deposit boxes opened

August 8: Jews excluded from medical professions

August 13: Jews forbidden to have radios

August 14: French Communist Party outlawed; manifestations against Occupation begin to appear

August 20–23: Second *rafle* of Parisian Jews (4,300 arrested on German orders) takes place, in 11th arrondissement

August 21 and 28: First German serviceman, Alfons Moser, assassinated in a public place: "Colonel Fabien," a *résistant,* kills him at the Barbès-Rochechouart Métro stop; thirteen hostages executed at Mont-Valérien, outside Paris, where there would be many such executions over the next four years

August 29: First Free French (Gaullist) agent, Honoré d'Estienne d'Orves, shot by Germans at Mont-Valérien

September 5: Opening of exhibition *Le Juif et la France* (will run until June of 1942)

November 21: Bomb explodes in a Left Bank bookstore that features German publications; probably set by Tommy Elek of the Manouchian Group

December 8: United States declares war on Axis powers (Germany, Japan, Italy)

December 10: Jews not allowed to change domicile; word JUIF or JUIVE must be stamped in red on ID cards

December 15: Germans arrest 743 affluent French Jews in Paris

1942

January 20: Clandestine publication of Vercors's *Silence of the Sea*

February: Relegation of Jews to last Métro cars; Jews forbidden to leave home between 8:00 p.m. and 6:00 a.m.

March 1: Opening of *Le Bolchévisme contre l'Europe* exhibition in Paris

March 3–4: Allies bomb Boulogne-Billancourt, suburb of Paris where Renault factory is located

March 27: First deportation of French Jews to Auschwitz from Drancy

April 18: Pétain reappoints Laval as vice president of the Council of Ministers—in effect, the prime minister

May: Drancy, outside Paris, becomes a major collecting point for deportation to Auschwitz; more than five hundred hostages have been shot since Moser's assassination in August of 1941; Jews forbidden to possess bicycles

May 5: SS general Reinhard Heydrich visits Paris to introduce SS general Carl Oberg to the Occupation authorities; police matters removed from army control and put under German police control; French police put under German command

May 15: Arno Breker (Hitler's favorite sculptor) exhibition opens at l'Orangerie in Paris

June 25: Thousands of Jews sent from Drancy to Auschwitz; also ten thousand from Unoccupied Zone delivered to Nazis

June: *La Relève,* a call by the Vichy government for volunteers to work in Germany in exchange for French prisoners of war (three workers for one prisoner); weak response

End June: Adolf Eichmann in Paris to coordinate "final solution" there

July 16–17: *Grande Rafle* (27,000 foreign Jews sought; 13,200 rounded up)

July 21–25: Arrest of Jewish orphans (of deported, escaped parents)

July 28: Camus's *The Stranger* (*L'Étranger*) appears

August: Jews forbidden to have telephones

August 6: Inauguration of Paris's new Musée d'Art Moderne

August 26: Arrest of 6,600 foreign Jews in Unoccupied Zone

September 14: Beginning of Battle of Stalingrad

November 11: Germans occupy *Zone libre* (Unoccupied Zone) after Allied invasion of North Africa

November 27: French navy sabotages its fleet in the port of Toulon

1943

January 11: Thirty Métro stations closed

January 30: Milice française established (right-wing militia of Vichy government)

February 2: Surrender of German marshal Friedrich von Paulus and his armies at Stalingrad

February 16: Vichy establishes Service du travail obligatoire (STO), obligatory draft of young workers for Germany

April 4: Outskirts of Paris heavily bombed

May 27: Establishment of the Conseil national de la Résistance, organized under Gaullist leadership; most resistance groups had theretofore acted independently

June 21: Arrest of Jean Moulin, de Gaulle's chief negotiator with all resistance groups; he would die after having been extensively tortured

June 25: Sartre's massive philosophical work *Being and Nothingness* appears

July: About six hundred examples of *art dégénéré* burned in Jeu de Paume garden

November: Arrest of the Manouchian Group, a resistance network

December 15: All French citizens must have *cartes d'identité*

1944

February: Trial of Manouchian Group; twenty-two executed

March 8: Berr family arrested

March 27: Hélène Berr deported on her birthday

April 26: Pétain visits Paris for first—and last—time as *chef de l'État français*

June 6: Allies invade Normandy

July: Operation Valkyrie (assassination plot against Hitler by dissident elements of German army)

August 17: Laval's last Council of Ministers meeting at the Hôtel Matignon in Paris; SS officer Alois Brunner leaves Drancy on a train with fifty-one deportees; 1,386 Jews at Drancy survived after Brunner's departure (of 75,700 Jews deported from France, 97 percent died in Auschwitz and other camps)

August 19–25: Battle for liberation of Paris

August 22: De Gaulle's first meeting with his Council of Ministers in Paris

Major Personalities

Parisian and French

Berthe Auroy: Retired Parisian schoolteacher

Simone de Beauvoir: Novelist and essayist

Hélène Berr: Jewish teenager

Brassaï: Photographer

Jean Bruller (aka Vercors): Author and *résistant*

Albert Camus: Author and clandestine editor

Jacques Chirac: Fifth president of the French Fifth Republic, 1995–2007

Jean Cocteau: Poet, dramatist, and filmmaker

Colette: Novelist and journalist

Marguerite Duras: Writer and *résistante*

Charles de Gaulle: Leader of the Free French; first president of the Fifth Republic

Benoîte and Flora Groult: Novelists and journalists; sisters

Jean Guéhenno: Lycée instructor; diarist

François Hollande: Seventh president of the French Fifth Republic, 2012–

Dominique Jamet: Commentator who writes about his youth in occupied Paris

Vivienne Jamet: Bordello madam; no relation to Dominique

Maurice Jouhandeau: Pro-Vichy author and professor

Sarah Kofman: Philosopher and memoirist

Roger Langeron: Prefect of Paris police when Germans arrived

Pierre Laval: Two-time president of Council of Ministers under Pétain

Philippe Leclerc de Hauteclocque: Commanded Deuxième Division Blindée (Second Armored Division), which helped liberate Paris

Jacques Lusseyran: Blind teenager who ran one of the largest resistance groups

Missak Manouchian: Resistance leader; born in Armenia

François Mitterrand: Fourth president of the French Fifth Republic (1981–95), early member of Vichy government and later a *résistant*

Guy Môquet: Teenage *résistant*

Philippe Pétain: President of the État français (Vichy); hero of Verdun (World War I)

Georges Pompidou: Second president of the French Fifth Republic (1969–1974)

Henri Rol-Tanguy: Communist and leader of the Free French Forces at the Liberation

Nicolas Sarkozy: Sixth president of the French Fifth Republic (2007–12)

Jean-Paul Sartre: Philosopher

Liliane Schroeder: Parisian memoirist

Françoise Siefridt: Parisian teenager

Jean Texcier: Journalist

Jacques Yonnet: Writer and *résistant*

André Zucca: Photographer

German

Otto Abetz: Third Reich's ambassador to France

Arno Breker: Sculptor

Dietrich von Choltitz: Commander of Paris at the Liberation

Joseph Goebbels: Head of Reich's Ministry of Public Enlightenment and Propaganda

Hermann Göring: Head of the Luftwaffe; heir apparent to Hitler

Felix Hartlaub: Historian and soldier assigned to Paris

Gerhard Heller: Propaganda bureaucrat in Paris

Adolf Hitler: Tourist

Ernst Jünger: Novelist and aide-de-camp to military administrator of Paris

Friedrich Sieburg: Author of *Gott in Frankreich?* (To Live Like God in France)

Albert Speer: Hitler's architect and city planner

Hans Speidel: Chief of staff to general commanding German troops in France

Other

Josephine Baker: American entertainer in Paris; member of the Resistance

Jacques Biélinky: Russian-Jewish journalist

Dora Bruder: Immigrant Jewish teenager and runaway

William Bullitt: American ambassador to France at time of Occupation

Edmond Dubois: Swiss journalist; visited Paris often during the Occupation

Hélène Elek: Hungarian-born mother of Thomas Elek

Thomas Elek: Teenage *résistant* and member of the Manouchian Group

Janet Flanner: Columnist for *The New Yorker;* Genêt was her pseudonym

Albert Grunberg: Jewish barber who hid in an attic room on the Left Bank of Paris for two years

Ernest Hemingway: American novelist

A. J. Liebling: American journalist

Irène Némirovsky: Russian novelist and Jewish; wrote in French; deported from France and died in concentration camp

Raoul Nordling: Swedish diplomat in Paris during the Liberation

Pablo Picasso: Spanish artist

Gertrude Stein: American novelist and essayist

Preface

Almost everything we know we know incompletely at best.
And almost nothing we are told remains the same when retold.
                                                    —*Janet Malcolm*[1]

My affection for and personal experience of Paris led me to wonder what it would have been like to live there under German Occupation during the Second World War. I remember being an especially green and curious twenty-year-old Alabaman walking along the Boulevard Saint-Germain on the Left Bank in the early 1960s. I noticed the evidence of the intense street battles that had briefly occurred in the Latin Quarter at the city's liberation in late August of 1944. I would look for traces of the impact made by shrapnel and bullets on the grand facades of those magnificent buildings that led up to the Boulevard Saint-Michel. Plaques on buildings all through the 5th and 6th arrondissements announced that some young man or other had died near that spot at the hand of retreating German soldiers or Vichy supporters. But it was not until I had read more about that war, and about the destruction of other major European cities by both Axis and Allied powers, that I began to wonder how Paris had managed to survive the twentieth century's greatest conflagration almost unscathed.

On my way to Paris to study at the Sorbonne, I had stayed for about six weeks with a family in Dijon, the capital of Burgundy. There I heard for the first time about the military occupation of France from those who had lived it. The mayor of Dijon was a cleric, Canon Félix Kir (for whom France's popular aperitif is named), who welcomed our group of young Americans to the city hall. Before we went, my host family informed me that their mayor was a hero of the Resistance; that a group of French hirelings of the Vichy government had tried to assassinate him at one point, but the wallet (some said a breviary) he carried near his heart had stopped the bullet. Every Dijonnais knew the story.

The head of my host family would take me into the woods of Burgundy to show us the place where he and his young friends used to lie in wait for German traffic. At the same time, the family and I would watch news reports of young African Americans standing courageously against the brutality of segregation. It was during this period that the Birmingham, Alabama, civil rights demonstrations were at their height. At the same time, the Algerian War, during which Algerians tried to push the French off the African continent after more than a century of colonialism, had just ended. I found myself trying to define, as a son of the state governed callously by George Wallace, what was just becoming clearer to me—namely, that the South was changing, and radically so, while my host family was explaining patiently how Algeria was really French. I was explaining the South's slow progress toward equality; my hosts were trying to justify benevolent colonialism. But we both agreed on one thing: the Nazis had been evil, and Europe and America had done well to rid that continent of Hitler and his cohort. Though blind to our own partial answers about contemporary social change, we were, on the other hand, confidently in solidarity about the German Occupation of France.

I remember, too, that while roaming France and Paris I would frequently find myself before some centrally located monument, maybe one that was topped by a stone sentinel, bearing an endless list of names of people from that community—many with the same patronyms— who had been lost during the great conflict of 1914–18. The towns and villages and cities of that epoch had officially remembered every local male who had died or disappeared during that horrendous conflict. Standing before these sad memorials, I wondered why there were not similar monuments raised to the local casualties of the Second World War. Yes, in post offices and other official buildings, in museums and some schools, we find names of those affiliated with a particular institution who died during World War II; but, more often than not, that list is tacked onto a First World War plaque or monument almost as an afterthought. Furthermore, the lists are for the most part composed of names of those who died in deportation or who publicly or violently resisted the Occupation. Rarely do you find lists of the region's military who died during the war. One senses the lack of a widespread communal and patriotic desire to remember, as if World War II had had a much more modest impact on national and local history.

This should not be surprising. Even today, the French endeavor both to remember and to find ways to forget their country's trials during World War II; their ambivalence stems from the cunning and original arrangement they devised with the Nazis, which was approved by Hitler and assented to by Philippe Pétain, the recently appointed head of the moribund Third Republic, that had ended the Battle of France in June of 1940. This treaty—known by all as the Armistice—had entangled France and the French in a web of cooperation, resistance, accommodation, and, later, of defensiveness, forgetfulness, and guilt from which they are still trying to escape. The word *collaboration* (the Germans first used *Zusammenarbeit,* "working together") evolved into an epithet. One French veteran told me, with conviction, that it might have been better, at least for French memory and morale, had an armistice never been signed—had the French fought to defend Paris, then the Loire Valley, then central France, retreating, if necessary, all the way to the Mediterranean and North Africa.

But the Third Republic did sign this agreement, and it did agree to an administrative division of French territory, and it did legally vote to end the Third Republic itself, established in 1871 after an ignominious defeat by the Prussians the previous year. For the first time since the Renaissance, France in 1940 was a geographically incoherent nation.*

---

* The very northern part of France was attached to the military government of Belgium; the eastern provinces of Alsace and Lorraine (which Germany had assimilated in the Franco-Prussian War and lost in the 1918 armistice) were reabsorbed into the Reich. Sections of southeastern France were put under Italian control. But the most significant division was between what became known as the Occupied and the Unoccupied Zones (which lasted until November of 1942): the northern zone ranged from the Rhine to the entire Atlantic and Channel coasts, down to the Spanish border, and of course included Paris. The Unoccupied, Vichy, or "Free Zone" comprised essentially central and south-central France to the Pyrénées, including most of the Mediterranean coast.

France dissected. *(Creative Commons)*

This administrative and geographical division would be replicated as a moral and psychological division for decades after the war as collective memory endeavored to rewrite history.

In what ways did Paris in 1940 pass from being a city known for its freedoms to a closed, uncanny, unfamiliar place? What effect did the open-endedness of the Occupation, the uncertainty of its duration, have on Parisian daily life? And how did this "uncanniness" affect both Parisians and their occupiers? Films and novels, memoirs and diaries, photographs and letters of the period, all make some reference to how the atmosphere of the City of Light changed with the arrival of German soldiers and, soon afterward, of the Nazi bureaucratic apparatus. To the

Parisian, the Germans might have been ethnic "cousins," but they were not French, and they certainly were not Parisians. Not since the late Middle Ages, during the Hundred Years' War, had the city had so many unwanted military visitors for such an undetermined spate of time. That, coupled with factors such as curfews, food shortages, air raid drills, a lack of automobiles, and the "repedestrianization" of a modern metropolis, turned the city into a quiet, eerie warren of sinister places and anxious citizens. Questions and facts such as these have guided my research and the story I relate.

Since the sixteenth century, Paris had become the standard by which other European cities — and, eventually, other world cities — measured themselves, both in terms of its aesthetic qualities and its political shenanigans. It was a very old capital city, attaining its permanent status as such at the beginning of the sixth century during the reign of Clovis I. Every French monarch since then had enhanced his reputation by spending lavishly on marking Paris as a major cultural and commercial center. Beginning in the Renaissance, French became the lingua franca of the European intelligentsia, gradually replacing Latin. French adventures abroad had shown that the nation could mount formidable obstacles to the incursions of their neighbors. The French had established massive colonies in America and had followed the Portuguese, Spanish, and Dutch as international entrepreneurs and colonial capitalists. For more than three hundred years Paris had created the impression that it was the European center for luxury, fine living, subtle diplomacy, advances in science, and innovations in philosophy. It became a beacon for all those who were "trapped" in less progressive nations. During the European Enlightenment of the seventeenth and eighteenth centuries, Paris's philosophes had shown that the city, though under the rule of an absolute monarch, was a center of progressive ideas, and this well-deserved reputation had mesmerized the world. From around 1750, to go to Paris for study and conversation was a sign of intellectual adventure and seriousness. On the other hand, Paris was a city that seemed addicted to revolt if not revolution; it had to put its ideas into action.

Largely because of this history, Paris was, of all of the capital cities that suffered during the Second World War, the most beloved, most familiar, and most mythical in the eyes of the world. Warsaw Oslo, Amsterdam, Brussels, and Prague—all fiercely occupied by the Nazis—were not as much in the world's concerned gaze. To watch as the Luftwaffe bombed London in 1940–41 evoked massive anger on behalf of those who treasured the cultural patrimony of that large city; though relentlessly attacked, London would never be occupied. Leningrad would be surrounded, starved, and bombarded for almost a thousand days, but never occupied. Moscow would be within hours of being seized before Stalin finally eked out a vicious defense. But by mid-June of 1940, the Germans—the Nazis—were strolling comfortably through the boulevards and gardens of Paris. The fear that Paris, too, might be bombarded had waned, but the images of its Occupation evinced, from Buenos Aires to Shanghai, a different sort of visceral protectiveness on behalf of Europe's urban jewel.

The historian Philippe Burrin describes three approaches to writing a history of military occupation: the first is to elucidate through comparison—that is, to use a variety of examples that will illuminate constants and differences; the second is to describe "the structural effects of occupation on the occupied society's environment and living conditions"; and the third is to call on what he describes as "the face-to-face interaction between occupiers and occupied people, dealing with both groups on the level of... lived experience and symbolic representation."[2] *When Paris Went Dark* falls within the third group and has cousinship to the second. This narrative aims to give an account of how the Parisians viewed the Germans and vice versa; of how the Parisian figured out a code of daily conduct toward his nemesis and effected it; of how the citizen of the Occupation handled his psychological and emotional responses to the presence of a powerful enemy; and of how each side perpetuated real and symbolic violence on the other. A prominent French historian of the "black years" noted that "an occupation is not defined alone as the imposition of a foreign authority over individuals. It is first and foremost the investment★ of a space, taking possession of a place, the affirmation of a presence by its signs and its symbols."³ Are we capable of imagining and describing the claustrophobic trauma of living in a familiar environment that has suddenly become threatening? One chronicler of the period, writing in 1945, thinks not: "[The psychological atmosphere] of Paris during the Occupation...changed from one year to the next, one month to the next, and, in critical periods one hour to the other. No one, no matter his or her learning or his or her intuition, is capable of evoking that atmosphere if he had not himself breathed it."⁴ This is the challenge to the contemporary chronicler: how to depict the intangible qualities, often inarticulately expressed, of a military occupation. Improvised hiding places, prison cells, hotels, doorways, elevators, apartments, cemeteries, schools, convents, theaters, offices, nightclubs, bomb shelters, sewers, Métro stations, restaurants, cabarets, bordellos, bookstores, arcades, department stores, small shops, automobiles, public parks, public bathrooms — all demanded a new ecology of the Occupation, underlining how systemic such an event was.

In order to help my readers learn about Paris's topography, then and now, I have cited specifically the quarters, neighborhoods, and arrondissements (administrative sections) of the city in which the events occurred. Parisians know the personality, the history, and the social identity of each of these divisions. The Occupation authorities' intention — though often haphazardly implemented — was to reduce spatial freedom. An occupying force cannot allow the free use of public spaces, and it makes every effort to restrict the liberties one expects in private spaces. Spatial disorientation brought the disintegration of psychic comfort, thereby multiplying the oppressive effect of being occupied. As one astute teenager noticed: "The silence caught you by the throat, made sadness press into your thoughts. The houses had grown too tall, the streets too wide. People were separated from each other by spaces that were too big. Even the air which flowed down the

---

★ *Investment* is an underused English term for a military blockade or the imposition of a controlling authority.

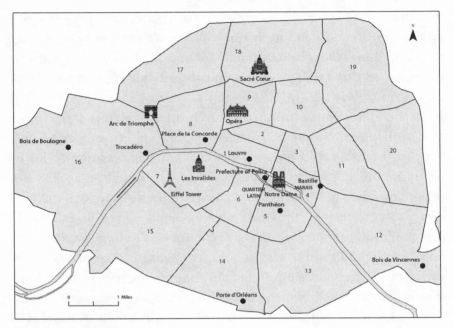

Arrondissements of Paris

empty streets was furtive and kept its secrets."[5] The natural rhythms of life in rural settings—e.g., seasons, diurnal and nocturnal changes, large open spaces—can sequester daily living from constant surveillance and interruption, but those patterns do not pertain for an urban existence. Early twentieth-century sociologists of everyday city life attempted to isolate and define the perpetual discomfort that can prevent one from feeling at home in a modern city. Many of their observations pertain even more so to a city under military, cultural, and political control by an outsider.

My sources include diaries, memoirs, essays, newspaper articles, histories, letters, films (fictional and documentary), archives, interviews, photographs, maps, novels, songs, paintings, drawings, and anything else that helped me understand what it was like to "live the Occupation." My hope was to create a framework for understanding the heartbeat, the intangible rhythms, of life during a period of sustained urban anxiety. As a consequence, I have been obliged to bring a mixture of interpretive strategies to bear: close reading—often between the lines—of texts, drawing conclusions that others have been perhaps too cautious to make, and using archival and historical data for purposes other than establishing or repeating facts. This is a work of reasonable interpretation, of reasonable judgments that I trust will enable readers to question assumptions, bromides, and received theories about what happens when a city is "occupied" by strangers, armed or not.

I do not claim the mantle of historian but rather of storyteller and guide; I have perused with care what others have written and have teased out stories that have always been there but had settled under the dust of memory and history. I have plumbed the extraordinary archival work done by others and done some of my own, always looking for fissures in texts that allow for a richer reading of a traumatic period in European history. Here are the famous and unknown voices of adolescents and adults, Germans and French, men and women, Jews and non-Jews, visitors and residents, collaborators and patriots, novelists and historians, journalists and diarists, the still living and the gone. Some appear repeatedly, some occasionally, and some only once. I have interviewed men and women who lived in Paris at the time. They offered anecdotes that became bright tiles in a vibrant mosaic that reveals more clearly how a familiar and beloved city became, even temporarily, threatening and uncanny. As one person raised in Paris during this period answered when I asked if her parents ever discussed the Occupation: "It [the memory of the Occupation] was like a secret garden whose gates were always closed to us." *When Paris Went Dark* makes an effort to look over that garden's walls.

"The Last Time I Saw Paris," written in 1940 by Oscar Hammerstein and Jerome Kern and played frequently on the radio late that year, summed up not only the nostalgia that the world had already developed for the City of Light but also the effects that the Occupation itself must have been having on Parisians themselves:

A lady known as Paris, Romantic and Charming,
Has left her old companions and faded from view.
Lonely men with lonely eyes are seeking her in vain.
Her streets are where they were, but there's no sign of her.

She has left the Seine.
The last time I saw Paris, her heart was warm and gay,
I heard the laughter of her heart in every street café.
The last time I saw Paris, her trees were dressed for spring,
And lovers walked beneath those trees and birds found songs to sing. . . .
No matter how they change her, I'll remember her that way.
I'll think of happy hours, and people who shared them. . . .
And those who danced at night and kept our Paris bright
'Til the town went dark.[6]

Paris is the primary protagonist of this narrative. A city is unable to speak for itself, but we can take from the written and oral memories of others how it was changed by, how it adapted to, and how it survived the German Occupation of 1940–44. This book brings those memories, real and imagined, back to light, offering a narrative that, in the best of worlds, Paris herself might tell.

WHEN
PARIS WENT
DARK

Introduction

NACH PARIS!
— "To Paris!" Signs plastering German railroad cars
carrying the Kaiser's troops to France, 1914–18

Faux Paris

Paris is and always has been obsessed with itself—its place within France, within Europe, within the world, and within the imaginations of those who have visited it or who want to. As a consequence, even though the city has in modern times survived siege, civil disorder, and military occupation, the French, and especially the Parisians, retain a magical belief that the City of Light is impervious to destruction. Exceptions to this fantasy cause bewilderment and generally incoherent or confused responses. When, in the last year of the First World War, German artillery, in the guise of Krupp's gigantic howitzer, Big Bertha, began dropping enormous shells on the city with considerable destructive force, the first reaction was outrage. Earlier, rather ineffectual bombing at night from zeppelins, and even from the more accurate Gotha aircraft, had inured the Parisians to occasional disruption from above. In the first quarter of 1918, when the Germans made their last great attempt at a breakthrough to reach the French capital, more than two hundred bombs had been dropped from aircraft on Paris in order to break the city's morale.

But the most terrifying bombardments appeared out of nowhere and capriciously peppered the city beginning in late March of that year. The 260-pound shells seemed to fall most often on the quiet streets of the comfortable 7th arrondissement: the Rue du Bac, the Rue

Barbet-de-Jouy, and the Rue de Vaugirard. (It was later discovered that the Germans were using Notre-Dame Cathedral as their major orienting target; thus many of Big Bertha's shells landed in the city's center.) Where were they coming from? There were no airplanes, no air raid alarms; they were just falling from the sky. No artillery shell was known to travel more than twenty-five miles or so, and the German army was almost a hundred miles away.

The population was much more disoriented by these mysterious bombardments than they had been by the air raids; and when it was discovered that the shells were indeed coming from more than seventy miles away, Parisians suddenly felt a vulnerability they had not felt since the early days of the war.* And then on Good Friday, one of the gigantic shells landed atop one of Paris's oldest churches, Saint-Gervais, in the Marais. More than 150 worshippers, including foreign dignitaries, were killed or injured. A historian of Big Bertha's late–World War I impact writes:

> The place was crowded. It was just 4:30. Suddenly the hundreds of kneeling worshippers were startled by a terrific crash overhead, an explosion. A projectile had struck the roof. Those looking up quickly saw a stone pillar crumbling, beginning to fall. Scores of tons of stone, some blocks weighing a half ton, were pouring upon the mass of people.[1]

Even after the cause was discovered, and the French were able to target the howitzer and the rail tracks needed to move it, Parisians would remember that distinct feeling of helplessness.

In fact, for some time before the war ended, French military leaders had begun planning how to dupe German reconnaissance airmen who, in a time without radar or any sort of sophisticated night vision equipment, had to use rail tracks, reflections off the river, and the lights of Paris to find their targets and guide their new and powerful artillery.

---

* French astronomers, engineers, and the artillery corps began using a combination of guesswork, physics, geometry, and air reconnaissance to discover the site from which the Germans were lobbing these shells.

By 1917 the French army had already begun looking for an area near Paris that, from the air, might be mistaken for the capital. They found one such site northwest of the city, near Saint-Germain-en-Laye, where the Seine makes a deep loop on its way to the English Channel, similar to the well-known curve that it creates as it passes through Paris. False train stations, tracks, and streetlights were constructed; plans were made to enhance this *faux* Paris, but the end of the war interrupted them and they were but desultorily continued for a few years afterward. Yet only two decades later, the fanciful idea of constructing another Paris as a protection for one of the world's most famous cityscapes would be reborn. For in occupying the capital of France, the Germans themselves would try to invent a *faux* Paris, one that would serve as an example of Nazi benevolence while, behind the facade, they pillaged a grand treasure house.

Sequestering Medusa

On a clear morning, April 26, 1937, the citizens of a small Basque town in northern Spain and their neighbors from the countryside were doing what they habitually did on Mondays: shopping, bargaining, and exchanging gossip in an open-air market. When a low, droning sound first entered their consciousness, theirs was not the automatic response that would soon become common throughout Europe—to look toward the skies for danger. Rather, they looked around to find the source of that loud, unfamiliar mechanical noise. Before they could protect themselves, warplanes from the Luftwaffe and the Italian air force began indiscriminately dropping concussive firebombs and splinter bombs on the town. After five raids, the allies of Franco's army had left Guernica three-quarters devastated and had killed between four hundred and one thousand civilians. (Historians still debate the final figures.) News of the event and its aftermath, thanks to a trenchant article by George Steer of the *New York Times,* flashed around the world. Steer's piece made one especially salient point, unrecognized then as being predictive: the bombing was meant to demoralize the populace, for the little town had no military value. For the first time, indiscriminate bombing of civilian populations was a reality, whereas before it had been but a theoretical assumption. "In the form of its execution and the scale of the destruction it wrought, no less than in the selection of its objective, the raid on Guernica is unparalleled in military history."[2]

The Spanish Civil War, particularly the bombing of Madrid and Barcelona, along with the devastation of Guernica, forced museum curators and protectors of all cultural treasures to think about how to protect their patrimony from arbitrary destruction. It also warned military commanders that they should pay more attention to protecting their cities from the air. After Guernica, the bombing of Madrid, and with the destruction of two great cities in 1939 and 1940 (Warsaw and Rotterdam), Europeans were learning from relentlessly replayed newsreels that war was no longer a matter just between armies* and that their historical confidence in the general impregnability of large metropolises had been misplaced. During the First World War, most of the casualties were soldiers; but it became clear this time around that civilians would not be spared the fury of combat. This new type of warfare was erasing the boundaries, as fragile as they had been, between the battlefield and the home. Indeed, the phrase "home front" would soon become a cliché.

The Occupation of Paris during the Second World War has provided us with a rich array of photographs, many of which have been repeatedly reproduced. Often, they provide unintentionally ironic commentary on the complexities of urban life when a foreign enemy threatens a familiar city. A photograph of curators emptying the Louvre in 1938 only two years before the Germans arrived does just that. A nation's material culture has always been the target of opposing nations and peoples, and this period in French and German history was

---

* Warsaw had been bombed into submission in 1939. On May 14, 1940, the Luftwaffe conducted a devastating air raid on Rotterdam, Europe's largest port. The old center of the city was destroyed; hundreds were killed and tens of thousands made homeless. The Dutch government surrendered the next day. The scenes of shattered cities were thereafter embedded in the minds of Europeans under Nazi threat.

Sequestering Medusa. *(© Ministère de la Culture / Médiathèque du Patrimoine, Dist. RMN-Grand Palais / Art Resource, NY)*

no exception.[3] The protection of national treasures had begun in Paris in the late 1930s: sandbags were used to surround public statues, monuments, churches, and other buildings; many public statues were dismantled and put in safe places; precious stained-glass windows were covered with wire or removed. Found more often than not in the centers of its cities, Europe's great museums—the National Gallery and Tate Gallery in London, Paris's Louvre, Leningrad's Hermitage, the Rijksmuseum of Amsterdam, and the Royal Museums of Fine Arts in Brussels, to name only the best known—were like sitting ducks, vulnerable to bombardment, fire, and air attack, so they had to be emptied as thoroughly as possible. Soon their walls were denuded. And there was another threat: looting. It was an open secret that the Reich sought to repatriate any painting or sculpture that it felt belonged to Germany—any work that had been itself looted over centuries of war or even sold legally. Small groups of German curators and art historians had fanned out all over Europe in the late 1930s, using their academic credentials to discover what museums held that might be called Germanic. The Third Reich was primed to reveal what it believed to be the lies and fantasies of provenance.

A first glance at the photograph shows a group of men struggling to pull a very large canvas through a door of the museum. On closer

Géricault, The Raft of the Medusa. *(Erich Lessing / Art Resource, NY)*

The Louvre denuded. *(© Roger-Viollet / The Image Works)*

investigation, we see that the painting is none other than Théodore Géricault's mammoth *Le Radeau de la Méduse* (*The Raft of the Medusa*), painted in 1819 and exhibited in the Salon of that year. Much has been said about the relationship between this painting's subject—a terrible shipwreck—and the dark, romantic style of its fabrication. It shocked many who saw it, both artists and the public, and amazed many as well because of its forthright depiction of communal solidarity at its weakest point. Some wrote then, and have argued since, that the painting was Géricault's critique of the failure of the Napoleonic experiment, which was followed by the hasty reinstallation of the Bourbon monarchy in 1815. Others have seen it as a dour commentary on the slave trade, which France did not abolish in its overseas colonies until 1849: "Much has been read into this painting: an allegory for a wounded France, the fatherland at the moment of its mortal failure, the disarray of a lost generation.... But aside from these political meanings, is not 'The Raft' above all a representation of horror?"[4] This magnificent canvas, one of the largest in the Louvre, had hung on the museum's walls for more than a hundred years as a reminder of moral, political, and personal despair and humiliation.*

The photograph of the complicated attempt at removing the painting captures, predictively, what the next four years of the German Occupation of Paris would entail. Here we see the curators of France's national museum methodically trying to remove and hide an artwork that had represented the French nation at another political low point. Themes of the Occupation are present in the painting: a sense of abandonment; false hope for succor; struggles among fellow sufferers; the implacability of the enemy (in this case, the ocean, thirst, and hunger); the betrayal of nature itself; death and humiliation. The Louvre's curators would be more successful at protecting the nation's patrimony (they moved Leonardo's *Mona Lisa* all over France to keep it out of German hands) than would the Third Republic at protecting the nation's geographical, military, and political integrity. Like the Parisians who would soon follow it in their exodus before the arrival of the Germans, Géricault's canvas would seek refuge in unfamiliar and restricted spaces, in this case, some dusty room in an even dustier château. Yet more hauntingly, the sequestering of this great canvas was itself a terrifying revelation and prophecy of what was to come.

---

* What was the historical event that had occasioned this work? A French naval vessel, the *Méduse*, had foundered off the coast of western Africa. Crew and officers had escaped onto a hastily built raft with only enough water and food to last a few days. Although the men had intended to float to shore, the improvised raft moved farther out to sea. Before long there was a mutiny against the officers, who were killed. Many of the rest died before the raft was finally rescued. A subsequent trial brought out horrible stories of desperate attempts to survive, including murder and cannibalism. These published accounts tarnished the reputation of the French navy and the legacy of the French Revolution: *Liberté, Égalité, Fraternité.*

Paris *Was* Different

Paris's arrogance made it a metropolis more difficult to "occupy" than any of the other European cities the Nazis controlled by force between 1939 and 1945. Nevertheless, Adolf Hitler brought German civilians and German soldiers by the thousands to the city, attempting to colonize it culturally, using it as a model for the greater Berlin that the Reich would soon begin building. Parisians themselves tried to avoid as much as they could the fact of the Occupation, presenting a "city without a face," accepting—some say too "collaboratively"—but not welcoming the presence of a confident enemy in their midst. For four years, both sides—the Germans, with their French collaborators, and the average Parisian—lived in this *faux* Paris, attempting to create a lure for the other, a trap or decoy in which to snare an antagonist.

Der Deutsche Wegleiter für Paris: Wohin in Paris? (The German Guide to Paris: What to Do in Paris) began publication within a month of the Occupation (July 15, 1940). At first it was only sixteen pages long, but it would grow to more than one hundred pages by its last issue, two weeks before the Liberation. The purpose of the guide was to "offer" Paris to the thousands of soldiers who would be visiting the capital for the next four years.*

> For the majority of us, Paris is an unknown land. We approach her with mixed feelings: superiority, curiosity and nervous anticipation. The name of Paris evokes something special. Paris—our grandfathers saw it at the time of the war that offered the imperial crown to the kings of Prussia [the Franco-Prussian War of 1870]. And in their mouth, the word "Paris" had a mysterious, extraordinary sound. Now we are there and we can enjoy it at our liberty.[5]

---

* The guide contained information about Paris's most chic shops and services, Métro maps, lists of French phrases, cultural advice (e.g., how to deal with Parisian police), and many, many ads for bars, restaurants, and cabarets (even those featuring Gypsy music; while their fellows were murdering Romanies in eastern Europe, the touring soldiers would line up to hear Django Reinhardt and other "approved" Gypsy musicians).

But the author of this little article also warns the soldier not to be seduced by this untrustworthy city. Remember, it intones, that there are many other beautiful places you will visit as a Wehrmacht soldier, so "in the middle of the sweet and easy life of the City of Lights...keep in your heart, as every German should, a motto: 'Don't fall into sentimentality; the strength of steel is what we need now; direct yourself to clear and sure goals; and be ready for combat.'"[6]

Guardians of Nazi morality would remain concerned that the world's most attractive city would turn its soldiers into the same decadent military that they had defeated during the Battle of France.

Hitler had several reasons for breathing a sigh of relief that Paris had fallen with nary a shot fired even before the Armistice had been signed. First he wanted to enhance the image of National Socialism worldwide—to show that he and his cohort were a sophisticated and cultured race, worthy of continental leadership. In addition, he sought to mollify the bellicose Winston Churchill, for Germany was still desperately seeking a cessation of hostilities with Great Britain now that France had been subdued. Perhaps allowing a retreating British Expeditionary Force to escape from the port of Dunkirk had been one of the Führer's signals to the English; treating Paris with respect was definitely another. But a stubborn Churchill refused to read such signals favorably. And so the Occupation of Paris would last for more than fifteen hundred nights, much longer than any of the parties had foreseen.

We shall see how Nazi ideology was quite ambivalent about urban centers: they imagined building cleaner, more idealized city environments so as to reduce the filthy, the foreign, and the aberrant. When confronted with a site such as Paris they were truly befuddled. But had they not occupied other major metropolises, other centers of art and the gay life? What was different about Paris? The difference resided in the place Paris had in the world's imagination—that and the fact that it was the capital of one of Germany's most powerful and traditional foes. Now the German Occupation of Paris sought to freeze Paris, to make it static, less dynamic, and to reduce it to a banal tourist site. For a great lot of the Germans, the city remained a sort of El Dorado. Many had visited Paris as tourists before the war; a substantial number of the elite had studied there. Many of the upper echelons of the Occupying forces spoke excellent French. Those who only knew the city secondhand still recognized it as the ideal city of freedom, charm, and beauty.

Nevertheless, Paris confronted Hitler with a conundrum that he and his acolytes would never completely solve. How does an occupier vigorously and efficiently control a city while maintaining the appearance of a benevolent trusteeship? By its very nature, a metropolis is difficult, if not impossible, to govern predictably. The Occupation authorities had organizational problems; these were evident from the day the first German motorcyclist entered the city. In his study of the period, the American historian Allan Mitchell explains that the administration of the Occupation never fully recovered from early mistakes, despite the myth of German precision and efficiency: "The basic problem was that the German command itself was in virtual chaos. The first phase of the Occupation was therefore characterized by a welter of titles, acronyms, ill-defined prerogatives, and overlapping duties as the German bureaucracy struggled to adapt itself to the particular circumstances of occupied France."[7] As France's civic and cultural capital, Paris demanded a more flexible and entrepreneurial management than its occupiers were prepared to develop. Their administration of the capital was more layered and confusing than elsewhere in France, particularly because of German bureaucracies overlapping with their Vichy counterparts. The Nazi government's concern for its image as the new custodian of the world's most recognized city added further complications. The occupiers were organizing to take material advantage of a conquered city while ostensibly protecting an important part of the world's patrimony. They also had to ensure that they not appear beguiled by Paris, for such lack of martial attention might encourage restless residents of other occupied cities.

The history of the Occupation is, in part, a melodrama about an often feckless bureaucracy attempting to remake an iconic city into a Potemkin-like hamlet. City planning, as any urban historian will confirm, is an oxymoron. There had been no greater example of planned urban reconstruction than that effected by Baron Haussmann, under the aegis of Napoleon III, between 1852 and 1870. Yet in 1871, the forces of the Paris Commune (the world's first communist government), in retreating before the French army could crush it, would use the city's modern accoutrements (fountains, cobblestones, lampposts, kiosks, benches, and other street furniture) to construct barricades across widened boulevards. They also set this new Paris afire. So the Nazis had occupied a city steeped in the blood of revolt and massacre, of civil strife, and had somehow convinced themselves that they could succeed where even the French themselves had failed. They were both seduced and apprehensive.

But they were not fools: they knew that to occupy was to establish relations with sympathetic and ambitious citizens as well as those who feared and loathed them, and they were quite adept at it. Cities under occupation demand new urban identities of their stressed inhabitants. Often those identities can take on attributes of the occupier; those individuals, for whatever reason, become integral to the confidence of the "foreign" visitor. In writing a history of this period, one needs regularly to remember that there are many less visible lines of demarcation between "occupier" and "occupied." Language and uniforms are but the most obvious markers of "otherness"; the less obvious—the occasional, accidental, and coincidental acts of "cooperation" and "accommodation"—remind the student of this period that his effort can only suggest the complexity of human relations in such a stressed environment. Daily life was—is—always a matter of accommodation to unexpected and noxious events; the Occupation inflected the small and large decisions that constitute daily life in myriad ways. It imposed an attuned sensitivity on the French that raised moral issues that, to their credit, are still being debated.

A citizen of a city as robustly occupied as was Paris must "accommodate" himself continuously to an unpredictable reality. Just obeying Nazi and Vichy injunctions was an example of such accommodation; but was answering the occupiers' innocuous questions or having affective or sexual relations with them or selling them bread or shoe polish also a form of collaboration? Is there a hierarchy of activities that makes one a collaborator rather than just an accommodator? Is a quick date or a one-night stand more "accommodating" than selling coffee to the same officer day after day and even occasionally offering him a free croissant? These are questions that demand thoughtful answers, and thoughtfulness, as we will see later, was not prevalent in the postliberation period. Jean Dutourd's astutely satirical novel *Au Bon Beurre* (*The Best Butter,* 1952), written less than a decade after the events it describes, was a bestseller in France even though it satirized the compromises made by many Parisians. The owners of a dairy shop adapt themselves to every change that occurs in Paris during that period, but they do so to benefit from opportunities to make money, not for ideological reasons. "In exceptional times, exceptional actions," reasons Monsieur Poissonnard, the grocer.[8] Living under surveillance for four years stymied and disfigured earlier ethical certainties; all decisions demanded new justifications.

Paris during the Second World War survived many grievous injuries, but its most serious were not the visible wounds left behind by air raids, bombardments, fires, and disease. There were subtler marks, more difficult to evaluate, easier for history to ignore. These effects were often deeper, more traumatic. An occupation numbs a city's vitality, the vitality that makes urban life attractive. Soon the citizen begins to feel alienated, disconnected from a familiar environment; though he is still physically engaged with the city, his emotional attachment to it weakens. Previously confident of his urban sophistication, which had allowed him to navigate a complex environment, he becomes tentative, anxious, angry, and impatient as he wonders how long before "his" city returns to him. One of the ironies is that an occupied city brings its citizens closer together physically—in lines, in movie houses, in cafés for warmth, in smaller living spaces, in crowded buses and trains—but separates them emotionally and sentimentally. Suspicion becomes the norm; openness diminishes. Generosity turns to covetousness; racial and ethnic markers become clearer and thus more compelling; objects—things—take on almost ethical value: "If I can't have my city, then at least I can grab part of it, find something to call mine."

There are eloquent examples of French people who lived not in Paris or Marseille or Lyon but in small towns and villages accommodating themselves to the sudden proximity of those with power over their daily lives. In her stunningly prescient novel *Suite Française* (1942, but unpublished until 2004), the French-Russian novelist Irène Némirovsky gives us a view of how intimate the Occupation became in rural settings: "The Germans had moved into their lodgings and were getting to know the village. The officers walked about alone or in pairs, heads held high, boots striking the paving stones.... They inspired in the inhabitants of the occupied countries fear, respect, aversion, and the amusing desire to fleece them, to take advantage of them, to get hold of their money."[9]

Another book, the novella *The Silence of the Sea,* distributed clandestinely during 1942, was credited to a certain author named Vercors (in reality, Jean Bruller, a writer and member of the Resistance). A young woman and her uncle, who narrates, are forced to accept as a tenant a German officer who makes every effort to befriend them. Deciding early to resist the only way they can, they provide every courtesy to their tenant except to speak to him. Finally von Ebrennac, an anti-Nazi but proud German officer, decides that honor demands he ask to be transferred to the Eastern Front—in other words, to probable death. He announces this to the old man and his niece, and tells them:

> "I wish you a good night." I thought he was going to close the door and leave. But no. I was looking at my niece. I stared at her. He said—murmured: "Adieu." He did not move. He remained completely still, and in his still and tense face, his eyes were even more still and tense, connected to the eyes—too open, too pale— of my niece. This lasted, lasted—how long?—lasted until finally, the girl moved her lips. Werner's eyes shone. I heard: "Adieu." You had to look for the word in order to hear it, but finally I heard it. Von Ebrennac heard it too, and he stood up straight, and his face and his whole body seemed to relax as if he had just had a restful bath. And he smiled, so that the last image that I had of

him was a happy one. And the door closed and his steps disappeared into the depths of the house.[10]

French programs on BBC Radio would read *The Silence of the Sea* on the air with touching enthusiasm. Those who had not signed on to the Vichy experiment believed that it presented a France that still had the wherewithal to struggle against apparently impossible odds. It boldly put forth the ethical questions that would haunt France for decades: Which actions, exactly, constitute collaboration and which constitute resistance?

Living in cities, where so many serendipitous encounters occur, is different from living in more intimate villages and towns. Knowing a city by maps alone cannot explain or contain the on-the-ground facts of that city; too much is unseen by the innocent visitor, even less by an occupier. Not only cul-de-sacs and alleys but also the daily lives of a city's inhabitants are invisible to the mapmaker. *Stadtluft macht frei* (city air makes one free): a totalitarian regime can only partially rule a metropolis. Conquerors tend to forget this age-old belief.

Perhaps the most informative and moving accounts of the war in Europe came from the dispatches and journals of A. J. Liebling, correspondent for *The New Yorker*. Liebling stayed in Paris until forty-eight hours before the arrival of the Germans. Throughout the war, he traveled to the United States, to North Africa, and England; he landed at Normandy on D-day and was one of the first journalists to enter the liberated city. For four years, though, he had been frustrated about not knowing what was going on in his beloved Paris. His only information came from tales brought back by escaped prisoners and from the dozens of little newspapers published clandestinely in France during those years. Reading those scraps of information was as if "one were to try to piece together a theory of what is going on behind the familiar facade of a house across the street where a friend is held prisoner by a kidnap gang. These tiny newspapers are like messages scrawled on bits of paper and dropped from a window by the prisoner."[11] I know how he felt, for even though we have learned much about what was going on since the war, there remain so many contradictory stories and theories, so many attempts at explanation and exculpation, that unraveling them seems at times to be an exercise in frustration. But the stories themselves are worth remembering, for they speak of a period and a place—Paris—that still demand our sentimental and intellectual attention.

Chapter One

A Nation Disintegrates

It is with anguish that I tell you that we must lay down our arms.

— *Maréchal Philippe Pétain*[1]

Preludes

How did this debacle happen, and so rapidly?

When Hitler invaded Poland on September 1, 1939, feverish diplomatic efforts were engaged to obviate the treaty obligations that would force Britain and France to come to her defense. After declaring war on Germany a few days later, both nations almost desultorily began preparations for a European war. The French had increased their already large army to about 2.5 million men. They pushed past their own Maginot Line in eastern France and moved cautiously a few kilometers into Germany, where they met little resistance, for the Luftwaffe and the panzers of the Wehrmacht were firmly engaged in Poland.* Thus began nine months of the "phony war" on the Western Front, as Hitler bided his time before taking on the combined Allied forces of Holland, Belgium, France, and the United Kingdom. One of the lasting effects of Poland's treaty partners' lack of resolve to help the country more aggressively—except for a few naval and land sorties by

---

* The Maginot Line was an extensive series of massive forts built into the terrain in the 1930s from the border of Switzerland to Luxembourg. This was France's first line of defense against a German invasion. The Germans, of course, went around it in 1940.

the French and British, Poland fought Germany alone during that deadly month—was not only a wariness on the part of other Allied nations toward the "big two" but also an internecine distrust between France and Great Britain themselves. Nevertheless, there was a general confidence, born of years of propaganda, that France's army—believed to be the greatest fighting force in Europe, if not the world—was invincible and that England's navy only increased that invulnerability. It was widely argued that the Germans would be embarrassingly battered should they try to invade any nation other than Poland, which, after all, had been fought over for centuries, its boundaries changing with the vagaries of the political strength of its most powerful neighbors, Germany and Russia (later the USSR).

Still, Paris was nervous. A national mobilization was imposed, and recruits from all over the nation were arriving at train stations and leaving hourly for the Maginot Line and other fronts. The government was introducing the public to "passive defense" training—that is, showing them what to do in case of an air raid. Blackouts, air raid sirens, and other interruptions of daily life became de rigueur. Métro stations were turned into shelters, and almost every apartment house had an *abri* (shelter; the word can still be seen painted in the basements of many Parisian buildings). Dozens of concrete blockhouses were hastily constructed on the major roads leading into Paris. But these were offhand, almost casual attempts at forestalling an invasion that no one believed would really happen. France was just too strong. But within barely six weeks, the German juggernaut would have breached Paris's gates, and a quickly agreed-to armistice was signed.

Many saw the armistice that Maréchal Philippe Pétain, newly named head of government, had confirmed with the Germans as a respite, necessary for France to get its household in order while the Germans pushed their war against England. The decision to call for an armistice was not welcomed by everyone, but most French were confident that this political arrangement with Germany would be necessary for only a limited period. Parisians in particular had been through a rough patch of political disagreement during the 1930s, including bloody street confrontations. At least a dozen French governments had been installed and dissolved since Hitler's ascension to the Reich's chancellorship in 1933. For many French, the example of a stable Third Reich seemed to promise the sort of national pride and civic predictability found lacking on their side of the Rhine. In 1939, the Third Republic, established in 1871 after the civil war that had followed France's defeat in the Franco-Prussian War, was at the nadir of its popularity. The Armistice would allow a harried nation to catch its breath.

But many on the left in 1940 suspected that the Armistice was the French right's revenge—a way to undermine the legacy of the Third Republic, which they despised. Since the Dreyfus affair (1894–1906), when a Jewish army officer was framed for distributing illicit intelligence to the Prussians, the political right, composed essentially of the military, the very Catholic, the aristocratic class, monarchists, and industrialists, had seen or imagined their power wane. The emphases of the Third Republic on public education, support of labor, secularism, and a social safety net appeared to them to have doomed the nation to mediocrity. In addition, once European fascist savagery erupted, France had welcomed tens of thousands of immigrants from Spain (Republicans fleeing Franco) and from Germany and eastern Europe (Jews and other political dissidents). Their presence infuriated the right, enhancing French nativism. A new government, this time headed by a respected military leader, could put the nation back on a more conservative track.

One of those who most fretted during this confusing period was the thirty-one-year-old Simone de Beauvoir, a brilliant schoolteacher and writer then unknown to the French public. (She would not publish her first work, a novel—*L'Invitée* [*She Came to Stay*]—until 1943.) A confidante and lover to Jean-Paul Sartre, the existentialist philosopher who had gone off to war in 1939, de Beauvoir has left us detailed descriptions of her reactions to the way confused Parisians, especially intellectuals, schoolteachers, writers, and artists, felt as they saw their city invaded by the minions of a gang of thugs. Assigned to meteorological duties near Nancy, in the eastern part of France, Sartre himself would be taken prisoner when the Germans finally invaded. He was then shipped off to a German prisoner of war camp (from which he would be released in April 1941). De Beauvoir worried about Sartre, though she regularly received letters from him, at least during the so-called phony war (the French called it *drôle de guerre*)—the period between September of 1939 and May of 1940, when the only major battles in Europe were the Polish campaign and the Russo-Finnish ("Winter") War.

De Beauvoir noticed almost immediately a change in Parisian temperament as its citizens awaited with anxiety, but not yet dread, the results of their mutual defense pact with Poland. In the diary that she kept during these lonely months, she noted that there was a "mini exodus" out of Paris—nothing like the one that would empty the city nine months later, but still a symptom of Parisians' bafflement at the threats from new types of warfare. As she accompanied Sartre to his mobilization reporting station in late 1939, she noticed that

> Passy [part of the fashionable 16th arrondissement] was completely deserted. All the homes were closed up and not a single soul in the street, but an unending line of cars passing on the quay, crammed with suitcases and sometimes with kids.... [Later] we walked up Rue de Rennes. The church tower of St. Germain-des-Prés was bathed in beautiful moonlight and could be mistaken for that of a country church. And underlying everything, before me, an incomprehensible horror. It is impossible to foresee anything, imagine anything, or touch anything. In any case, it's better not to try. I felt frozen and strained inside, strained in order to preserve a void—and an impression of fragility. Just one false move and it could turn suddenly into intolerable suffering. On Rue de Rennes, for a moment, I felt I was dissolving into little pieces.[2]

This feeling of anxiety and of alienation from her familiar environment, of a "narrowing" of her sentient world, would soon spread to all Parisians, before and during the Occupation itself. With these sentiments came another that de Beauvoir was especially attuned to: the fact

De Beauvoir and Sartre. *(Creative Commons)*

that anticipation of war, military occupation, and resistance called for a recalibration of psychological as well as physical senses of time. She said often in her diary that she felt "out of time"; that she desperately wanted to know the future and not be seduced by past happier memories, and that she wanted to mitigate her impatience at having constantly to live in the present. "Boredom," she wrote on September 5, "hasn't set in yet but is looming on the horizon."[3] By November, she was writing: "For

23

the last two months I had lived my life simultaneously in the infinite and in the moment. I had to fill the time minute-by-minute, or long hours at a time, but entirely without a tomorrow. I had reached the point that even the news of military leaves, which gave me hope by defining a future-with-hope, had no effect on me and [was] even painful to me, or almost."[4]

Another prescient chronicler, Edith Thomas, an active French Communist and archivist, kept a daily journal of the Occupation that came to light only in the early 1990s.* Thomas described what Paris was like on May 8, 1940, only two days before the Blitzkrieg would end and the taking of Paris would begin:

> The desert of the streets, and the dead squares at night. Paris [after the grand exodus] is like...a city become too large for those who live there. They walk along under the funereal streetlights covered in blue paper, which give no more light than the candlelight of my childhood. Steps sound as if they are coming from empty rooms where it seems that no one will ever live again. Everything is too big; frightening, bluish, dark, and the shadows of men are lost as if they were in the deepest of forests.[5]

We know how things would end, but back then Parisians had no concrete information, so rumor, guessing games, BBC propaganda, and news bulletins took the place of planning. This waiting was one of the most enervating aspects of the Paris during the war, especially after the Germans arrived. It would not end until Allied tanks were seen on the outskirts of Paris in late August of 1944.

---

* The French Communist Party was the best-organized political group on the political left. Its support of the leftist *Front populaire* government in 1936–37 and again in 1938, and of the Spanish Republic during that country's civil war (1936–39), had given it much moral authority as an antagonist of fascism. Its membership growing in the late 1930s and early 1940s, the Party had been hog-tied by Hitler's cynical 1939 nonaggression pact with Stalin, signed just weeks before the invasion of Poland. Nevertheless, it continued to organize. The largest anti-fascist organization in France, it was also the most feared by the new, collaborationist Vichy government.

Three Traumas

Before the Occupation of Paris per se, though, France experienced three almost simultaneous traumas that would thoroughly demoralize the capital's population: the lightning defeat of the French and Allied armies in May and June of 1940; an ensuing massive civilian exodus southward from northern France and Paris; and, as a result, the collapse of the Third Republic. The effect of these events was to impart a sense of helplessness and confusion that would enable the Germans to occupy Paris even more efficiently and calmly than they had anticipated.

As we have seen, the period between the German attack on Poland in September of 1939 and the first Blitzkrieg incursions into the Low Countries in May of 1940 was defined by an irresponsible lack of preparation by the French high command, confident in their retrofitted First World War strategy—attack and defeat the Germans in Belgium, with the help of the British—and in the technical brilliance of the Maginot Line, they confidently waited for the Germans. Unfortunately for them, Hitler's generals did not move their armies as the French had projected. The Wehrmacht skirted the Maginot Line, rolled unchallenged through the dense Ardennes forest into northeastern France, while at the same time invading the Netherlands, then Belgium, and moving south speedily. They thereby cut the Allied forces in half. Within seven days, the French army and the British Expeditionary Force, sent to help it in extremis, were thrown on their heels so quickly that a stunned world could barely keep up with the news reports of German advances. As early as May 18 (eight days after the German attack), French generals, to the stunned horror of their British allies, were seriously and openly stating that the Battle of France was over. It would actually last another grisly month, as a weakened French army retreated slowly southward. Rather than focus attention on the restaging of their still large army and adapt quickly to the new strategies of Blitzkrieg, Allied military leaders and politicians spent most of this period arguing over whether to continue fighting in France itself, fight from its colonies, or sign an armistice with Germany.

Within no time German troops had reached the English Channel, where the frantic evacuation at Dunkirk in late May and early June of 1940 managed to save the British Expeditionary Force as well as many French soldiers. The retreat by sea of almost half a million French and British troops rescued an army, but it demoralized two exhausted and weakened nations. Churchill, in office only a week, had tried everything to bolster the French government and its army. But the fact that the British did not evacuate more French citizens was one of the several events during this hectic period that would drive a wedge between England and France. Numerous French right-wing politicians opined: "The British want to fight to the last drop of French blood."

By June 8, the Germans had crossed the Somme, north of Paris, and then the lower Seine, east of the capital. A German journalist exalted the pace of Hitler's legions:

> Incredibly, the campaign is playing out quite differently than in 1914: miracles are now on our side. Each milepost gives witness: Paris 70 km, Paris 60 km, Paris 58 km....The horses of our Eastern Prussian cavalry are already drinking from the Seine....I feel a hand on my shoulder. Turning, I look into the smiling face of...the commander in our section: "'Do you want to go with me to Paris?' 'What?! Really?' 'Yes! To ask the city to surrender,' he said with an air of triumph."[6]

As the capital slipped into imminent danger of being surrounded, the confusion that settled in at French army headquarters at Vincennes, on the western edge of Paris, was startling. The absence of a radio (wireless) connection with their armies, even the lack of carrier pigeons (used with some success during the Franco-Prussian War and the First World War), compounded the cluelessness of France's general staff. Within five weeks of their first incursions into Luxembourg, Belgium, and the Netherlands, German forces would reach the Loire, roughly halfway into France. Unable to duplicate the miraculous stands of 1914 and 1918 that had saved Paris, the French army would be swept away like chaff in a brisk spring wind.

Meanwhile, the Third Republic politicians were angrily divided; in varying degrees, their opinions were affected strongly by pacifism, a fear of communism, their hatred of the English, the fecklessness of their own military leadership, political ambition, and a stubborn admiration for Hitler's National Socialist experiment. All these factors froze Prime Minister Paul Reynaud's government. The interrogatories were endless: Does the army continue to defend French territory, eventually to the Pyrénées and the Mediterranean? Does the government leave France to lead the country from their African and Asian colonies? Or does it seek an armistice with Germany and save some French autonomy? Should Paris be defended in order to buy time for more English or eventual American intervention? Or does the army declare the city "open," crossing its fingers that the Germans will treat the French capital with respect?

Whatever answers emerged became concretized in the personalities of two leaders. The best known was the revered though mentally diminished eighty-four-year-old Maréchal Philippe Pétain, who had been leader of all French forces in the Great War and the victor at Verdun, the fort in eastern France that had withstood all that the Kaiser's armies could throw at it. The other was almost a nonentity, a young, recently promoted brigadier general, Charles de Gaulle, who flew back and forth between France and England at the behest of Prime Minister Reynaud to strategize about how to save France from defeat. But the pacifists and "dead-enders," those who would fight until death, did not have the weight of the others, nor did they have Philippe Pétain. The last cabinet meeting of the Third Republic in Paris was on June 9; it had only a month of life left. And then on June 10, Italy belatedly attacked France from the southeast.

Winston Churchill, who had only become prime minister on May 10, had flown several times to Paris and then to the Loire Valley, where the government had retreated on June 10 and June 13 — five quite dangerous trips amid an already intense war in order to buck up the French resistance to the Blitzkrieg. He pleaded with Prime Minister Reynaud to keep the French fighting, even defending Paris, and then, as events cascaded, Churchill urged him not to sign an armistice with the

Maréchal Philippe Pétain. *(Courtesy of the Library of Congress)*

Général Charles de Gaulle. *(Courtesy of the Library of Congress)*

Germans. Yet the British leader likely recognized the futility of his pleading. On his first visit to Paris, looking out a window of the Ministry of Foreign Affairs on the Quai d'Orsay, Churchill had watched as dozens of diplomatic staff members collected papers that had been thrown into the courtyard; he stared fixedly as they managed a bonfire that fiercely burned the dossiers. As the smoke cast a pall over the Left Bank, Reynaud assured him that the government was not going to leave its capital, an affirmation the British prime minister, in office but a few days, saw only as bravado. His thoughts punctuated by the heavy thuds of files landing in the courtyard, Churchill must then have realized that only England now stood between Hitler and European domination. But he had to ask, even if he knew what the answer would be; he had to exhort, even though he knew the eventual result.

An exhausted Reynaud was persistent in his telegrams to President Roosevelt that he would not leave Paris to the Germans without a fight, sending a message through American ambassador William Bullitt as late as June 10: "Today the enemy is almost at the gates of Paris. We shall fight in front of Paris; we shall fight behind Paris; we shall close ourselves in one of our provinces to fight and should we be driven out of it we shall establish ourselves in North Africa to continue the fight, and if necessary in our American colonies."[7] On his last day in Paris, before leaving for Tours, where the government had retreated, Reynaud wrote one final pathetic letter to President Roosevelt, imploring him to come to his nation's aid. The answer, as everyone knew, was that America would sit on the sidelines as France headed toward an armistice.

One of the major conundrums facing both the pro-armistice and the pro-resistance groups was what to do with the French capital. To let it go without a fight would be so disheartening, so humiliating to the French, not to mention the Allies, that France might take years to recover. Yet to defend it would mean bringing destruction upon the world's best-known urban masterpiece. Some generals argued for the latter decision, saying that it was time the world saw how relentlessly uncivilized the Third Reich was. Let the French experience what the Poles and the Dutch have endured! But the Germans did not want to attack Paris, either; as early as May 26 or 27, Hitler had a discussion with his military leaders:

> We must defer the decision to continue toward the west of Paris, the Führer firmly declared. A large city like Paris can hide a thousand dangers: the enemy can throw at us between four hundred thousand and five hundred thousand men at any moment. Our tanks cannot carry on an intense combat in the streets. It's a trap.... On the contrary, our armies east [of the city] must be ready for an important armored force to take Paris quickly, but only if necessary.[8]

And two weeks later, once he knew the Battle of France had been won, Hitler reiterated: "I have no intention of attacking the beautiful capital of France. Our war machine is operating in the vicinity of the city. Paris has nothing to fear, provided that, like Brussels, it remains an 'open city.'"[9]

Taking Paris provided dilemmas for both sides. A small but destructive German air raid on Paris on June 3 had given a vision of what air bombardment could do to the City of Light. At the automobile factories of Renault and Citroën, near the fashionable neighborhoods of the 16th arrondissement, more than a thousand bombs had fallen, killing about forty-five civilians. Though this would be the last time until the Liberation that the Germans would bomb central Paris under Hitler's orders, curious residents could, and did, see "the smoking debris of an apartment house on the [fashionable] Boulevard Suchet, bordering the Bois de Boulogne, a gutted mansion in the Rue Poussin, in Auteuil: spectators then knew directly the violated intimacy of a bedroom cut in two, with its armoires, its broken dressers and chests from which hung against the empty skies a bathrobe, a coat or a pair of curtains."[10]

Recessed in the collective memory of the average Parisian was Guy de Maupassant's story "Boule de suif" ("Butterball"; 1880), about the Franco-Prussian conflict of 1870. Everyone who had attended the Third Republic's schools during its great initiative to establish universal public education knew this tale. At the beginning of the story, Maupassant describes the retreat of the French army as it pulls back across the Seine at the Norman capital of Rouen, fleeing before a relentless Prussian enemy:

> For several days in succession, remnants of a routed army had been passing through the town. They were not disciplined units but bands of stragglers. The men's beards were unkempt and dirty, their uniforms in rags, and they slouched along without colors or regiments. All of them seemed crushed and exhausted, incapable of thought or resolve, marching only out of force of habit, and dropping with fatigue as soon as they stopped.... Their leaders— former drapers or corn merchants, or sometimes dealers in soap and tallow—were only temporary warriors.... They talked in loud voices about campaign plans, and boastfully declared that they alone were carrying their dying country on their shoulders. But they sometimes went in fear of their own men, thoroughgoing scoundrels who were often incredibly brave, though given to looting and debauchery.[11]

Such depictions of the uninspired being led by the incompetent, both marching under the empty platitudes of patriotism, succinctly reinforced what was happening before Parisian eyes in late May and June of 1940. The French fought courageously, with high casualties: the Battle of France lasted a bit more than six weeks, but between 55,000 and 65,000 French and colonial troops had met their deaths, and maybe as many as 120,000 were wounded.* Almost two million were taken prisoner. But the conscripts' individual courage and sacrifice, and the resistance of some units, could not compensate for a

---

* Because a census of the dead was not taken immediately after the debacle, estimated numbers have bedeviled historians seeking certainty about the human cost of the Battle of France on the French army. Death figures have ranged between fifty thousand and ninety thousand. For details, see Jackson, *The Fall of France*, and Azéma, *1940: L'Année noire*.

paucity of planning and a lumbering, unimaginative battlefield response to the Blitzkrieg.

The departure of the central government left the capital bereft of political leadership. Overnight, Parisians realized that they had been comforted for weeks with misinformation and patriotic bombast. Spoken and unspoken questions permeated the city's marketplaces and cafés. How had the Germans advanced so rapidly? Where are they now? Who is between them and Paris? Is there a "fifth column" now in the city?★ It took a while for residents to believe that such a calamity, the collapse of their capital's defenses, could be allowed to happen, despite intimations to the contrary. Most Parisians—white- and blue-collar workers, bureaucrats, small businessmen, students, and the elderly—still held to the narcissistic notion that they and their city were not part of the war. When the Communists organized an anti-Nazi propaganda campaign, the reaction had been ho-hum. "What's the use of defeating Hitler if we wind up with the *Front populaire* [the Socialists and Communists]?" was a common observation. Another: *"Mieux vaut Hitler que Blum"* (Better Hitler than Blum—a Socialist prime minister and a Jew). Nor did the weather help prepare Parisians for disaster: many observers mentioned the clear, blue skies and mild temperatures that had favored the capital during the last weeks of May and early June. At first quietly, then less and less so, reality began to pierce this veil of lassitude. French cinemas had been showing newsreels of the German air bombardments of Warsaw in the fall of 1939 and then their flattening of Rotterdam in May. Concerns had been heightened by scenes of deeply frightened civilians, especially women and children, fleeing burning buildings with a few belongings—still, after all, this was Paris, and the French army was reputed to be at least equal to anything the upstart Germans could put in the field.

The war came inexorably closer to a Paris still locked in the false comfort of imagined protection. Irène Némirovsky describes how

---

★ "Fifth column" was a term that had originated during the Spanish Civil War, when a rebel general remarked that when he took Madrid his four columns would be supported by a virtual fifth—civilian supporters and guerrillas inside the city.

difficult it was for Paris to realize that it was itself part of the war and that it could be harmed:

> An air raid. All the lights were out, but beneath the clear, golden June sky, every house, every street was visible. As for the Seine, the river seemed to absorb even the faintest glimmers of light and reflect them back a hundred times brighter, like some multifaceted mirror. Badly blacked-out windows, glistening rooftops, the metal hinges of doors all shone in the water.... From above, it could be seen flowing along, as white as a river of milk. It guided the enemy planes, some people thought.[12]

The little hill villages of Auteuil and Passy had only been part of Paris since 1860, when they became the city's western 16th arrondissement. Then, as today, they included the most prestigious addresses, the sites of many embassies and consulates. By late May of 1940, the boulevards and streets of this cosseted area had become even quieter and certainly emptier than usual. Just two weeks after Hitler's invasion of Belgium, on May 10, chauffeured limousines, trunks filled, had begun easing efficiently southward, toward the Porte d'Orléans, Paris's gateway to the Loire Valley, where it was believed any German offensive would be stopped. How did these well-connected and affluent Parisians come to take to the roads even before the larger refugee lines would enter Paris from Flanders and northern France? Their highly placed connections had informed them that the city was in imminent danger and that, despite what the radio and newspapers were saying, the Battle of France was over. At the same time, in the eastern, working-class arrondissements of Paris, there was concern but not yet panic. After all, had not the government repeatedly promised that Paris would not fall, that the army would make the same ferocious stand it had made in 1914, when the taxicabs of Paris had brought reinforcements to the Marne to finally break the back of the German offensive? Besides, most of the working-class population of eastern Paris had no automobiles, little free time from work, and little money to buy train tickets. While one side of the city was quietly closing its shutters, locking its doors, emptying its safe-deposit boxes, and heading south out of town, the other was living daily in the expectation that everything would work out.

The massive and unanticipated defeat of its vaunted armed forces would have been enough to cause paralyzing anxiety in any besieged city. But hundreds of thousands of refugees from the Netherlands, Belgium, and northern France plodding relentlessly southward toward hoped-for sanctuary mesmerized the Parisians. These desperate northerners sharing roads with the remnants of a disorganized and dispirited French army drew a collective gasp from the theretofore complacent Parisians. It was not much longer before they too began joining that exodus, almost like metal filings pulled toward a strong magnet. This panicky act of running away would forge a profound sense of embarrassment, self-abasement, guilt, and a felt loss of masculine superiority that would mark the years of the Occupation.

Slowly, the news of military collapse spread to the middle-class and working-class neighborhoods as rumors flew about German paratroopers disguised as nuns and about Communists ready to take over the city hall. Newspapers warned of the ever-imagined "fifth column," ready to turn Paris over to the Germans, and, at the other extreme, of the resisters, ready to fight the Wehrmacht down to the last alleyway of the invaded city. Public anger grew, and citizens became much more vocal about the government's pusillanimity. The panic was more palpable because its cause was so unclear: Were Parisians supposed to stay and defend the city? Or hide? Or leave? Was the entire army retreating? Would there be a siege, as there was in 1870? Wrote a historian: "Those who leave are still making up excuses: the children, a sick relative, family business in the provinces. But, in the *beaux quartiers* especially [e.g., the 16th arrondissement], the streets are lined with building after building, shutters tightly closed, as if in the grip of a contagious illness."[13]

Stunningly, almost four million inhabitants fled Paris and its environs in late May and early June rather than await the increasingly inevitable occupation of their precious capital.* Several memoirists mention that Parisian boulevards soon resembled empty movie sets—an ironic comment given the reputation of the city as a somewhat artificial but beautiful exemplum of urban life. Groceries and bakeries were closed, their entrances barricaded; automobiles had vanished; dogs ran unleashed (if they had not been poisoned by their owners); diplomats and ministries burned so much paper that a smoky pall

A strangely empty Champs-Élysées. (Verlag der Deutschen Arbeitsfront)

---

* Again, estimates vary according to which historian is doing the figuring and whether or not Paris per se (ca. three million inhabitants) or the entire Paris region (ca. five to seven million inhabitants) is being considered. The point is that millions of families took to roads already crowded with a retreating army. For details, see Diamond, *Fleeing Hitler*, and Leleu, et al., *La France pendant la Seconde Guerre Mondiale: Atlas Historique*.

unnerved the citizens who believed that the Germans were at their gates. Distilleries and oil storage farms added greasy clouds to the mix. Rumors outran attempts by the remaining authorities at calming fears; a few citizens committed suicide. Everyone, it seemed, suddenly wanted to leave their city before it was attacked and invaded by a relentless foreign army.

Again, one of the most compelling narratives that we have of this, the largest civilian exodus in modern times up to that point, comes from Némirovsky. We should remember that she wrote her novel while the events were still fresh in her mind, just a year or so afterward, and the vividness of her descriptions of the panic that took hold of northern France and Paris is incomparable. She describes a world turned upside down, where lost or abandoned children ran wild, mothers stole gasoline, the elderly were left behind, self-interest and greed were rampant, and class divisions were exacerbated; where the fear of strafing planes, marauding French soldiers, and other looters dominated life minute by minute. And no one knew exactly where he or she was heading—toward what or whom, or how far to run. When would times return to normal? The exodus, in Némirovsky's hands, takes on an almost mythical cast for those who later heard of it:

> Occasionally the road rose more steeply and they could see clearly the chaotic multitude trudging through the dust, stretching far into the distance. The luckiest ones had wheelbarrows, a pram, a cart made of four planks of wood set on top of crudely fashioned wheels, bowing down under the weight of bags, tattered clothes, sleeping children.... [Poor and rich] had suddenly been gripped by panic.... None of them knew why they were bothering to flee: all of France was burning; there was danger everywhere.... These great human migrations seemed to follow natural laws.[14]

And further on, one character likens his joining the exodus to those who escaped Pompeii under the ash of Vesuvius, leaving behind all that was important to them, not knowing when they would return or if their homes or possessions would be the same when they did.

Fleeing uncertainty. *(© LAPI / Roger-Viollet / The Image Works)*

French and foreign Jews felt especially vulnerable. Most just stayed put, praying somehow that the French government and its republican traditions would protect them from Nazi racism. But a few read the writing on the wall more astutely than others. One was a Jewish diamond merchant whose family had been French for generations and who was prescient enough to understand that not only was his business about to suffer, so were his wife and children if the Nazis instituted their racial policies in France. He had quietly procured exit visas for his family and had hired automobiles to drive them from Paris to the Spanish border and safety. One major problem remained. Border guards all over Europe had discovered how easy it was to demand bribes from fleeing Jews and other hunted persons, and the merchant knew that he would not be able to successfully carry his valuable stock of diamonds over the border. He had to leave them hidden in Paris—but where? Taking a rather risky chance, he decided to rely on a friend, a soccer buddy from his lycée years, a Gentile.

The plan he devised was audacious. Heating up a large amount of lardlike unguent, he poured the mixture into a tall, clear jar. Then he dribbled the clear, precious stones into the liquid, constantly stirring it as it cooled, so that the gems would not settle to the bottom. Soon the concoction congealed; from the outside, the suspended diamonds were invisible. He arrived at his friend's home, holding the apparently innocuous bottle as if he were carrying a child.

His friend welcomed him with the warmth he had expected. After they worried together about the current state of Paris and France, the diamond trader said: "I must leave France, for obvious reasons. I am unsure about when I will be able to return, but I do know that I would like to have this jar of a family remedy, an unguent for all that ails you, waiting here for me. It means a lot to my family and to our memories. Could I ask you to keep it?" Bemused, his friend accepted the consignment, relieved that the request was as simple as storing a bottle in his house. The merchant left, unburdened but apprehensive. Had he outsmarted himself? Should he have told his friend what the jar contained? What if...? But more immediate concerns dominated. Fortunately, the merchant's escape with his family was a success. Making their way into and across Spain, they set sail from Portugal for the United States, where they remained for five long years. Around the dinner table, hundreds of times, the family wondered about that apparently innocuous bottle sitting in a dark cupboard back in occupied Paris. In early 1946, when our merchant could finally return to the city, he found himself once again in his friend's kitchen. For a while they exchanged stories of the war years. After a bit, the Jewish friend broached the subject that had preoccupied him for half a decade: "Do you recall that jar of unguent I left with you in June of 1940?" At first, his friend looked puzzled. "Jar? Unguent?" Then he remembered what had not crossed his mind since his friend had left. Getting up from the table, he rummaged around in a remote cupboard, mumbling: "I hope we didn't throw it out when we moved things around during the war." The merchant politely waited, his guts in a knot. "Aha! I found it, I think. Is this the jar?"

"Oh, yes," the merchant answered, holding it, once again, as if it were a fragile Ming vase. "Now I have a story for you. Could you light up your stove and get me a sieve and a pan?"

Soon the contents of the jar were bubbling away over a low flame. Taking the sieve, the merchant poured the pot's contents into another container, and there, nestled in the mesh, was his diamond reserve, the gems sparkling as if they had never been covered with animal fat and salve. The grateful merchant selected the brightest, largest diamond from the pile and handed it to his speechless host. "Take this one for your dear wife."

Most stories of fast and permanent exits were not to have such happy endings. The great majority of those fleeing before the Blitzkrieg were women and children, for most men had been drafted; many were already in POW camps or in hiding. Those who had obtained leave from conscription because of important civilian jobs were advised to flee rather than be sent off to work in Germany. Scenes of babies, toddlers, and teenagers clinging to their parents, or of grandparents sitting on the family's cart or in a packed automobile, filled the population with a self-perpetuating panic. A journalist wrote that "houses emptied themselves of women and children, burdened with luggage, who ran toward the Métro. Families piled in and on their automobiles packages, bags, luggage, and mattresses,* even birdcages...!"[15]

With Germany not yet at war with the United States, the American ambassador to France, William Bullitt, and Roger Langeron, the prefect of police, became in effect "mayors" of the bewildered city during the few hectic days between the government's retreat to the Loire Valley and the arrival of the Wehrmacht. Bullitt had already refused Roosevelt's suggestion that he follow the government to Bordeaux. This loyalty (though it would freeze his own career in the diplomatic service) ensured trusted communication as the diplomat and the police chief tried to figure out how to keep peace in a city filled with leaderless

---

* Mattresses, always mattresses—the sight is so attached to images of refugee flight that we have become used to it. There is probably no action more symbolic of leaving home in distress. What prompts refugees, even today, to load themselves down with their bedding? Refugees in 1940 may have brought their mattresses with them as pitiful protection against strafing planes or, especially, as temporary bedding. But it also makes sense that when being forced to leave home, one clings to some symbol of the private life that has been upended. An uncertain future demands a secure place in which to wait for it. (See O. F. Bollnow, *Human Space*.)

and retreating French soldiers, savvy but worried Jewish citizens, frightened eastern European refugees, stubborn French patriots, and antsy looters. One of the best eyewitness accounts we have of those few days comes from Langeron's diary, published in 1945. It gives a week-by-week account of the ways in which the French police "accommodated" themselves to the German presence. Strongly positive when it came to his department, the diary nevertheless reveals the frustration of not knowing how to turn over a major metropolis peacefully to a confident invader. Langeron opens his diary with a sardonic description of the government's strained justifications for leaving Paris. It was June 10, 1940, only four days before the first German soldiers would enter the city. Across from his desk at headquarters sat a man he much admired, Georges Mandel, the recently named minister of the interior and thus his immediate superior. The sky over the city remained heavy with the acrid smoke from burning mountains of files and dossiers and from munitions and fuel depots. Ash could be seen floating in the mild winds that swept over a peaceful Île de la Cité, site of the Préfecture de police. A chagrined Mandel officially informed his friend that the country's government was moving south toward the Loire, abandoning the capital. He reminded the police chief that his task was to "retain order" should the Germans arrive before either an armistice or an improbable French victory. Langeron respected, even admired, Mandel, but he observed in his journal, with a dab of black humor, that this was the twelfth minister of the interior under whom he had served since his appointment in 1934.

Having already taken careful notice from his office window of the thousands of refugees heading southward, like the government, Langeron recognized the possibility of urban chaos. The predictable environment that a police chief covets was disintegrating before his very eyes. The police were responsible for ensuring that the city was supplied with food, that its utility services and public and private transportation were maintained, that access to clinics and hospitals remained unencumbered, and that laws were enforced. Traffic, snarled by thousands of confused refugees and retreating French soldiers, must remain orderly; looting had to be controlled; those left behind had to be monitored. Though confident that he and his cohort were primed for these tasks, a nervous Langeron continued to resent that the government had abandoned Paris. It was one thing to lose a city in honorable battle; it was quite another to desert the nation's capital in a panic. To forsake Paris was to forsake the whole French empire. He had received little intelligence about the German advance, even less about their plans for Paris, other than what he could glean from his own patrols and from information coming in from outposts in the near countryside. The military command of the city was as clueless as he. He could call on no precedent, no instructions, no guidance about how to prepare for transferring administrative and police powers to the Occupation authorities.

Confusion reigned at the highest military levels. Policemen were given rifles to carry; city buses were ordered to block main arteries; plans for bombing bridges were bruited about. General Pierre Héring, commander of Paris, told the police prefects of the region on June 11 that "the capital would be defended to the last," but a day earlier, General Weygand, supreme military commander, had announced that "Paris [will be] an Open City. In order that Paris preserve its character as an Open City it is my intention to avoid any defensive organization around the city on the belt of the old fortifications or on that of the ancient forts."★ [16] We can only imagine how frustrating these contradictory messages from the military authority were for the average Parisian eager for usable information — not to mention for those responsible for civil order. Such confusion was amplified by the fact that posters informing Parisians of the proclamation of an "open city" would not appear on walls until June 13, only a few hours before the first Germans would appear on the arteries of the metropolis.

To finally declare Paris an open city was a political rather than a

---

★ The concept of an "open city" has an ambiguous place in international jurisprudence. It relies on two opposing armies to agree that a major conurbation will not be defended and thus not be bombed. The agreement has a logic for both sides: the attackers will not have to waste time, materiel, and men to take a heavily fortified metropolis, and the retreating army saves its citizens, its nation's patrimony, and leaves a potential thorn in the side of the occupying forces. Of course, delicate negotiations have to precede such an arrangement, and such situations are rife with the possibility of misunderstandings.

military decision. Such a decision made sense militarily; politically less so unless we understand the obsessive concerns of the army, the Catholic Church, the industrialist cadre, and the conservative right wing about the Communists (and the Socialists, whom they believed to be Communists in sheep's wool). Should the city be left to its own defenses, even under army control, it could quickly institute another Commune-type government, as it had after the long Prussian siege in 1870, and could instigate thereby another civil war, making France even more vulnerable to German intervention. On June 12, Langeron learned from French military headquarters about the open-city declaration. Not having been notified in time to prepare his officers, he saw the pronouncement as yet another feckless decision made by a timorous government in order to cover its own retreat. The three conditions that the Germans had imposed so that Paris might remain "open" were blunt: no destruction of bridges, no looting, and the population must remain indoors for forty-eight hours. Easier said than done. How was Langeron supposed to control remnants of the French army that might want to resist, or angry Parisians, or agents provocateurs, or citizens who needed milk, bread, and other necessities? What if German units were fired, stoned, or spat on? What if Parisians took to the streets to form human barricades to forestall the military occupation of their city? What if civil war broke out between those who were satisfied with the Armistice and those who despised the Nazis? What about the tens of thousands of refugees from Nazi Germany and eastern Europe? How would they react? These thoughts kept Langeron nervously awake as he tried to make sense of an unprecedented event.

The government itself having decamped on June 10, the rest of the city was now in full flight. One historian has put it succinctly: "The entire social fabric to which people were accustomed, all the points of reference on which they had been socialized to depend, suddenly collapsed without warning in a way they could not understand."[17] The citizens would return, especially after the Armistice went into effect on June 25, but slowly, and they would return abashed. The hangover from this mass exit would affect the relationship between the Occupying forces and the Parisians for months to come. On returning to Paris, after having joined the exodus, the pro-German writer and publisher Jean de la Hire described what he saw, when, too late to venture into the streets after curfew, he had to spend the night in the train station:

> A Paris prodigiously empty and silent appeared outside the closed gates of the station, guarded by two policemen in capes and képis. At 5:30 a.m., the gates open. And the crowd spreads out into Paris, or is swallowed up by the Métro. I wait in front of the station.... German motorized patrols. Not one civilian car, not a bistro open. What Paris is this? My heart sank. A sudden noise as a large black airplane appears and passes overhead, skimming the roofs.... French police, alone, watch over absent traffic.[18]

A number of small merchants who had not fled told him that they had had no option: they couldn't leave their businesses or their families. They had lived through worse; this, too, would pass.

During the last two weeks of June, meeting in Bordeaux, with the German army closing in on that city, the French government watched as events unfolded almost surreally. The first stunner: Churchill and his cabinet offered, if France would not sign an armistice with the Germans, to form a political union between Great Britain and France. De Gaulle phoned Reynaud from Paris and read him the agreement proposed by Churchill's government:

> At this most fateful moment in the history of the modern world, the Governments of the United Kingdom and the French Republic make this declaration of indissoluble union and unyielding resolution in their common defense of justice and freedom.... The two Governments declare that France and Great Britain shall no longer be two nations but one Franco-British Union. The constitution of the Union will provide for joint organs of defense, foreign, financial and economic policies. Every citizen of France will enjoy immediately citizenship of Great Britain; every British subject will become a citizen of France.[19]

Reynaud was ecstatic, but by then the forces in favor of an armistice had taken control of the cabinet, and Maréchal Pétain was asked by President Albert Lebrun to form a new government on June 17. The next day the Maréchal inexplicably announced on national radio that an armistice was already in effect (though he had not yet negotiated with the Germans) and ordered French troops to lay down their arms. The result was even more chaos in the ranks, for although many French soldiers followed his instructions, many did not, unsure who was in charge of the government. The Germans, of course, were delighted, and they drove into towns waving white flags to broadcast that the Battle of France was over. One of my sources told me that the Germans would enter a town, call the next town's city hall, and ask if they were going to defend it. If the answer was no, the German officer would respond: "Good. We'll be there within the hour." On June 18, a few days before the signing of an armistice, Hitler met in Rome with Mussolini about the next steps regarding France. Il Duce demanded that Italy be permitted to occupy the Rhône Valley, Marseille, even Corsica. But Hitler was firm, for he recognized that the French must be kept from falling into Britain's arms and that the French Mediterranean fleet must not join the Royal Navy. He needed "to secure...a French government functioning on French territory. This would be far preferable to a situation in which the French might reject the German proposals and flee abroad to London [as de Gaulle had already done] to continue the war from there."[20]

Poor Pétain thought he might still have some leverage with the Germans, but given his eagerness to stop the hemorrhaging of his own armed forces, in the end, on June 22, at Compiègne, only fifty miles northeast of Paris, the Third Republic signed an agreement that in effect divided France into multiple zones. Hitler was ecstatic; in one of the most frequently shown film clips of the war, he is seen doing a little jig outside the railcar where the Armistice had been signed—the same railcar where the Germans had acceeded to a similar armistice in November of 1918. Two days later, an Italian-French armistice was signed.

All fighting was declared to have ceased at 1:35 a.m. next morning. Hitler proclaimed the end of the war in the west and the "most glorious victory of all time." He ordered bells to be rung in the Reich for a week, and flags to be flown for ten days. As the moment for the official conclusion of hostilities drew near, Hitler, sitting at the wooden table in his field headquarters [in Belgium], ordered the lights extinguished and the windows opened in order to hear, in the darkness, the trumpeter outside marking the historic moment.[21]

Less than three weeks later, France's Third Republic cravenly voted itself out of existence and installed in its place yet another quasi-fascist regime in Europe, only twenty-two miles from Great Britain:

The National Assembly [of the Third Republic] gives all powers to the Government of the Republic under the authority and the signature of Maréchal Pétain to promulgate by one or several edicts a new constitution of the French State [henceforth, the so-called Vichy government would be officially known as the État français]. This constitution will guarantee the rights of Work, Family and [Nation]. It will be ratified by the nation and applied by the assemblies that it will create.[22]

The Armistice, as we have seen, divided France into several occupied and unoccupied regions and was unique in Nazi Germany's relations with other occupied nations. No other conquered nation was permitted to have its own sovereign territory after a Nazi victory.

For rather mundane reasons—because it was a spa town that had a plethora of hotel rooms and superb rail connections with most of France—Vichy, almost at the geographical center of France, became the seat of the new État français, successor to the legislatively abolished Third Republic. The name of this dowager city would forever be associated with that new state, the word *Vichy* still evoking memories of national shame, guilt, and anger. It is difficult to explain to someone who does not intimately know French culture how even such rather mundane terms as *eau de Vichy* and *vichyssois* still retain just a hint of the odor of a repellent government. But as France seemed to be dissolving under the German Blitzkrieg, the Armistice was welcomed by most as God-sent, especially when incarnated in the person of the "victor of Verdun," Maréchal Philippe Pétain. His reputation was impeccable.* He vigorously requested that his government be located in Paris, or at least in nearby Versailles, but Hitler refused this request, and the État français would remain in the backwater of Vichy for the duration.

Thus did France begin its collaboration with the regime that had defeated it.

---

* It is hard to believe, but it was only in March of 2013 that the last street in France named for Pétain was "debaptized." Christened Rue du Maréchal Pétain in the 1930s, before he became associated with the Vichy government, the little avenue is in Belrain, a village of about forty inhabitants in the northeast of France, about twenty-five miles from Verdun. The town will rename the avenue, most likely after someone who resisted the Vichy government.

Chapter Two

⋆⟿⟞⋆

Waiting for Hitler

Paris worried Hitler.

—August von Kageneck[1]

"They" Arrive, and Are Surprised

In mid-June of 1940, the German army arrived before Paris, exuberant but stunned. They could see in the distance the Eiffel Tower, standing as confidently over the world's most recognized cityscape as when it had first appeared there just fifty-one years earlier. The Wehrmacht had been almost as surprised as the French at the ease of their foray into the Low Countries and France. Their victory had not been a foregone conclusion. Hindsight has given us a quite benign view of what the Allies and Germans expected in 1940: "The campaign was won so swiftly and decisively that, retrospectively, both sides came to view its outcome as inevitable."[2] More imaginative and forceful leadership on behalf of the Allies could well have stymied even the panzer-led Blitz-krieg the Germans had so brilliantly planned. The Battle of France could have bogged down in the same area as it had in the First World War, and Germany could have been quickly bled and spent to death before realizing its aims. But luck and Allied pusillanimity made Hitler into a military genius, and now another German army was ready to occupy, this time for years, the capital of France.

Just a generation before, the Kaiser's troops had lost major battles in their attempt to take the city. Still, the Germans were a bit abashed at their new responsibility as occupiers: "The German generals, of whom many had fought in the First World War, had psychological difficulty in realizing the depth, and especially the rapidity of their victory [over the French Army]." One young lieutenant wrote home: "My thoughts are turning in on themselves. My mind truly wants to understand. We are the victors. But our heart is not yet ready to seize the immensity of this fact, all the grandeur of these events, the full significance of our victory. We talk about it amongst ourselves, we try to understand it, but without success."[3] The fact of their victory was in effect more intimidating than had been the armed forces of their enemy.

There had been almost no French military defense of Paris, so there had been no excuse for the Wehrmacht to hesitate in driving right into the prize. But an awkward lull had briefly prevailed. Waiting outside the city on June 13, a day before his army would formally enter it, one young lieutenant was impatient. Asked to make plans for his battalion's quarters when they entered the capital, he borrowed a BMW motorcycle, and using the Byzantine dome of the Basilique du Sacré-Coeur as his guide, drove straight into Montmartre, on the city's northern edge. The streets, he felt, were strangely empty, but when he stopped in the neighborhood's most famous plaza, the Place du Tertre, a crowd instantly gathered. They were looking at their first German soldier— who suddenly lost his earlier exuberance. Turning around, he sped back behind his lines to safety.

Because French authorities had devised few sensible plans about how to protect against the military capture of Paris, they had been forced to resort at the last minute to the open-city strategy. Had Parisians fought to defend their capital street by street, at least for a while, the sense of helplessness, despair, and humiliation that they would feel for years might have been somewhat mitigated. Many of the eyewitness accounts we have from the first Germans to enter the city underline both their surprise at the ease of occupying the world's best-known capital and their pleasure at being able to enjoy its advantages from day one.

Not one shot had been fired in the city's defense. Now Teutons were riding brazenly through the streets of the City of Light for the first time since 1870, with plans to stay much longer. Their own curiosity was manifest in every action they took: How should we treat the occupants of a city that had not lifted a finger against us? Later in the day, when regular army formations began to roll more confidently down the city's grand boulevards, Wehrmacht soldiers expressed consternation, even derision, at the many smiling, waving French: Don't they have any pride? But the French were amazed—and relieved—at the handsome, "correct," and well-behaved German ranks. To some, they almost seemed to have deserved victory over the poorly led and poorly trained French army.

That first morning, Roger Langeron's assistant informed him that two official German army automobiles had driven up to the Préfecture. Four officers had gotten out and walked calmly into the reception area, where they made a polite request to speak with the police chief. Langeron had been waiting for some sort of official communiqué since news had reached him earlier that German patrols had entered the city proper. They had taken up positions throughout Paris, but no official contact between his administration and the conquering army had yet occurred. When the young German officers arrived in his office, they were almost deferential, he thought, too young to have fought in the Great War and thus too green to understand the enormous symbolism of their victory over the French. The present German army was filled with men born during the last war or right after—youth who had been brought up on hatred for the way the French had treated their fathers in defeat and anger at the occupation of the Rhineland in the 1920s. Langeron also wondered if these officers might be from the German provinces rather than from a large city, for they seemed uncomfortable in the nerve center of Paris. The Germans politely requested that Langeron appear at the Hôtel de Crillon, their temporary headquarters on the Place de la Concorde, at 11:00 that morning to meet the general in command of the army that was supervising the Occupation. Finally, Langeron thought, he would receive instructions on protocol and his legal responsibilities. The Germans would tell him what the French military command of Paris could—or would—not do.

Reports had continued to arrive at the Préfecture that German troops and vehicles, both logistical and armed, were entering Paris from the north and northeast. Strangely enough, horses and mules pulled much of the materiel. The wagons had pneumatic tires, but Parisian observers were startled and not a little amused by the disjunction between the reputation of the highly mechanized Wehrmacht, with its notorious panzer divisions, and this nineteenth-century mode of transport. The city remained quiescent; the citizens who had not left stayed inside, shutters closed. German foot and motorcycle patrols were traversing the city, from the Boulevard Saint-Michel on the Left Bank to the Avenue des Champs-Élysées on the Right Bank. Advance units of Germans were lowering French flags from official buildings and replacing them with a striking red flag bearing a black swastika inside a white circle. (Purported French sabotage of the Eiffel Tower's elevators meant that the Nazi flag had to be carried up the one-thousand-foot monument on booted feet.) German cars fitted with loudspeakers circulated, demanding the surrender of private arms and threatening with the death penalty any hostile acts against the Occupation authorities. Germans were putting up signs in their language to help direct the new, massive military traffic. Nevertheless, Paris remained calm, almost somnolent. Even passive resistance was minimal, if it occurred at all. The Wehrmacht was able to move into the city with alacrity and precision and to establish firm control. Langeron took pride in maintaining order during this awkward period and in the fact that so few of his officers had left with the exodus. The French police maintained what remained of general traffic, occasionally with the polite assistance of their German counterparts. Were the police collaborating with a new authority, or were they protecting their city from the whims of a nervous occupier? The question would persist for years, and Langeron himself would be investigated for collaboration after the war.

Unbeknownst to those who had breathed a sigh of relief at the polite invasion of their city by the Wehrmacht, the Gestapo had followed on the army's heels.* Langeron, in his diary, presents a vignette that must

---

* The Gestapo (short for Geheime Staatspolizei, or secret state police) was a political police arm of the Third Reich, founded by Hermann Göring and greatly enhanced and led by Heinrich Himmler. It operated both in Germany and in the occupied countries.

have been repeated throughout the city in those early days. He was in his private apartment, in the Préfecture de police, when he was informed that a high Nazi official wished to see him downstairs in his office. The police chief took his time to get dressed and had to be called once again. Finally he showed up to confront an exasperated representative of the Occupation authorities, this time a civilian, not an army officer.

Langeron surmised that his guest must be from the Gestapo. Sitting down at his desk, the chief watched as the smug bureaucrat, whom he had left standing, grew more and more agitated at this lack of respect. Finally the German sat down and asked if Langeron still believed himself to be under the orders of that "Jew Mandel." The man added, "We know you are anti–German, Monsieur Langeron." Earlier, in September of 1939, when the German diplomatic delegation was leaving Paris for Berlin at the beginning of hostilities, the head of the legation had offered his hand to the Parisian police chief, who had refused to take it. That minor sign of resistance had been noted in the Gestapo's files. Langeron was amused at the pettiness of his new bosses, but then the German asked a much more serious question: "Where are the police files?" Langeron wrote that his heart beat faster with pleasure, for he had outsmarted this pompous secret policeman and his cohort. A few days before, the French police had loaded onto two barges, docked at the Quai des Orfèvres, right alongside the Préfecture, a large consignment of the police files; on one boat were those of foreigners, on another those dealing with delicate matters of espionage and politics. The barges had proceeded downstream, loaded with explosives in case of capture. He told the agent that the police files had been evacuated with other official dossiers when the government decamped to Tours and Bordeaux, and he had no idea of their whereabouts. Red-faced and blustering, the agent demanded to see Langeron's department heads. Brought in, they repeated the same story. When the German official left, in more than a huff, Langeron was quite delighted at his initial effort at resistance but also sadly aware that the tone of the Occupation would change inexorably from one of genteel accommodation to one of mutual suspicion.

51

As the refugees began returning or through Paris in late June and early July, they were surprised to see a city more relaxed than the one they had so quickly left behind. After two or three weeks on the crowded roads south of Paris, they were exhausted and fearful. Yet everything seemed to be as it had been, except for the gray-green uniforms of thousands of foreign soldiers. The swastika was indeed flying from the Eiffel Tower, and the German language was everywhere. One American, married to a prominent Frenchman, was especially offended by the plethora of red, white, and black German standards: "The horrible and hideous symbols of German domination made the city I loved hateful. They did not float over the housetops and towers like the flags of civilized nations so that one had to raise the eye to see them, but hung in the direct line of vision, suspended like huge carpets waiting to be beaten."[4]

But while there was no doubt that the Germans were there, none of the anticipated destruction or panic or shortages were manifest. This

Swastika banners were everywhere. (Musée de la Résistance nationale)

would be one of the major contradictions that would define the early Occupation. The newsreels of the German army's advance through Europe that Parisians had watched for months in movie houses had not prepared them for a "correct" invasion. Once again, they felt separated from a government that had persistently lied to them. Perhaps it would not be so bad to have the Germans here after all. At least now there was order, precision, and predictability.

For the next four months or so, until October of 1940, Langeron juggled three important responsibilities: maintaining distance between his police and the Occupation authorities; keeping the newly instituted État français (Vichy) government at arm's length; and establishing a sort of "secular" order in a bewildered city. The return of the thousands of Parisians who had fled, though a welcome sight, placed increased and complex demands on the police forces. Once again, he had to worry about whether this new influx would be carrying a dangerous animus toward the Germans that could ignite an urban revolt. Working out an agreement with a novice and nervous Occupation force about how to reassimilate this enormous population demanded Langeron's most subtle diplomatic skills. And the repopulation of the weary city proceeded with only minor disruptions.

One Who Stayed, One Who Left

His closest friends had slipped out of town before the arrival of the Germans, so the well-known Spanish artist Pablo Picasso had also escaped, traveling to Royan, on France's southwestern coast, far from Paris, ostensibly to ride out the occupation, which did not yet have a capital O. The Germans, most thought, would leave Paris soon, after the British had surrendered or had also signed an armistice. Yet even that "soon" was not enough for Picasso, who decided to return to Paris in August of 1940, where he remained for the duration. The question persists: Why did this timorous artist, whose masterpiece, *Guernica,* had blatantly criticized the muscular fascism of the Germans at the Exposition Internationale des Arts et Techniques dans la Vie Moderne in 1937, scurry back? He was world famous, which might provide a degree of protection, but he was also an outspoken supporter of those who opposed Franco. Rumors continued to persist among many on the right that he was Jewish or Communist—or, maybe worse, both; he was certainly on the left. Yet he refused repeated offers to wait out the war in New York or South America.

Picasso told his friend Brassaï (the pseudonym of the brilliant Hungarian photographer Gyula Halász) that he had returned to Paris because he could only get certain materials for his work there, that he trusted only the printers and foundries of Paris. Whatever the reason, the draw of the city was too strong to resist for the Spanish genius. Still, he was never quite at rest in the changed capital. One can only imagine the vacillations that accompanied his decision to return to Paris only two months after the Germans had arrived. As the art historian Rosalind Krauss has suggested, Picasso's fine-tuned sensitivity dominated his every waking moment (and most likely his dreams): "[Picasso's anxiety] is there in what [Françoise] Gilot [his mistress] calls 'the disease of the will that made it impossible for him to make the slightest domestic decision', a disease that produces...frequent scenes during which Picasso argues with an irrational persistence that reduces [his] interlocutors to tears."[5] After the war, he would assume a mask of boldness that put to rest many questions regarding his apparent "neutrality" while living in the city during the Occupation: "He explained how he had been able to work in the face of Nazi occupation and [that] party's antagonism to all forms of modern art, saying: 'It was not a time for creative man to fail, to shrink, to stop working,' and 'there was nothing else to do but work seriously and devotedly, struggle for food, see friends quietly and look forward to freedom'."[6] He was fined once, for eating a steak in a restaurant on a meatless day, but this was as close as he came to confronting the Occupation authorities. In fact, having remained in Paris during the Occupation, then joining the Communist Party immediately after the Liberation, gave Picasso a postwar cachet of courageous resistance that is generally belied by the low profile he kept during the dark years. He had only one, very discreet, gallery show between 1940 and 1944, and though he received many visitors and kept up relations with a wide variety of artists—many of whom were openly anti-Vichy, if not anti-Nazi—Picasso's silhouette was gray against a dark background.

Picasso established a studio on the Rue des Grands-Augustins, in the Left Bank's 6th arrondissement, right next to the Seine, and he would walk there daily from his much fancier apartment in the Rue La Boétie, across the river. Soon he abandoned the latter and settled in a large, loft-like apartment on the Left Bank, quite near his favorite restaurant, Le Catalan, and the bustle of the Saint-Germain-des-Prés crossroads. And he did work during those four years. On the top floors of this old building (which one may now visit), he put a sign at his door that said simply: ICI ("Here"). German officers would stop by (and even, against orders, so would German enlisted men), as would other admirers who were in

Picasso in his Left Bank studio. *(© Pierre Jahan / Roger-Viollet / The Image Works)*

Paris during those troubled years. Indeed, the home of the world's best-known artist became a required tourist stop in the occupied city. He adroitly used his notoriety to protect himself from those who did not wish him well, who could not understand why he was allowed to continue to live a free man given his anti-fascism. He was protected, too, by some of the Reich's own artists, most notably the sculptor Arno Breker, one of Hitler's favorites. And he was discreet. There is an anecdote in the diary of the Russian-British journalist Alexander Werth describing how Picasso even stood in line to request French nationality, just as any other foreigner had to do: "He's fed up with being a Spaniard. But you know what our red tape is like. Not long ago, I found him standing in a long queue at the Préfecture [de police]; and I had to rescue him. Do you know that Picasso is one of the very biggest taxpayers in France? Last year he paid 750,000 francs in income tax."[7]

Still, though the reasons why he stayed there were never clear—either to his friends or, perhaps, even to himself—Picasso's presence in Paris reassured other artists and writers that there could be life and productivity under the Germans. (The Germans might have tolerated his presence as part of their mission to make their Occupation seem relatively benign. Picasso probably intuited this was true.) Henri Matisse, almost as well known as Picasso, had also elected to remain in France during the war, residing in Nice and Vence, in southeastern France. That area was a bit safer, for the Italians controlled it, and they were much less restrictive than the Germans. He, too, ignored pleas from all over the world to emigrate. Matisse, however, was French, not Spanish; he was never considered a Jew or a leftist, as was Picasso. In his conversations with Picasso and his friends, Brassaï quotes an exchange he had with the poet Jacques Prévert. They were discussing Picasso in October of 1943:

We should be grateful to [Picasso]. [Staying] was an act of courage. The man is not a hero. Just like anyone who has something to say or to defend. It's easy to be a hero when you're only risking your life. For his part, he could, and can still lose everything. Who knows what turn the war will take. Paris may be destroyed. He's got a bad record with the Nazis, and could be interned, deported, taken hostage. Even his works—"degenerate" art and "Bolshevik" art—have already been condemned and could be burned at the stake. . . . And the more desperate Hitler and his acolytes become, the more dangerous, deadly, and destructive their rage may be. Can Picasso guess how they might react? He has assumed the risk. He is with us. Picasso is a fine guy.[8]

For the Germans, even the most ignorant of them, Paris was not just any city; it was an idea, a myth. By serendipity, creative planning, and massive amounts of public funding, the French capital had come to represent tolerance, liberty, and a crucible for the imagination. No one represented this image more than a young African American woman who came to Paris at the age of nineteen in 1925. Josephine Baker arrived fresh, seductive, and very brown to a jazz-obsessed city. Straight

Josephine Baker. *(© TopFoto / The Image Works)*

from Saint Louis, Missouri, she became an overnight sensation at the Casino de Paris and the Folies Bergère with her production *La Revue nègre*. Brilliantly playing upon the contradictory European fascination with and abhorrence of black sexuality, she adapted her style and performances to the newfound Parisian love for American popular music, imported by African American soldiers during the First World War. Her sensuous dancing elicited an almost hypnotic response from white male audiences all over Europe. By 1940, after the enormous success of her revue, the provocative Baker had become a transnational celebrity.

Wrote one critic:

> With Miss Joséphine Baker everything seems to change. The rhythmic spurt comes from her, with her frenzied flutterings and reckless, dislocated movements. She seems to dictate to the spellbound drummer, to the saxophonist who leans lovingly towards her with pulsating language of the blues, [whose] insistent ear-splitting hammering is punctuated by the most unexpected syncopations. In mid-air, syllable for syllable, the jazz players catch hold of the fantastic monologue of this crazed body. The music is created by the dance. And what a dance!...This brief *pas de deux sauvage* in the finale reaches the heights with ferocious and superb bestiality.[9]

The *Revue nègre* offered other black bodies, often half nude (or more), sweating in exotic dances devised by Baker, who exploited the stereotypes that Europeans had about "primitive savages." The posters that plastered Paris, and that made their way across Europe, reproduced all the stereotypes of Africanness: jutting buttocks, thick lips, wide eyes, shiny teeth, kinky hair. Seeing these joyful ads for the revue at the Music-hall des Champs-Élysées, our smile becomes embarrassed when we realize that the Nazis would use the same stereotypes for their attacks in the 1930s on "degenerate art."

Soon after their Parisian triumph, Baker's producers realized that there was more money to be made throughout Europe, so an extensive tour was planned. In 1926, her troupe was a sensation in Berlin, where the freedom of the Weimar Republic art scene was at its height. Baker and the show had visibly influenced German musicians and artists, who livened up their own productions in efforts to catch her energy and style. But on her return to Berlin in 1928, when she was the featured artist, not just part of a show, Baker found a new, less tolerant city. She had always brushed off hysterical newspaper reviews, but now the audiences were themselves belligerent. The Depression had made Europe tenser, less tolerant, and more ready to look for scapegoats. Eastern Europe welcomed her with an aggressive, almost palpable hatred, where, in Germany especially, blacks were looked on with unmitigated scorn.

When she appeared in Berlin, after having been to Budapest, Basel, Belgrade, Lucerne, Amsterdam, and Oslo, trouble began. In some cities, proper critics expressed their distaste of her performances, but only on "artistic" grounds. In Berlin, Nazi brownshirts in the audience whistled and hooted at the show (this was the period when the Nazis were seen primarily as a nuisance, certainly not a major political party). Baker represented what the Nazis most despised and most feared about the influence of Paris: the "degeneration" of racial and moral standards, the loosening of ethical certainties, and the freedom of expression, both artistic and political. Blackness and Frenchness—racial mixing that caused degeneration—became firmly connected in the German mind, this despite the fact that there were fewer blacks in Europe than there were Romanies or Jews. Hitler had reserved his most heinous comments for the "subhumans" that had slipped into European culture; the fact that black musicians, artists, and performers were immensely popular drove him to inarticulate fury. And it was Paris where this suggestive dancer, who threatened the "white race" with her blatant sexuality, became popular. One of the world's best-known and most photographed women, she was like a traveling billboard, advertising her lifestyle throughout Europe, performing in a way that threatened to ruin centuries of dogmatic tradition. She may have been American-born, but she was now Parisian, and Paris in the 1920s and 1930s began to become, in the eyes of fascists, a prime site of hedonism and political threat. Just a decade later, when the Germans would arrive in Paris, they had Baker in mind, for she represented, in many ways, the "other"; she was the forbidden, the dangerous, the diseased, and the profligate. She had even married a Jew.

Nazi ideology sought to destroy the Bakers of Europe, yet the Nazis also wanted some of them to remain in Paris to keep up the image of that city as being just as gay under Nazi control as it had been before. But by June of 1940, the most famous Baker of them all was no longer in Paris. It appears that the advent of the war caught her by surprise. Though still popular, her shows had come to seem somewhat passé.★ Still, she knew that, given her race and her husband's ethnicity, she would not be able to perform in Paris under German Occupation, despite their program to "keep Paris Paris." Baker's last show in Paris was a small revue in the fall of 1939 costarring the popular song-and-dance man Maurice Chevalier (who would stay and perform in the city until 1943, when he became nervous about appearing to support the Vichy regime). Like Picasso, Baker thought the Germans would depart in a few months, but it would be years before she appeared again on a Parisian stage. She would not perform again on French soil until the Germans had left. Volunteering for the Red Cross, and doing a little intelligence work, she was soon moving throughout North Africa and the Middle East, entertaining the Free French and eventually catching the attention of Charles de Gaulle. (After the war, he awarded her France's highest honor for members of the Resistance.) She had left Paris, but only to serve her beloved France better.

"They" Settle In

Seeing a German soldier in his field uniform for the first time must have been searing, for every memoir, journal, and commentary about the invasion mentions the experience in its first few pages. This was

---

★ Billy Wilder, the Austrian-born American director (who had left Paris in 1933 for the United States), is reputed to have suggested that her performances were throwbacks to "those far off happy days in Paris when a siren was a brunette, and when a man turned off the light, it wasn't on account of an air-raid" (cited in Hammond and O'Connor, *Josephine Baker*).

visual, almost tactile proof that France was no longer in charge of its own destiny. With the division of the country in 1940 into Occupied and Unoccupied Zones, it would be more than two years before citizens in the latter areas would catch much sight of Germans other than in newsreels. But in northern France, and in Paris, there was an almost eerie preoccupation with the behavior, dress, and physical characteristics of this "other." For several of those whose journals I have used in this work, their first sight of a German was not in Paris itself but in the small village or town in which the writers found themselves in June of 1940, having left Paris on the verge of the Occupation. There is something even more intimate about coming face-to-face with one's nemesis in a rural village, on a country road, or on the streets of a provincial city.

Irène Némirovsky builds her story "Dolce," part of *Suite Française,* around this very point. The Germans arrive in a village during Sunday mass, and their heavy boots can be heard as the communicants try to follow the sermon:

> The men seemed very young. They had rosy complexions and golden hair. They rode magnificent, well-fed horses with wide, shiny rumps, which they tied up in the square, around the War Memorial. The soldiers broke ranks and started to make themselves at home. The village was filled with the sound of boots, foreign voices, the rattling of spurs and weapons. In the better houses, they hid away the linen.[10]

"Dolce" recounts in mesmerizing detail how the intimacy of country living enhanced the sense of being "occupied," of having to make place where there was not much place to be made, where "accommodation" became unavoidable, and where one could fall into "collaboration" almost casually. Némirovsky wrote this piece almost contemporaneously with the events; she had left Paris (where she had seen her first Germans) to hide in Burgundy, where the French police would later arrest her.

Simone de Beauvoir, having joined the exodus, was in the Pays de la

Loire, a region southwest of Paris, when she saw her first Germans close-up:

> [In La Flèche was] where I saw the first steel-gray uniforms; all the Germans in La Pouèze [another village nearby] had been wearing Italian-green. Those in La Flèche, in their beautiful uniforms and their beautiful cars of the same color, had an elegant look about them; they were not blond as were the Germans in La Pouèze. There were many different kinds of them, and of all I saw afterward these showed the greatest diversity.[11]

She comments further on how their laughter, their clicking heels, their confidence, their near joy in victory made French humiliation manifest.

Jean Guéhenno, a literary critic and lycée instructor, witnessed his first Germans in Clermont-Ferrand, a city in central France: "I don't want to comment here about these grey men that I have been passing in the streets. It's an invasion of rats."[12] (This image, of course, presages by a half decade Albert Camus's allegory, *The Plague*.) And another Parisian schoolteacher saw her first Germans in Moulins, a village in Burgundy:

> An uninterrupted flood of tanks, armored cars, cannons, trucks, motorcycles filing by with a hellish noise and at a fearful speed.... The soldiers riding them stand proudly, arms crossed as fierce victors. Others, more magnanimous, smilingly throw packets of chocolate (chocolate looted from our shops) to stunned kids.... I have just realized the totality of our poor country's defeat. I feel crushed by these tanks.[13]

The Parisian sisters Benoîte and Flora Groult (both would later become journalists and writers) produced a journal that gives us a day-by-day account of the rising anxiety as war news befuddled a waiting populace. Their parents had taken their two teenage daughters to Brittany in May, to a grandmother's home, fearful for the young girls' safety should the

Germans reach Paris. Settled in the quaint town of Concarneau, everyone listened assiduously to the radio. The French newscasters bragged frequently about the "enormous losses" incurred by the Germans, while the news the family was receiving from fleeing refugees and passing soldiers implied the opposite. As one of the sisters wrote: "How much longer can an army have 'enormous losses' without being bled to death?"[14] The sisters wondered what would happen if the soldiers reached Paris while the family was in Brittany: Would they pillage the family's apartment there, on Rue Vavin, in the 6th arrondissement?

Eventually, as the first Germans arrived in little Concarneau, and everyone ran to the town square to look them over. Wrote Flora, age fifteen: "I was in town; I saw them, on grey vehicles — camouflaged with branches, stiff, red, immobile, completely normal-looking men. Handsome for the most part, with stiff necks and identical equipment, impressive. They did indeed have the arrogant gaze of a victor, they were impassive, accomplishing their mission."[15] She notices, too, that town girls were flirting with the handsome German boys, climbing onto their trucks, teasing them with oranges. Flora was horrified, calling her peers "bitches in heat," but the image is a strong one and indicates a fact: there was a sexual frisson that passed through many of the crowds that watched those handsome, virile young men take over town after town. The unspoken comparison with the demasculinized, defeated French army would remain fixed in the imaginations of most French people right up until the end of the war. (We will see, too, how the Groult sisters reacted to the new soldiers on the block, the Americans, when they helped liberate Paris in August of 1944.)

Meanwhile, back in Paris: "I've just seen one," murmured a stunned maid to her employer, who had run to see why her servant had cried out. "He came into the courtyard, Madame, looked around, and then walked out."[16] Nervous citizens gazed at nervous invaders. A German tank commander described what he saw:

Everywhere we find the same scene [as we crossed into Paris]. The populace watches as if frozen by astonishment and fear. Then, suddenly, they are all running away! Mothers snatch their children from the street to hide them in their houses. Doors and windows close. Finally, realizing that there is no gunfire and that our column is rolling peacefully along, people come back out and line up with curiosity on the sidewalks. . . . On the place in front of the [Paris] City Hall . . . the French standard that had been flying over the building is lowered, to be replaced by a German flag. A crowd of the curious gathered in front of the building, and when the swastika slowly rises on the pole, we felt coming from that crowd something like a heavy sigh.[17]

The Germans' precision and efficiency awed Paris. The invaders swept through the city on that Friday morning in mid-June with all the efficiency for which the new Germany had become known. Official and unofficial histories of the period state, or strongly imply, that the German bureaucracy had indeed run a network of spies inside Paris before the war, taking careful notes of buildings, apartments, crossroads, transport, and Métro stations. "They knew where everything was" was a sentence repeated by the stunned Parisian spectator. Their assumption of the spaces of the city was breathtaking. They knew which crossroads were crucial, which buildings were to be immediately requisitioned; they knew where important archives were to be found, which art galleries were Jewish-owned, which museums still had important collections; they had dozens of signs already painted, with black borders, directing traffic in the German language. They set up traffic police at every major intersection and moved with confidence into government buildings. They organized military parades around the Arc de Triomphe, using all twelve of Haussmann's radiating avenues as staging grounds. They set up bands and orchestras in key places—the Rond-point des Champs-Élysées, in front of Notre-Dame Cathedral, and in the Jardin des Tuileries—to entertain both their troops and curious Parisians. Still and motion pictures were put to immediate use; scaffolding for cameramen and photographers was set up on the Place de la Concorde to record the spectacle of German officers and troops coming and going in the great eighteenth-century

German directions on the Place de la Concorde.
(Editions Granger / Collection Claude Giasone)

palaces that border the northern side of that plaza: the Hôtel de Crillon (still perhaps Paris's most prestigious hotel) and the Hôtel de la Marine (until recently, the Ministry of the Navy). They showed off their technological sophistication by having three small Messerschmitt reconnaissance planes land in the Place de la Concorde itself; one even carried the general in command of Paris during the first days of the Occupation.

The Battle of France was still going on elsewhere. So the Germans immediately sent motorized loudspeakers throughout the city, repeating the admonitions of thousands of previously distributed leaflets: "You have been completely betrayed. There is no longer any

Wehrmacht on the Place de la Concorde. *(Bundesarchiv)*

efficacious resistance you can mount against German-Italian military superiority. [It is useless] to continue the struggle.... Think of your poor children, of your unfortunate wives. Demand that your government end this struggle that has no hope of success."[18] Despite their apprehension, such large crowds of citizens surrounded German traffic controllers, soldiers on assignment, and their vehicles that orders had to be given to the public to allow the Wehrmacht to perform its jobs so that newly occupied Paris might return to normal as soon as possible.

The Nazi hierarchy wanted the Occupation to appear almost seamless, not only to influence world opinion but also to give the impression to the English and Russians that the Third Reich could be a flexible and compassionate European ally. "Keep Paris Paris," the order, both implied and specific, rolled out from the propaganda office in Berlin. Tourism was immediately encouraged, and the city was soon filled with busloads of wide-eyed, curious German troops wishing that they had been assigned to this sensual, beautiful oasis. Even those who had never been to either city realized that Berlin was no Paris; it was too far east, too isolated, too Prussian. Vienna could compare in some ways with Paris, but it shared its influence with Budapest, in the barely unified remains of the former Austro-Hungarian Empire. It, too, was in the east, too far away from the mercantile giants of England, France, and Holland to be but an attractive shadow of Paris. And Hitler knew this, too: one of his generals would ask him in late 1941 what his first impressions of France's capital had been; the Führer answered, "I was very happy to think that there was at least one city in the Reich that was superior to Paris from the point of view of taste — I mean, Vienna. At present Berlin doesn't exist, but one day she'll be more beautiful than Paris." He went on about how he had saved Paris and would have no compunction about destroying Moscow or Leningrad. "On the whole," he concluded, "Paris remains one of the jewels of Europe."[19] This attitude would dominate the early Occupation. The "correct" military investment of Paris was to be an example of the Reich's respect for Europe's non-Bolshevik civilization. The Germans would present themselves immediately, and up to the end, as the protectors of this architectural gem. They were not barbarians but rather the shield against those who would undermine centuries of tradition. As if blessed by the gods, Paris continued to benefit from a magnificent spring that year. Even nature seemed to welcome the new regime.

In an article, "Tourists in Uniform," published in the magazine *L'Illustration* a couple of months after the arrival of the Germans, we read one version of the early Parisian reactions to their occupiers:

What struck us at the sight of these military moving among us was their obvious youth. Under the *feldgrau* [field gray] uniform, we couldn't distinguish social class, or profession. But we could sense that there were many intellectuals, among these young people, university students, who would take up their interrupted studies and who would profit from their visit to learn about French culture and to increase their learning and experience. They probably had only a bookish knowledge of our culture. This occasion would help them, to their benefit, to see the real face of

France, to be able to get to know its citizens, and to familiarize themselves with our customs and our spirit.[20]

The Vichy-German propaganda machine had easily introduced itself into popular Parisian culture. "Visitors" and "tourists" are not the first terms that came to mind for most Parisians, but this editorial fantasy would prevail for most of the Occupation.

French propaganda prior to the Occupation had been telling its audience for months that the Germans were undernourished, poorly armed, and uncommitted to the Nazi regime. File after file of smart-looking, cadence-stepping, evidently well-armed young men belied these canards and further undermined confidence in the leadership of the Third Republic. There were not a few Parisians relieved that they were seeing fascist rather than communist soldiers marching through their streets. The fear of another Commune of 1870, when communist cadres had briefly ruled the city, was not uncommon, and there was hope that a well-trained and well-led army, even though foreign, would keep away the threat of a leftist takeover of the city. To add to this sense of a reasserted security—one that seemed to put to rest almost overnight the residual fear of the Huns of the First World War—was the near total absence of any French military or guerrilla resistance to the invasion of Paris. There were no gunshots in the night, no sounds of careening vehicles, no insistent police sirens, no air raid warnings, and no troops running from building to building. It seemed as if Paris had literally opened its city gates to a benevolent victor and that its generosity was being repaid in kind.

Of course, there were many other citizens who were mortified at what had happened, especially among the older veterans of the Great War; tears streamed down their faces as they watched, with their medals pinned to their suit coats, a spectacle of arrogance: smug victors revealing their superiority to a befuddled and morally weak population. Thierry de Martel, one of the most prominent surgeons in France and the director of the American Hospital, killed himself and made sure his friends knew why: he could not bear the sight of German uniforms infecting Paris. There were other reported suicides. (Including, some say, the old security guard at the Pasteur Institute, who as a boy had been the great scientist's first rabies patient.) And, of course, most of the population of Paris was not in the city when the first troops arrived but was caught somewhere south, between the retreating French army and the advancing German one. Soon seen on the streets again were the children of those who had stayed, fascinated with the smart-looking soldiers and their shiny equipment. Stores were reopening, most victuals (except milk, which had to come from the still-war-ravaged countryside) were available; rationing had not yet been set up. The Germans set immediately to shopping—another Blitzkrieg—eager to snap up what had been rationed in their country for almost a year. Paris had become "Germanized" almost overnight, with only small incidents reminding them that they were interlopers.

Still, many Parisians felt ill at ease. Some were more aware of what was to come than others; many hoped that the worst had passed. These were the foreign immigrants who had been arriving for years in Paris from Germany and Austria, then from Czechoslovakia and Poland. They were socialists, communists, intellectuals, Jews, and other adversaries of Nazism. They were in Paris because the city had attracted them by virtue of its reputation as the European center for artistic and intellectual tolerance. French Jews, of course, were for the most part unworried, for they were French first, Jews second, and surely any French government would protect them as they would all their citizens. Nor were recently naturalized French citizens from Europe and North Africa overly concerned—after all, they were French as well. And of course a French government would protect decorated veterans despite their religion or political affiliation. However, anxiety was almost palpable in the immigrant sections of Paris, especially in the working-class quarters, where rent was affordable and where many immigrants had settled. What would happen to them should these "correct" Germans attempt to impose the rigorous limitations they had already imposed in Germany, Austria, and Poland?

The Armistice had demanded that all anti-Nazi German citizens be immediately arrested and handed over to the Occupation authorities.

Americans were unconcerned and would remain unmolested in Paris for another year and a half, until Pearl Harbor. But there were not a small number of citizens of the British Empire, still a belligerent force, caught in Paris. Archives in the Imperial War Museum in London contain several diaries and letters that offer a non-French perspective on the Occupation of Paris. One particular document details how much effort Nazi propaganda—almost instantly on the walls of Paris—forcefully and directly sought to drive a wedge between Great Britain and France. Posters reminded the French that it was the British who had executed Joan of Arc and that it was Churchill who was interested only in protecting the British Empire and not its "ally," the loyal nation of France. "How painful it was to see our brave men so falsely represented and read such ignominious lies. No sooner were these posters put up than they were torn to pieces or covered with mud but ever to be renewed, until the day came when circumstances absolutely prevented anyone from touching them," the diarist wrote.[21] British citizens were required to go daily to the local police station and to sign a register. They could, of course, be arrested at the drop of a hat, but women were generally left alone as long as they regularly signaled their residency and kept low profiles. Once, our diarist forgot to make her daily trudge to the station; so the next day she appeared tentatively, expecting at any minute to be challenged. Unnoticed, she took the register from an inattentive clerk's desk, retired to a bench, and signed it twice, hoping no one would notice. It worked. A daily signature meant a ration card; without one, getting food was almost impossible. Such cards were even more important than an *Ausweis,* the pass one received to move about in certain monitored areas.

Our "English civilian" also recounted that a large number of dogs and cats roamed the Parisian streets; feeding them had become an awkward burden in a time of rationing. Concierges often woke in the morning to find a basket or dustbin filled with puppies or kittens at their doorsteps, for the city's apartment-building gatekeepers were known for their love of animals. Later, the police put out warnings that eating cat meat was not healthy because cats fed on rats, animals known for carrying deadly diseases. But upon arrival, the Nazis were more focused on what they saw as a more immediately worrisome sort of "vermin." As the English diarist records:

> No time was lost by the Germans before occupying the luxurious homes of the wealthy Jews....Huge pantechnicons [moving vans] were soon seen stationed before their houses....Beautiful tapestries, carpets, busts, masterpieces, china, furniture, blankets, sheets, all were taken away to Germany.... [In the home of a friend, two German officers] went to the wine cellar, the contents of which they evidently knew; they asked for all the Burgundy, etc., and then made for the Benedictine, Chartreuses and Hungarian Apricot Liqueurs....After, the Germans visited the garage. One of the officers stepped inside the Delage, had the pictures and bottles carried there and departed. A few hours later the little Simca was fetched by two German soldiers.[22]

Like so many others, the diarist was staggered by the Germans' sinister preparations. "The knowledge revealed by the Germans of the interior of flats and houses was astonishing." This "comprehension" of a major metropolis is one of the reasons that Parisians felt so helpless, almost benumbed, in the summer of 1940. The combination of an effortless assumption of the control of Paris with the invaders' apparently "correct" behavior, coupled with an armistice that had preserved some French honor, all worked together to make the Occupation of Paris seem embarrassingly easy both to Parisians and their new masters. Upon closer examination, we see that perhaps the vast assertion of authority lacked focus (too many entities too eager to put their units' imprints on the newly acquired jewel), but an unmistakable message came through: as if by magic, Paris had become a suburb of Berlin.

In notes for her great novel, Irène Némirovsky took notice of how ready the French were for an end to the brief war that had devastated their country and how fed up they were with the incompetence of a failed government: "The French grew tired of the Republic as if she were an old wife. For them, the [Pétain] dictatorship [that followed] was a brief affair, adultery. But they intended to cheat on their wife,

not to kill her. Now they realize she's dead, their Republic, their freedom. They're mourning her.... Who will win out?"[23] It would take
four long—very long—years to find out.

Hitler's Own Tour

About 6:00 a.m. on Friday, June 28, 1940, a convoy of convertible
Mercedes limousines almost mockingly entered nearly abandoned
Paris, zigzagging around military barriers and passing a few staring
Parisian police officers and bystanders. They had come from the
northeast, speeding down Avenue de Flandre, then Rue La Fayette, to
their first stop, the Opéra de Paris. Adolf Hitler was tense with
excitement.*

Just two weeks before this visit, Hitler's Wehrmacht had occupied
Paris almost without firing a shot, and only a week earlier, at Compiègne, he had watched as his generals signed an armistice with a sullen
French military, a reversal of what had happened in the same place
twenty-two years earlier. The German leader had already toured
Belgium and northern France, where he had spent the youthful years
he most liked to recall. He had been a battlefield runner during the last
war, the soldier given the dangerous task of carrying messages between
headquarters. For his courage under fire, he had been awarded the Iron
Cross. In 1940, as German armies pushed southward toward France, he
had established a headquarters, named Wolfsschlucht (Wolf's Lair), in
the village of Brûly-de-Pesche, near Brussels. From there, by air and
by car, he revisited each of the places where he had been billeted during the Great War, and he had also toured Belgium's capital. He had
taken a leave in Brussels in 1917; using his memory of that time, he
carefully planned his return as its conqueror. As he would in Paris, he
stopped before the city's great state buildings, including the mammoth
Palais de Justice, testimony in stone to the excessive fantasies of a

---

* Though hard to believe, confusion still surrounds the exact date of this visit. For years
the date was thought to be Sunday, June 23, right after the signing of the armistice, but
subsequent historians, especially Kershaw and Fest, have generally coalesced around the
later date, Friday, June 28, though the former remains the most often cited.

colonial state yet fascinating to him, for it fed the visual megalomania that he was already directing toward the construction of a new, more monumental Berlin.

During this nostalgic tour through prostrate Belgium, Hitler passed through the city of Ghent. A Belgian witness describes a convoy of armored carriers, motorcyclists, and a large convertible Mercedes with a special passenger holding on to the rim of the windshield. He was "standing upright, very straight....He looked like the ancient statues of regal, imperial figures, like, if one could admit it, a Germanic Napoleon....A black mustache, stoutly built, rigid cap visor. Hitler is passing in front of us; I see his somber, yet passionate look, between the mustache and visor. I think of the images of Roman civilization that I found in my grandfather's library."[24] We know from one of his companions on the trip that Hitler was not only reviewing his present success but also revisiting a reassuring past. We do not have a similar eyewitness account by a Parisian of Hitler's visit to that city, but we can be certain that it held none of the emotional nostalgia of this one.

On the day of Hitler's Paris tour, the city was nearly empty. Estimates agree that somewhere between 70 and 80 percent of Parisians had fled in fear of the Nazi advance, leaving the capital uncannily silent. A nervous Arno Breker, the favored sculptor, accompanied his Führer on the trip. He describes how Gestapo officers had awakened him in Munich, then rushed him by special plane to front headquarters in Belgium. Hitler had wanted someone at his side who had lived in the French capital, as Breker had while studying art in the 1920s. Breker, too, was taken aback by the city's appearance on that early Friday morning: "Paris seemed dead. Not a soul. Groups of buildings that life seemed to have abandoned passed by, ghost-like and unreal....As if he shared my reflections, Hitler remained silent and sullen."[25] Had the Nazi leader expected at least a modest welcome from the curious? If so, why had he come so early in the morning? Nighttime curfews did not end until early morning, around six o'clock; only the hardiest citizens or most urgently needed personnel would venture onto the streets before that time. The anticlimax of entering almost furtively the world's best-known city must have removed some of the pleasure derived from the conqueror's review. Hitler must have felt a mixture of disappointment as well as awe. Rather than a vibrant metropolis, before him was vacancy and facade. Compared to his adulatory entry into Vienna in March of 1938 and his review of a triumphant parade of his army in a devastated Warsaw in November of 1939, this visit tended toward the pathetic.

Films of Hitler's Parisian tour were shown widely in Germany immediately after the visit. Soon they were being seen in America and even Britain, but they would not appear in France until later in 1940, after the Occupation had been firmly seated. By then the message had made its impression around the globe: the Nazis were benevolently in charge of one of the "civilized" world's most important sites. There is, in the films and photographs, a sense of entitlement, of situational arrogance. Yet one could argue that Goebbels underestimated the visual disjunction between his Führer's brisk roll through a captured Paris and the stark emptiness of a city whose reputation had been built as much on its effervescence as its architecture.[26] The visit was intended to make clear that the Germans were in command, but the visual record also showed a city turning its back on its new conqueror. For a while, the first message would dominate world opinion; later, the second vision would begin to mitigate the arrogance of this Occupation.

His may have been a *visite éclair* (lightning visit), but it had been minutely prepared and perfectly enacted. Hitler seems to have ignored any possibility of assassination during his visit, riding with apparent sangfroid in an open limousine, one that often stopped so he could stand and look around. He would leave his car at the most public places, entering through the most public doorways. The formal uniforms, the impressive limousines, the streets as if emptied for the conqueror, the easy accessibility of some of Paris's most revered monuments, the posed photographs that implied ownership of the cityscape: all combined to project not only a strapping image of martial self-confidence but of inevitability. Still, one senses a smallness, a half-hidden tentativeness in the lonely cortege's progress through this magnificent built environment.

In his diary from Spandau (the Berlin prison where he served his postwar incarceration), Albert Speer writes extensively about Hitler's

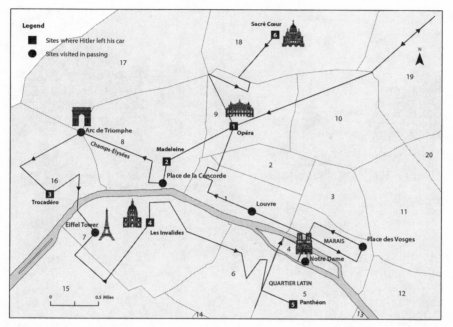

Approximate route of Hitler's tour

visual intelligence: "[His] passion for the theater,...[his] amazing knowledge of stage-craft and especially different lighting techniques" had enthralled his entourage.[27] Whenever he attended a theatrical or operatic production, he first analyzed, then criticized, the stage setting and the lighting before commenting on the actors or musicians. Performance was at the heart of Nazi self-projection, and it would be an essential part of the Occupation. So it made sense that the group's first stop was at the Palais Garnier, site of the Opéra de Paris, constructed between 1861 and 1875. This beautiful building sits regally in the midst of the 9th arrondissement, near the center of the city. Then as now, this Right Bank neighborhood is the site of some of Paris's most elegant department stores and borders the city's wealthiest sections — where many German bureaucrats and officers were already finding luxurious lodging. The opera house is positioned at the head of the Avenue de l'Opéra, one of the best-known boulevards of Paris. Slicing through packed neighborhoods when it was built by Haussmann's engineers in the late nineteenth century, the broad thoroughfare was repeatedly and

The tour continues. *(United States Holocaust Memorial Museum)*

imaginatively painted by such artists as Pissarro, Monet, and Caille-
botte, each trying to capture on canvas a newer, modernized city. The
only major avenue in Paris not bordered by trees, it was specially constructed to draw attention to the Opéra building itself and, as one looks
southward, to tie this new building with the massive Louvre on the
Seine. Hitler could not have chosen a more typically monumental site
as his first stop.

Films show Hitler quickly leaving his car and climbing purposefully
the stairs of the imposingly baroque building, as if it alone had been the
sole reason for his visit. His entourage was impressed at how intimately
familiar he was with the structure, inside and out. (The German leader
knew so well this great temple to opera, built by the architect Charles
Garnier, that he claimed to have no use for the French guide who had
been assigned to welcome him.) He wondered at the edifice's spacious
interior and its neo-baroque decoration; he remarked in detail on its
public and private spaces, even noticing that a small alcove that he

Happy Easter from the Paris Opera House. *(Editions Granger / Collection Claude Giasone)*

remembered from his study of blueprints had been removed. He stayed at the Opéra longer than he stayed anywhere else on his tour; the newsreels of this visit emphasize a connoisseur carefully examining an architectural masterpiece, one dedicated to the mannered, neo-baroque art of the late nineteenth century.

Why did Europe's most celebrated opera house so enthrall a military conqueror? Goebbels and his cultural machinery had made National Socialism into a spectacle—indeed, its ethical mandate demanded an imposition of visual order to heal a disordered world. This meant stunning uniforms, grand parades, intricately designed mass rallies, nighttime events, and a generally brilliant use of lighting and music to accompany these performances. It also meant that special attention was paid to the particular militaristic and traditional tastes of the youngest and the oldest of German citizens. Yet Hitler's visit also reminds us of how much of Nazi art was kitsch—that is, a cheapened, unironic appropriation of traditional aesthetic forms for mass consumption. Kitsch plays exclusively to the emotions; it is a hollowed-out, sentimental expression, not an intellectual one. Garnier's opera house was the final visually extravagant monument of Napoleon III's own kitschy reign—baroque-like statuary and decoration, gilt everywhere, massive stairways leading to red velvet seats and boxes—thus it was in sync with the Nazi attempt to revive dated architectural and artistic traditions. Having organized the devastatingly pejorative show of the *entartete Kunst* (degenerate arts) in Munich in 1937, which derided jazz, cubism, Bauhaus, and other modernist expressions, Hitler had already imposed on German society a Nazi "modernism," one whose antecedents he was especially eager to find in Paris. He did not begin his tour at the Louvre (which anyway had been emptied of many of its treasures in anticipation of his army's "visit") but rather at this site, where his knowledge of architectural history and his belief in the transformative power of the performing arts—vocal, physical, theatrical—could be admired. The great opera houses of Europe were, for this upstart bourgeois, the locus of "nondegenerate" artistic expression.

Hitler's love for nineteenth-century opera is well known, and his passion for Wagner continues to mark that genius's reputation. (It seems that the German people, who preferred Verdi and Mozart, did not share widely this Wagnerophilia.) Opera, an opulent combination of several forms of art, was to be used by the Nazis to inculcate a "popular" culture, one that did what many of the public performances of party events themselves did: create a cohesive and seduced multitude riveted by imposed taste. According to a historian of Nazi aesthetics, Hitler believed fervently that "a community [should] regard its opera house as an object of civic pride.... 'An opera house is the standard by which the culture of a city or civilization is measured,' was how he once put it to Speer."[28] Hitler's obsession with opera houses even affected his war aims:

> "The bombing of an opera house," Speer recalled, "pained him more than the destruction of whole residential quarters." Whenever this occurred—in Berlin with the State Opera in 1941 and the German Opera in 1943, in Mainz and Saarbrücken in 1942 and in Munich in 1943—he ordered their immediate reconstruction. To

Goebbels's argument that this would not be popular in light of the catastrophic housing shortage resulting from air raids, Hitler responded, "...the theatre is not merely a communal achievement but the one structure that belongs exclusively to the community. From this point of view, reconstructing housing would not achieve as much as reconstructing opera houses and theatres....Of course, all this opera house construction means a loss of material for war production; but so be it."[29]

Garnier's building was thus an appropriate first stop for another "phantom of the opera."

Hitler wanted to see examples of Paris's past, not its present or future, to understand how it had arrived at the center of the world's urban imagination, how it had melded architecture, ideas, fashion, style, and revolution to become the model of metropolitan sophistication. The Occupation would be defined, in part, by similar attempts at "freezing" Paris in its past, by trying to limit change, ignoring the fact that all metropolises must change in order to prosper. Hitler's visit, then, introduces two major strategies of the Occupation: one, to keep Paris in stasis as an example of the ideal city, and two, to undermine a metropolis's most distinctive trait, its porosity—that is, its openness to new ideas and to foreigners.

The Führer's next stop was down the street from the Opéra. Breker notes that "the Boulevard des Capucines, empty of people, without traffic, seemed a stage set" as they approached the imposing eighteenth-century Église de la Madeleine.[30] Again, Hitler jumped out of his car and vigorously mounted the steps to the temple's portals. Looking southward, he could see the Place de la Concorde, with its Egyptian obelisk, and, farther across the Seine, another eighteenth-century building, the former Palais Bourbon, then the seat of the Chambre des députés (most of whom had by then fled to Bordeaux). The view before him remains one of the most imposing vistas one can enjoy of neoclassical Paris, and it must have been especially compelling then, for there was almost no traffic. It was as if a museumlike replica of Paris had been especially prepared for the Leader's eye. From there, the cortege sped down the Rue Royale, past the restaurant Maxim's, which would become one of the favorite spots of German officials. They circled the impressive Place de la Concorde—where Louis XVI and Marie Antoinette had lost their heads—passing in front of the Hôtel de Crillon and the Hôtel de la Marine, the first headquarters of the occupying army. At each of the four corners of the grand square stand monuments to the major cities of France, among them Strasbourg, the capital of Alsace, then part of the new Reich, as it had been part of Germany after the Franco-Prussian War. At the square's entrance to the city's most famous thoroughfare, the Champs-Élysées, Hitler's limousine paused; standing in the car, he grabbed the windshield and gazed pensively at what was before and behind him. His cameras find two or three Parisian police officers on the sidewalk. We do not know if they were there coincidentally or by order. Then a figure in a dark cloak crosses our field of vision, almost certainly a member of a religious order, rushing across the street before the cortege continues.

Hitler proceeded slowly up the Avenue des Champs-Élysées toward

Gazing at his prize. *(United States Holocaust Memorial Museum)*

A popular German tourist site. *(Editions Granger / Collection Claude Giasone)*

the Arc de Triomphe.* The cavalcade approached the Place de l'Étoile, where it slowly circled the Arc de Triomphe, host to the Tomb of the Unknown Soldier, a memorial to a war whose loss Hitler was avenging. For the rest of the Occupation, German civilians and military would obsessively and respectfully visit this site. One of their most frequently photographed Parisian monuments would be the eternal flame,

---

* The Führer knew well the world's most famous urban thoroughfare. He had remarked as early as 1936 that "the Champs-Élysées is 100 meters wide. In any case we'll make our avenue [Berlin's Unter den Linden] 20-odd meters wider." Albert Speer writes that he was ordered to measure the width of the avenue during Hitler's tour (Speer, *Inside the Third Reich: Memoirs* [New York: Macmillan, 1970], 76).

often covered with bouquets and wreaths. It might seem perverse that Germans in the 1940s would show such respect to an army that had defeated them in 1918 until one remembers the fervent belief in military honor that informed the Wehrmacht. For the Nazis, also, such visits and respect were obviously a political move, meant to keep the French as quiescent as possible.

By way of the elegant Avenue Foch, where the Gestapo and other Occupation authorities offices were already in residence, and the Avenue Raymond-Poincaré, the cortege arrived at the Place du Trocadéro, a large open space between two curved buildings that provided a magnificent perspective over the Pont d'Iéna and, across the Seine, on to the Eiffel Tower. This should have been a familiar site to Hitler; it certainly was to Speer, for here, in 1937 — to showcase Nazi ingenuity and products to the visiting millions — the Germans had erected a massive hall for the international exposition. On Trocadéro Hill, the French government had constructed two enormous buildings, still used today as museums and conference halls. Standing between these curved edifices, one can look down the slope toward the Seine and then across the river up at the imposing Eiffel Tower. Tourists still do it as Hitler did then, with cameras rolling.

By 1940, the fifty-one-year-old Eiffel Tower had become a metonym for Paris. Design experts often stated that, along with Charlie Chaplin's bowler and Mickey Mouse's ears, its silhouette was the most recognized in the world's visual archive. The very "uselessness" and "meaninglessness" (its architecture was without any symbolic interest) of a tower built essentially as an advertisement for an engineer's genius were suggestive of the contemporary art so despised by Nazi aesthetics. Yet Hitler could not resist — nor could he avoid — posing with the tower in the background. Of the nine times he got out of his car on his tour, this one would produce the most iconic photograph. The juxtaposition of the conqueror of France in a tourist shot with Paris's best-known monument wavers, once more, between the sinister and the kitschy. Though the photograph became the most reproduced of all the day's images, its irony was not evident to Hitler and his entourage. Highly desirous of being recognized as connoisseurs of beauty, deeply

A tourist at the Eiffel Tower. *(© AKG Images / The Image Works)*

moved by their new responsibility to protect the world's best-loved city, the group was oblivious to the moment's contradictions. Time and subsequent events would give this famous snapshot an aura of the absurd. Here was Hitler, arrogant yet respectful, a tourist yet a conqueror, posing in front of a French structure whose monumentality belittled him.

The cortege next crossed the Seine for the first time, traversing the Pont d'Iéna, to stop at the Hôtel des Invalides, constructed by Louis XIV in the seventeenth century for his aged and ill soldiers. Hitler left his limousine here and walked carefully around the massive church that was at the center of the old soldiers' home. Ascending the steps on the building's south side, the group solemnly walked into the massive chapel to look down on the sepulchre of the Führer's great antecedent. In another of the visit's most reproduced photographs, a thoughtful Hitler, wearing a light duster rather than the leather coat he had had on earlier, stands out from his entourage. (So many visiting German soldiers would repeat this visit during the Occupation that a wooden covering had to be laid over the chapel's precious marble floor to protect it from the hobnailed boots of the Teutonic tourists.) Looking down on the porphyry sarcophagus, Hitler must have seen the list of victories inscribed around the emperor's tomb, one of which is MOSCOWA. This staged scene reflects another major strategy of Hitler's brief visit, namely, to be seen paying respect to a leader who had also sought to create a "new Europe" held together by military strength and his own charismatic leadership. In 1806, prints had been made and published of a similarly somber Napoleon visiting the grave, in Potsdam, of Frederick the Great. The French emperor had also been a radical leader, seeking to derive legitimacy by proximity to the remains of a mythical predecessor.

For a closer look at the sarcophagus, Hitler then descended into the crypt, whose entrance is inscribed with the famous words from Napoleon's will—JE DÉSIRE QUE MES CENDRES REPOSENT SUR LES BORDS DE LA SEINE, AU MILIEU DE CE PEUPLE FRANÇAIS QUE J'AI TANT AIMÉ (May my ashes rest on the banks of the Seine, among the French people I loved so well). Then, leaving the Invalides, the group sped along the fashionable and narrow Rue de Lille, passing by the German embassy, sited in the Hôtel de Beauharnais (another Napoleonic connection; Josephine's first husband was a Beauharnais), then down the Boulevard Saint-Germain to the Rue Bonaparte and the Latin Quarter.* The group headed next for the neighborhood of Montparnasse and its well-known

---

* Some have suggested that the Führer got out of his car again to walk along the Boulevard Saint-Michel, the famous Boul' Mich', which runs beside the Sorbonne and the prestigious Lycée Saint-Louis, but most accounts do not confirm this.

Hitler channels Napoleon. *(The Granger Collection)*

expatriate hangout, the Closerie des Lilas, where Hitler teased Breker about his dissolute days as a student in the Latin Quarter. The cars then turned north again to the Île de la Cité, the mythical center of Paris. They cruised past the exquisite thirteenth-century Sainte-Chapelle, and drove even more slowly in front of Notre-Dame Cathedral, but Hitler did not set foot on the Île de la Cité. Was the tour taking too much time? Or was the medieval genius of the place too foreign to his sensibility? He once again impressed his entourage with his knowledge of the rather unknown—and mediocre—Palais du Tribunal de

Visiting a famous tomb. (Musée de la Résistance nationale)

Commerce, another Second Empire building on the island's Quai de la Corse. (Few Parisians today could tell you where to find the Tribunal de Commerce, or, in fact, what it is.*)

Breker reiterates that Hitler entertained his companions with an almost continuous architectural patter; he mused openly about each building and monument they slowed down to see. Yet this was partly— if not predominantly—why Hitler left the city without seeing or understanding what made it an exceptional expression of urban energy. Monuments alone do not define a city. They crossed the Pont d'Arcole to return to the Right Bank, passing by the Hôtel de Ville, Paris's city hall. Then, surprisingly, the group turned into the Marais, a decrepit neighborhood chockablock with crammed tenements housing eastern European immigrants, mostly Jews.† A sad irony of this particular

---

* It was built to house, and still does, the chief commercial law court of the city of Paris.

† I know of no other example of Hitler having passed through what he feared and despised the most, the ghetto, filled with undesirable non-Aryans.

detour is that the future victims of Hitler's pathology were asleep while he was within meters of what they had thought was a haven. In two short years, one of the largest roundups of these "undesirables" would bring terror to the same narrow streets.

The limousines then paraded up the mansion-laden Rue des Francs-Bourgeois to the Place des Vosges, a perfectly landscaped square bordered by one of Paris's first and most coveted apartment complexes. They turned west onto the Rue de Rivoli, the wide artery that serves as the major east-west axis of the city, taking them to the neighborhood of Les Halles, the famous food marketplace known as the "belly of Paris." Like the rest of the city, the vast market was almost empty; but the cortege did pass some fishwives waiting for their delivery. The women stared at the shiny automobiles as they slowly passed by; according to Breker, a young man setting up his newspaper kiosk suddenly recognized whom he was seeing, and yelled: "It's him. Oh, it's him!" before running off to hide from the devil himself. Here the entourage began their climb to Montmartre, the highest hill in Paris, site of the Place de Clichy and the Place Pigalle—the latter infamous before, during, and after the war for its plethora of streetwalkers and garish cafés. (Allied soldiers would call it Pig Alley.) Overlooking the city from the Butte Montmartre is the Basilique du Sacré-Coeur, "a surprising choice," wrote Albert Speer later, "even given Hitler's taste."[31] Speer (like almost every Parisian I know) held in unconcealed distaste the quasi-Byzantine, quasiclassical, brilliantly white "wedding cake" at the top of hill, one of the two or three most photographed and thus most representative Paris landmarks.* Consecrated in 1919 it was only about two decades old when Hitler saw it. One of the most compelling reasons for the Führer's visit to this bizarre temple is that the basilica's large parvis offers a spectacular natural view of the city. Here

---

* This strange-looking building was built at the end of the nineteenth century and the beginning of the twentieth, funded in large part by individual donations from all over France. The government had passed a "national vow" to build a church as penance for national "sins" committed during the Franco-Prussian War, especially for the brief Paris Commune (the first ever communist government) that had followed in 1871 the siege of Paris. So the church had its own peculiar connection to Franco-German history.

he stood and congratulated himself on having saved this magnificent metropolis for Western civilization.

Again, Hitler alternated between the gaze of the tourist—who seeks to make as banal and nonthreatening as possible the object contemplated—and the gaze of the conqueror, who seeks to command what he sees before him. The tourist is curious, adventurous, and yet anxious before an unfamiliar phenomenon. His intellectual interest combines with his pride at having arrived at a new site. But this exhilaration is tempered by timidity, partially prompted by a fear of the unknown city and its unfamiliar inhabitants, and an anxiety about

Église du Sacré-Coeur. *(Creative Commons)*

appearing ignorant. On the other hand, the conqueror seeks to control with a glance, to impose order by virtue of his will rather than his imagination. He temporarily represses thoughts of insurrection, of provisioning, and of governance in order to assume spiritual ownership of a heterogeneous, labyrinthine urban center. The exhilaration Hitler must have felt made him "generously" offer the city back—at least metaphorically—to its citizens, from whom he expected to receive kudos. Speer later wrote about how startled he was that Hitler seemed to treat the glorious city as though it were a plaything: "Maybe I'll protect it; maybe I won't. It's up to me." This is, of course, the attitude of any megalomaniac.

Assuming Hitler's first-person point of view, Breker reported the chancellor's musings as he contemplated Paris from Sacré-Coeur:

> Paris has always fascinated me. For years, I had the strongest desire to go there. After 1918, the political era I entered and the evolution of events made this desire impossible [to act upon]. Now, the city's gates are open to me! Since the news [of its capitulation] I have had no other idea in my head than to visit this metropolis of the arts with my own artists. Paris for me is a model. I'm sure we will learn many lessons from her. We can [use her] in planning the transformation of our most important cities, a project that has already begun. I have a strong interest in understanding the structure of [this] city, one known to me in theory, and to feel [in my visit] the force of its energy. I could have marched at the head of my troops under the Arc de Triomphe—the classic event of all victory parades—but I did not want, under any pretext, to inflict this humiliation on the French people after their defeat. I want no obstacle to the *entente franco-allemande,* which will happen, I am sure.[32]

In these observations, there is a tone of envy, an almost palpable recognition that Germany was a new country, jerry-built into a nation by Bismarck and others less than a century earlier. Berlin had only been a national capital since then; its history could not begin to compare to that of Paris, even though much attention had been paid to it during the

Second Reich (1871–1918) and thereafter. But Hitler was planning that Berlin would become a major capital soon, after the victories of 1939–41; what had been a barely disguised wish would become a certainty.

Many of the German observers of Paris during the Occupation glowed with satisfaction that this old, respectable, and beautiful capital would be overshadowed by the majestic example of a resurgent Berlin. Tobin Siebers has argued that "Hitler's Germany was a dictatorship of the aesthetic...[but one where] beauty was a thing of the blood."[33] A fascination with decadence (which extended to racial and ethnic qualities), with the decline of a civilization remembered nostalgically, informed Nazi ideology; this obsession was transferred to those who, they thought, represented the decline of that Western civilization. On the other hand, the attraction of Paris was so powerful that some sort of ethical and aesthetic compromise had to be made by the arrogant, though impressed, Occupiers. To admire Paris was fine, but to admire the French ingenuity that had created it was not. This contradiction subtends not only Hitler's short tour but also German conduct during the city's fifty-month Occupation. Part of Goebbels's general cultural project for the "new Europe" was to reduce the influence of French culture, which had led, he believed, to the weaknesses that had allowed France to be overrun by the purer Nazis in less than a month. Nazi ideology demanded an unbreakable link between racial purity, ethical certainty, and cultural expression. Yet Paris represented, as it had for more than a century, a site of impurity, moral relativism, and cultural radicalism.* Though the French may have fielded ineffectual armies, they had succeeded through their "decadent" arts, including jazz and cubism, in colonizing the European imagination. Goebbels spent a considerable amount of time devising propaganda and a machinery for artistic appropriation that would make Berlin, not Paris, the art, film, and fashion center of the "new Europe." He would in the end fail, to the world's relief.

After fewer than three hours, the Führer's cavalcade sped back to the airport at Le Bourget to fly to its Belgian headquarters. As his plane

---

* "Weimar" Berlin—that is, Germany's capital during 1919–33, that nation's brief period of robust democracy—had been just as "decadent" as Paris had ever been. But the Nazis had cleaned up the city, brutally.

rose from the field, Hitler asked his pilot to make a slow turn over Paris so that he could see it again. Once more, the German leader captured in his glance the panorama of a mythical city, lying below him in a bright sunlight, cut in two by the silver meandering of a strong river. It would be the last time he would gaze upon Paris, though the city never left his imagination. Until the final days in his bunker, Hitler would still dream of the city he thought he had conquered, unaware to his death how the City of Light would vanquish him.

The Führer's Urbanophobia

The memoranda of Hitler's private (recorded) conversations are replete with offhand and direct references to Paris. Sometimes he implies that Paris is simply an architectural congeries of beautiful buildings and monuments; at other moments, he muses that it is the model for all cities, or he might compare it unfavorably to Rome. He never mentions its vibrancy or the exhilarating confusion of daily life; instead, he reduces the image of Paris to that of an open-air museum, the result of centuries of good taste.

The First World War had given a new dimension to the fascination Germany and France have historically had for each other: Were they now to be brothers in peace, standing in opposition to Bolshevik Russia and imperial Great Britain, or were they forever to be locked in an embrace of scorpions, at any moment ready to sting the fraternal other? After that devastating war, books and essays had been published in Germany, especially in the late 1920s and 1930s, that had a great effect on how the Germans would consider and treat France once they had her in their thrall. For the most part, these works depicted France as a once-great country that had lost its way. It had degenerated, had become an empty plaster cast of its former greatness. By far the most widely read of these books, including by Hitler, was the journalist Friedrich Sieburg's *Gott in Frankreich?* (To Live Like God in France; 1929).* Written

---

* Almost immediately, it was translated into French and published in 1930 as *Dieu est-il français?* (Is God French?), with a lengthy and critical afterword by its editor, Bernard Grasset. Its title refers to the German aphorism "Wie ein Gott in Frankreich leben"

from the perspective of someone who purportedly loves France, it is patronizing and vigorously pro-German. The Vichy government republished it, for it outlined their own conviction that France had lost much of its former claim to glory through moral decay, leftist politics, and unfounded arrogance. A typical description of the Parisian cityscape follows:

> Will the fixed forms of this city's life ever be shaken? Certainly not, as long as the house-fronts retain their precious silver-grey, as long as the domes of the Panthéon and the Invalides force their way up through the heavy mist, as long as the Place de la Concorde has the sky for a roof, as long as the gentle crumbling of the stone softens even the most glaring new buildings, as long as the Champs-Elysées take one in a straight line through the Arc of Triomphe into the middle of the dream of Glory, as long as the tangled paths offer a green refuge to the despairing and the idle, as long as the river Seine gives the citizen his Sunday dram of fish, as long as there is red wine and white bread to be had. But a lover's anxious eye can already detect cracks in the everlasting structure.[34]

The passage not only outlines the tour itinerary that the future Führer would take a decade later, during his only visit to the city, but also insinuates that the glory that was Paris was passing. It was time for a new capital of Europe.

Great urban sites attracted Hitler but intimidated him as well; many of his recorded conversations about cities reveal a need to criticize as well as to exalt the human achievement that cities represent. In *Mein Kampf,* he describes them as sites of teeming apartment buildings and restive populations. When he remarks favorably about them, he analyzes their structures and their built environments. For him, the most

---

(to live like a god in France) — that is, to have the best possible life. It was published in the United States as *Who Are These French?* in 1938.

interesting metropolis would be empty of its innumerable, often churl-
ish citizens. Coincidentally, the Paris he visited that early Friday morning, while most of its inhabitants were either asleep or fleeing
southward, would come close to that ideal.★ *Mein Kampf* sparingly
mentions the massive urban resurgence during the late nineteenth and
early twentieth centuries, but a close reading shows a general distrust of
cities and of the masses that congregated in them. It is common knowledge that the early National Socialist electoral successes came from the
rural areas and small towns of Germany. Hitler always appeared a bit
befuddled by large cities, including the German capital.

Hitler had not spent much time in Berlin before his appointment as
chancellor; the two major Germanic cities he knew best were Munich
and Vienna. The latter held a complexly nostalgic place in the Führer's
mind. He had spent his formative years there as an aspiring artist, but
poverty and rejection had left less pleasant memories. His fraught relationship with the capital city of his native Austria can give us another
window into his general attitude toward cities. On March 18, 1938,
two years before he would sneak into Paris, Hitler arrived in a motor-
cade before rapturous Viennese: "Many hundreds of thousands were
on their way to hear him. Streets are dipped in a frenzy of color. The
Heldenplatz could not hold the masses. . . . Sieg Heil shouts storm across
the square, many thousands of arms are raised in the German salute."[35]

Vienna was the best-known metropolis swallowed by the Third
Reich before Paris, to which it was often compared, and in his oration
to the crowd, Hitler referred to it as the Reich's second city. The Austrians, for the most part and at first, were ecstatic, and showed their
enthusiasm about the Anschluss (the political union of Germany and
Austria in 1938, forming the greater Reich) through many violent acts
against Jews, Socialists, and Communists both preceding and during

---

★ In May of 1938, Mussolini had organized an elaborate tour of Rome and Florence for
his friend from Germany. The preparations actually changed aspects of the cityscape to
present a new facade to the curious Führer. An amusing account of that visit may be
found in the journal of art historian Ranuccio Bianchi Bandinelli, part of which was
recently published in Paris as *Quelques jours avec Hitler et Mussolini*.

the union. However, what followed after the annexation was a transparent, brutal Aryanization (the ejection of Jewish business owners and their removal from teaching and other professions) of Hitler's "pearl" city, an attempt to make it into a cultural beacon for the entire Third Reich. Not long after, these two goals—making Vienna a free-spirited sister to Paris as well as a stepsister of the Reich's capital—came into conflict, and, sooner rather than later, Vienna increasingly became a problem for the Berlin government, a site of tough and tenacious resistance to the Nazi regime. It began to promote itself as the "first" cultural city of the Reich, and the previously delirious Viennese Nazis were soon impatient with rule from Berlin. "I can't afford to have a mutinous large city at the southeast corner of the Reich," Hitler supposedly told Baldur von Schirach, his choice for *gauleiter* and *reichsstatthalter* (boss) of Vienna.[36] The Austrian capital would remain a problem, so Hitler's attention focused on the much smaller Linz, his Austrian birthplace, as a "counter-Vienna," one he would rebuild along the lines of Berlin and Paris. Indeed, Hitler's reaction to the Occupation of Paris, both his joy and his anxiety, may well have been influenced by his frustrations with a persistently querulous Vienna.

In general, the Germans sought to appropriate and then to fix Paris in a time that was embedded in the collective memory of the cosmopolitan world. In so doing, they hoped to slow down the unpredictable energy that defines metropolises and thus to provide more security for themselves and their motives. Cities were too porous, too difficult to control. The author of *Mein Kampf* wrote in the mid-1920s that "the meaning and purpose of revolutions is not to tear down the whole building, but to remove what is bad or unsuitable and to continue building on the same spot that has been laid bare."[37] Using an architectural metaphor, he is speaking of ideas; but the Nazi anxiety would translate into a desire to "cleanse" cities as well as minds, just as they were "cleansing" through ethnic removal. Continued Hitler:

How truly deplorable the relation between state buildings and private buildings has become today! If the fate of [imperial] Rome should strike Berlin, future generations would some day admire the department stores of a few Jews as the mightiest works of our era and [the large buildings] of a few corporations as the characteristic expression of the culture of our times. Just compare the miserable discrepancy prevailing in [even a city like Berlin] between the structures of Reich and those of finance and commerce.[38]

Cities, according to Hitler, are filled with citizens who frequently change addresses and, thus, in his mind, identities. (Throughout occupied Europe, Jews were forbidden to sell, rent, or move from their apartments.) This undermines the authority of the state that must protect itself against the anonymity of its citizens. Immigration threatens the state's promise to provide its urban citizens a secure, consistently recognizable, and "nonsinister" environment. City life can weaken the bonds that are essential to a well-managed and predictable political and cultural entity. Urban centers should be spaces of cultural greatness, as long as the culture is imposed by tradition and the state and not by the city's unpredictable population. Without the dominant hand of a confident ideology, they risk becoming only "human settlements," sites of rootlessness and passing through. Nazism sought to reconstruct the urban environment through application of a nationalistic culture that would bind citizens more securely than did such human needs.

So with Paris, Hitler found himself confronted by a "monumental" urban center, recognized across the world as a carefully planned conglomeration of private and public buildings modernized (by Baron Haussmann and Napoleon III) according to the very principles of an imperial monument-city. Yet it was as well a haven for a massive influx of immigrants from eastern Europe and elsewhere; it was teeming with all he hated and feared: anti-Nazis, Jews, homosexuals, mixed-race degenerates, and "modern" artists. As a consequence, the newly arrived Germans set about mediating those aspects of Parisian life that most threatened their presence as well as those that could be manipulated to strengthen their defenses: movement through the city, nourishment and bodily comfort, personal identity, signs and symbols, pastimes, entertainment, even time itself. These restrictive regulations demanded of the Parisian a constant, fatiguing, and stressful reorientation vis-à-vis their own city. The German occupiers wanted to unmake dynamic Paris, to create a static simulacrum, preserving its most banal characteristics for their own enjoyment. They thought they could persuade the world that they, too, were culturally and aesthetically sensitive while keeping Parisians literally in line. For a time, the strategy seemed to work.

Chapter Three

⋅⟶⟹ ⟸⟵⋅

Minuet (1940–1941)

On one hand the city was swept clean by the police, by official authority, while on the other, the people each day traced the contours of a city that it redesigned according to the season, or some crisis, even sometimes an angry outburst. Thus [Paris], in its bistros, in its neighborhoods, escaped the powers that organized and repressed [it].

—*Pierre Sansot[1]*

How Do You Occupy a City?

Article 43 of the regulations enacted at the Hague Convention of 1907 states succinctly: "The authority of the legitimate power having in fact passed into the hands of the occupant, the latter shall take all the measures in his power to restore and ensure, as far as possible, public order and [civil life], while respecting, unless absolutely prevented, the laws in force in the country."[2] Such benign language assumes that all occupying forces see their primary duty as maintaining a semblance of antebellum everyday life. Yet it suggests that the occupier might well read in the innocuous phrase "as far as possible" a loophole that would permit him to do whatever he wants. Also, there is no reference in this article to the notion of time: How long is an occupation? Can it go on forever? Is it an implied temporary state, or is it open-ended? One of the cruelest impositions on an occupied nation is the idea that time is also an enemy, a heretofore anodyne phenomenon that becomes a

97

patient, insatiable consumer of hope. A military occupation is no longer just the temporary appropriation of sovereignty.*

Initially polite, the Occupation authorities in Paris became more and more exigent. The newly returned population noticed immediately that many of the city's elite hotels and luxurious private residences had been confiscated by the Germans—for the Wehrmacht, the Luftwaffe, the Kriegsmarine, the Gestapo, the Foreign Office, the propaganda ministry, and so on—and that whole sections of the city were closed off to the casual pedestrian. Next they became aware of yellow signs affixed to the shop windows of all Jewish-owned enterprises.[†] The Germans wanted the residents to know which businesses were Jewish-controlled in the hope that "proper" French people would not shop there. Later, these yellow notices would be replaced with red ones announcing the presence of an "Aryan manager," that is, someone selected by the authorities who had paid for the rights to the establishment's management and profits. Strictly enforced food rationing began within weeks, revealing, though no one knew it then, a German strategy: to use the bounty of French agriculture to feed the armies of the Reich and to reduce the French to a minimal caloric intake. Eventually, Parisians had to accept hunger as a price for staying on the Seine.

Accounts of the months following the first surprise of the Occupation mix self-disgust and political despair to create an almost palpable despondency. It was one thing to see German soldiers in expected places—before major buildings, monuments, crossroads—but quite another to run into them on side streets or in one's favorite café. They seemed to have come out of nowhere, silently, to infest the city. For every Parisian who had welcomed them with surprise and respect there

---

* The First World War had already introduced the practice of very long military occupations; northern France, but not Paris, was in German hands for almost four years, and Allied—especially French—forces had occupied Germany's Rhineland and the Ruhr Valley until 1925.

† A still-remembered and much-repeated story tells of a French family, primarily known for its optical shops, that placed advertisements in French newspapers attesting that their name was Lissac, an old, respected French family name, and assuredly not Isaac, or newcomer Jews. The shops can still be found all over France.

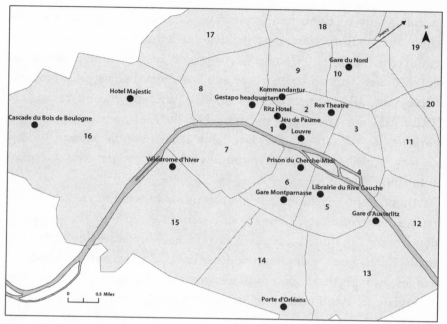

Sites of the Occupation

were now a dozen who felt bereaved, lost, forgotten. How had Paris, the heart and brain of France, been so effortlessly occupied? No counterattacks, no street-to-street fighting, not even a sign of a fruitless but symbolic resistance. How could this have happened in Paris, of all cities? Jean Guéhenno, in his *Journal des années noires* (Diary of the Dark Years), describes his return to Paris once the Armistice allowed him to leave the French army. He found Paris saddened and bleak, not the place a few had described as relieved, even happy, to see the Germans. He lived near the Bois de Boulogne, on the western side of Paris; almost offhandedly he noticed that something was not quite right, though there were no signs of Germans in the neighborhood. Then he figured it out: birds were no longer singing on those hot September days. Had they, too, fled?

Though physical resistance to the enemy was almost nonexistent, verbal and graphic expressions of anger or of a stubborn refusal to accept the obvious were soon present—and often humorous. Graffiti, flyers, and small tracts glued to lampposts almost immediately began to appear. Many of these first expressions of discontent were from the hands and imaginations of adolescents, delighted to have a patriotic reason to cause mischief. In his sad biography of the young Communist Guy Môquet, later to be executed as a hostage at the age of seventeen, Pierre-Louis Basse describes the exhilaration of teenage resistance: "[After] the surrender and the arrival of the Germans in Paris...the working-class youth of the 17th and 18th arrondissements wasted no time in playing cat-and-mouse with the French and German authorities."[3]

Mimeograph machines became precious and were hidden imaginatively all over the city; their stencils were inserted into the pumps of bicycles coolly ridden past the authorities. *Papillons* (butterflies) — small, toilet-paper-thin documents — were dropped from rooftops, bridges, and speeding bikes onto Germans and Parisians alike. There is an ingenious contraption on view at the Musée de la Résistance nationale in Champigny-sur-Marne that was designed to project these *papillons* from balconies and rooftops long after the perpetrator had left the area. The machine is constructed of a mousetrap weighted down by a tin can with a hole in its bottom; the can is filled with water, and as the leaking liquid lightens the can, the gadget pops the container of messages on the other end into the air. To the great amusement of the young *résistants,* bits of anti-Nazi propaganda would fall like snowflakes onto the heads of a German marching band or foot patrol.

For Some, Paris Was a Bubble

We know from several sources written during the Occupation that there was an often warm relationship between many of France's most talented citizens and the better-educated German occupiers. The upper echelons of society, if they were not Jewish, enjoyed a comfortable life, even though they could not get every foodstuff they wanted or have their drivers pick them up every morning. What we know less about is how difficult materially the Occupation was for the middle-of-the-road Parisian. There was more illness, to be sure, more malnutrition, but there was never starvation, nor were there massive roundups of average citizens.*

Still, the city did change measurably in the first year of the Occupation. For example, the cinema had never been so popular, yet before too long, lights would be turned up in the auditorium when Nazi newsreels were shown, to intimidate those who would laugh or hoot at them. Cafés, one of the few places where one could go for predictable warmth (churches having turned off their furnaces for lack of coal soon after the first harsh winter of 1940–41), were often frequented by Germans, in uniform and not. Cafés were also one of the few places one could go for a bit of privacy. From the seventeenth century onward, they had attracted police spies precisely because of their reputations for enabling private conversation about dissidence and revolt. The same pertained during the Occupation: real and potential resisters used them as mail drops and as places to hold discreet discussions about tactics. Care was taken, for one might be seated next to a German soldier or bureaucrat or, worse, a French collaborator and thus be seen or heard. This newly "uncanny" atmosphere persisted elsewhere, too. Streets that had been previously anodyne, e.g., Rue de Rivoli, Rue des Saussaies, Boulevard Raspail, even the Champs-Élysées, acquired a sinister aura because of official German presence. The same was true for certain quarters, such as the 3rd, 4th, 8th, and 20th arrondissements, known to be filled with "foreigners"—i.e., recent immigrants and expatriates—which were likely to be raided unpredictably.

The more expensive quarters, areas where many Germans had seized apartments and homes, notably in the 8th and 16th arrondissements and in Neuilly, had almost taken on the air of a neighborhood in Hamburg or Munich. In historian Cécile Desprairies's census of private and public buildings "acquisitioned" by the Germans, a good third of her six-hundred-plus pages cover only three arrondissements: the 8th, 16th, and 17th, still today the most coveted of neighborhoods, while only about forty pages cover the Latin Quarter's less affluent, more

---

* One of my interviewees, a pharmacy student during this period, opined with a sardonic smile that there was less obesity, less diabetes, fewer STDs, less asthma, and so forth during this time.

crowded 5th and 6th arrondissements.* Interestingly, for the nervous Parisian, the Left Bank (which included the Saint-Germain area, Montparnasse, and the Latin Quarter) was believed to be "safer" than the Right Bank, where the largest number of Jews, eastern European immigrants, and German personnel lived. This was more of an instinct than a fact. In his idiosyncratic memoir-cum-novel, *Rue des Maléfices* (published in English as *Paris Noir;* 1954), petty crook Jacques Yonnet describes how he, a spy for the Resistance, managed to stay one step ahead of the authorities by losing himself in the labyrinthine streets and neighborhoods of the Latin Quarter. Bars and cafés were his meeting places, his "offices," even though he was fully aware of the presence of collaborators; one just had to be careful. The presence on the Left Bank of many lycées, several universities—notably, the Sorbonne and its various institutes—and such *grandes écoles* as the École normale supérieure and the École libre des sciences politiques (now the Institut d'études politiques de Paris) meant that there were thousands of young people in the area eager to establish their independence from any dominant ideology. This sense of shelter was mostly an illusion, yet the Left Bank retained its aura of safety from oppressive authority, of a "less German" Paris, throughout the Occupation.

In general, the architectural integrity of Paris was not nearly as marked by the Occupation as were the physical and affective qualities of living in the city. A large swath of the area around the *grands boulevards,* between the Avenue de l'Opéra and the Avenue de la République, was closed even to bicycle traffic. Other major avenues were barred or heavily guarded, but most remained accessible to Parisians, at least on foot. Few sites were renamed, though the Théâtre Sarah-Bernhardt did become the Théâtre de la Cité, and some street names

---

* Since the early nineteenth century, the western sections of Paris had become the haven of the wealthy Parisians. As a consequence, many large mansions had been built in the 8th, 16th, and 17th arrondissements, where the most prestigious hotels were located. The Germans confidently—and shamelessly—appropriated many homes (especially those owned by wealthy Jews) and most hotels in this area. The Latin Quarter, on the other hand, though with pockets of affluence, remained a warren of student housing, church property, and schools and colleges, affording much less hospitality to the selective Occupiers.

were *déjudaïsées*—that is, "de-Jewed." Métro stops kept their original names, though many were closed either for reasons of security or to serve as air raid shelters (*abris*) or storage facilities. As noted, the Germans constructed many ugly concrete bunkers and other defensive structures around their encampments and headquarters. There were even plans to build a new German embassy on the Place de la Concorde, but apparently Hitler never approved them. The Occupier did raze many of the shanties that surrounded Paris (where the poorest of the poor lived), in the zones created by Haussmann's annexations of 1860. There was also substantial destruction by air raids in the near suburbs, where most of Paris's industry and railroad yards were located. But the capital's built environment was mostly left untouched by wary Occupation authorities. This fact reinforced the uncanniness: Paris looked the same, but it "had left the Seine." The *ville des lumières* had become the *ville éteinte* (the extinguished city). It was a darker city— gray and brown, not to mention *noir* (black), were required adjectives to describe the absence of ambient light.

In his memoir, *Un Petit Parisien* (A Little Parisian Boy), the journalist Dominique Jamet describes coming of age during the Occupation and how buffeted his life was between the ages of six and eleven. He especially remembers how quickly Paris had become another city:

> Paris without light, but Paris without cars, Paris without traffic jams, Paris without pollution, Paris without accidents, Paris without stoplights, Paris without noise, Paris made younger by the cleaning of its arteries where thrombosis no longer threatens, Paris, under its veil of soot and the calcified crust of its black facades, reveals its most beautiful, truest appearance, the larger perspective of its avenues made languid by good weather, returned to their proper proportions, the alignment of its palaces, of its houses, the curve of its streets, which have found again the purity of its lines.[4]

The city could be perceived in ways impossible since the end of Haussmannization; the original ideas behind the reconstruction of

Paris, to project it as an imperial city, with attempts through a coordinated architecture to imply that Paris would never end, that it was eternal. This Paris could be glimpsed again during the Occupation. There are many references to a changed Paris, to one where sounds previously smothered under loud urban noises could be heard, where one could walk more safely because only bicycles clogged the streets, where walking itself imposed a new rhythm of urban consciousness. It is a bit ironic that Paris—hungry, tired, and embarrassed by its shortages—could still nevertheless show its "bones." Its original beauty remained and provided occasional solace for those enmeshed in a strange, sinister environment.

By the middle of the nineteenth century, cities were increasingly being described as threatening, the blame going to the ravages of industrialism. No longer places to seek unfettered fortune, they became, in novels and essays of the period, sites of unhealthiness, physical danger, political instability, and immorality. And one of the most commonly cited reasons for these phenomena was the absence of light at night. Such lack of illumination was characteristic of most cities, and few offered as much vibrancy in the midnight shadows as the French capital. Paris had defined its very modernity, attractiveness, and pleasure in terms of the safety of its well-lit streets and boulevards. To live, then, in a newly darkened Paris, a city that had been known for its taming of nighttime, was unnatural and disorienting to both visitors and inhabitants. The unreliability of electricity and the need for defensive measures meant that streetlights were intermittent at best, absent most of the time. The headlights of the few automobiles running at night were covered with a blue material that let only a strip of light through. A constant darkness meant that one had to learn anew how to navigate familiar streets and neighborhoods. Tentativeness became a habit; everyone had a story about how someone had tripped, fallen into a hole dug by a construction crew, or bumped into someone while negotiating the murky streets. One writer described to a friend what it was like to look out a window and see not the Parisian glow but the much smaller, indiscriminately bouncing beams of flashlights (less frequent after batteries became impossible to obtain). He wrote: "You cannot imagine the little streets of the Montagne Sainte-Geneviève, Les Gobelins, the Canal Saint-Martin, the Bastille neighborhood, without any light except that of the moon! You can walk for hours without meeting anyone....Despite the darkness and the disorientation I'm afraid of experiencing this evening in places that were so familiar to me, I still feel my way, though carefully."[5]

One day in his studio on the Left Bank's Rue des Grands-Augustins, the fretful Picasso noticed that his flashlight was gone. He flew into a rage, accusing his secretary, visitors, and servants of having misplaced it or, worse, filched it. He stormed around the apartment for hours, fuming and refusing to see visitors or to paint. He stopped speaking to any of those who lived around him. For Picasso, to lose a flashlight was to have to admit how much he and others had to depend on the device, not only to get around outside but also to get around inside. A flashlight was not just a tool, it was an embarrassing necessity, as important to living in occupied Paris as a bicycle. The day was one of the most tense his entourage had ever experienced, but the next was better: Picasso had found the missing flashlight right where he had left it.

Another urban characteristic, the cacophony of daily urban engagement—passersby, hawkers, street minstrels and performers, construction work, and especially traffic noise—was severely diminished during the Occupation. The patina of urban noise affords the urban dweller another sort of anonymity, a sensory cocoon that provides a feeling of protection from the interjection of unwelcome sounds. Urbanists often ignore inhabitants' aural engagement with their city, but it is as important in how we negotiate a city's complexities as our senses of sight and touch. Writers of the period, such as Colette, emphasize how quiet Paris became during these years. Sometimes the silence brought benefits, when pleasant sounds—birdsong, music—were able to reach Parisians' ears. And there are many mentions of how clearly radio broadcasts could be heard (especially problematic for those listening to the BBC). But mostly, the new silence in such a vital capital must have been confusing and intermittently frightening. Police sirens were more menacing, airplane engines meant danger, a shout or scream provoked a more nervous response.

Dancing the Minuet

Despite all the signs, Parisians were still caught flat-footed by the surrender of their city, and it would be months before they realized what a
military occupation really meant. A young Parisian wrote in her
journal:

> How those first days...have been disillusioning, sad, and differ-
> ent! To try to express, to render, this suffocating ambience would
> have only rendered it more insufferable....More than ever, the
> "I've heard," the "I've been told," the "it seems that" are taken
> seriously. They are in effect useless, but they test the resistance
> that one has built up. In spite of oneself, one dreams, laughs, and
> then falls back into reality, or even into excessive pessimism,
> making the situation more painful.[6]

The time of year—late spring, summer, and fall—helped lull Parisians into a sense of well-being. Food was still easily available; despite
the relentless shopping by the occupiers, the stores were still stocked,
and there was no need for coal or large amounts of electricity. The
Germans had immediately put France on Berlin time, so there were
even more daylight hours available well into the autumn. Curfews
were generally later and predictable, and the Métro was running after a
brief stoppage. Apartment windows were being unshuttered as those
who had left during the exodus returned (in fact, the state railroad system was activating more trains to accommodate the returning hordes,
even offering free passage back home to Paris). Maybe this Occupation
would not be so onerous. After all, suggests a historian of the period,
once the Brits signed their own armistice or surrendered, life would
return to normal. The Germans would go back over the Rhine, and a
"new Europe" would bring order and prosperity:

> To create a climate favorable to a productive colonialization by
> seducing [Parisian] souls appears to be one of the first concerns of
> the occupier. To place between the German authorities and the

Parisians a screen that would mask, more or less totally, the important role the former was playing in this process was equally important to the Occupation. They intervened directly in our cultural life, but discreetly so, notwithstanding the heavyhandedness of some of their representatives.[7]

The German war machinery—panzers and paperwork—was quite happy to insist to the French and the world that their presence would be as unobtrusive as possible, except for political immigrants and Jews. Still, it was impossible to "miss" the Occupation if one stayed in Paris during that period. The Germans were visitors, wandering curiously with guidebooks in hand, who would not leave for home. They "were everywhere, and they had purposefully selected the most sumptuous buildings, the best-known mansions; they intervened, directly or indirectly, in all the city's activities; people spoke, sotto voce, of the Gestapo, but they scarcely were aware of the inner workings of the machine that was controlling them."[8] This new administration of Paris was a confusing one, and not only to the occupied. The Reich's Ministry of Foreign Affairs and the Ministry of Public Enlightenment and Propaganda, as well as the Gestapo, the Wehrmacht, and other military services, were all vying to control aspects of Parisian life and the French economy.* They were also competing for Berlin's attention. The Occupiers—innocently and purposefully—collided and often duplicated efforts. Recently, the historian Max Hastings has succinctly addressed the contradictions that hampered German administration of both the Reich and its occupied countries:

---

* Studying this period is frustratingly complicated by the plethora of acronyms used by both German and French bureaucracies, both as shorthand and as a means of covering up nefarious activities. ERR (Einsatzstab Reichsleiter Rosenberg), MBF (Militärbefehlshaber in Frankreich), OKW (Oberkommando der Wehrmacht), Sipo-SD (Sicherheitspolizei Sicherheitsdienst), not to mention the better-known Gestapo (Geheime Staatspolizei) and SS (Schutzstaffel), festooned official posters and documents, along with the acronyms of dozens of their co-occupying agencies. Acronyms can be, and often are, a means to make banal the shameful.

There is a striking contradiction about Germany's performance in World War II. The Wehrmacht showed itself the outstanding fighting force of the conflict, one of the most effective armies the world has ever seen. But its achievements on the battlefield were set at naught, fortunately for the interest of mankind, by the stunning incompetence with which the German war machine was conducted.[9]

The Germans were nothing if not planners. Even before the Occupation their spies had long been at work in Paris, and Berlin had been studying the public records of the city of Paris's architectural office for months in advance. They knew who lived in which apartment houses, which buildings were publicly owned, and which were private. They knew the location of every bank, art gallery, record-keeping depot, insurance company, and warehouse. They had studied blueprints and site drawings so they knew which buildings had multiple entrances. They knew the sewer system and the underground railroad and even

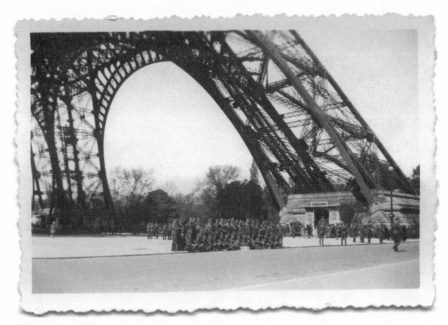

We're only tourists. (*Musée de la Résistance nationale*)

understood the labyrinthine nature of Paris's mined-out limestone quarries. They knew the specialties and locations of all major hospitals and clinics. They had learned which lycées and schools had extensive playing fields. They had a list of all of the bordellos of Paris and had already selected those that would be reserved for their own men. They had decided which restaurants and which cinemas would be open only to German authorities. They had the names of every wealthy Jewish family and which bank vaults contained their most valuable belongings. They knew which works of art had been removed from which museums and in most cases where those works had been taken. They knew of the census that the French had taken of foreign immigrants. They knew the numbers of rooms that each hotel contained. They knew the telephone and pneumatic-tube systems of the city. They knew who had telephones and where the switchboards were. They knew the intricacies of the river that passed through Paris, its docks and warehouses.

This sight of the Occupier living and working in their city, rather than the much rarer scenes of force, continuously disturbed the Parisians. Appropriators of familiar spaces, the Germans made the City of Light *unheimlich* (uncanny) for its longtime residents. There was no "ordinary," and as a consequence the Parisian had to take unfamiliar measures to deflect a regular interruption of daily routines and expectations. Many observers of this period—both French and German—remark that Parisians soon assumed a sort of blindness toward the innumerable uniformed men in their midst. Here begins the myth of *Paris sans regard,* the *Stadt ohne Blick*—the city without a face—discussed in the next chapter. Yet we must be careful not to assign a monolithic response on the part of the Parisian populace. Many Parisians benefited from the German presence in their city. Not all Germans were Nazi thugs; they needed entertainment, food, clothing, and other comforts, including human contact. For propaganda purposes, for morale, and for the economy (which the Germans had to support if they were to skim hundreds of millions of francs off the French GDP every month), Paris barely skipped a beat in maintaining a vibrant entertainment industry (films, theater, vaudeville, cabarets,

Looking for a good deal. *(Musée de la Résistance nationale)*

bordellos, radio variety shows, even an incipient television industry). Horse racing was a major divertissement again by the second year of the Occupation; the fashion industry, even under severe material shortages, still prospered. The bimonthly German guidebook *Der Deutsche Wegleiter für Paris* included pages of advertisements for fashionable designers and what remained of luxury items in the occupied city.

Every major economic, political, and military unit needed a place to work and to collect; countless Parisian buildings were used for this purpose. The traumas of the Occupation were entombed in the apparent banality of these mostly Haussmannian edifices, clad in the *pierre de taille* (carved or freestone masonry) that gives Paris its character. The authorities chose most of these buildings, too, because they were conveniently located at the intersection of two or more streets, thus providing multiple entrances and exits. They served multiple functions: "The same spot could be a place of torture, of pleasure, or of business."[10] But no structure was too small or insignificant to escape

Nazi attention. They even requisitioned newspaper kiosks to ensure the distribution of their newspapers and magazines. (Other kiosks, the significant remnants of Haussmann's "street furniture," were often removed for fear they might be too close to official buildings.) The military constructed concrete blockhouses at key junctions and before key buildings throughout the city. Massive underground bunkers were constructed under the streets and rail stations of the city. They set up warehouses everywhere, especially near major train stations, in which to store the household goods they had "appropriated" from Jewish and "foreign" families. These goods would be sent to Germany to replace what had been destroyed by Allied bombing.

The Germans and their outposts were in almost every Parisian quarter and neighborhood. Every district had an office of the Occupation authorities or an apartment building that had been totally or partially requisitioned by the Germans; the city was dotted with Jewish businesses and residences that had been seized. Wherever she looked, there was a reminder of France's complete subservience to the Occupier. Hundreds of buildings were requisitioned or "Aryanized"; thousands of apartments were turned over to new owners, either Germans or their sympathizers. Later, changing the purpose of a building, putting a new sign on it, or even razing it rarely erased the memory of its former use, no matter how innocuous that use might have been.

Like the minuet, a dance with precise moves but little touching, the Occupation involved two parties—the Parisian and the German— trying to avoid stepping on each other's toes. That does not mean that there were not strong feelings individually expressed on both sides. Small signs of resistance—teenagers on their bikes whistling when they passed Germans in uniform, graffiti on the city's walls, stony stares—cropped up against the inevitable arrogance of the conqueror: pushing ahead in line, making bad jokes, speeding carelessly in their cars on the city's arteries. Such early signs foreshadowed what was to become a much more bitter interaction.

Soon after the army and the bureaucrats arrived, German women auxiliary workers—Red Cross nurses, secretaries, telephone and telegraph operators—began to appear on Parisian streets. Dressed in gray uniforms, with perky little caps on their carefully coiffed heads, they soon became known as the "gray mice," or "little maids." They walked through the streets with the same patronizing purposefulness of their fellows, eschewing any of the stylishness that defined so many young French women, even in a time of austerity. Parisians gossiped about their "real" purpose, given the large number of men in the German contingent, but, at least for this early period, German couples were rarely seen on the street. These young women lived in hotels that were like dormitories (and even in actual dormitories, such as the one at the recently built Cité internationale universitaire, in the 14th arrondissement); they frequently ate in separate canteens and, like nuns, walked in pairs or groups while shopping. Their presence might have softened the image of the hard soldier whose main task was to impose order, but they also tended to remind the Parisian of the permanence of the German Occupation authorities.

Probably the first major adjustment, in July and August following the Occupation, had to do with automobile transportation. Parisian owners of large cars (in particular, models from 1938, 1939, and 1940) were ordered to take them to the Vincennes hippodrome, on the outskirts of the city, for evaluation and "purchase" by the Occupation authorities. Buses were transformed from gasoline power to wood and charcoal power (*gazogène*), which was provided by large containers atop the vehicles, giving them the look of some sort of humpbacked exotic animal escaped from the zoo. (The mature trees of some arteries had to be trimmed radically in order for these contraptions to pass.) New tires and retreads could no longer be sold to civilians; driver's licenses were parsimoniously issued. Professions that had lived by the gasoline engine become dead ends: taxi driver, bus driver (many city and intercity bus lines were canceled or shortened), deliveryman, and moving man. The bicycle—soon de rigueur for anyone not walking—became even more prevalent, and in the Occupied Zone every one of them had to be registered; they carried small yellow tags on their rear mudguards. (After two more years of the Occupation, with an aluminum shortage, license plates would be issued in heavy cardboard and were no longer required to be posted.) It was obvious that bikes would be used increasingly for harassing the Occupiers, but there was no way to forbid them, or Paris would have ceased to function. Still, all bicycles were carefully monitored, and rules became more stringent: hands must be kept on handlebars at all times, feet on the pedals; no second riders; no latching on to passing trucks or cars; no riding abreast, only in single file.

One of the major mistakes made by Berlin was its failure to define its role in two key ways — a failure that would end up exacerbating the unpleasantness of the Occupation. First, it did not give specific guidelines to the Occupation authorities to do anything in Paris but "maintain order and security"; and second, it refused to clarify for the Vichy government its future in a Paris and in a Europe ruled by the Reich.[11] Such lack of precision combined with the unique presence of a separate État français led to one exquisitely melodramatic episode that embarrassed key political figures — Hitler himself; Otto Abetz (the German ambassador to Paris); the prime minister, Pierre Laval; and Maréchal Pétain. It concerned the decision to return the remains of the King of Rome, Duke of Reichstadt, and only recognized son of Napoleon I (who designated him Napoleon II upon his abdication) to the Invalides, where he would lie beside his father. Arno Breker recalled the Führer gazing on Napoleon's tomb:

> Witnesses to this historical moment, we were secretly hoping and even waiting for Hitler to find words appropriate for the occasion and the site. Something absolutely unexpected then happened. He spoke of the Duke of Reichstadt, Napoleon's son, whose remains were in Vienna. A magnanimous gesture of reconciliation with the French people seemed to him to be what the occasion demanded. . . . Hitler's order was a gesture of reconciliation, but events did not allow it to find a positive echo from the French.[12]

This last sentence is an understatement, for the event caused the first serious contretemps between the German Occupation and the Vichy government.

Coincidentally, Pétain was at that moment in the process of reorganizing his cabinet with the aim of ridding himself of the oily, subversive Pierre Laval, a close confidant of Otto Abetz, Foreign Minister Ribbentrop's man in Paris.* Laval had supported the idea of returning the ashes when Abetz mentioned it. (It remains unclear how much more Hitler had thought about his suggestion after he made it in June.) By mid-December, Laval had contrived for Hitler to send the following letter to Pétain:

> *Berlin, December 13, 1940*
>
> *Monsieur le Maréchal, the 15th of December will bring the centenary of the arrival of Napoleon's body at the Invalides. I would like to honor that occasion by letting you know, Monsieur le Maréchal, that I have decided to offer the mortal remains of the Duke of Reichstadt to the French people. Thus the son of Napoleon, leaving surroundings that during his tragic life were foreign to him, will return to his native country to rest next to his august father. Please accept, Monsieur le Maréchal, my personal esteem.*
>
> *Signed: Adolf Hitler*[13]

Pétain, for once, was incensed at the arrogance of the German leader. Informed that he was expected to be at the Invalides to receive the coffin on behalf of a grateful France, he haughtily refused: to appear under the Nazi flag, surrounded by German military, would have offended even the most neutral French citizens. And, to put it bluntly, Pétain couldn't have cared less about Napoleon II's ashes (the French use the

---

* The internal political machinations of the Vichy government were byzantine. The government was divided between those who saw themselves as allies of the Germans and those who were faithful and traditional French patriots, though quite conservative. Laval was in the former group and had enemies in the latter cohort influential with the doddering Pétain. For a variety of reasons, Pétain fired Laval, his prime minister, in December of 1940. But in April of 1942, Laval, like an unsavory phoenix, rose again to that position and would remain head of the government until the end of the war.

term *cendres* to refer to the mortal remains of major figures, even when there has been no cremation). He had other things on his mind: getting rid of Laval, for one, and persuading the Germans to allow him to move his government from the backwater of Vichy to Versailles, nearer Paris, as the Armistice agreement had suggested. To the embarrassment of the newly fired Laval and Ambassador Abetz, Pétain, for once, stood his ground.

What followed was nearly comic, a combination of the ghoulish, the pompous, the hypocritical, and the amusing—one of the few events of the Occupation that can inspire a small smile. The heavy bronze coffin was taken from the Capuchin Church in Vienna, where the Duke of Reichstadt had lain for more than a hundred years next to his mother, Marie-Louise, grandniece of Marie Antoinette. (There were wags in Paris who asked, after the transfer had been announced: "Why move him away from his mother? Why not move them both? Or move Napoleon to Vienna—keep the family together.") Placed on a special armored train, the coffin made the slow trip from Vienna to Paris through a freezing European winter. One Frenchman remembers that his father, a railroad worker, bundled him up and took him to the Gare de l'Est that cold morning to watch the train come in. His father asked his fellows when the young Napoleon's body was arriving. "What Napoleon? We're expecting an important train with the body of some German big shot, the Duke of Reichstadt." As one historian has pointed out, the French knew more about the Duke of Windsor than they did Napoleon's boy.

The heavy coffin, which had been surrounded inside the car by a small forest of Austrian pines, was placed on a special caisson that was pulled through Paris by the light of torches down major boulevards, along the icy Seine, past the Louvre, to the Invalides. The scene was right out of Leni Riefenstahl's (Hitler's favorite filmmaker) and Goebbels's lugubrious performance manual: darkness, torches, slow pacing, cadenced drumming, all hints of ancient Teutonic tradition. This parade happened right after midnight, and, of course, there was no one in the streets, only the slowly pacing cortege, led and followed by military vehicles. It was wicked cold, with persistent sleet falling on the

115

catafalque. When the parade reached the Invalides, the coffin was brought in by German soldiers, formally delivered to the elaborately uniformed Garde républicaine, who laid it at the chapel's altar, where finally a tricolor flag was draped over the casket. (An exception had been made to allow the French flag to be used ceremonially.)

Somberly, an official placed at the bier a wreath from Philippe Pétain, chef de l'État français. But shouldn't there have been one, equally ostentatious, from the Führer, whose brilliant initiative this had been? Indeed, a late night delivery had been made, before the chapel had been opened. A wreath with the name of Adolf Hitler prominently displayed had been left outside the gate. The story is that the wife of the Invalides's caretaker saw it and quickly removed and burned it in her fireplace. In turn, her husband gathered the wires on which it had stood and buried them on the grounds. So there was no wreath from the magnanimous Nazi manager of this ghoulish farce.

The next day Parisian newspapers described the arrival and the disposal of the remains; soon there were long lines of French and Germans waiting to see the coffin. But overall, this meticulously planned spectacle had, as Pétain knew it would, little impact on the French. ("We asked them for coal and they sent us ashes" was a typically Parisian response.) An especially imaginative rumor, one believed by many, was that de Gaulle had been killed in the bombing of London and his ashes had been spirited to Paris, placed in the Duke of Reichstadt's coffin, and were now resting next to Napoleon!

So the minuet had miscues and slipups. For about a year, until Germany invaded the USSR in June of 1941, both sides tried to follow the other's lead, if suspiciously. As the summer months of 1940 passed, many Parisians found themselves increasingly preoccupied with figuring out how to meet the normal demands of everyday life. Larger questions such as resistance, political concerns about the new Vichy government, and philosophical notions about liberty were put aside in favor of worrying about finding nourishment, fretting about the million and a half French soldiers still in POW camps, and adjusting to new and less efficient means of transportation. But there were Parisians who had other, more immediate concerns.

Correct, but Still Nazis

Jacques Biélinky was born in Russia in 1881 and had immigrated to Paris in 1909, primarily to escape the anti-Jewish violence that was frequent in that part of Europe. He became a French citizen in 1927 (not that such a choice would help him escape deportation and death in the camp at Sobibòr in 1943) and began to write for Jewish papers, both in French and in Yiddish. When the Germans arrived in Paris, many Parisians were curious, angry, or neutral. But Jews knew that the web of Nazi racism was encroaching on them in one of the continent's most progressive cities. Within two months of their arrival, the Germans began a census of all foreigners, "with the assistance of the owners of apartment buildings, apartment managers, and concierges."[14] The effort made even French Jews apprehensive. By the end of September, the Vichy government had passed specific anti-Jewish ordinances defining "Jewishness" and setting up regulations regarding property ownership. From July of 1940 until December of 1942, Biélinky kept a meticulous journal of the effects of the Occupation on the complexly heterogeneous Jewish population of Paris.

The number of Jews in Paris at that moment is a difficult statistic to pin down, even given the intensive effort of the Vichy and German police to establish the aforementioned census. In general, we can work with these numbers: in October of 1940 there were about 150,000 Jews in Paris, and many more were coming daily from Alsace-Lorraine, from which they had been expelled. Of that number, about 86,000 were French nationals (though some, like Biélinky, had been citizens only since the early twentieth century), and about 64,000 were foreign immigrants, many of them recent. They spoke many languages and held varying degrees of allegiance to Jewish religious practices. They were mostly poor, but a significant number of them had businesses and other affairs that had brought wealth. The many synagogues of Paris ranged from the modest to the opulent, and there were definitely social prejudices on the part of some groups toward others. In fact, many of the poor Jews had convinced themselves that the rich ones would be the targets of Nazi looting and arrest—certainly not they, who had nothing.

Biélinky's diary gives us a detailed account of life in the first year of occupied Paris as he tried to gauge the dangers for Jews, which were harder and harder to ignore. His journal is a cross between an anthropological study of an urban environment under duress and an analysis of the status of Jews within the capital. Strangely enough, he found that in the beginning, Gentile Parisians gave Jews and their situation little attention, showing disinterest rather than hatred or scorn. He hears almost no anti-Semitic remarks while waiting in shop queues; he even learns that patrolling French police occasionally kept right-wing thugs from intimidating Jewish students and merchants.

There were definitely targeted ordinances—Jews could not sell their buildings or apartments, Jewish musicians were fired from classical and popular orchestras—but on the whole German soldiers themselves seemed unconcerned with those whom their government considered their greatest mortal and moral threat. For instance, in the Rue Buffault, in the working-class 14th arrondissement, a German garage was right across the street from a synagogue. Jews were at first skittish about going to worship, but the Germans barely took notice of them; there were no incidents. When there were a few anti-Semitic outbursts in a soup line, German soldiers would at first protect the Jews.

Despite the bright yellow signs on the outside of Jewish shops, reminding potential patrons that their owners belonged to the hated race, their business grew. Was it because of Parisian solidarity, or was it a form of Parisian resistance? Biélinky did not know, but perhaps it was both, and the examples reflect how difficult it is to suggest a seamless tableau about Parisian anti-Semitism and apathy. For the most part, non-Jews seem to have ignored the regulations imposed on their *Israélite* neighbors. Even visiting Germans and their wives shopped in those stores, and, unbelievably, some Catholic shop owners put the same yellow signs up because they seemed to attract more customers than other types of advertising. One Jewish woman said that the fact that her parents' restaurant had a yellow sign meant they never had to worry about German clients. Should a German soldier walk in obliviously, her parents would point to the sign (in German as well as French); he would mumble an apology and leave.

That does not mean that the Germans did not do their dirty work. Rumors were rampant, and Parisian Jews were always waiting for another shoe to fall. Biélinky heard of Jewish bookshops being raided and apartments being targeted with alacrity and precision. Rabbis enjoined their congregants not to talk politics at worship, and not to stand around outside the synagogue drawing attention. Still, our optimistic (or, at least, hopeful) journalist remarked as late as May 19, 1941, that despite increasingly inclusive dragnets targeting Jews, perhaps the worst would not happen in Paris: "On the day of mass arrests of Jews for internment, around one hundred Jews—especially artists and intellectuals—were arrested at the city hall of the 14th arrondissement. Outside, the French crowd, very Aryan, violently protested against these arrests."[15] But Parisian solidarity and sense of justice would not be enough to keep these roundups from increasing, nor would the Wehrmacht, though not unhelpful in some of the SS's actions, be able to stop their fanatical brethren from trying to remove every Jew, French or foreign, from the streets of Paris.

"To Bed, to Bed!"

In another part of the city, Sidonie-Gabrielle Colette (known universally by her last name alone), France's best-known woman writer, a feminist and a gifted narrator, was also interested in recording what was happening in her beloved city. She had decided to return to Paris after the exodus and, like Picasso and her close friend Jean Cocteau, who lived nearby, to remain there. She did not wander very far from her enclave: the Palais-Royal. This former palace, built by Cardinal Richelieu in the seventeenth century, is located in the center of Paris, just a stone's throw from the Louvre. The site of some of Paris's most idiosyncratic shops, the building had several apartments on the upper floors; although they were not grand, they had the cachet of location. The Palais-Royal was to Paris what Paris was to the rest of war-ravaged Europe: an island of relative peace and calm despite being in the 1st arrondissement, among the most infested by the German presence. The Occupation authorities had requisitioned about two dozen hotels

Colette and her friend Jean Cocteau in the gardens of the Palais-Royal. (Serge Lido/Sipa Press/Sipa USA)

The Palais Royal and its secluded gardens

for offices and billeting in that district—among them the capital's most famous establishments: the Ritz, the Continental, the Meurice, the Lotti. This geographically small neighborhood contained the Ministries of Justice and Finance, the Louvre, the headquarters of the Banque de France, the Police Judiciaire, on the Quai des Orfèvres, and the Palais de Justice, on the Île de la Cité. It encompassed the luxurious Place Vendôme and the popular Les Halles. And it was home to the Orangerie and the Jeu de Paume museums (which Göring would visit more than twenty times during the Occupation). But the Germans did not lay their hands on the Palais-Royal: no hotel in the neighborhood was requisitioned, nor were any apartments or any businesses appropriated. For years, Colette and her husband, Maurice Goudeket, a Jewish journalist, lived at 9 Rue Beaujolais, in a small apartment she affectionately called *le Tunnel*. One of France's best-known chefs, Raymond Oliver, ran Le Grand Véfour restaurant, located on the ground floor, under Colette's apartment. High-ranking Germans and French collaborators often lunched and dined there, and Oliver would on occasion send dishes to his friend upstairs. From time to time, a German military band would play in the garden, and military personnel could be found there playing chess outdoors. But the wall around the old palace's garden seemed to have kept the Occupiers at a distance.

At her second-story window on the northern edge of the enclave, Colette would sit on her chaise longue and write her letters, stories, and newspaper columns. (During the war, she composed "Gigi," the story that would bring her wide international fame.) From October of 1940 until her husband's arrest in December of 1941, she wrote a series of articles for the collaborationist newspaper *Le Petit Parisien*. As one of her critics says: "This collection... is not among those that would have allowed Colette to pass into posterity."[16] Yet it provides an important glimpse of the first reactions of Parisians to the sudden arrival of the German occupiers. To the chagrin of many who were less sanguine about the invader, Colette wrote a sort of advice column to her women readers, suggesting how to make do during this difficult time. The columns make little reference to the political nature of the Occupation; after all, they were being published in a newspaper controlled by

German and Vichy censors. But they do let us know how soon the Occupation began to wear on Parisians and in what ways many of them coped. Twin concerns dominate her pieces: winter cold and the paucity of good nourishment. Colette suffered much from an arthritic hip that kept her inside her apartment. She could barely navigate the steps down to the shelter during air raid warnings and rarely ventured into the Métro because of the stairs down to the tracks. Yet she maintained, at least in her columns, an optimism that would, as a friend said after the war, be seen as a sort of heroism, a keeping of one's sangfroid during difficult times. She repeated her commonsensical mantra: despair, sorrow, and penury teach us how to live better than do joyous moments, and things would get better. "I have known happy Paris too well to worry about unhappy Paris," she famously wrote.[17] Colette had always challenged in her work the bourgeois hypocrisy that defined elite Parisian society, and this comment is a perfect example of her devil-may-care attitude about the Occupation.

Her columns also introduce another subject in need of more attention: the role of women in Paris during the Occupation. More than a million and a half French soldiers had been captured in just over a month, most of them spirited away to Germany. They would be released in dribbles for the next four years, used as bargaining chits by the Germans to ensure, through blackmail, as much quiescence as they could from the French population. The large absence of men (in stalags, in hiding, or working abroad) meant that Paris became a significantly feminized city, yet another major consequence of the presence of a masculinized other. Women, then, had to leave the hearth and venture out into the world to find jobs, food, and companionship if they were to survive physically as well as psychologically. Raising children became more burdensome; the temptation to accommodate oneself with the German Occupier became harder to resist, less ethically severe. Colette suggests in her columns that Parisian women should follow her strategy: lie low, find food, and stay at home as much as possible. "Au lit, au lit!" (To bed, to bed!), she half seriously offered as advice. What most of her readers did not realize, of course, is that in addition to her physical infirmities Colette had the anxiety of worrying about her Jewish husband, a journalist, too, who had been "relieved" of his job at the daily *Paris-Soir* by the Germans as soon as they arrived. Her neighbors and nearby merchants offered him a hiding place every night if one were needed, for they knew that the police—French or German—arrived while you were still in your bed. One young woman on the floor above even told Maurice that he should come "jump in bed" with her if surprised by a raid. Sure enough, Goudeket was arrested by the Gestapo in December of 1941 and imprisoned for two months. Colette's prestige and the respect German ambassador Abetz's French wife had for her enabled his release in February of 1942. For the rest of the war, they lived anxiously, awaiting another ominous knock on their door.*

From her second-floor window prospect, Colette knew that there were stories "out there," as her readers tried to adapt to a new set of daily occurrences. For example, just because the Germans were everywhere did not mean that crime had disappeared: one of her best friends was mugged in one of the Palais-Royal's arcades. And because she religiously believed that to eat meant more than to nourish the body—it meant nourishing the imagination as well—one had to know the black market and other sources (friends in the countryside, for example) intimately in order to obtain impossible-to-get foods such as garlic, cheese, and pork. Colette also wrote of how much more sensitive she and others had become to sounds, both human and nonhuman—loud, unexpected sounds as well as quiet ones, which had become audible because of the diminution of traffic in the empty streets—sounds such as the occasional gunshot kept her from concentrating on her work. (Children in the garden, with their constantly popping cap pistols, did not help.) But she still refused to leave Paris for the country; the city, even in distress, continued to provide inspiration for her work, which dealt with how people love and live under seemingly depressing circumstances. Even though her connected friends kept her and her husband, Maurice, protected from further Nazi harassment, and even

---

* Otto Abetz was officially the German ambassador to France, both occupied and unoccupied. He had substantial authority over all aspects of French politics and culture and served in Paris throughout the Occupation.

though she finally gave up writing her newspaper articles, the anxiety never totally disappeared.

Colette and others also took notice in their journals and memoirs of the subtle changes that occurred in daily social interactions between Parisians as well as between Parisians and their German "visitors." A new sort of awareness had to be developed: checkpoints for papers were more frequent; looking ahead as one walked familiar streets became routine. There was a reorientation of the habitual use of the senses as Parisians made their way through a changed city. One's hearing had to adjust to the unfamiliar, disorienting silence caused by the absence of traffic noises. Memoirists even mentioned that the sound of wooden — as opposed to rubber, a material that was rationed — soles pounding on the pavement allowed one to track the number as well as the speed of passing pedestrians. (In December of 1942, the singer Maurice Chevalier would introduce his song "La Symphonie des semelles de bois" [The Symphony of Wooden Soles].) Sight and touch were more often put to use as citizens became aware of what their neighbors were wearing, how their fellows were coping with the new restrictions the war economy had produced, from foodstuffs to textiles. Private motorized transportation having been radically restricted, densely packed public transportation became an environment in which Parisians of all social and economic classes were aware of the body odor of their compatriots. As a historian of everyday life in this period has convincingly posited: "To break a plate, tear a pair of pants, choose one café over another, speak with any neighbor can have grave consequences. The simplest gestures in a time of peace are no longer at all trifling in an occupied, pillaged, destroyed country."[18]

Wit, humor, and a sense of the absurd soon become expressions not only of a sense of fatalism but also of resistance. Jokes and pranks (some of them cause for imprisonment) were soon part of the Parisian response to the invaders. Perhaps the most repeated joke of the period managed to knead enemy, victim, and ally into a single confection:

Hitler, searching for a way to invade England, calls in the chief rabbi of Berlin and asks him how Moses parted the Red Sea. If he can get that information, the Führer will end his harassment campaign against the Jews. The rabbi answers: "Give me a week, Chancellor." Returning a week later, the rabbi announces that he has both good news and bad news. "Well," insists an impatient Hitler, "do you have the answer or not?" The rabbi replies, "Yes, sir—it was the staff Moses always had with him that had the power to create a path through the waters." Demanded Hitler, "Where is it?" Answered the anxious rabbi, "Well, that's the bad news. It's in the British Museum."

A more ghoulish joke:

A Parisian reports to his friend a rumor that at 9:20 the previous night, a Jew attacked and killed a German in the Métro. He even ate part of his entrails, including his heart. The friend says with a laugh, "You'll believe anything you hear, Pierre."

"But it's true!"

"No, my friend: it's impossible."

"Why?"

"First, Jews don't eat pigs; second, Germans have no heart; and, third, at 9:20 everyone is listening to the BBC."

An Execution in Paris

Yet humor only went so far. On Christmas Eve day in 1940, Parisians awoke to find the following notice pasted on kiosks and in Métro stations:

> The engineer Jacques Bonsergent, of Paris, received a death sentence by the German military tribunal for an act of violence toward a member of the German army. He was shot this morning.
> Paris, 23 December 1940
> The Military Commander of France

What strikes us about this announcement is that it does not refer to any political affiliation, nor does it imply that Bonsergent was a terrorist.

He was simply a young French engineer. Parisians were left to wonder whether he had struck a blow for France or whether he had acted out of personal pique.

It remains unclear today as to what happened in the streets abutting the Gare Saint-Lazare that Saturday evening, November 10, when Bonsergent was arrested; official reports and recollections vary. What we can be sure of is that a group of young Frenchmen, coming out of the station after having gone to a wedding in the country, ran into a group of German soldiers heading back to the barracks after a bibulous evening. Liquored up, the groups confronted each other, or bumped into one another, or exchanged a few comments. Bonsergent's friends skedaddled, but he was caught by the Germans and immediately brought into the lobby of the nearby Hôtel Terminus, where he was held for the military police. He refused to give the names of his comrades, and he was hustled off to Cherche-Midi Prison, on the Boulevard Raspail, in the 6th arrondissement.

Unfortunately for Bonsergent, two significant events occurred between his rather routine arrest and his surprising death sentence. The day after he was caught, World War I Armistice Day, students rallied on the Champs-Élysées for the first—and, during the Germans' reign over Paris, the only—large popular demonstration against the Occupiers. The exodus had wound down, families were returning to their city, and schools were reopening, though later than normal. Arguments were increasingly heated as a wide range of French men and women—pacifists, "wait-and-see" holdouts, anti-German patriots, Communists, and even vigorous supporters of the new Vichy regime—worried more and more openly over the military and political debacles they had just seen take place. Many frustrated and angry young Parisians saw the annual celebration of Armistice Day as the perfect moment to show French solidarity against the German presence in their city. Primarily at the initiative of high school and university students, the word passed quickly that a large crowd would march up the Avenue des Champs-Élysées to the Tomb of the Unknown Soldier under the Arc de Triomphe and, on their way, lay flowers at the statue of the great prime minister Georges Clemenceau, leader of France in late 1918, when Germany had had to sign its own armistice. Sometime on November 8, the only "call to arms" that historians have been able to track down was distributed in lycées and universities across the city:

> Student [sic] of France! November 11 remains for you a National Holiday. Despite orders from the oppressive authorities, it will be a Day of Memory. You will not attend classes. You will go to honor the Unknown Soldier [at the Arc de Triomphe] at 5:30 p.m. 11 November 1918 was the date of a great victory. 11 November 1940 will signal yet another. All students are in solidarity that France must live. Copy and distribute these lines.[19]

Having heard rumblings of such an event, the Free French in London encouraged, by way of the BBC, a big turnout. (Subsequent investigations have left doubts about how many Parisians actually heard the BBC's call to demonstrate.) Estimates vary, but perhaps as many as one thousand to three thousand young people showed up, first to lay wreaths at the statue of Clemenceau and then to continue their march up the wide avenue to the Arc de Triomphe.* "The Marseillaise," by then outlawed by the Vichy government, was whistled, sung, and played on improvised instruments. Many students carried two fishing poles, called *gaules*, signaling with their *deux gaules* solidarity with de Gaulle, the increasingly well-known general who spoke to the French frequently from London.

But the Vichy government had heard of the possible demonstration and had warned the Paris police and the Germans. As a result, the authorities were waiting for the crowd. Initially surprised at the numbers, the police soon realized that the group was not organized; composed of many small groups of friends, classmates, members of youth organizations, and so forth, the march was easy to disrupt by police action. At first the French police seemed to have everything

---

* The symbolism of honoring Georges Clemenceau was evident: he was "the Tiger," "the father of victory," who had stood fast against the last Teutonic invasion of France; he had helped devise the Treaty of Versailles, which had devastated Germany diplomatically and financially.

under control, but soon the crowd felt the stern hand of German police and soldiers who charged the groups as they approached the Arc. The demonstrators scattered. Some were protected by merchants who opened their doors; other merchants and bystanders pointed out the miscreants. Those who could not escape felt the blows of police billy clubs and fists. The authorities fired shots, and several youngsters were wounded. As always, among the victims were the innocent. I was told of one mother, out shopping, who was caught in the crossfire and shot in the thigh; she would have bled to death had not bystanders waved down a car to take her to a hospital. How many of the *manifestants* were killed, if any, has never been confirmed.

The other significant event that had an effect on poor Bonsergent's fate was that Philippe Pétain and his Vichy ministers had insulted Hitler by not showing up to receive Napoleon's ashes on December 14–15, 1940. The commander of occupied France, General Otto von Stülpnagel, under intense pressure from Berlin for being too soft toward such incipient expressions—nonviolent and violent—of noncompliance and rebellion, decided to make an example of young Bonsergent, and he did. The French had their first "resistance" hero—one with the solid and popular name of Jacques and a patronymic that implied decency and military rank.

By midwinter of 1940–41, days had indeed shortened; surprise arrests had become more frequent; friends and colleagues had disappeared into the Parisian prison system; sentences had been meted out for purported offenses toward the Occupation authorities; but no one had yet been put to death for them. The authorities' poster had announced not only the death of a young professional but also the beginning of the end of the "correct" minuet that had theretofore defined the Occupation.

A minuet demands exquisite timing and subtle appreciation of the movements of one's partner. It permits a limited number of steps; it suggests intimacy without allowing it. It is the perfect dance for strangers or almost strangers; whether or not a second dance follows depends on the comfort established with the moves and signals of the first.

Minuets were meant to introduce casual acquaintances at large gatherings; if nothing came of one dance, then the disappointed twosome sulked patiently and waited for better partners. Yet in this case, for one of the minuet's participants, the dance was not one in which there could be a voluntary separation. The darkness that blanketed Paris was increasingly both tangible and intangible. More lights were soon to be extinguished, and the minuet would cease.

Chapter Four

City Without a Face — The Occupier's Lament

The glacial politeness of a patiently waiting bookseller... has a paralyzing effect. Strong nerves and a thick skin are absolutely necessary.

— Felix Hartlaub[1]

Paris Had Already Welcomed the Nazis — Before the Occupation

In 1937, for the last great international exposition before the war, Germany had been invited to build a massive pavilion just below the promenade on the Place du Trocadéro, where Hitler would stand for his iconic photograph on June 28, 1940, during his brief visit to Paris. (Opposite this Speer-designed edifice of fascist taste and ideology would stand the USSR pavilion, topped by striding figures carrying the hammer and sickle.) One imaginative historian has insinuated that this pavilion represented the first "occupation" of Paris by the Germans. She argues that one of the main aims of the Third Reich's participation was to persuade the French of Germany's kinship as a cultural innovator and respecter of tradition.[2] Thousands of Hitler Youth were ferried to Paris for the fair; many of them would be back in just a few years for another sort of tourism.

The Berlin Olympic Games of 1936 had already impressed the world

Exposition of 1937: Germany confronts the USSR. (© *LAPI / Roger-Viollet / The Image Works*)

with the talents of Hitler's master image-führer, Joseph Goebbels, who brilliantly combined international spectacle with fascist ideology. The Paris Exposition, though on foreign soil, would provide Goebbels with another venue in which to dazzle the world with the positive qualities of National Socialism. And there was one more way in to the French political psyche for the Nazis: pacifism was a dominant political sentiment in the late 1930s. This tendency allowed Hitler to encourage the French to let him continue his machinations in central and eastern Europe without interruption. It is hard today to overestimate the vigor, passion, and confidence felt by many French pacifists during this period. Their nation had barely survived the First World War, having been almost bled to death. No matter how often we read them, the statistics stun: 1.4 million dead (almost all young men), 4.3 million wounded, three hundred thousand civilians killed or dying from the war's effects. The military casualties came to about 20 percent of the male population and about 10 percent of the population of France as a whole—by far the largest casualty rate of any of the Allies. As a result, after the war the nation was severely fearful of being overtaken demographically and industrially by its archrival. Yet strangely enough, the same French were supremely confident that they had emerged stronger militarily than their German rivals, especially given the strict terms of the Treaty of Versailles, signed in 1919; they now read the German effort to impress through cultural activity—perhaps naively—as a tentative foundation for a peaceful Europe, despite Hitler's rants about lebensraum (living space for a growing German population), and Jews.

International expositions were supposed to encourage peace among nations, emphasizing what they had in common and diminishing jingoistic reflexes. German visitors to Paris during the 1937 exposition were greeted with open arms, and, though the Spanish pavilion featured Picasso's devastatingly pertinent painting *Guernica* (about the cruel bombing of that little town by the fascists), the tendency was to think positively, not defensively, about a resurgent Germany.*

Of course, we do not know if the future Occupation of Paris was then well formed in the collective minds of the Nazi leadership, but certainly every attempt was made by the Nazis to attenuate international anxiety about their cultural, political, and, especially, military intentions. The massiveness of their pavilion, its emphasis on up-to-date technology, and its attempts at being "modern" and "traditional" at the same time made a hugely favorable impression on the French. Even though the German pavilion contained not one photograph or other likeness of Hitler—its primary symbols being the striking swastika and eagle—his muscular presence was subtly felt. The legacy of this exposition would last until the first Germans marched into Paris only three years later to find many French citizens more than curious about how the occupier might bring a similar order to the chaos of a humiliated France. This state of affairs played a major role in the early success of the Occupation.

---

* For reasons that are still unclear, Hitler did not attend the 1937 exposition, though most of his closest advisers did, basking in the light of French respect.

The Occupiers Are Surprised, Too

Beginning in the early 1930s, Paris was where Germans went to break out of the moral and artistic strictures imposed by the Nazis. Returning as conquerors reminded them of that freedom. Words like "paradise on earth" and "jewel" pepper the letters and memoirs of the first Germans to walk the streets of Paris in uniform. Even Goebbels's irrepressible braggadocio was muted: *"Paris ist gefallen"* (Paris has fallen) was so somberly repeated on German radio on June 14, 1940, that it was a while before Germans went into the streets in celebration. From the end of the Napoleonic Wars to the advent of Nazism, many young Germans from the upper middle classes and the aristocracy had spent time studying in Paris. "Paris envy" was a strong neurosis of the German imagination, and this state of mind never fully diminished until the last of them had slipped out of the city in late August of 1944.

Hitler's racial obsessions, unsurprisingly, carried over to his view of the French "race," which he believed had mixed unhealthily with *Neger* and Jewish blood. There were no more Joan of Arcs or Sun Kings for other nations to emulate. Paris had become so preoccupied with itself and its uniqueness that it had lost its sense of "Frenchness," which, for these observers, was derived from the hardworking, deeply religious, traditional peasantry. The latter had become frustrated with Paris and its demands on the rest of the nation; Hitler believed and insisted that when German soldiers and bureaucrats confronted the French they should be careful to distinguish between Parisians and their compatriots in the provinces. Observers such as Friedrich Sieburg, in his *Gott in Frankreich?* (God in France?), had revealed themselves impatient with the "myth of Paris," with its claim to superiority over other European cities and its casual disregard, as is clear in its history of revolts, for authority and stability. We have seen how metropolises were antithetical to Nazi ideology; the German city was not where the Nazis had found their most fervent supporters. Cities have always been resistant to autocratic control, and Hitler mistrusted them. A self-confident Paris would be even more threatening than other cities. And

Paris in particular was too "metropolitan"; its porousness had invited too many Slavs, Arabs, Asians, Africans, and Jews into its compass. General Fedor von Bock, the officer in command of troops entering Paris for the first time, had met Hitler in early June in Brussels and remarked later that the Führer was worried about the city, about its potential for taking his victory away from him.

At the height of the Occupation there may have been as many as twenty thousand German personnel in the city: everyone from the highest echelons of the Wehrmacht to the lowliest ranks of the supply offices. Ambassadors; representatives of all of the Reich's most powerful ministries; female secretaries, telephone operators, and nurses; medical personnel; archivists; intelligence officers; Gestapo; censors—the list was endless.* What was daily life like for these servants of the Reich? At first, they were delighted to be in a country with so many available consumer items; Germany had been at war for more than a year, and the sight of such excess meant that most of those first appointed to Paris spent every spare minute in department stores and other shops. The German mark had been set at a favorable rate vis-à-vis the French franc, and soon more Germans than French were shopping. This may have been the source of the first popular resentment toward the Occupier—a sense of "We know you are here because your army was stronger than ours, but it's quite another thing to appropriate buildings, apartments, goods, and foodstuffs because you have the power to do so." This negative dynamic soon became dominant, and more Parisians began to feel despoiled, insulted, and humiliated. The photographs of Germans browsing through the typical Seine book-stalls, negotiating with the *bouquinistes,* are only one example of how intrusive the military uniform must have been. Even when one tried to forget that "they" were there, an unanticipated sighting could throw one back into the state of despondency that afflicts the

---

* This information, on the numbers of Germans assigned to Paris during the Occupation, has been most resistant to resolution in my research. Estimates vary widely, especially because the demands of the Russian front and, later, the Normandy front, meant that reassignments were continually being made. The types of units and the quality of personnel changed as well.

Passing time. *(Editions Granger / Collection Claude Giasone)*

inhabitants of any occupied city. Many Germans understood this and went out of their way to be polite, helpful, and engaging to Parisians. But more often than not, these generous acts only reinforced the frustration and embarrassment of those under the thumb of a hateful bureaucracy.

There was also the black market, in which Germans were involved both officially and unofficially. The Occupiers had decided that they could not stop the surreptitious purchase and exchange of goods and services, so they set up special units that took advantage of shortages from black marketers and bought themselves. To a large extent this strategy worked, but what it gained for the German economy it may have lost in terms of offering an unflattering image of the German as just another wartime hustler angling for a good deal.

The Militärbefehlshaber in Frankreich* had taken for their headquarters Paris's tourist gems, its *grands hôtels:* the Majestic, the George V, the Prince de Galles, the Meurice, the Continental, the Lutétia, and others. They also requisitioned dozens of smaller hotels throughout the city, both for the office and living space these institutions immediately provided and because this strategy emphasized the connection between cultural tourism and military occupation. The Germans were there to stay, but only temporarily; they were visitors, yet they were permanent reminders of Paris's humiliation. Using tourism as a means of taming an occupied city is subtle and has psychological as well as practical consequences. Once the hard work of conquering has been done, the idea that one can enjoy a major cultural capital as a consuming visitor relieves a nagging guilt. It connects to the fanciful notion, in the minds of the Occupiers, that Parisians were, if not happy, at least complacent about the presence of so many Germans. "After all, you and your fellows are our best customers."

Within weeks of taking over the city, German diarists, journalists, essayists, and bureaucrats evinced an almost palpable need to describe what they found and how they felt. Most of them took up many of Friedrich Sieburg's assumptions, expressing their own fears that they might be seduced by a painted woman while trying to appreciate the art, history, and culture of Europe's most admired city. This trepidation worked at all levels: French women were generally criticized because of their makeup and seductive fashions; it was suggested that Zazous, young men who dressed in zoot suits and wore long hair, should be sent to work in Germany. Too much emphasis was placed on eating as a form of entertainment, on cuisine as an art form. Yes, all this had made the city great, but such a laissez-faire culture could be detrimental to the morals of young *Soldaten* coming into Paris on

---

* MBF—the German Military Command in France, which had policing responsibility for the civilian population, an arrangement that would not change until late 1942, when the Gestapo would take over that job.

permanent assignment or on leave. The Occupation authority immediately published guidebooks in German for Reich visitors to the newly
occupied city, including lists and descriptions of its most "decadent"
attractions (e.g., approved brothels for its officers and their men), and
Paris was soon filled with camera-toting, bargain-seeking, question-
asking, and naively curious German-speaking visitors. For the typical
soldier, photographs were their diaries, and we know that there were
thousands upon thousands sent back home. Perhaps the German
propaganda arm wanted to encourage their soldiers to further appropriate Paris and its environs by use of the omnipresent camera. The
Wehrmacht provided specially made photograph albums to their
soldiers (many of these have been on sale at auction houses and on the
Internet for years). Like any tourist, the soldiers in these modest records
banally "naturalized" their presence in an unfamiliar and intimidating
environment.

A second wave of soldiers on leave, along with civilian visitors from
Germany and Austria, followed the initial invaders, but Parisians continued to resist seeing their occupied city as a tourist destination for
their enemies. Stories about Parisians misdirecting the frequently disoriented German abound: "Yesterday, in the Métro, a German soldier
was hovering over his guide to Paris. He finally asked a laborer where
the Bréguet-Sabin station was. The old guy told him, but the German
couldn't understand. Then, overflowing with a sincere concern: 'My
poor boy. What an idiot you are. What the hell are you doing here?'"[3]
In 1968, the novelist Patrick Modiano chose as the title of his first novel
La Place de l'Étoile, the punch line of a well-known anecdote. A German tourist approaches a Jew to ask where the famous place is. The
young man points to his heart and says, "Here," referring, of course, to
the yellow star that Jews had been made to wear.

The same scene had repeated itself all over France; tightly disciplined formations of gray-green–clad, sturdy, and healthy young men
marched by the thousands throughout a country still reeling from
defeat and embarrassment. Goebbels and his sophisticated cadre of propagandists were well aware of the power that the city then had on the
world's cultural imagination. He wanted the world to recognize—and

be relieved—that the Nazis appreciated that Paris was part of the international patrimony. (In fact, he may well have ordered that the Wehrmacht select its best-looking soldiers to be the first to enter and march in the capital.*) But within the confines of a hypersophisticated capital city, their presence brought even more pride to the victor and a complicated combination of curiosity, apprehension, and shame to the Parisians. Very quickly, almost as if another Blitzkrieg had taken place, the German military had not only marched in with arrogant precision but also established itself "in the very interstices of daily life."[4] And they were there for the duration—not here and gone but established. This is the slowly understood certainty that forced Parisians to realize that their city, though unharmed and still familiar, was no longer theirs but rather *theirs.*

To further confound things, rules on informal interaction between Parisians and Germans were never made clear. Of course, the commander of *Gross Paris* promulgated warnings about inappropriate resistance to the authority of his troops, but the codes and protocols of day-to-day relations between citizen and soldier were left to the participants to establish. What rights did the citizen have to resist inappropriate orders or actions on the part of the German soldiers? Was a simple argument between a German and a Parisian a matter for harsh justice? What if a German soldier harassed a young Parisian woman or a woman refused his advances by making fun of him in public? Who had priority waiting in line or taking a seat in a bus or on the Métro? German punctiliousness often protected the daily civil rights of Parisian citizens, while German obsession with order undermined the greater freedoms of assembly, publication, and political action.

The average occupier was not a faceless Nazi focused on reducing French society to penury and humiliation. We, and especially the French, often accept a monolithic image of German repression, disdain,

---

* I have found no archival or other support for this premise, though it is an oft-repeated assumption in accounts of the initial Occupation.

and cruelty. Such an image enables us to remember history only superficially, and it deprives us of a more dimensional evaluation of the infinite variety of interactions that occurred during the four years of the Occupation of Paris. We must remind ourselves, too, that even though Nazi aesthetics and racial policy held that the French were racially weakened, they were still considered at least "cousins" to the Germans. In German terms, as we have seen, the French were like distaff relatives who had failed to guard the Teutonic side of their heritage and had allowed themselves to "degenerate" from pure origins. Nevertheless, Paris beckoned to the prim German ethos as though it were a huge amusement park.

The Wehrmacht had gone out of its way to provide special canteens for their soldiers; cinemas, theaters, and cabarets had been set aside for them, and they would have access to the French ones that had quickly reopened. Certain movie houses were set aside for German audiences only, the most prominent being the enormous Grand Rex on the Boulevard de Poissonnière, which held more than 2,500 seats. The Germans requisitioned it for their troops, on assignment and visiting; it became the most popular *deutsches Soldatenkino* in Paris, so much so that the Resistance chose it for a major bombing attempt in late 1942, which killed or wounded more than a hundred Germans waiting in line.

In essence, the Germans appropriated a vibrant, heterogeneous metropolis and then attempted to fix and stabilize the imagined version of Paris that had existed in the collective memory of the cultured world. In doing so the Occupier sought, intuitively or purposefully, to vitiate the unpredictable energy that defines metropolises and thus to provide more security for his own purposes. The Occupiers wanted to unmake dynamic Paris, to create a static simulacrum, while preserving for their own enjoyment some of its most engagingly decadent attractions (jazz clubs, cabarets, bordellos).*

---

* Amazingly, the *Wegleiter,* the German guide to Paris, repeatedly printed advertisements for cabarets featuring "Gypsy" music and bands. As the Romanies were being murdered in eastern Europe, their compatriots were entertaining SS troops in the City of Light.

Each and every soldier stationed in France was offered a visit to Paris as a sort of reminder of the magnitude of the victory over that nation. Soon after June of 1940, tour buses filled with gawking German soldiers were a common sight in the streets and around the best-known monuments. Hitler would later insist, after June of 1941, that every German soldier on the Eastern Front have a leave in Paris (*"jeder einmal nach Paris"* — everyone once in Paris). Whether this happened, especially as the war progressed, is difficult to determine, but the official message was clear: Paris was now in German hands. Yet while the German propagandists, especially Goebbels, had sought through economic and cultural policies to reduce French cultural influence in Europe to the advantage of Germany, they could not bring themselves to destroy completely the transnational image of a brilliant Paris. All the Reich's leaders, including Hitler himself, had made pilgrimages (and that is the word) to the city on the Seine. They went to show the flag, to buy (if not to loot), to indulge in the luxurious life still available to those with resources; they condescended toward the social laissez-faire of a quasi-degenerate populace. Through their own obsession with Paris, they unknowingly underpinned the notion that the city, though shackled, was still capable of resisting the imposition of Nazi orthodoxy, that Paris still possessed a strong immunity to noxious foreign influence.

Thousands of touring Germans visited the city during the Occupation. The journalist and former Wehrmacht soldier August von Kageneck describes how he and a few buddies were brought from their boring country assignment to the city:

One day in August [1940], they took us by truck to the capital. Hitler had preceded us as a tourist...in a deserted city.... We were set loose in Paris only after many instructions: we had [a total of] six hours to visit the city; an impeccable uniform was required; no relations with Frenchmen, and especially with Frenchwomen. And it was strictly understood that we were not allowed to seek out professional comfort.... Paris struck us with its general torpor. Few people were in the streets, only small groups of well-dressed German soldiers like us, following their guide.... I remember the Louvre and the Eiffel Tower decked out with flags bearing the swastika. I also remember going to Montmartre to find a willing woman. In vain. But I still see, in a street beneath the Sacré-Coeur, an Arab who wanted to sell us pornographic photos.[5]

After the Reich's invasion of the USSR in June of 1941, Parisians were both elated that Hitler had made such a huge mistake and depressed to conclude that the war would last a long time — now the Wehrmacht would certainly not leave the Atlantic coast unprotected and would thus stay in Paris. For the German soldiers serving on the Eastern Front, Paris took on an even more fantastic aura. One source tells us that the editor of the *Wegleiter*, the German guidebook to Paris, received requests from many soldiers on the Eastern Front eager for a subscription to the publication. If they could not be there, they could at least dream about being there.

On the other hand, those assigned to Paris were not always happy. There was too much division among cadres, too many officers, too few chances for young German soldiers to even bond with their comrades. Most spoke no French, and most Parisians would not answer questions in German or even respond to friendly gestures. A profound sense of alienation and loneliness developed, even with thousands of fellow Germans and Austrians around. When sitting in a café, it was as if a cordon sanitaire had been established around each German soldier, so ignored were they by other clientele, not to mention the servers. Even at church, unless it was one frequented by Germans, the occupier felt out of place. Paris was like a city without a face, a *Stadt ohne Blick* (literally, a "city without a glance") — a sentiment and a phrase that began to pervade letters, diaries, and even official reports. Young homesick Bavarians and Silesians, though happy not to be in Poland or Norway, were frequently abashed by the apparent rudeness of the Parisians.

Without the ideological arrogance of the true Nazi, the average soldier must have quickly realized that Paris's architectural beauty was no substitute for human contact. The daily *Pariser Zeitung* (Paris Times) was not much solace. It contained mostly stories from German newspapers, local advertisements, entertainment listings, and a few articles in French. There was none of the "hominess" that the average soldier needed. Even the museums were closed if not nearly empty. (By now, 80 percent of the paintings in the Louvre had been hidden elsewhere; many great sculptures had either been buried or hidden in the country.) One may ask: Don't soldiers always get homesick, always seek familiar bonding under the sign of danger, and yearn for a leave? Yes, but the danger in this case was not yet physical; the counterattack was literally muted. Surrounded by hundreds of thousands of perfectly pleasant people who paid you no attention day after day could be starkly discomfiting. To ignore someone's presence momentarily negated the whole idea of cooperation and thus subtly undermined the Occupier's authority.

Pariser Zeitung *with French pages. (Editions Granger / Collection Claude Giasone)*

A Dreamer in Exile

Felix Hartlaub, a young historian assigned as a record keeper in the Occupation bureaucracy, left us a diary of impressions that often mentions his efforts at trying to be just another face on the street.[6] He reconciles his memory of having been in Paris as a student with his present assignment, noting in 1942:

> The city...still has its charm, but it is a secret, sad charm....In the richer quarters, around the Place de l'Étoile, for instance, one only sees closed shutters. The same is true for the most elegant businesses and mansions. In the Rue de la Paix, a Luftwaffe lieutenant affirms: "Good God! Everything is closed here!" The [Place de la Concorde], the Champs-Élysées without cars or buses is almost incomprehensible. The Louvre, emptied for the most part except for some large, ancient statuary, the Cluny Museum closed; at the Carnavalet [the museum of the history of Paris, in the Marais], where I went to celebrate my return, half of its contents are gone, and everything that remains is in impossible disorder.... The theaters are not well heated and only half full. Attendance is split between Wehrmacht soldiers and Parisians.[7]

A typical recurring concern for the German occupier was whether to wear civilian attire when moving through the city. Memoirs and diaries that have come down to us reveal even the most self-assured German's anxiety about strolling through Paris in uniform. The proud victors soon realized that their uniforms brought them the blank if not hostile stares of a resentful populace. They heard Parisians refer to them as *doryphores* (beetles, because of the famous helmets), *verts de gris* and *haricots verts* (gray-greens and green beans, because of the color of the army's uniforms), and *bottes* (for their heavy and noisy tread). (The more familiar *Boche* [similar to the GI's "Kraut"] had been forbidden by both Vichy and German authorities from being spoken or written in public.) Even in mufti, Germans could more often than not be identified by other qualities: haircuts, posture, quality of civilian clothes, stoutness, and, of course, accent.

When not at work in their offices, many of the German bureaucrats who held military rank but were not themselves military men sought to melt into the crowd. Hartlaub describes how, in civilian dress, he would approach the ticket taker in the Métro with some apprehension. Germans rode free if they showed their ID cards, but Hartlaub tried to finesse this requirement by letting only a corner of the card peek from his wallet, hoping the ticket taker would allow him to pass through without comment. When she would hesitate, he felt the eyes of Parisians boring into his back. He walked along the station platform, avoiding eye contact with his uniformed compatriots, hesitating whether to offer a *"pardon"* or a *"Verzeihung"* when he bumped into them. He wanted to be an archetypical Parisian flaneur, an innocuous stroller taking in the pleasures of the Parisian streets, but he sensed that Parisians simultaneously recognized and ignored him. In the intimate crowding of the Métro, this sense became exaggerated; Hartlaub felt keenly that he was an object to avoid. Later, writing home, he was quite clear about these sensations:

> I was rather naïve to think that I could be taken for a native [in my civilian suit]. My way of walking and my demeanor betray me immediately.... And should, for an instant, one not be noticed, the following instant, a shudder of recognition will be doubly felt in return. In a way, it would be easier just to wear the uniform; all would be clear for everyone. For instance, in civilian clothes, I run the risk of being taken for a spy. My embarrassment renders me completely stiff, causes me to lose all of my French, and cuts me off from everything as if with rusty scissors.[8]

Though this mild paranoia on an occupier's part is rarely so carefully described, it must have marked everyone who was in Paris longer than a few weeks. It is ironic that the occupier sought to be part of the city where he did not belong, yet his attitude speaks to the psychological confusion from trying to combine conciliation with arrogance.

Hartlaub's memoir is filled with passages that describe a beautiful but imposing city, one that offers itself to the tourist but threatens the occupier. Desperate to be an inhabitant and not a tourist, he admits repeatedly to his desire's impossibility. For him, Paris is not just a physical, built environment, it is a malleable, flexible, kaleidoscopic site best invented and reinvented through the senses (more subtle than Hitler's sense of the city). His pages are filled with references to the hard-stepping hobnailed boots that impose their authority on the citizen; he compares them with the articulated clicking of wooden-soled shoes worn by civilians. Close your eyes, he writes, and still you can "hear" the Occupation, just as you can see it with your eyes open. It has invaded the sensual lives of Parisians, not just their bureaucratic and physical lives. The sound of boots, one of the most persistent of his images, which seems to ring false on the cobbled streets of Paris; the silence that reigns in a city known for its noisy traffic; the often embarrassed posture of German soldiers and officers trying to accommodate themselves to a city that simultaneously attracts and repulses them: these are the themes of this subtle, sad, yet compelling memoir.

Sexually Occupied

And then there was sex. Many Parisian eyes were attracted not only to the German soldiers' uniforms and their shiny accoutrements but also to their virile youthfulness. They evinced a sense of healthiness and physical beauty that mesmerized the French. Counterintuitively, the threatening German body became a desired one, especially once the Germans began taking off their clothes. They exercised and played football with bare chests; they marched together clad only in their underwear to rivers and pools; they were often seen nude sunning on rooftops or on beaches or riding horses in the countryside. The naturist ethic had long been part of German athletic culture, and the Nazis had appropriated it for its own purposes, to remind the Germans that their collective body must be healthy in order to fight the diseases of Bolshevism, Judaism, and anti-German sentiment. Soon, the Vichy government would also develop a highly athletic youth culture, emphasizing that a healthy body kept youth out of trouble. It kept youth patriotic and—why not?—pondering pleasures other than sex. Of course, the desired body is a sexualized body, and soon a new sort of "accommodation" and "collaboration" developed between young Germans and young French men and women.

Recent historians of sexuality have introduced us to a world that many intuited had existed; now, with more information, we have a much clearer picture of the libidinal Occupation.[9] The average Parisian might have tried to be as unaccommodating as he or she could to the German presence, but before too long they saw that these young men (especially in the first year of the Occupation) were not all monsters. Perhaps it was the humiliating demasculinization of the French soldier, in prison or otherwise absent; perhaps it was the desire to humanize the occupier; no matter, there is little doubt that much attention was paid to the sexualized German body, especially in 1940–41.*

Another fascinated audience was composed of Parisian male adolescents who frequented the troops, offering to help them, wanting their recognition. Remembered one Frenchman: "What adolescent of my generation did not dream, even if only briefly and shamefully, of being a young, twenty-year-old SS soldier, leaning on his tank, spreading butter on his bread with his dagger. Ten or so of us would just hang around to watch him and to look intensely at the death heads on his uniform."[10] And the homosexual population of Paris, one of long-standing and relative freedom, did not ignore the masculine attractiveness of these young men. In fact, gay French men recount that, despite the notorious harassment, incarceration, and even murder of homosexuals elsewhere in Europe, in Paris the Wehrmacht seemed to turn a blind eye to activity that was a capital crime in Germany: "The

---

* With the invasion of Russia, many of these young men left for the Eastern Front— reportedly a great loss for the *maisons closes* (bordellos) of Paris.

146

hypervirility of the German military, its taste for physical culture, its propensity to nudism, or almost, struck the imaginations of Frenchmen and was at the origin of a true cultural shock that would have an influence on the gestation of homosexual identity."[11] In many ways, the German body had become Nazism's earliest ambassador to the still stunned Parisians—particularly at night.

And the Germans were neither innocent nor adverse to the charms of Paris. Historians have estimated that between eighty thousand and two hundred thousand Franco-German babies were born in France during the Occupation.[12] *Enfants maudits* (accursed children), generally ignored or humiliated by both their French and their German relatives, were incontestable proof of a sexual liaison especially forbidden by the Wehrmacht. Going to a bordello for "relaxation" was one thing; an intimate relation with a French civilian was another, yet these relationships were widespread. Youths of both sides were attracted to each other. There was a paucity of young French men; the German soldiers were lonely and often despised; and there were so many occasions, both in the provinces and in the cities, where female and male bodies came into semi-intimate contact: daily business interactions, on the buses and Métro, at swimming pools, parties, and fairs. Paris might have been generally *sans regard* (without a glance) for the average German soldier, but there were many times when a soldier's own gaze was returned by an attractive Frenchwoman—or man. In fact, Colette, in the last essay in *Paris from My Window,* written in the spring of 1944, a few months before the Germans would leave, felt she had to comment on how Parisiennes had comported themselves:

> One of the singularities of the war is the...dangerously feminine quality that has come over [French] women. Is it because of the complete occupation of our territory, the omnipresence of a foreign and virile [army], that women have affected the appearance of kids and the actions of schoolgirls? I don't call into question their motives, knowing full well that they might hide good intentions. But the disorderly profusion of her hair, the indiscreet arrangement of her curls, her skirt of inappropriate length, whose

looseness allows the breeze to give her a certain look, are errors, though graceful, that have occasioned not a few arousals. One wants to say to these "girls" of all ages, windblown and uncovered: "Shh.... We are not alone."[13]

Some observers thought the heightened femininity of French women was a patriotic slap in the face to the occupier; others, like the increasingly prudish Colette, thought that females were playing a dangerous game. Whatever the interpretation, such libidinous exchanges were an important element in the new environment that the Occupation imposed, an element that complicated the task of its bureaucrats.

Not coincidentally, the Parisians were amused to learn that the Germans—both officially and personally—were obsessed with disease. It became a running joke that all one had to do to avoid their social importunateness was to sneeze into one's hand, pick one's nose, or cough deeply. The Wehrmacht papered all the places soldiers frequented with warnings about venereal disease; condoms were freely offered. Medical officers oversaw all bordellos. "For the Germans, France was not only the center of sexual amusement but also a country where [venereal] epidemics reigned, where clandestine prostitution was everywhere, and where the danger of venereal contagion was great—a country, then, where innumerable infected women represented a real menace for the health of German soldiers.[14] Yet the Wehrmacht also recognized the sexual needs and desires of its frontline soldiers, especially those on leave from the devastating Eastern Front. Indeed, what was the use of "having" Paris if you could not benefit from one of its most delectable products? Thus the Wehrmacht refused to close bordellos, not only because they were crucial to morale but also because they were valuable to intelligence services, which used them to garner information.*

One of the most humorous yet informative memoirs of the Occu-

---

* In eastern Europe, the Wehrmacht and the SS created their own bordellos, using Jewish and other "undesirables" as "comfort women," an irony almost too bizarre to believe.

pation was published by Fabienne Jamet, brothel madam par excellence and owner and manager of One Two Two, perhaps Paris's best-known bordello. Sited at 122 Rue de Provence, in the chic 8th arrondissement, it was known throughout Europe—not just as a bordello but also as a meeting place for the city's cultural elite. Soon after its opening in the 1930s, it had become the place where the upper-crust bohemian set gathered. On the first floor, there was an elegant café, where drinks, especially Champagne, were served to the sophisticated clientele, male and female, whether they were looking for sex or not. Most knew of the lavishly decorated rooms on the floors above—designed as harems, jungles, Roman baths, and so forth; as one climbed from floor to floor, the more "refined" the sexual offerings became. Having fled her business during the exodus in June of 1940, Madame Jamet returned to find the bordello still operating, albeit filled with German enlisted men, all wanting to taste one of Paris's most famous delicacies. "[The Germans]...had requisitioned the One Two Two and had installed themselves there the very day of their entry into Paris, as if we had been as well known as the tomb of Napoleon at the Invalides!"[15] Rather than be relieved that the Germans had allowed her establishment to remain open and in business, Jamet was furious that this high-class establishment had been "invaded" by common soldiers, men who could never have afforded to patronize the place before the war. Jamet marched down the Rue Auber to the Place de l'Opéra, where the *Kommandantur der Gross-Paris* had set up its offices (the bureaucratic center of the MBF). There she asked to see a high-ranking administrator and, surprisingly, was quickly received. She ran a very high-class establishment, she told the bemused soldier-bureaucrat; it was known throughout Germany and had even received many German aristocrats and businessmen before the war. She was appalled that it now would serve only enlisted men, for her more respectable clientele would now no longer come. This would be, she exclaimed, a disservice to the Occupation authorities themselves! Politely, the officer assured her that she would hear from his office within a month. (We note that he did not jump up in Nazi horror at the degenerate culture of Paris and order Madame Jamet to find another profession.) A month later, she received a note stating that henceforth the One Two Two would be accessible only to German officers in uniform.

At first placated, Jamet soon realized that this restriction would not provide enough income to keep her establishment in the black; many officers came and bought Champagne and hired her girls, but even though the officers seemed to be everywhere in Paris, they were not numerous or needy enough to keep her business afloat. So she returned to the *Kommandantur* to plead that French men as well be allowed to return to the bordello. The idea that German officers would be rubbing shoulders in a bordello with the Parisians and French they were supposed to have under surveillance caused some consternation within the offices of the German authorities. Another month passed. Two Germans in civilian clothes, obviously Gestapo officers, appeared at the house's door and asked for "Madame." They had arrived at a compromise, they told her. French men would be permitted to come to the house, but only when accompanied by a German officer.

> "Are you joking, Inspector? Do you really think that every time one of my French clients wants to fuck he is going to go up to a German officer in the street and say to him: 'Captain, will you go with me to One Two Two? I want to get laid. If you refuse, I guess I'll just have to....' This isn't serious. I'm ready to assume my responsibilities, but that goes for you, too. At any rate, if you maintain this position, I'll just close."[16]

Four days passed, and another official letter arrived: "Madame, from this date on, French citizens are permitted to enter your house. Officers of the German army may only present themselves in civilian attire."[17] One Two Two remained open during the Occupation, and both German and French men enjoyed the offerings of Paris's most renowned bordello.

These anecdotes—recounted by French madams as well as insecure Germans—refer to problems that were, for the most part, far removed from the daily preoccupations of Parisian citizens. When there is a paucity of foodstuffs, intermittent heat and electricity, a capricious foreign authority, a fear that one's source of livelihood could be instantly ended, a concern that the wrong word or the wrong friendship could land you in jail or worse, and a need to keep one's anger and frustration under cover, the last thing to worry about is how the poor Germans felt or whether or not a whorehouse is going to be successful. Yet to ignore the sexual aspects of the Occupation would remove a dimension that reveals a great deal about the forced intimacy between enemies living together in a city known for its libidinal energy.

A "Better" German

To assume his duties as a bureaucrat at the MBF, Wehrmacht Captain Ernst Jünger officially entered Paris, elegantly mounted on a horse, on April 24, 1941 (he had earlier visited in February for a weekend leave). Well known across Europe as a novelist and essayist before the war, he was, after soldiering in the Blitzkrieg, ready to enjoy an assignment in his favorite city. Jünger was an *Einzelgänger*—a loner—and deftly self-centered. Nevertheless he was well known in German and French literary circles, "a star among stars in the city of cities,"[18] and saw himself as representative of the most sophisticated European, not just German, elite. He had studied in Paris and visited it before the war; like so many other high-level German soldiers and bureaucrats, he felt that assignment to Paris was a just reward for his chosen life of intellectual sophistication. Working closely with the head of the MBF, he secretly kept a meticulous, if strangely cold, journal of his life as a *salonnier* (he visited everyone from Cocteau to Picasso and was always invited to the best openings and most exclusive dinner parties). At the same time, he was witness to the chronic infighting among the Occupational entities in Paris. His diary does evince a sorrowfulness that edges from beneath the gloss that the Germans put on their stewardship of Paris. But he keeps rather silent on the everyday life of Parisians, on his ethical concerns about Nazism, and on his emotional life. Still, Jünger provides subtle evidence of how conflicted many of the Occupiers were about their situation. Doubtlessly much of what he wrote helped alleviate his own sense of responsibility, small as it might have been, for the excesses of the Occupation. Most likely Ernst Jünger often felt himself in danger for his scarcely hidden scorn for Hitler, the National Socialist Party, the SS, and the Gestapo. Nevertheless he was part of the bureaucracy that executed "terrorists" and hostages, that looted the city of its foodstuffs and its valuables, and that imposed curfews and other impediments on the daily life of Parisians.

Jünger's diaries offer a kind of scaffolding for an understanding of how complex the Occupation was, one that gives shape and texture to an important though not universal German view of this long event, too often represented by most witnesses as engagement with a wall of implacable gray-green. Jünger was a true flaneur, engaged in a leisure activity (casual and purposeless walking through the city) that was open, for the most part, only to Germans, for Parisians usually had to have justifiable reasons for wandering the streets. He loved to visit cemeteries because of their pastoral atmosphere, to sit in cafés and tea shops, watching Parisians in their attempts to recapture their prewar élan. Tracing on a map of Paris the place names mentioned most frequently by Jünger reveals the trajectories of a man clearly enthralled with architectural beauty and cosmopolitan culture. Yet he, like his most sensitive brothers, remained anxious about how Paris received him. As much as he tried to remind his readers, himself, and Paris in general that he had appreciated the city *before* the Nazis came, he is incapable of imposing a completely anodyne image of his assignment there. Reading his journals, we get more than a glimpse of what it must have been like to move through an urban environment you love (he spoke excellent French) knowing that you are despised.

Married, with a family living in Kirchhorst, between Hannover and Hamburg, Jünger adored women and enjoyed the way Parisiennes succeeded in maintaining the elegance for which the city was renowned. He noticed that foreign women—Spaniards, Italians, and Germans— had assimilated themselves to Paris's myth of fashion and style. It was easier for them, for they had resources that the Parisian woman did not have; yet it was to the latter that they still looked for hints about elegance and fashionable savoir faire. For the most part, Jünger stays in the most chic quarters, the richest ones. He ventures rarely into more modest neighborhoods to witness and comment on the uneventful lives of the average Parisian. He frequents the cafés of the Champs-Élysées neighborhood, the Jardin des Tuileries, the Trocadéro, the gardens of the Château de Bagatelle in the Bois de Boulogne. He might venture into Montmartre from time to time, but only at night and only to those places most frequented by Germans. Or he might go south from his hotel to Montparnasse, mainly to visit the massive cemetery there but also to revisit the cafés and restaurants made famous in the 1930s by the Lost Generation. His domicile was in the elegant Raphael hotel on the Avenue Kléber, only two hundred meters from the Arc de Triomphe and still one of the most beautiful and elite hostelries in Paris; his nearby workplace was the even more prestigious Majestic Hôtel on Avenue des Portugais. It was from the rooftop bar of the latter that he so often watched the Allied bombing of the Parisian suburbs. Some of his most energetic descriptions concern the squadrons of Allied bombers flying over Paris as they crossed the city to attack its near suburbs. Firing at the Allied bombers resulted in tons of German shrapnel falling onto the streets, roofs, and gardens and cemeteries of the city; there are many stories of casualties among the civilians whose bad luck put them in the line of this "friendly" fire. Sometimes Paris itself was inadvertently hit: an RAF Lancaster bomber crashed onto the roof of the Grands Magasins du Louvre, a department store across the street from the Louvre museum. One of the store's two buildings was burned to the ground, and the bodies of the pilot and his crew were found on the roof of the Louvre itself.

Despite every effort to describe a mythical, timeless Paris, one he wants to enjoy, one that allows him to contemplate the human condition, Jünger cannot ignore that he is on an island protected from the conflagration surrounding it. This is especially true, and affecting, when he goes home on leave to Kirchhorst to find that the nearby cities of Hannover and Hamburg have been hellishly bombed, while Paris remains strangely untouched.

One of the most articulate and astute German occupiers, Jünger wanted to present himself as having been at odds, both in his musings as well as in his activities, with the gray plague that was sullying his

153

beloved Paris. Just two days after one of the Occupation's most thorough roundups of Jews, in July of 1942, he wrote in his journal:

> Yesterday some Jews were arrested here in order to be deported—
> first they separated parents from their children, so firmly that one
> could hear their distressed cries in the streets. At no moment must
> I forget that I am surrounded by unhappy people, humans
> experiencing the most profound suffering. If I forgot, what sort of
> man or soldier would I be? Our uniform imposes the duty to
> ensure protection wherever one can. [Yet] one feels that in order
> to do that one has to battle like Don Quixote with millions of
> adversaries.* [19]

How many Germans—and Nazis—felt the same way? Who knows? The important point is that not enough of them acted on their feelings to change the nature of the Occupation, let alone save any Jews.

Recollected Solitude

An assertive knock brought Madame Heller to her apartment door. It was November of 1940, and the Germans had been in Paris for five months. She had grown used to seeing them in the street, but she was stunned when she saw on her landing a man in the uniform of a Wehrmacht lieutenant. Quickly she called her husband. What could he possibly want with them? The officer politely saluted and asked if this is where a certain younger Heller lived. They answered yes, but told their unnerving visitor that their son was presently a prisoner of war. The German officer introduced himself as Gerhard Heller, who had known their son while he was studying medicine in Germany. Coincidentally, they had the same family name and had bonded because of it. Heller told the couple that he was new to Paris and that their son was the only person whom he knew to call on. The Parisian Hellers were confused;

---

* Cynically, we must remember that Jünger's journal was not published until 1949, after he had had the chance to edit his entries as well as his memories.

their son had never spoken of another student named Heller. At any rate, he was not there and would not be for a long time. They did not invite Gerhard in or show any interest in his story. The lieutenant turned away, still alone in the *Stadt ohne Blick*.

Lieutenant Heller recounts the anecdote in his memoirs, published in France in 1981, reminding us, as did Hartlaub and Jünger, of the other side of the Occupation. Of course we have to consider his memoirs with care: we are not reading contemporary documents but the memories of a man who wants to present himself as sympathetic, educated, highly literate, and generous. Nevertheless, his book presents anecdotes that help us to understand further the anxieties that affected many of the Reich's best officers. Heller was obviously a Francophile and, at least forty years later, an anti-Nazi. An important Wehrmacht bureaucrat, Heller was charged with the unpleasant task of preventing the publication of French literature that could be construed as anti-German or influenced by Jews. The physical result of this responsibility was a huge warehouse in Paris where thousands upon thousands of "unapproved" books were destroyed or left to molder. He found himself trying to keep French literature vibrant and respectable on the one hand while on the other hand using the blunt knife of censorship to chop away at originality and imagination. Soon after arriving in Paris, Heller had to accept that he was an outsider, not a tourist; not an innocent bureaucrat but a stranger, one who made the Parisians uncomfortable. "How relieved I felt each time I could dress in civilian clothes, especially after having to wear a uniform all day," he recalled.[20]

Germans spent a good deal of their free time in the bathhouses and swimming pools of Paris for the same reason: "In a swimsuit, no one could tell the difference between a German and a Frenchman."[21] He discovered that even his accent could be construed as Alsatian or Swiss rather than German. Heller and his cadre tried to separate themselves from their fellows, not only in an attempt to "pass" as French but also, perhaps, as a mild form of rejection of the Nazi presence. "One does not conquer Paris, but is conquered by Paris.... I lived then always alone, in a state of disarray and anguish.... How not to carry in one's mind or within one's body the marks of such tension when one knows that the Gestapo is spying on you, that your comrades or your superiors suspect you? Your conscience becomes dislocated."[22]

At one point Heller learns of a young Parisian bourgeois who offers his services to trusted Germans:

> He lived on a street adjacent to the Champs-Élysées, above a bank where his father was a director. He had arranged just under the roof of the building a little apartment completely separated from the lower floors. . . . It was tastefully furnished (wood paneling and pretty antique furniture). He carried on there, with a little group of French and Germans, a traffic in alcohol and, in particular, whiskey (i.e., Scotch). I went up there several times to taste the legs of lamb he got from the countryside.[23]

At the very end of the Occupation, this same French friend would offer Heller a secret room near his own isolated apartment where the German could stay until things calmed down; afterward, he naively argued, the German could resume his Parisian life. Heller tells us this story as an illustration of how friendly with each other many upper-class Parisians and Germans were—the Frenchman was not "collaborating" but simply trying to help a friend who just happened to be a key member of the Occupation forces. More interestingly, this anecdote reveals how secretive Paris was during this period. Everyone—Parisian and occupier—thought of a rabbit hole they could use in case things got worse: air raid shelters, the concierge's loge, basements, attics, outdoor sheds, sewers, Métro stations, relatives' apartments in Paris, or homes in the country.

At the end of his memoir, Heller leaves us with two similar anecdotes that can serve as apologues for the anxiety of the occupier as he contemplated the loss of the war, the necessity of leaving Paris, and the anticipation of returning to a devastated Germany. At night, as only a German officer could, Heller would often walk through the gardens that line the lower reaches of the Champs-Élysées, between the Place de la Concorde and the Rond-point des Champs-Élysées. During the day, then and now, these are playgrounds for children in the area, sites of stamp markets, kiosks that sell toys and newspapers, public conveniences, and chairs for senior citizens out for fresh air. But at night, under wartime curfew, with few vehicles on the streets, these spaces were empty and silent.

In these gardens, strolling at dusk, Heller had two strange encounters. They speak volumes about the loneliness he felt in Paris as well as about the patronizing attitude that many Germans took toward their French charges. The first concerned a young French girl of about fifteen. Heller had noticed movement in the bushes, and when he approached, he found the girl hiding behind them. "You'd best get home," he intoned. "The curfew will catch you outside, and you could be picked up." She explained that she had missed her train at the Gare Saint-Lazare, that she lived in the country, and that she had nowhere to stay in Paris. She was hiding until the curfew was lifted in the morning, when she could catch the first train back home. Heller took her to his hotel and asked the concierge to let the girl sleep in the lobby until the next morning. The girl left early, leaving a note for Heller—she had gotten his name from the concierge—thanking him and promising to call later. She did, and for several months, the two would have "dates": bicycle rides in the country, walks through Paris, café moments. "What was her name? Who was she? I never knew. Martine, Nadine, Aline, those seemed to be what I heard when she mumbled her name. I gave her the name of Reinette [little queen]. She was for several months my little queen, my Beatrice, accompanying me to the end of the road through a world that, each day, became heavier and darker for me."[24] Heller assures his reader that he never laid a hand on the girl, that they maintained a respectful distance (though they do skinny-dip in a country stream; for him it was an "innocent idyll"), but he describes her in terms that reveal his sexual attraction to her. Then she disappeared, and he never saw her again. A year later, in November of 1943 (a time when it was becoming clear that Germany had lost any initiative it had earlier gained in winning the war), Heller met another teenager in the same garden, this time a boy. A similar sort of attachment evolves. "We showed a lot of tenderness toward each other; he would take my hand [while we walked]; we embraced when we met, nothing more. Our rendezvous lasted until spring 1944; he, too, disappeared, forever."[25]

We have seen how the German authorities feared a sexualized Paris but could do little to overcome the image and the reality of that reputation. German journalists, soldiers, and visitors all made reference to what they saw as the overtly sexual demeanor of Parisian women: they wore stylish clothes and makeup; they felt comfortable walking unescorted and being alone in a major metropolis. The Germans were both fascinated and revolted, but there was always an undercurrent that admired the sexual self-confidence of the French. Heller's two anecdotes, at the very end of his memoir, speak to the loneliness, sexual and psychological, that often enveloped the occupier. Paris had proven, for this German at least, to be the decadent siren so feared by Nazism. By befriending children, perhaps he thought he was sanitizing his sexual loneliness.

Heller used his position — and the competition among the propaganda ministry, the German embassy, and the Gestapo — to his advantage. Not unlike Jünger, he gives his readers an itinerary through intellectual and artistic Paris as if to show that he and many of his fellow Germans (if not the Nazis) were sensitive to and protective of French patrimony. On the other hand, there is an almost pathetic quality to his awe and respect for certain writers, collaborationists or not. He met and frequented the artists Georges Braque, Aristide Maillol, Paul Klee, and Pablo Picasso as well as writers such as Jean Cocteau and Paul Valéry. Finding few friendly faces among Parisians on the street, he used his salon life as a means of learning about French culture and helping to protect it. Despite his star-studded, name-dropping notations, one senses underneath a deep dissatisfaction with being an occupier. Loneliness, suspicion, and, later, the threat of assassination weighed heavily on those senior officers and bureaucrats stationed in Paris. Heller recognizes, as do similar memoirists, such as Jünger, that no matter its surface, the city underneath was like a hidden wasps' nest: the sound of a constant, unidentifiable buzzing kept everyone on edge.

Heller would refuse the offered hiding place of his French "friend," but he would leave a piece of himself in Paris. Under a tree on the great esplanade that leads from the Hôtel des Invalides to the Seine, he buried a tin box filled with notes and a diary. In 1948 he returned, for the first time since the war, to Paris, but he never was able to find his buried treasure. Like so many of his compatriots, a part of his past lay hidden in a resurgent Paris.

During the war, Jean Paulhan, the publisher and poet, wrote a clear-eyed view of the way in which many Parisians saw their occupiers, one that gives us at the same time a view of the way many Germans felt when they were placed amid a group of apparently placid Parisians. He begins by imagining how an occupation of Paris might have been different under the Swedes or the Hungarians or the Javanese or the Hottentots or even the Italians. In those cases, he suggests, there would have been a sort of gay exchange of gestures, expressions, and rhythms that might have hinted at an affectionate indulgence on behalf of the occupied:

> But from [these Germans], no one sees what we can gain from them. Not even a tune or a grimace. The kid in the street doesn't even imitate the goose step. In the Métro, which has become, along with the grocery, our common meeting place, they never push anyone, while we still push or bump into each other! They even pick up our stupidly dropped packages. But we have no interest in picking up theirs. They are not very animated. They will have passed [through Paris] without a mark. As if they were already dead. Except that they are spreading around this death. It's the only thing they know how to do.[26]

The image devastates: the mask of death placed on the face of a polite young German bending over to gather the packages dropped by an old man. Perhaps, though, it is the best one we have to illustrate the discrepancy between the way many of the occupiers saw themselves and the fact that Parisians did all they could to ignore them.

Chapter Five

⊷≔◉⇐⊷

Narrowed Lives

The Parisian now knows the condition of being "occupied" in a city that does not belong to him anymore and that offers him the schizophrenic image of an environment suddenly foreign to his gaze. Constraints and humiliations, restrictions and punishments accompany this disorientation and the upending of daily routine.

—Jean-Paul Cointet[1]

Narrowing and Boredom

Sarah's Key (2007), Tatiana de Rosnay's bestselling novel about the weight of memory and unresolved guilt during and after the Occupation, begins with the roundup of Parisian Jews on July 16–17, 1942, known as the Grande Rafle. (The French verb *rafler* means "to collect" or "to bring together.") As in many novels and memoirs of the period, the sound of police—French police—beating on the door is the narrator's most vivid aural memory. Trapped in the apartment with her two children, her husband in hiding, a Jewish mother panics. "Wake your brother. Get dressed, both of you. Take some clothes, for him and you. Hurry! Hurry, now!" The little boy does not want to go, persuading his sister to let him hide in their "secret place," a tiny space under the eaves, its door hidden by wallpaper.

> The girl could see her brother's small face peeking out at her from the darkness. He had his favorite teddy bear clutched to him; he

160

was not frightened anymore. Maybe he'd be safe there, after all. He had water and the flashlight. And he could look at the pictures in [his favorite] book.... Maybe she should leave him there for the moment. The men would never find him. She would come back to get him later in the day when they were allowed to go home again. And Papa, still in the cellar, would know where the boy was hiding, if ever he came up.[2]

The reader soon intuits the result of this childish scheme: the boy will be locked permanently in the dark hole in the wall as his sister desperately tries to return with the key to let him out. This chilling episode represents vividly one of the subjects of this chapter: the fact that secret and narrow spaces became a fixation of Parisians and their families during the Occupation.

A recurrent refrain of the memoirs written by—and interviews conducted with—those who lived in Paris then is that physical and psychological space seemed to progressively narrow. Whether because of the sight of German uniforms, the closed-off streets, the insufficient nourishment, the cold winters, crowded transportation, long lines—or just the suffocating feeling of being suspicious of one's acquaintances, neighbors, and even family—the city seemed to be contracting, closing in on Parisian lives, as the Occupation dragged on. The very term *occupation* connotes "taking a place," and the most compelling stories of this period concern how "places"—apartments, shops, subway trains, bookstores, buses, parks, cafés, streets and sidewalks, restaurants, cabarets, even brothels—were taken over by foreign soldiers and bureaucrats as well as by smug French collaborators. From physical displacement to psychological displacement is not a great leap: once you find that your body is no longer "at home," your mind tends to feel disoriented as well. Gaston Bachelard, a French philosopher of space and its connection to the imagination, writes of spaces we conceive of as "felicitous," those that make us feel secure, comfortable, and protected; whereas in "hostile" spaces, we feel ill at ease, threatened, off balance.[3] The stories of the Occupation recount the often subtle movement from a felicitous to a hostile environment, not only for Parisians themselves but also for the Germans who were assigned there or who passed through.

The discomfort that comes from being "out of place" changes the way we comprehend, even imagine, our immediate surroundings. Imagine yourself blindfolded, touching your way through a familiar setting. You know where you are, but not quite. You feel remembered objects, but you run your fingers along others that seem unfamiliar because you have never taken the time before to touch them or look at them closely. You take cautious steps even though you have been down this hallway or around that corner countless times. Your temporary blindness not only slows you down; its very fact causes an almost paralyzing uneasiness. Memory and habit enable you to move, to reach a modest level of comfort, but nothing really seems the same as before. Parisians and their occupiers both felt this sense of spatial, tactile, and psychological unease.*

Another philosopher, the German O. F. Bollnow, has also thought about how important space is to our identity and feeling of affective security. He believes that our humanity is determined by the way we act within specific, lived-in spaces. Man needs room to move, but so do his fellows; this tension is a normal part of everyday life. But it is manifestly and uncontrollably more tense to live in proximity to an outsider, an enemy, or a culturally different group of humans. Habitual, instinctual activities such as stepping out onto the street from one's dwelling become less habitual, less instinctual. When the individual no longer can take comfort from the predictability of movement, another set of anxieties is created. To illustrate, Bollnow addresses the notion of "narrowness": "Narrowness...always refers to the prevention of free movement by something that restricts it on all sides....Man perceives restricting space as a pressure which torments him; he seeks to break through it and to press forward into the liberating distance."[4]

Marcel Aymé, a popular writer active during the Occupation, published in 1943 a fantasy entitled "Le Passe-muraille" (The Man

---

* The French refer to this sense of alienation as *dépaysement*—not feeling at home, or feeling like a fish out of water.

Who Walked Through Walls). The tale appears in a collection of stories that rely on the Occupation for their narrative suspense. The story offers the best fictional, though indirect, description I have found of the frustration and spatial restrictions experienced by Parisians under the Occupation: a person's isolation is leavened by a desire to resist freely, especially when one has nothing left to lose. The protagonist is a very minor Parisian bureaucrat, Dutilleul, who unexpectedly—and inexplicably; after all, the tale is a fantasy—acquires the ability to pass through walls, no matter how thick. Cautious at first, he only avails himself of this trick when he has forgotten the key to his apartment. But one day, frustrated by his boss, a martinet with a "brush mustache," Dutilleul terrorizes him by pushing his head through his superior's wall, threatening that "the werewolf," as he referred to himself, was going to destroy him. The poor manager finally is taken away to an asylum, and Dutilleul's job has no more inconveniences. Having, however, acquired a taste for surprising those who never had taken him seriously, our hero turns to burglary, escaping from prisons, and visiting beautiful women in their boudoirs. One day, as he passes into a house where a married lover awaits him, he senses something is not right: "He begins to feel an unfamiliar rubbing on his hips and shoulders, but decides not to pay attention. . . . On going through a thicker wall, he began to feel some [more] resistance. He seems to be moving in a fluid matter, but one that becomes pastier, taking on, as he progresses, more thickness."[5]

At this moment, terror strikes him: he remembers that he had failed that morning to follow exactly the detailed prescription for a medicine that his doctor had given him; he had taken aspirin instead. He slowly realizes that his strangely acquired powers had weakened, and that he would be unable to get through the wall to his lover's room:

Dutilleul was frozen inside the wall. He is still there, incorporated into the stone. Nightly strollers going down the Rue Norvins when the streets of Paris are especially quiet hear a muffled voice that seems to come from the other side of a tomb; they take it to be the wind whistling around the hills. But it is Dutilleul lamenting the end of his glorious adventures.... On some nights, [his friend] the painter Gen Paul, unstrapping his guitar, goes out into the silent Rue Norvins to console the poor prisoner with a song, and the notes, sent on their way by his swollen fingers, penetrate the very heart of the stony wall like drops of moonlight.[6]

This sense of being frozen within a narrowed space, of being unable to act, of being abandoned, with only the occasional sound of music for consolation, began by the winter of 1940–41 to describe many Parisians, and their number would increase rapidly.

The most prevalent psychological response to this narrowing might be identified as a sort of ennui. Apprehension, limitations—e.g., curfews—interruptions of normal activities, absence of nourishment, and difficulty of movement through the city: these and other phenomena imposed a new sort of boredom on Parisians, who, like many urban citizens, thrived on the actual and implied vibrancy of their city. In her journal, Edith Thomas writes in late 1941:

Who would speak now of time must speak of distress, of disgust, of boredom. And perhaps this epoch's boredom is stronger even than our horror. Horror is a paroxysm; boredom a state of mind. One gets used to all sorts of things, even indignation, which is only the persistence of disgust.... [The knowledge that they are] impotent witnesses [to what is happening in Europe] is visible on the thin and tired faces that rush to the Métro or stand in shop queues: too passive and resigned, just waiting.[7]

Malnourishment, unpredictable regulations, conflicting rumors and news reports, the absence of more than a million men locked away in German stalags, suspicion of neighbors—all combined unhealthily, and the Parisian responded by shutting himself or herself down, affectively. Boredom became as much an internally imposed as an externally imposed state of mind—sometimes for reasons of survival. The slightest effort to appear different, especially if one were Jewish or in hiding or a foreigner or a Gaullist or a Communist, had to be repressed. To be recognizable was to be at risk. Victoria Kent, a Catalonian Republican immigrant hiding out in Paris, writes in her semiautobiographical narrative, *Quatre ans à Paris* (Four Years in Paris):

> One must be neither too well nor too badly dressed, neither too well groomed nor too sloppy. To go out, one needed camouflage; so much for any singularity in one's appearance or way of speaking or walking or dressing. If you do not want to be suspected, don't risk giving your opinion on even the most trivial topic, for the man that you have opposite you is not you; he is in the other camp, and as soon as your singularity is evident, it becomes suspicious....Let your appearance be like those of others, your reactions like those of others.[8]

All those habitual, casual actions that set one apart, that give some variety to one's life, had to be muted. Spontaneity had to be repressed; generosity reduced.

This was especially hard for parents who had to worry about their children's inventiveness and their artless attitudes toward official authority. Discussions between parents were muted, new codes invented; an aura of secrecy—and of an undefined danger—became a common atmosphere at home. A child's casual remark or an adolescent's insolent retort could bring minor as well as serious problems to his or her family. Children are easily bored, and in a world where boredom becomes a daily survival strategy, their own impatience and frustration intensify. And, of course, their enforced social isolation brings an even more unnatural atmosphere to their families and neighborhoods. For youngsters the Occupation seemed unnecessarily, inexplicably restrictive; for their parents, living in the city took on aspects of uncanniness.★

Thanks to those who had permanently left the city, either willfully

---

★ In his work on the "personality" of urban spaces, the architectural historian Anthony Vidler argues: "The uncanny [is]...precisely the contrast between a secure and homely interior and the fearful invasion of an alien presence..., [a space] of silence, solitude, or internal confinement and suffocation" (Vidler, *The Architectural Uncanny*, 4, 39).

or not, a large number of beautiful apartments were available during the early months of the Occupation. The middle-class Jamets (unrelated to Fabienne, the bordello madam) had the good fortune to find themselves in a spacious apartment on the Rue Vavin, in the 6th arrondissement. As we observed earlier, Dominique Jamet recalled that as an intelligent but naive young boy—Gentile and thus less personally threatened by the occupier—he was still aware of a changed Paris. For example, he wrote with amusement about the public idolatry of Philippe Pétain:

> The Maréchal is everywhere. He's on stamps. He's on the postal calendar. He reigns from chimney mantels among family photos. He decorates shop windows; he is already in history books, and his image opens the movie news; he won the war of 1914, a good augury; he planted his marshal's baton on coins; he's in everyone's head; he's on all lips; everyone's had it up to here with the Maréchal.[9]

Not only in private residences but also in public sites and on the very symbols of the French state, the venerable warrior fixed his starkly blue eyes on his nervous subjects. A new watchfulness, with its passwords— *"Étes-vous plus français que lui?"* (Are you more French than he?)—became part of the social negotiations of daily urban life. Pétain's image symbolized the moral surveillance that was endeavoring to turn Paris into a bourgeois *ville de province*. A visual vocabulary of the newly occupied Paris (of which Pétain and the Vichy government were part) had suddenly imposed itself.

Dominique Jamet remembers that after the shock of the defeat and the initial occupation, he felt, as a youngster, that

> life in occupied Paris regained its ocean liner rhythm. Theaters, cinemas, music halls are full, cabarets and racecourses, too.... [But] the reserves of altruism are at their lowest, the fund of compassion exhausted. Families huddle together in homes that have become lairs. [It's] everyone for himself, or for his family, or for a close

circle of friends he cares about. Generosity does not run through the darkened streets.[10]

The quarters of Paris, geographically close, had become separated in the imagination. The young Jamet speaks of familiar neighborhoods as if they were somewhere in eastern Europe—names he recognizes, places he may have visited before the Occupation, are now only distant Métro stops on a map:

We live in a bourgeois quarter. We study in a bourgeois lycée.... The news [of the roundups of Jews] never got to [us]. The arrests made on the Rue des Écouffes, the Rue de Turenne, the Rue de Belleville, or the Boulevard Barbès did not trouble summer doldrums of the Place Saint-Sulpice, the Rue Notre-Dame-des-Champs, or the Avenue de l'Observatoire. Even less were they the subject of conversations when we went back to school in the fall.[11]

The quarters' names may have had resonance for Jamet, but their physical reality remained weirdly distant and essentially unknown. Paris reverted to being a congeries of villages and lost much of its metropolitan aura. Parisians noticed many alterations to their city but remained distant from its darkest, most inhumane corners.

Narrowing—the constriction of the vital energy of a society—is a hallmark of living under military occupation and intensive police surveillance. Four years is a long time for any society to experience this state of affairs "temporarily," and the Occupation's length was especially cruel. There was always the hope that the Occupation would end soon, that political pressure would weaken some of the more invasive measures of the Vichy government, and that the war would come to a close. But when? How long did people have to live that way? This anxiety of longing for a resolution of a state of affairs that was obviously *not* temporary is perhaps the most important component of the concept of narrowing, and the Occupier knew this well.

The Apartment

The Parisian apartment figures prominently in recollections of the Occupation. An apartment was more than a place of expected physical comfort; it was also a site of psychological retreat from confusion and uncertainty. Yet at the same time the apartment could be a trap, and many wrote of feeling closed in there by events and police, always worrying about how they would escape should there be an ominous knock at the door. And there were more mundane concerns, such as how to heat and live comfortably in apartments during a time of enforced penury.

The apartment building has been a site of sophisticated Parisian life since the 1840s; it "embodied the continuity between domestic and urban, private and public spaces."[12] The private apartment, a rather inexpensive real estate investment for a rising bourgeois population, was situated among other such units in a large building or a group of buildings. From the street, a row of apartment buildings presents a facade of regularity and order; Parisian streetscapes are noted for the uniformity of their external architecture, conferring a mask of sameness on a heterogeneous collection of private dwellings. But this was only the outside; entering a Parisian apartment complex brought one often to a "courtyard, carved out of the space where the undecorated, cheaply constructed back walls of up to four different buildings met and were irregularly punctuated by [multiple doorways]."[13] Later, elevators were added to many apartment buildings, as was indoor plumbing, both of which enhanced privacy. The several exits and entrances, reconfigured stairways, and hidden or seldom used spaces, often confusing to the visitor or newcomer, make the Parisian apartment building an ideal place to study the spatial anxieties of the Occupation.

A professional gatekeeper enabled the "public privacy" of the Parisian apartment building: the concierge. (*Gardien* and *gardienne* are the current, socially correct terms.) The profession of concierge takes us back to the Middle Ages and the guardians of a castle's gates. The position soon became a sign of wealth, of separateness from the hoi

A concierge's lodging. (Pierre Gaudin; CREAPHIS)

polloi, and was always held by a male. With the advent of the apartment house in the mid-nineteenth century, it became obvious that a *portière,* or gatekeeper—later the concierge—was needed to help bring some order to the potential chaos of a large, multidomicile building often with dozens of owners, renters, and their staffs. More than any other private figure, the concierge (generally a woman, though men were also guardians) was the person—and face—offered to the outside world by the apartment house. She lived on the ground floor in her own small set of rooms, called a loge, from which she could see and hear, through her glass door, the comings and goings of tenants and their visitors. She delivered the mail, received packages, kept the public spaces clean, let in visitors, acted as nanny, and kept keys to all the apartments. The concierge was the equivalent of a public telephone, a mailbox, a message service, and a counselor. She knew who had late-night visitors, who had money problems, who was ill (and who was malingering). She knew the merchants in the neighborhood, knew other concierges (and thus was privy to what was happening in other buildings), knew children (who often told her more than they should), and was the first person the police came to when they had questions about tenants. The Occupation authorities officially obliged all concierges to help the police. For example, each had to report within twenty-four hours the arrival of a new tenant, identify "visitors" who stayed more than a night or two, and be responsible for removing any anti-German or anti-Vichy graffiti from her building or the sidewalks in front of it. If she did not inform the Occupiers of a new tenant, and that tenant turned out to be a "terrorist," then she was liable to be imprisoned or worse. Such activities would often unfairly mark her as a *collabo* (popular term for a collaborator).

Responsibilities were expected of her from the Occupied as well as the Occupier. The concierge was an extremely useful friend for all Parisians to have. Wily, knowledgeable, often courageous in the face of pressure, she was smart enough to realize that her relationship with the Germans had to be proper if she were to be of use to herself and her tenants in cases of emergencies. Stories of the Occupation are replete with anecdotes of good, bad, and indifferent concierges. Some hid Jewish children; others betrayed Jewish families. Some protected empty apartments; others looted them, even moved into them. Some confronted the Germans fearlessly; others collaborated as much as they could. One Jewish girl remembers watching through closed shutters as a concierge across the street pointed out the apartments in the vicinity where she knew Jews lived. Another concierge betrayed her tenants so that she could get into their apartment, rummage through their belongings, and then, when they returned, blame the Germans. Yet another tells the story of a concierge who kept tabs on all empty or emptied apartments in the neighborhood so that she could move her threatened Jewish clients from one to the other, one step ahead of the police.

Hessy Taft and her Jewish parents, recently emigrated from a much more oppressive Berlin, lived in a very upscale part of Paris, on the Avenue de Messine, in the 8th arrondissement, just south of the elegant Parc Monceau. One Sunday, the family went out for a visit, and by chance Hessy's father told the concierge, who was sitting in the sun on the stoop, "I'll be *chez* your friend Jacques for a while." Jacques had visited Hessy's family often and had always been polite to the concierge, so she remembered him and considered him her friend, too. Within a few minutes of having arrived at Jacques's apartment, Hessy's family heard the phone ring. It was the concierge. "Don't come back, monsieur," she told Hessy's father. "They are here waiting for you." This phone call made it possible for the father to hide and for the family to return to the apartment innocently, *sans père*. Later the whole family was able to escape to America. Hessy just shook her head when hearing about concierges who had exposed or given up Jewish tenants. She firmly told me: "They weren't all that way; I'm here because one of them respected my family, especially my father."*

Of course, not all apartment houses were the same. Some were sturdy, well-maintained buildings providing homes to middle-class tenants. Others were luxurious, perhaps containing only two or three apartments. Then there were the apartments in poor communities, built on the same principle but much more porous and thus more easily raided. The same opportunities and constraints existed in these buildings as in the others. Proximity bred solidarity but also suspicion. Most apartment buildings in these neighborhoods were deplorable rabbit warrens of false turns, stairs leading to hidden doors—and, as the police became more diligent, specially constructed hidden spaces.† In

---

* Hessy Taft was one of about two dozen persons I interviewed both in the United States and France about their memories of the Occupation. These generous persons are listed in my acknowledgments.

† There is a stunning homemade film in the Jewish Historical Museum in Amsterdam that shows how a group of Jewish residents (in the end, caught and deported) used their hearths and chimneys as secret passageways, enabling them to move between apartments and secret rooms.

any roundup, the French police were especially useful to the Vichy government and the Germans because many of them had grown up in such environments and knew them intimately.

Another characteristic of the apartment was its role as a prospect—that is, a site from which one could look out upon occupied Paris in relative safety. Down on the streets, expressing an undue curiosity—to walk slowly, or to look or stand for more than a minute in front of shop windows or with a group of people, or to turn around in order to avoid the inconvenience of a police control—could attract official attention. Those apartments whose balconies or large windows gave onto the street would permit their owners to catch a glimpse of the city without having to go downstairs and outside. They were frequently used, too, as lookouts for clandestine actions or as sites from which to throw leaflets. On the other hand, the open windows also exposed residents to shrapnel from antiaircraft shells exploding or missing their targets. Everyone seemed to know of a case of someone who, unluckily, had been standing at a window at the wrong time. But watching and seeing what was going on from the relative security of apartments could alleviate the ever-present sense of claustrophobia that characterized daily life during the Occupation.

Apartments and apartment buildings were the scenes of some of the most touching, frightening, and horrifying events of the Occupation. To avoid arrest and deportation, a few terrified Jewish mothers threw their children from windows and then jumped out after them; the sound of pounding footsteps—or stealthy creaking—on stairways provoked panic; neighbors betrayed neighbors, even those living on the same landing. Tales of those who were hiding Jews or downed pilots or Resistance fighters often revolved around apartments and how they could be adapted to the new exigencies. For example, in October of 1943, two young women members of the Resistance thought they were safe deep in the wealthy 16th arrondissement, on the Rue de la Faisanderie, surrounded by Germans living in requisitioned apartments. They met a third conspirator on the street and invited him back to their building, where one of the girls wanted to collect her mail. The concierge told her that everything was okay, that no one had been by. No sooner were they in the apartment than the bell rang. Suspicious of the concierge's casual attitude, rather than answer they tried to escape by the service door, but it was stuck, and the two young women were arrested. The young man left by a window, climbed up to the next floor, and then took the elevator down. Passing by the seventh floor, he caught a glimpse of two men in the gray coats and hats of the Gestapo. When he reached the *rez-de-chaussée* (the ground floor), he casually walked out of the building, ignoring cries to stop from a policeman who had been left there on guard; he was arrested at gunpoint a few steps away. Fortunately, many others would evade capture, thanks to the porousness of the massive apartment buildings dotted with escape hatches.★

In another episode, on the Boulevard Raspail in the 7th arrondissement, an apartment house was used for a getaway.[14] Jean Ayrol, a resister, was arrested and taken for interrogation to the Hôtel Cayré, requisitioned by the Abwehr (Wehrmacht counterintelligence). He was led to a back room, where he found three other arrested men plus three guards. They sat staring at each other for hours. Then one of the prisoners asked to go to the toilet, and a guard accompanied him. Another guard left to answer the phone: three prisoners, one guard. Overpowering the guard and taking his pistol, the three men left the room and reached the street through the hotel's revolving doors. Knowing he had but a few minutes at most to lose himself, Ayrol walked through the first porte cochère he passed, crossed the courtyard, entered an apartment building without seeing the concierge, and, three steps at a time, rushed to the eighth floor—the highest. A curious renter opened the door to her room. (Most Parisian apartment buildings had tiny rooms right under the roof for servants; then, as now, they were rented to students or kept as maids' apartments.) Without a word, Ayrol jumped onto a chair and pushed open the hatch leading to the attic, where he crouched to hide. But someone had seen

---

★ The opening scenes in Roberto Rossellini's great film *Roma, città aperta* (1945) make use of what was common knowledge: escaping from an urban apartment house, across roofs into labyrinthine streets and alleys, had become a survival tactic in many European cities.

him enter the building, and soon he heard loud voices, barking dogs, and the cries of tenants rousted from their apartments. The door to his hideaway opened...but no one saw him in the darkness, and the door then closed. Soon the noises disappeared, and he waited there, tensely. About an hour later, the door opened again, and this time he saw the face of the building's concierge, who knew he had to be somewhere. She had been searching for him; taking him to her loge, she fed the young man and let him take a bath. Early the next morning, Ayrol slipped out and disappeared into the sleeping city. This time, an apartment building had been first a refuge, then a trap, then a passage to escape.

The Rue Lepic, in Paris's 18th arrondissement, where Montmartre is located, rises gradually and sinuously from the Place Blanche toward the hill that gives the quarter its name. A middle-class street, it had a different clientele at night than in the daytime. Because of its bars, its bordellos, its strip clubs, and its jazz venues, German enlisted men constantly frequented the neighborhood. Living on that street, Berthe Auroy, a spinster schoolteacher, kept a thorough record of day-to-day life in Paris during these hard years. She had just retired from the all-female Lycée Jules-Ferry down the hill and had first seen German invaders in the country while visiting Chartres, an hour by car outside the capital. In the fall of 1940, she returned to Paris and, writing with the acuity and acerbity of a concierge watching every move made by her tenants, detailed the German invasion of her quarter.

The small squares and narrow streets of Montmartre had been spared the renovations effected by Baron Haussmann in Paris during the nineteenth century, and one could almost imagine, while walking through the area in 1940, still being in a hilltop village. (It even had—and still has—vineyards.) Cheap rents had made Montmartre the center of the bohemian art world in the late nineteenth and early twentieth centuries. The famous rambling Bateau-Lavoir (Laundry Boat), the building where every avant-garde painter from Picasso to Modigliani seemed to have had an apartment or studio in the 1900s and 1910s, was only a few short blocks from Auroy's apartment building. The area's artistic, cultural, and populist energy drew many there to escape some of the rigors of the Occupation, but it also brought together, almost intimately, Parisian and German.

Auroy's journal, which runs from June 10, 1940, to August 15, 1945, expresses her frustration, anger, and humiliation at being locked up in her own apartment, sequestered in her own neighborhood. She pulled no punches: "The Occupation has made us like wooden robots."[15] What made it worse, of course, was that she lived alone, and her neighborhood had become a tourist and nightlife mecca for the despised Germans: "Gray uniforms are everywhere. They come out of shops, their arms filled with packages.... Every day, around 5:00 p.m., many trucks filled with soldiers park in front of the Moulin de la Galette [a nightclub just a short walk from her apartment]."[16] Out spilled Germans, drenching the neighborhood with their boisterous enthusiasm.

As with other memoirs and diaries, we should pause to ask ourselves why they were written, hidden, rewritten, trusted to others, and in some cases unpublished for years. In a world where there has been a short-circuiting of normal connections, blank pages can offer the freedom that one misses in an unpredictable occupied city. But the danger always remains that a person's writing can be found and act as an instrument of betrayal. Finding a task that would bring habit to a disrupted environment led many Parisians of all ages to keep scrapbooks in which they pasted maps, drawings, and newspaper clippings and to write secret diaries, journals, and unsent letters depicting daily life. In the past decade or so, more and more of these texts have come out of closets, attics, and forgotten chests of drawers to be published for generations that have never known a bereft Paris.

Auroy was not a dispassionate chronicler: her journal is rich with detailed examples and analysis of the anxiety caused by trying to live some sort of "normal" life in German Paris. In 1943, for example, she returned from shopping to discover that neighbors from the floor above hers had been arrested. No one knew why. They were not Jewish and had expressed no stronger anti-Nazi sentiments than anyone else. A day or two after they had been taken away, Auroy watched as Germans, or their acolytes, emptied the apartment of anything valuable. "Germans love to loot," she observed, and she wondered what happened to the modern paintings, including one by Picasso, that had covered her neighbors' walls. (It turned out that a cunning neighbor had saved them from the ignorant movers.) This arrest was very close to home — too close; happily, the Gestapo would never knock at her own door, but she was always on the alert for the sound of unfamiliar boots in the stairwell.

The curfew was one of the most successful—and pesky—means devised by the Occupation forces to control a population. To further discombobulate Parisians, curfew times were arbitrarily changed; Auroy and her friends often had to hurry home earlier than the announced hour in case a street might be blocked or a Métro station closed. Being caught on the street after curfew was no minor infraction. In an unpublished memoir of a British woman who had remained in Paris after the Occupation, the author relates how she had stayed past curfew at a friend's home in the near suburbs; she decided nonetheless to walk back to Paris with a companion. Before too long, they were stopped on the near-empty streets by a French policeman and asked for their passes. They had none, but they showed their ID cards, and insisted that as British citizens they were in order, having gone each day to a police station to register. The policeman smiled, reminding them that he had the authority to have them spend the night in a police station. But taking pity, he decided to walk with them to the end of his route, pass them on to another group of cops, until they finally reached their destination. Later, our lady discovered a favorite technique of less generous policemen: they would pass innocent breakers of the curfew from one escort to another all night, making them walk miles and miles before the curfew lifted.[17]

Such tales must have led Berthe Auroy to reason that it was best just to stay at or close to home, in her neighborhood, within her narrow community. Wrote another observant Parisian about that period: "Occupied Paris is on its guard. Inviolate down to its core, the city has grown tense, surly and scornful. It has reinforced its interior borders, as the bulkheads of an endangered ship are closed.... Left Bank and Right Bank are not two different worlds any more, but two different planets."[18] The city was like a submarine, with major sections closed off by watertight doors. A year after the Germans had arrived, Auroy would no more have thought of casually venturing south across the river to the Latin Quarter than she would have thought of boarding a train to Berlin; she might leave for the suburbs, but venture into another Parisian neighborhood if she did not have to? Not on her life.

This psychologically disturbing readjustment of one's sense of space, of having to redefine where safety was assured and where it was not, is one of the most persistent themes gleaned from those who lived in Paris during the Occupation. One's neighborhood, the Métro, one's apartment house, one's private rooms: all had to be reconsidered. What had been benign now seemed strangely dangerous. Long-repressed agoraphobia and claustrophobia began to reemerge; the spatial awareness of the citizen under Occupation became almost as acute as that of the soldier under fire.

Parisians, in secret, must have taken out thousands of maps and marked them with ink or pins to show the constellation of troops grinding across the continent and, at last, the inexorable retreat of the Reich's forces. A new geography festooned apartment walls; children learned place names because of the nervous excitement with which their parents pronounced them. After the D-day invasion in 1944, Victoria Kent wrote:

> I'm looking quickly for my map. Where is my map of France? I bought it a few months ago and put it aside: it seemed a bit premature to hang it up in my room with the others. I think that if the Gestapo had suddenly burst into my room, they would have a clear idea of my life during the last four years. [My maps of Russia, Africa, and eastern Europe] were all covered with arrows, circles, and special marks that I added day after day during the war.[19]

Closed up in their apartments, so many Parisians, in hiding and not, used such charts and visual representations to expand their limited horizons.*

Albert Grunberg, a Jewish hairdresser, whose salon was right in the center of the Latin Quarter, on the Rue des Écoles, soon found himself a target of German interest. Fortuitously, Grunberg, who had married a Gentile after emigrating from Romania twenty years earlier, had anticipated his roundup. Seeing agents enter his shop, he escaped— barely—running next door to the adjacent apartment building and up to its seventh floor, where there was a small, semihidden room. On the same floor where he had been told earlier he could hole up were three other apartments. For the next two years, thanks to the assertive benevolence of the building's concierge, Grunberg lived in a room of eight square meters (about eighty-five square feet).

Cramped in his hideaway, Albert Grunberg was continuously alert; his journal offers us a very good account of how life for every unhappy Parisian—in hiding or not—must have changed. Compelled to live clandestinely—always aware of his surroundings, counting the minutes, the hours, the days, and the weeks until something or someone would bring a new order—he exhibited a daunting patience. Fortunately, his friends had also drilled a hole in the wall joining Grunberg's room to the kitchen so that he could have electricity. He had to be very careful that his radio was not heard, that lights from his bedroom were kept to a minimum, that the snoring of his brother, Sami, who after several months would join him in hiding there, not disturb his neighbors as much as it disturbed him, and that he walk only on the piles of carpets that the concierge had laid in the tiny room and in the kitchen of the neighboring apartment, which he could get to unseen. (He could not cook in the kitchen unless the neighbor was there for fear of sending tattletale odors out to the building's other tenants.)

---

* I was especially fortunate to be offered a collection of high school notebooks filled with newspaper clippings, drawings, and photographs. The young student who kept this journal, Philippe Lemaire, was meticulous in following the trajectory of the war as the Germans were pushed back home.

Parisian apartment buildings are built around an inner courtyard and maybe a rear courtyard; they form a natural echo chamber, and sound carries with startling efficiency throughout the building, especially when windows are open. There was no air-conditioning in those days, so windows were often left open, especially during the hot summer months. Grunberg could only use his one small window—which opened onto the inner courtyard and through which he could see only the apartments opposite and a small panel of the Parisian sky—to listen and watch for any disruption that might presage a raid. The Gestapo and the French Vichy police were relentless in their patrols and round-ups; they received dozens of letters a day suggesting that some Jew or communist was in hiding. The Nazis would cordon off whole quarters or apartment houses or set up barricades at Métro entrances and exits, for they were under persistent orders to provide a quota of foreigners and Jews for the detention and transit camp in Drancy, north of Paris, or for work (or death) in Poland and Germany.

Even concealed, the hairdresser was still in his neighborhood, though no longer a visible part of it. He was able to see his wife almost weekly, and from his small chamber he had contact with his concierge, her family, and a neighbor or two. Awaiting safe release, Grunberg began a journal to "kill time," writing, as many others did, to lighten the sense that he was not free. He was fortunate enough to have a radio, and half his journal is taken up by descriptions he heard on news broadcasts of the victories of the Western allies and Russia against Germany's war machine.

Grunberg and other victims of the Occupation of Paris did not examine philosophically the effects of physical isolation, but through their writings, we can begin to fathom what was the most intangible, though most prevalent, inconvenience of living in an occupied city: that of not being able to control and order one's time or space. This unease undermined the "spacefulness" of a richly built and lived urban experience. For these chroniclers and their fellows the pleasure of living in Paris had gradually narrowed, or diminished, and, in some cases, it had been erased.

There was a persistent dearth of food and heat sources for most

Parisians between 1940 and 1945. No one starved, but the majority experienced hunger or at least an absence of satiety. Every winter seemed to last longer and be more frigid than the one before.* As a result of the scarcity of nourishment, apartment rooms and—when the temperature allowed—balconies were turned into gardens; space was given over to growing food or raising rabbits and chickens. Public parks, too, were tilled and planted. The city took on the allure of a huge greenhouse as public spaces took on practical functions.

Of the four winters during which Paris was occupied, three were exceptionally cold, colder than any winter in memory. One writer describes vividly what it must have been like to have been unable to get enough coal or charcoal, even in the finest apartments. Having received a bouquet of pink carnations, a lady placed them in a glass vase and set them on a living room table. The apartment became so cold that the glass burst, but the flowers remained fresh and bright in a block of unmelting ice. Furniture makers soon began running advertisements about a new contraption:

> A tiny cabin. A sort of mini room, with wooden partitions, a door, and a low ceiling, closed on all sides; made to be placed inside an apartment, where its reduced dimensions would allow the concentration of heat. The photograph in the ad showed people wrapped in winter clothes up to their ears, seated face-to-face, as in a railcar, around a narrow, rectangular table in this very restricted space. How many buyers were attracted to this device?...
> Even rabbits had more room in their cages![†] [20]

---

* In interview after interview, I would first be told, without fail, about how cold it was in Paris in the early 1940s, how large apartments became smaller as rooms were closed off, how few public spaces—cafés, churches, offices—were adequately heated. When I began to wonder if this was just a strategy to keep from talking about more controversial topics, an interlocutor retorted: "Being cold and hungry often pushes other considerations—political, ideological—to the side."

† In Jean-Pierre Melville's captivating film about the French resistance, *L'Armée des ombres* (Army of Shadows, 1969), there is a long scene that takes place inside one of these compartments within a cold apartment.

Berthe Auroy's memoir contains a remarkable series of entries about how her apartment shrank as she began to live in fewer rooms and finally consolidated her life in the kitchen, a place she describes with the detailed intimacy of a Balzac.

> In order not to lose any heat, I live exclusively in my kitchen. I look like an Eskimo in her hut, the only island of warmth in this Spitzberg that is the apartment. The enemy [cold] is there, who watches me behind the door in order to pinch and bite me.... Dressing, undressing, toilette, meals, visits, correspondence, etc., everything happens in the kitchen. At night, I jump into my bed, heated with hot water bottles...in order to escape from the enemy, which wants to bite my nose and the nape of my neck.[21]

It makes little difference whether the "enemy" she feels closing in on her is the cold or the Germans; her world has become much smaller because of the Occupation and its deficiencies.

The Germans and their Vichy partners requisitioned hundreds of apartments; entire apartment buildings were even put under seal, both for housing and for looting. A protocol of "minding one's own business" prevailed, but uncomfortable, even dangerous encounters were unavoidable. On the top floor of an elegant apartment building in the block-long Rue de Buenos-Ayres, right under the Eiffel Tower in the fashionable 7th arrondissement, a Jewish family hid in plain view. Having emigrated from eastern Europe with papers, forged by an Eastern Orthodox priest, that made them "Christians," they had not registered when Jews were required to do so in 1940. To their despair, Germans requisitioned apartments on the lower floors of their building. For years, they would pass each other in the elevator or on the stairway, but the occupiers took no undue notice. Then, one evening, a heavy knock at their front door sounded. Gently, the lady of the home opened it to find three slightly drunk, smiling German officers on her landing. They were surprised at the sight of the woman, and she was terrified. They were just returning from a night out and, laughing out loud, excused themselves—"We are on the wrong floor. Please excuse our rudeness, madame"—as they stumbled back down the stairs. The refugee family never completely forgot this incident and how intimately they were living with those who could arrest and deport them at a whim.

A Crowded Métro

The Métro—a vast system of underground trains and stations—was only forty years old when war came to Paris. A subway system has an immutable trajectory, unforgiving as it controls the direction and the pace of the passenger. Yet it provides, too, an apparent freedom, for one can get on or off wherever one wishes. One can take any line, change cars, wait for another train to pass, ride around all day on a single ticket, or remain in a station. One can direct a glance or ignore one; avoid physical contact or encourage it; talk with others or ignore them; read, eat, sleep, daydream. Here, on these predictable tracks, Parisians experienced the most freedom from official surveillance during the Occupation. Not that there were no thefts, arrests, roundups, attacks, and assassinations on the trains and in the stations, but more than a modicum of anonymity still prevailed as one rode under the streets of Paris.

In the guidebook *Wegleiter,* the Métro is often described as an inescapably useful means of getting around in a city where even Germans had trouble obtaining other means of transportation (except bicycles). "The Métro is the alpha and omega in Paris," intoned the anonymous writer.[22] Be careful, he warned his readers: you may get lost in its labyrinthine underground stations, but it can be a place of adventures and pleasant encounters with the French. (This was, of course, before the roundups and assassinations that would make the Métro quite dangerous for both sides.) The soldier was advised to procure a subway map as soon as he arrived in Paris and to study carefully how to get past the ticket puncher (all Germans in uniform could ride free), how to get on and off the train, and how to find his way out of the station. He also learned that about a hundred of the 350 Métro stations had been closed (because of the "difficulty of the transmission of electricity"—only

Midcentury Métro trains. *(Creative Commons)*

one of the reasons) but was also urged to admire that there were more than 1,800 train cars that ran over 110 miles of track and carried, in 1942, more than 1.25 million passengers.

The Métro was a subterranean microcosm of what was occurring up in the city's streets. Using the mostly underground railway had always forced Parisians into cautious engagement with others, both familiar and unfamiliar.* Paris's Métro trains were composed of five cars each;

---

* Aside from the Métro lines, there were more than two thousand kilometers of sewers and underground caverns (most left over from centuries of limestone mining) underneath Paris; these places could be reached through more than five thousand entrances. During the first half of the century, many of the caverns had even been major mushroom-producing farms. Many had been mapped and were known; others were secret, forgotten, or had never been discovered. Today, Parisian police still keep an eye on these underground paths and rooms, for young people use them as art colonies, movie theaters, performance spaces, and places to smoke, drink, dance, and do other interesting stuff. *Cataphiles* (cave lovers) of all types roam these spaces, which were not unknown to the Germans: they used them for storage, just as the Resistance used them to hide their meager arms supplies. For example, between September of 1941 and March of 1942, German and French police said they found thousands of revolvers and rifles and even nineteen machine guns in subterranean Paris. As in Hugo's *Les Misérables* (1862), those seeking safety took to the underground, either surreptitiously or legally, this time on the Métro.

until the Socialists became the ruling party in 1981, the red middle car, with thin leather cushions, was reserved for those who had bought a first-class ticket for about three times what a regular ticket cost. Almost immediately after the Occupation, the Germans—who could travel free, in uniform or not—occupied that car as if by right. Two years later, in 1942, those with yellow stars were relegated to the last car, just as blacks had been from the beginning of the Occupation.

The five-car train replicated some aspects of the city's newly reorganized society. Many were forced to take the Métro who had never taken public transportation before or who had only taken the bus, the more bourgeois conveyance. One French woman remembers her mother recounting the horror she felt when a German officer reached down to pick her up in a crowded train. "I, too, have a little girl at home, whom I miss so," he told the tense mother. The others in the car watched, trying not to stare, as the Frenchwoman refrained from wresting her child from the grasp of the friendly officer. However trivial, these episodes raised blood pressure and thorny ethical concerns about collaboration—or *Kontakt,* as the Germans called it—as well as questions about the boundaries separating social interaction and political expression. A series of paintings by the artist Jean Dubuffet depict blank-faced passengers in Métro cars sitting under signs that order DÉFENSE DE FUMER and VERBOTEN RAUCHEN (No Smoking) in two languages, an innocuous linguistic reminder that French travelers were still tied to the Germans.

During the Occupation many of the stations were closed because they were used by the Germans for workshops and storage or as air raid shelters or for security purposes. Consequently, Parisians could not easily make the transfers (*correspondances*) that allowed them to go from one line to another; and there was of course no predictability as to when stations or lines would be open or closed. No one knew when he or she might have to walk a long distance after learning that a stop had been closed. Citizens found themselves in neighborhoods only a few blocks from their own that they had scarcely known before the war.

Germans learning the Métro. *(Wegleiter)*

Nonetheless the system was essential to the productivity of Paris. Without it, the city would have been shut down, for the absence of gasoline and private vehicles made efficient travel on the surface cumbersome and slow unless one used a bicycle.

A Swiss journalist, Edmond Dubois, described his return to Paris in 1942 after a two-year absence. He noticed that the streets were emptier; the taxis had disappeared; there was more use of muscle than engines. But when he took a Métro train, he instantly recalled the Paris he had left two years before:

> We are swallowed by a Métro entrance. The bustle of the crowd is unbelievable. We advance step by step through long corridors broken up by stairways.... In the Métro [there is] immediate contact with the new life of the capital. The first-class car, where I am, offers a perfect tableau of the equality imposed by the transportation problem. All the seats are occupied.... The first thing

that strikes me is that the crowd looks healthy...because the women have remained attractive, and, despite the early morning hour, they have put on makeup, without which Parisiennes would not be Parisiennes.[23]

Dubois and others reveal a dichotomy that repeatedly manifests itself in accounts of the period. There was an awareness that Paris had changed, that everything, from fashion to the daily clock, had adapted to the Occupation. In spite of these disruptions, some minor, some major, Parisians felt they had shown a resistance to the invader that gave them a sense of moral comfort, necessary in any situation where one's individual liberty had been so severely abrogated: "Everywhere possible, Parisians would ostentatiously turn their backs on the Germans. It was considered good form to use second class in the Métro, as it was to leave a museum gallery when [German groups] appeared on guided tours. Parisians never mixed with the army."[24] This is only one point of view, and a somewhat affected and pretentious one, but it speaks to the recurring question: How did the typical Parisian live under Hitler's thumb? Dubois, amusingly, plays to the prejudices of his Swiss readers (comfortably ensconced in their neutrality), whose idea of Paris is limited to their superficial knowledge of a gay, fashionable, aloof city temporarily inconvenienced by a boorish Occupier. But he still reminds us of the daily accommodations every Parisian—except for the most cosseted—had to make with the German interlopers.

The Informer

One has only to live in a Parisian apartment for a week or so to discover how obsessive the French are about locks and doors. Lock shops in Paris are fascinating places to visit; they reflect the preoccupation that the French have always had with security, not only against the malfeasant but also against neighbors. To be offered a *trousseau de clés* (a key ring) is to be entrusted with the secrets of the owner; to lose a key is a minor disaster. Still, no bolts or chains could keep gossip from circulating, and the rumor economy became very robust during the Occupation. A French term for denunciation is *délation,* and the practice of reporting on neighbors, strangers, family members, business associates, Jews, Freemasons, Jehovah's Witnesses, and one's own clients—not to mention political refugees, those in hiding, and resisters—was endemic in occupied Paris.* This was another type of narrowing, the kind in which looking over your shoulder was not just a casual habit.

In late 1943, less than a year before Paris would be liberated, the film *Le Corbeau* (The Raven), directed by Henri-Georges Clouzot, brought in a very impressive seven million francs (selling about 185,000 tickets in just over three weeks in Paris alone). In spite of—or because of—its popularity, *Le Corbeau* was never shown in Germany, and the Catholic Church in France attempted to ban it. It was also immediately censored at the Liberation by Free French authorities, and not until 1947 would it be shown again in France and abroad. After the Liberation, its lead actor, Pierre Fresnay, spent six months in jail, partly for having participated in the film, which had been financed by Continental, the German-controlled French studio that made many—and many good—movies during the Occupation. Clouzot himself was not imprisoned, but he was forbidden to produce or direct films for the rest of his life, a sentence that was soon annulled. Around 1968, *Le Corbeau* finally became a staple in rerun houses and *cinémathèques.*

Le Corbeau is an unsettling film, even for today's viewer: it depicts the moral, social, and psychological disintegration of a fictional small town, Saint-Robin, in the French provinces. Though not set in Paris, it obviously touched the nerves of Parisians. The plot line runs like this: anonymous letters begin to appear in the village's mailboxes; they

---

* The Freemasons threatened the Nazi regime because they were believed to be heavily influenced by Anglo-Saxon values, defenders of a bourgeois parliamentary democracy, and adversaries of the Catholic Church (and thus of any totalitarian regime). They counted among their membership, especially in Germany and eastern Europe, where they were very strong, influential Jewish intellectuals and financiers. Right-wing adherents believed, without a doubt, that Masons were part of a plot to destroy Christian "democracy." Jehovah's Witnesses, of course, admit to no temporal power higher than God and his Son.

accuse a recently arrived medical doctor of adultery; then more letters (eventually dozens over the course of two months) detail the illicit and immoral activities of the town's most important and influential politicians and professionals.

In a real-life parallel to the film, police files in the provinces and in Paris were crammed with letters of denunciation from supposedly "well-meaning" but willfully malicious informers. They were sent to authorities for a variety of reasons and were both useful and a pain in the neck for the police. Encouraged early in the Occupation by the Germans and the Vichy government, the *délation,* anonymous or not, lost much of its effectiveness as the war dragged on. Surprisingly, recent research has suggested that there were relatively few denunciations of Jews; that Christian French men and women were criticizing, informing on, and betraying each other, mainly for personal reasons. Most letters contained reports on those who had criticized the Germans or Maréchal Pétain, who were illicitly listening to the BBC, or who were engaged in some imagined resistance activity. Though denunciation did happen in the provinces, it was much more prevalent in cities, where collaboration was more frequent and intimate. Indeed, what makes the atmosphere of *Le Corbeau* so intense for viewers is that it captures the aura of claustrophobia that comes from the social intimacy of the most respected citizens of the small town. "Our city is in a fever," offers one of its leaders. "Little squares of white paper have been raining down on this town." And, in real life, such denunciations would of course meet counternarratives, and both would confuse and befuddle the Germans.

Whose narrative of the Occupation was going to be dominant? Was French society composed of petty snitches, focused on themselves and their personal needs and expectations? Or was that society composed of patriots who used overheard information to undermine the authority of the Occupation? One of the primary criticisms of Clouzot's film is that it revealed a fractious France, obsessed with the narcissism of small concerns, a country that had deserved its defeat and had been conquered by a morally superior nation. Yet the soft but continuously repeated theme of moral indignation was also heard: Do we have to act this way, even though we are defeated? The film, like its plot, is morally ambiguous. For this reason, if not for its artistry, Clouzot's *Le Corbeau* remains fascinating to French audiences.★

Examples of letters of denunciation have appeared extensively in print since the end of the war. The missives are often appalling in their blunt carelessness about the lives they are disrupting:

[To:] Commissioner of Jewish Questions; Paris, January 28, 1943

Monsieur le Commissaire: I am the concierge at 4 Rue Saulnier, Paris 9th arrondissement; my owner is a Jew, and I must declare to you that in the building there is an active synagogue. The owner's name is Lucien Feist and he has left for the Free Zone.

My deepest respects, Renée Berti[25]

What strikes one first about this note is that the concierge signs her name, invoking the authority of her position—a concierge, someone who definitely should know what is happening in the building she is responsible for. One wonders if she has considered the possible consequences of her actions: maybe the building will be assigned to an "Aryan manager" who might have his own concierge put into place. Also, there is an assurance in the note that reveals how comfortable individuals were in exposing others. Somewhere along the line Renée Berti had learned that she had more to gain in reporting this possible "crime" than in remaining silent.

The suspicious atmosphere created by a hovering Occupation gave opportunities for shenanigans at best and malicious behavior at worst. Broken hearts, romantic rivalries, bad business relations, desire for rewards, envy among neighbors—these were just as prevalent as betrayal of one's political or religious beliefs. There were so many incidences of denunciation—both anonymous and proudly

---

★ Amusingly, the *Wegleiter* gives a positive review of this subversive film. Calling it a *policier* (detective story), the reviewer writes that the anonymous letters "are amusing unless one is the target!...The ending is surprising and very satisfying!" See Laurent Lemire, ed., *1940–1944 Der Deutsche Wegleiter* (Paris: Alma, 2013), 119.

signed—that police forces became increasingly inured to them; indeed, there were not enough officers to check every accusation. Yet the Gestapo did stay alert to charges of anti-German behavior and certainly used these letters and notes to track down Jews in hiding. Sometimes even newspaper articles or radio programs would point out "suspicious" occurrences or sites. Of course, anonymous denunciation occurs in peacetime, but the uncertainty of a military and civil occupation offers opportunities, and often rewards, that in this case produced thousands of letters, notes, phone calls, and person-to-person betrayals.

The Queue

Waiting in line is not just about waiting in line. Indeed, the psychological stress of those waiting for service or a product is a major subject of marketing research. What happens when we wait in line? Why we are obsessed with lines that move faster than ours? Why will we always choose the shorter one, even if the longer is moving and the shorter one isn't? When standing in line, we also become more judgmental of others: the lady who opens her chaotic purse only when she reaches the cashier; the guy with expired coupons; the person who asks questions but cannot understand the answers; and so forth. Waiting in line makes us impatient and unfriendly—our greatest fear is that the line will stop right before we get to it: the cashier will take a break, or the produce we are waiting to buy will be sold out. One can only imagine how these stresses were multiplied in a period where waiting in line could mean the difference between sickness and health or even life and death. The lines were not only sources of information about supplies, but also sites of potential danger, especially if one happened to say something one shouldn't have said. Every memoir, journal, or work of fiction about the Occupation mentions the trouble, if not anxiety, of waiting in line. Lengthy and slow lines in an occupied city reinforce the idea of being a prisoner, of having one's will continuously thwarted. The Occupiers knew that lines were a means of control—of one's time, one's space, and one's desires.

Given the situation, the Parisians' famous système D (*système de débrouillage;* a system for getting by) kicked in, and myriad methods were invented for beating the lines. Professional "waiters" offered for a fee to stand in line; others brought small chairs on which to sit; children were used as placeholders; some, if able, even rented hotel or other rooms near popular bakeries and butcher shops. One concierge rented out her basement for those who wanted to be first in line for the horse butcher across the street. Then there were the bumptious, who broke in line or used pregnancy, military or civil decorations, or a physical handicap to push ahead. Complaints to the French or German police often led to shouting matches and threats of fistfights or hair-pulling. Vichy, always sensitive to public opinion, was especially nervous about the threat of civil unrest. They believed that arbitrary action by the Germans would pit the French state against its own people, further weakening its slowly declining prestige. Low morale—brought on by having to wait in line for inferior or unavailable products—could lead to a resistance that would reveal the tenuousness of the Vichy state's control of the French.

In a remarkably prescient 1941 book, *La Queue* (The Line), censored and thus unpublished during the Occupation, the journalist and novelist Paul Achard described the pervasiveness of standing in line as part of Parisian culture during the war. He presents conversations overheard while waiting in line, suggesting, among other things, that those interminable periods, those lost minutes and hours, provided the gossip necessary to overcome the paucity of credible news from official reports, radio broadcasts, and newspapers. A new type of solidarity was implicit in queuing up, a replacement for forbidden political gatherings. The lines forced people, mostly strangers, to be close to each other, which meant that Parisians were more sensorially aware of those around them. Queuers could check out clothing to see how their fellows were making do in a city known for fashion. They caught each other's scent, touched each other, and exchanged meaningful glances. Social hierarchy became muddled. It was often unwise to talk about anything in line other than the weather; but waiting in line was infinitely boring if one could not chat. Parisians endured the queue, so

Lines, lines, lines… *(Roger Schall / Musée Carnavalet / Roger-Viollet / The Image Works)*

derided and hated, as "a course in philosophy, [fomenting] eloquence, self-control, courage, and patience. Its motto should be 'Wait [in order to] do without.' "[26]

The line was a sign, too, of how much a wealthy agricultural nation had been looted by a foreign enemy; a reminder of the scarcity, lack of choice, and humiliation imposed daily on a proud populace that had theretofore been vigorous and selective. Waiting in line had its own rules; casual conversation—especially complaining—was at first forbidden in the lines. Orderly queues must be maintained; a slight infraction could mean being asked to leave. There are many tales of breaking curfew in order to be first in line, of having to pay someone to hold your place while you went to stand in another queue for another product, and of having to keep your children close at hand in the cold or rain because there was no one with whom to leave them. The French police often watched lines closely. Body language and whispering became the primary modes of communication. As the Occupation continued, official Paris viewed lines as potential congregations of malcontents.

Most of those in line, of course, were women. As noted earlier, Paris—indeed, all of France—had been severely "de-manned" by the war and its effects. By the fall of 1940, more than a million men were in stalags and *oflags* (for officers) in Germany, far from their homeland; about two-thirds of them would remain five years in captivity. In addition, women had few political or financial rights in France during this period, so they had to learn how to "be a man" in a very short time while continuing their traditional roles as homemakers and nourishers. In the countryside, they were responsible for everything from clearing fields to bringing in harvests. In the city, they were forced to leave their homes, often in the face of criticism from traditionalists, to earn a living. Taking care of young ones was difficult, especially when school was not in session. Despite the Vichy regime's emphasis on maternity and the hearth as the centers of French life, the state provided little social or financial support to these overwhelmed women. It is no wonder that so many "little Fritzes," offspring of French women and Germans, were born during this period. Finding succor demanded compromises that would not be respected at the war's end.

The food line was where female solidarity had its most palpable manifestation. More concerned about unhappy men—released and wounded prisoners, crucial employees, and others—the Germans and their Vichy supporters overlooked the potential for disruption inherent in a line of tired, frustrated, and angry women. Since everyone—or at least everyone who was not actively cooperating with the Germans or the Vichy government—had to wait, social orderliness and excessive politeness were imposed on those who lined up. But there was also a barely hidden assertiveness required to maintain one's place or even to squeeze up. (This collective cultural memory affects Parisians even today; it does not pay to allow your mind to wander when waiting in a French queue.) Standing in line was useless unless one had "tickets," or ration cards, with their scissorable sections marked with dates and amounts. The merchants wore scissors around their necks, tools soon recognized as the symbols of the inevitable amputation of one's access to food or clothes or shoes or fabric. The daily papers were filled with warnings and stories about stolen packets of tickets, counterfeit tickets, and the black market for tickets. Elsa Triolet, poet and wife of the poet Louis Aragon, wrote that *tickettomanie* (ticketmania) had taken over France.[27] That's all people wanted to talk about, she reported; some even waited in line because it broke the monotony of their day. Others took tickets worth nothing in their own provinces and traveled to places where they were worth more. Dinner invitations would often have a request printed next to the RSVP that asked the guest to bring tickets for 250 grams of bread.

Standing in line was not optional; it was a necessity of daily life. And it exposed the individual citizen by taking her out of the relative comfort of her home. If a mother could not find a friendly neighbor or concierge to take care of her children, they had to accompany her. To lose one's place in line was a small tragedy, so children had to learn to stand like soldiers, holding hands, not daring to leave their mothers or fathers. Often children were sent to stand in line themselves, but there was always the danger that adults, including merchants, would take advantage of them. Because of their small hands, easily adaptable to the minute artisanry needed for forgery, some children were urged to counterfeit the stamps necessary to print phony tickets. Merchants were often sharper at discerning these games than the officials themselves.

"Everything is heard in line," wrote Achard, and this, of course, is where rumors could most efficiently be passed on.[28] Parisians were desperate for news affecting them directly—news about curfews, shortages, arrests, the war, the progress of the Allies—and the effectiveness and speed of reports true and false remain stunning to students of the period. But there were also spies in those lines, official and unofficial police and Gestapo informers. Jean Galtier-Boissière, a French journalist, recounts a "true" story: a formerly rich old lady, down on her luck, registered at a "Society for the Help of the Middle Class," run by a respected Vichy officer. The organization furnished jobs for petits bourgeois under economic stress, and a few days later, she was called to the *Kommandantur* (headquarters of the Occupier's bureaucracy), where officers proposed that she denounce anti-German comments she might hear in lines; for this she would receive sixty francs a day.[29] We do not learn if she agreed or not, but the story speaks at least to the paranoia of the Parisian line stander as well as to the ingenuity of the Occupation bureaucracy.

For millions of French men and women, the bars and confinement of prisons were replicated in the city by means of ukases, posters, radio announcements, layers of police authorities, reported gossip, and denunciations. So, too, followed their sisters, agoraphobia and claustrophobia; with fear came an insistent desire to avoid what caused it. The result was just what the Occupation authorities desired: a potentially powerful adversary—the French citizen and patriot—was intimidated, frustrated, and disheartened. But not everyone was willing to stand silently in line.

Chapter Six

‹›⇒◦⇐‹›

The Dilemmas of Resistance

In war as in peace, the last word goes to those who never surrender.

— *Georges Clemenceau*[1]

Quoi faire?

In July of 1940, not long after the arrival of the first German troops in Paris, a mimeographed flyer was stuffed into apartment mailboxes, slid under doors, and placed on café chairs. Created by Jean Texcier, a journalist from Normandy, "Tips for the Occupied" was one of the earliest signs of French resistance to the foreign occupier. These ironic suggestions introduced some of the formative themes of the Occupation just as the German bureaucracy was eagerly setting it up. Texcier lists thirty-three *conseils,* or tips. Among them:

• Street vendors offer them [German soldiers] maps of Paris and conversation manuals; tour buses unload waves of them in front of Notre-Dame and the Panthéon; each one of them has a little camera screwed to his eye. Don't be fooled: they are not tourists.

• They are conquerors. Be polite to them. But do not, to be friendly, exceed this correct behavior. Don't hurry [to accommodate them]. In the end, they will not, in any case, reciprocate.

• If one of them addresses you in German, act confused and continue on your way.

• If he addresses you in French, you are not obliged to show him the way. He's not your traveling companion.

• If, in the café or restaurant, he tries to start a conversation, make him understand, politely, that what he has to say does not interest you.

• If he asks you for a light, offer your cigarette. Never in human history has one refused a light, even to the most traditional enemy. . . .

• The guy you buy your suspenders from has decided to put a sign on his shop: MAN SPRICHT DEUTSCH (we speak German). Go to another shop, even if he doesn't speak the language of Goethe. . . .

• Show an elegant indifference, but don't let your anger diminish. It will eventually come in handy. . . .

• You complain because they order you to be home by 9:00 p.m. on the dot. You are so naive; you didn't realize that it's so you can listen to English radio? . . .

• You won't find copies of these tips at your local bookshop. Most likely, you only have a single copy and want to keep it. So make copies for your friends, who will make copies, too. This will be a good occupation for the occupied.[2]

Texcier had intuited early that resistance did not have to be violent, that standing against the occupier did not require a grenade in one's hand. The flyer wittily and temporarily answered the question "Quoi faire?" What to do? What is the protocol for daily living in a city occupied by a formidable and arrogantly victorious enemy? The massively defeated French found themselves in a quandary. Had not their government signed an armistice with the Germans? Had not a war hero, the estimable Maréchal Philippe Pétain, become chef de l'État français? Were not the Germans acting "correctly," at least now, at least toward the average French person? Of course it was a bit galling that German signs were popping up all over Paris, that certain avenues and boulevards were closed, that private automobiles had been requisitioned, that a palpable sense of entitlement was emanating from the thousands of German soldiers and bureaucrats assigned to the city. But most Parisians believed that to be a temporary price of defeat once the fighting and bombing had stopped. Texcier had captured the mood of the moment: be polite but unwelcoming; the Germans were not tourists, but they would be leaving soon. No one dreamed in midsummer of 1940 that more than 1,500 days would pass before Parisians would be free of their hereditary enemy.

French resistance against the Nazis has been asked to serve crucial functions in that nation's collective memory. After the liberation of the country, the myth that a large majority of the French population from the beginning actively had opposed the Occupation was important in tamping down serious civil disorder, as the political right and left once again fought for control of a new government. The myth was also necessary to salve national pride over the breakthrough defeat of 1940 and in order to earn a place at the table with the European Allied powers—the USSR, the United States, and Great Britain—as they decided the fate of postwar Europe. In fact, this myth served to postpone for a quarter of a century deeper analyses of how easily France had been beaten and how feckless had been the nation's reaction to German authority, especially between 1940 and early 1943. Finally, the myth of a universal resistance was important to France's idea of itself as a beacon for human liberty and as an example of the courage one needed in the face of hideous political ideologies.[3]

French historians continue to tie themselves in knots as they work to define and explain the Resistance. They parse the term itself, arguing about when the small r became a capital R. They use anthropological, psychological, and cultural methods to identify and categorize varieties of opposition to the presence of victorious Germans on French soil. They struggle over the antithesis of resistance: is it cooperation, appeasement, acceptance, accommodation, collaboration, or, worse, treason? Is resistance a moral or a political choice? Could one not resist in good conscience? Is nonviolent resistance really resistance? The historical and popular narratives surrounding these questions are complex, gripping—tortured, even—often misleading, and sometimes mendacious. Add to this the fact that many *résistants* were not French citizens but immigrants, often Jewish, and that saving Jews was not a stated aim of "official" resistance organizations, and the story becomes even more complicated and blurred.★ [4]

One recent French historian has meticulously analyzed how long it took for the idea of the Resistance to take hold in France. Public opinion moved slowly from a comfortable, benign belief in the leadership of Maréchal Pétain, even with early evidence that his political colleagues were anti-Semitic, anti-leftist, and even pro-fascist. His revered persona obfuscated political distractions, at least for the first year or so of the Occupation. What resistance there was, especially in the Unoccupied Zone (that part of central and southern France still controlled by the Vichy regime), was limited to a propaganda campaign to keep up French morale:

> The power of the myth of Pétain in that part of France that remained "free" [that is, unoccupied] limited the Resistance to the use of propaganda [instead of force]. Before dreaming of fighting again, they had to convince a public largely comfortable with defeatism and *attentisme* [waiting it out]. Success in this direction was slow to come.[5]

To judge, even today, can lead to ethical headaches. We must always keep in mind that we know the outcome of the Second World War; our judgments are influenced by that reassuring knowledge. No such comfort was available to those faced with the devastating fact of massive defeat and military occupation.

Other historians have argued that the term *resistance* has entirely different connotations when applied to different parts of occupied Europe. Writes Jean-Pierre Azéma:

★ I have endeavored to capitalize "resistance" whenever the term refers to the organized, quasimilitary opposition to the Occupation by French irregulars. I do not capitalize it when I am referring to the concept itself or to those who were not part of a formally recognized group. Many of the sources I cite do not make these distinctions, and, indeed, I occasionally slip up, too.

Given that the Nazi occupation is founded on a racist as well as an imperialist ideology, the logic of occupation in western Europe diverged from that of the east. In the part of Europe peopled by Slavs, the conqueror not only annexed but expulsed, colonized, and exterminated those it considered subhuman: resistance became a vital imperative. In the west... resistance was not seen as a means of surviving.... One could "accommodate," and many did.[6]

Using German terms, Azéma argues for the difference between actively, often violently, "withstanding" or "standing against" a foreign host (*Widerstand*) and quietly maintaining a state of nonacceptance, of "resisting"—that is, refusing to concede to the fact of and even ignoring the German presence (*Resistenz*).[7] To explain how exquisite some of these distinctions can be would take us further from our subject—resistance in Paris—but it is necessary to be aware of how important the concept was and continues to be to French identity.

Perhaps the origins of this complexity began in the radio war that occurred in June and July of 1940 between two French military men, an upstart "temporary" general (*général à titre temporaire*) speaking on the BBC from London and a venerable, widely respected Maréchal de France (the highest military rank) speaking from Bordeaux and later from Vichy. These speeches, or *appels* (calls to action), introduced the three major terms that would come to define this debate during and after the war: *résistance, occupation,* and *collaboration.* The speakers were, of course, the relatively unknown fifty-nine-year-old Charles de Gaulle (he had been promoted to brigadier general during the brief Battle of France and would later be demoted and cashiered by the Vichy government, although he would continue to use the title of general) and Maréchal Philippe Pétain. One of the earliest uses of the term *resistance* had entered official parlance when Churchill wondered aloud after Dunkirk if there would be anyone left in France to "resist." Then, in his famous national allocution of June 17, 1940, after he had hastily called for armistice talks, Pétain himself, assuming authority over a defeated France, used the term: "Certain of the affection of our admirable army, which still struggles with a heroism worthy of its long military traditions against an enemy superior both in numbers and in arms; confident that by its magnificent resistance [that army] has fulfilled its obligations toward our allies,... it is with a deep sorrow that I tell you today that the fight must end."[8] Of course the concept has an entirely different meaning in Pétain's discourse from the one it will later take on, but it is interesting that a day later, in his rapid radio response, the famous "Appel du 18 juin," de Gaulle picked up the word: "Whatever may happen, the flame of French resistance must not go out; it shall not go out." And four days later, in another BBC address, without using the term specifically, he reiterates: "Honor, common sense, patriotism demand that all free Frenchmen continue the struggle wherever they are and however they might."[9]

Punctilious analysts of de Gaulle's speeches and of his politics in these early days of a Free France differ on what he was calling for. Did "free Frenchmen" refer to those who were in the empire's colonies or abroad rather than to those already under the yoke of the Germans? Or did the term refer to *all* French who refused to accept German domination, within and without France? The reason this question arises is that de Gaulle, throughout his four years in exile, harbored a very conflicted view of "internal resistance," that is, of the anti-German activities of organizations and individuals within France. It would take him almost three years, until mid-1943, to bring most of those independent resistance groups under his bureaucratic command. His greatest fear was that the best organized of them all, the French Communist Party, would offer strong political alternatives to his already developing vision of postwar France. De Gaulle's anti-Communism was not ambivalent; the organizational and ideological strength of the French Communists, especially after Hitler invaded the USSR in June of 1941, would preoccupy him until and after the end of the war.

One other point should be made about the reputation of French resistance. Overwhelming attention by journalists and military historians—both then and later—to the June 1944 Normandy invasion helped to elevate the idea that there was a powerful secret army at work in France during most of the Occupation.* It can be argued that the Resistance was probably never as effective as it was in those few hours and days preceding and immediately following the Allied invasion. Indeed, Operation Overlord needed every scant advantage it could find, and Eisenhower made canny use of the armed and unarmed units in France to help disrupt German response to his massive invasion, one that could well have been stymied or pushed back into the Channel several times before July of 1944. In fact, Ike was quoted widely as estimating that the war had been shortened by two months because of the French resistance fighters. In his postwar memoir, *Crusade in Europe,* he wrote: "Throughout France the Resistance had been of inestimable value in the campaign. Without their great assistance the liberation of France would have consumed a much longer time and meant greater losses to ourselves."[10] But that estimable success was an anomaly; for the most part, the intra-France resistance of the years 1940–44 definitely harassed, but was in no way permanently detrimental to, the Occupying forces, either in northern France or, after the Wehrmacht occupied it in November of 1942, the southern part of the country. As one of our best historians of both the resistance and the Resistance, Matthew Cobb, writes: "For most of the war, the vast majority of the French did little or nothing to oppose Vichy and the Occupation....Less than two per cent of the population—at most 500,000 people—were involved in the Resistance in one way or another."[11] On one hand this could seem a rather significant number (out of a population of about thirty-eight million), especially if it had been an organized, deftly led force of armed and unarmed men and women. But it wasn't. This number includes independent, often individual, actions during almost five years of the Occupation, supported by some French citizens but also criticized by many of them as well. Resistance attacks brought reprisals, horrible ones, prompting the Free French government to warn from London

---

* In fact, until 1944, the Free French themselves referred to the combination of guerrillas and nonviolent members of resistance movements as *une armée secrète,* changing the name later to Forces françaises de l'Intérieur (the FFI, or Fifis).

that disorganization, lack of coordination, and the emphasis on only short-term goals could be detrimental to the central purpose of liberating France.

De Gaulle, himself an army man, distrusted the independence and freewheeling nature of resistance groups while recognizing that they did have some positive effect on the morale of a people still recovering from the humiliations of 1940. Without a doubt, there was a strong, courageous, and tenacious minority who did resist. About one hundred thousand men and women whom the Germans and the Vichy government designated as "terrorists" may have died—in battles, in camps, or as a result of executions—during the war, but the public was decidedly split over the efficacy of their actions and was often angry at their valiant but frequently foolhardy deeds.[12] Toward the end of the war, as the Germans were slowly retreating through France toward Germany, the audacity and cunning of the so-called *maquis* (the guerrillas who lived off the land) caused apprehension among ordinary German soldiers and often brought brutal reprisals.★ Yet the Germans and their Vichy allies had been very effective in keeping the various resistance organizations at bay throughout the Occupation; their intelligence services, relying heavily on the French themselves to denounce their fellow citizens, were remarkably successful.

Resistant Paris

To limit discussions of moral and violent resistance to the Occupier to its effectiveness at undermining the German war machine misses an

---

★ The best known of these reprisals was the massacre in June of 1944 of almost all the residents of Oradour-sur-Glane, in south-central France, and the destruction of the village itself. Das Reich, a division of SS soldiers rushing north to Normandy after the D-day invasion, reacted to suspected Resistance actions by rounding up, mowing down, and burning alive 642 men, women, and children; only five inhabitants escaped to tell the story. The new town was not rebuilt on the site of the martyred one but next to it; the destroyed village stands today as an official state monument to victims of Nazi war crimes.

important point: the decisions and actions taken by French men and French women, and by new immigrants, against the Occupation (especially of Paris) did keep the Reich and their Vichy allies on the alert and did send a message to the world that Paris was not being benignly held prisoner. Everything from whistling at Germans while they marched in step to printing and distributing dozens of anti-Nazi tracts to throwing grenades into German crowds to assassination: these actions, though often uncoordinated, created an atmosphere of tension and a sense that one's life was not totally in thrall.

Roger Langeron was concerned enough about the possibility of a violent resistance to the arrival of German soldiers to warn his men to be especially alert. As chief of police, he feared that hotheads would set off a merciless response from an overconfident German army. But the exodus of May and June, 1940, had cleared Paris of three-quarters of its inhabitants, and early summer was a time when the schools were closed. The doldrums of the season did the rest. The Germans found a quiescent, even polite population, and the only reactions they had to parry were an occasional rude remark or pointed stare. Until the early fall of 1940, all seemed in order. By October, though, Paris had regained a good deal of its population and some of its élan, and a palpable feistiness stirred its inhabitants. The shock of seeing Germans, in uniform and in mufti, walking casually or marching confidently throughout the city's arteries began to fade, and resentment began to build. On public holidays, an occasional French flag could be seen or a whistled "La Marseillaise" heard. At first the Germans took these mild expressions of resistance to their presence calmly; one report sent back to Berlin even mentioned that in general the French were, in these first few months, "correct," "loyal," and "courteous."[13] Soon, though, the strain began to tell. Unable to ignore these scattered but recurrent protests (they correctly intuited that small signs of disrespect could presage a more vigorous resistance), the MBF, the German military administration of Paris, demanded that Chief Langeron put a stop to the impudent practices of the mostly young Parisians who mocked their occupiers. Otherwise, they threatened, there would be strong repercussions.

But this was easier ordered than done. The Wehrmacht was not a police force, and its generals resented having to keep civil order in Paris while having to maintain military preparedness.[14] They increasingly relied on—and put enormous pressure on—the Parisian police department (which on paper reported to the Vichy minister of defense but which had significant independence from the central government). Soon these police officials, as well as mayors and prefects, were receiving so many arbitrary, unpredictable, nervous, and furious phone calls from German officials that they asked collectively in mid-1941 for more formal, less idiosyncratic requests. At the same time, increased demands were coming down to arrest Jews, find escaped prisoners, ferret out downed Allied pilots, check out letters of denunciation, and investigate minor acts of sabotage. There is no doubt that many in the French police force responded with assiduousness, even eagerly. The Germans remained suspicious that French efforts at controlling the intransigence of their compatriots were not as vigorous as they should be; that there were Gaullist and Communist moles throughout the force (indeed there were) and that the bureaucracy's pursuit of Jews was unenthusiastic. The apprehensiveness shared by both the Vichy police and the Germans grew in intensity just at a time when the Germans needed complete and enthusiastic cooperation: the invasion of the USSR in June of 1941 had drawn the best-trained and youngest soldiers from France to the east. As a result, manpower had to be husbanded, and excessive demands were placed on the French authorities to do the repressive work of an occupying force. So even though there was no formal resistance early in the Occupation of Paris, individual acts of disrespect, insolence, and rudeness were taking their toll on *Zusammenarbeit* (working together—the German version of "collaboration").

As early as the fall of 1940, the first organized team of Parisian resisters was created among the curators and administrators of the Musée de l'Homme, the anthropological and natural history museum situated on Trocadéro Hill, site of the 1937 international exposition, overlooking the Eiffel Tower. They were especially astute about publishing and distributing anti-Vichy and anti-German tracts, including five numbers of a little paper named *Résistance*. These tracts called on French patriotism to encourage resistance against the Occupier; they also included news of the war gathered from English and Swiss radio stations broadcasting in France. They were successful at helping downed pilots escape back to Great Britain—forging papers, lodging them with sympathizers, and passing them beyond borders. But within a few months, a French spy in their midst would denounce the group; its members were arrested, and eventually executed in early 1942.

De Gaulle's June 18, 1940, appeal had little military or political impact, but it did give those young people in France, especially in Paris, a name to throw up on the walls, a name to pit against those of Hitler and Pétain. Most French might barely have heard of de Gaulle, but nevertheless they began to adopt him as a symbol of a nascent French resurgence against the Germans and their Vichy lackeys. By early 1941, his was almost a household name, especially in Paris. Soon the words *Vive de Gaulle* and depictions of his adopted symbol, the two-barred Cross of Lorraine, began appearing insolently on Parisian doors, inside public urinals, and on Parisian sidewalks. Little by little, the upstart general was, mainly through the force of his amazing will, becoming the symbol of resistance throughout France and its colonies. For his part, Churchill found de Gaulle impressive though obdurate, but he had nowhere else to turn for a French leader who might keep the fight alive in the French empire. Roosevelt's distrust of de Gaulle was even deeper; FDR persisted until his death in seeing him as a right-wing general only slightly less offensive than his former Vichy colleagues.

In chapter 3, we learned of the only major public demonstration that occurred in Paris during the Occupation: the manifestation on the Champs-Élysées on November 11, 1940, Armistice Day. Other, smaller "spontaneous" marches and gatherings were held throughout France, but they were carefully monitored and controlled. Hundreds of these protests were patronizingly called "marches by housewives" and were held in opposition to the cost of and scarcity of food. The authorities were concerned that such expressions of frustration could turn into

De Gaulle's Cross of Lorraine. *(© Roger-Viollet / The Image Works)*

general opposition, and, sure enough, some, particularly those in large cities, were actually organized by resistance groups, especially the Communists. One was planned in mid-1943, on Paris's Left Bank, near the Place Denfert-Rochereau. There stood a huge grocery store, part of the popular chain Félix Potin, with as many shelves empty as full. Appearing to lead a "spontaneous" event (almost like today's flash mobs), Lise Ricol-London jumped onto a trestle table just as the store's doors opened. Several accomplices threw hundreds of leaflets into the air as she called out to frustrated Parisian housewives:

> The Occupation, with its cortege of misfortunes, restrictions, [and] crimes, has lasted long enough!... It is time to act! The French must refuse to work for the German war machine. By so doing they expose their lives and those of their families to Allied bombing.... Women! Stop your husbands, your sons from going to work in Germany. Help them hide, to escape to the country-side, where they can use their hands.... It is the moment to begin

an armed struggle against the *Boches* [i.e., "Krauts"] in order to boot them from the country. The Second Front will soon arrive. Liberation approaches! *Vive la Résistance, vive la France!*[15]

Although she was attacked by Potin salesmen and others, Lise managed to escape the police. But she left behind evidence of a fiercely patriotic, and fiercely feminine, Parisian resistance, one that would grow slowly during the final eighteen months of the Occupation.

Resistance, especially this sort of hit-and-run strategy, is much easier in a city than in rural areas. Cities are, as Hitler and his cohort recognized, primed to stymie a rigid system of controls. As we have seen and will see, the metropolis offers many boons to those who would resist authority. First is the gift of anonymity. Strangers in cities are not immediately noticed; neighbors may be likely to pick out aliens, but the city provides so many covers for an individual that he or she can "pass," often with audacity. There are also many places to hide in a city, many shortcuts, hidden and public, that allow an individual to escape quickly when pursued. We have already seen how porous apartment buildings can be. The subway system—in fact, all public transportation—provides secure ways to lose oneself and one's pursuers. But the advantages of moving in a crowd, of jumping on and off transportation, outweigh the dangers of being trapped in a dead end when being checked or pursued. In addition, an old European city such as Paris is a labyrinth of streets, alleys, and byways, many unknown to foreigners no matter how carefully they study Michelin maps and Baedeker guides. And the capital offered a maze of sewers, Métro tunnels, and abandoned quarries that provided the same sense of protection as a countryside's forests, ravines, and mountains do.

Paris, too, was dotted with many very public sites—such as cemeteries, large churches, flea markets, parks, river quays, marketplaces, large restaurants, and cafés—that could all serve as private meeting places for not-so-innocuous conversations. As well, the demographics and social personalities of neighborhoods can provide a sense of solidarity eminently useful to those on the run or seeking refuge.

The city itself has many entrances and exits: train stations, ports, and highways. The Germans did try to build barriers and controls to check vehicles at all the *portes* (major entrances) of Paris, but alternate routes were quickly and cunningly found. The Seine, which divides Paris, was a major resource for those who would escape the police; passengers could hide on barges as they glided through the city or be deposited at urban ports along with the cargo. Paris is a small city, about thirty-four square miles (not including its two large forested parks, the Bois de Boulogne and Bois de Vincennes), and can easily be traversed on foot in a day, north to south or east to west. This would seem an advantage to the Occupier, but with a population of about two million, easy access to the suburbs, and—despite Haussmann's great renovations of the late nineteenth century—a labyrinthine street layout, it was not a metropolis conducive to mass surveillance. It had a very large student population and an equally large immigrant population, both of them sympathetic to resistance or resentment toward an occupying army. This "shadow" citizenry, themselves anxious about discovery, served often as protective coloration for others hiding from the authorities. As a result, cells of resistance began to develop almost immediately once the fact that Germans were to be in Paris for a long time began to percolate through its inhabitants' psyches.

The mimeographed tract was an early sign of nonviolent resistance. By the end of the Occupation, dozens of these one-to-four-page "newspapers" had appeared on the streets of Paris. Their distribution was only one challenge for their editors. First, paper had to be found, and large amounts of it had to be hidden from authorities who were already seeking to control its allocation. Virgin stencils were priceless, and because they could effectively produce only a few hundred copies, they had to be replenished constantly. Most important, mimeograph (or *ronéotype*) machines and printing presses had to be "borrowed" or stolen and moved from safe house to safe house. The noise associated with printing machines was another problem; isolated apartments and the basements of shops and apartment houses were used, but they were searched with increasing attention by the authorities. One prominent editor hid a small printing press in his apartment; soon he heard that he had been denounced, so he and a friend dismantled it and put its pieces in their pockets and briefcases. Making several trips to the Seine, they threw the pieces into the fast-flowing river. When the Gestapo arrived, there was no press, no sign of ink or stencils, and no ink on the hands of the editor or his friends. They nonetheless arrested the printer and questioned him for several days before he admitted that he had thrown the infernal machine into Paris's river. At that confession, surprisingly, the police let him return home. It was as if they were more afraid of a wandering printing press than of the man who had wanted to use it.

Some writers wanted to do more than print tracts and news sheets with names like *Pantagruel, Résistance,* and *Valmy* (site of a great victory over the Prussians in 1792). One of them was Jean Bruller (a.k.a. Vercors). Bruller, as noted earlier, was the author and publisher of *Le Silence de la mer (The Silence of the Sea)*, perhaps the best fiction ever written about passive resistance. To publish a hundred-page story was going to take more than a mimeograph machine; Bruller needed a printing press. He first sought out a printer who had access to paper, but he did not want to print the small book. Once he had a commitment for the paper, enough for three hundred copies, Bruller inquired about other printers who might help. His supplier asked him to return in eight days. Bruller was not too concerned, because the manuscript was still in his hands and he could always claim, if denounced, that he was going to use the paper for printing something innocuous. Eight days passed; he returned to the first printer. "I've found a press for you. Let's go," said his new collaborator. Soon Bruller found himself outside Paris's largest hospital complex, the Pitié-Salpêtrière, on the Left Bank, just southeast of the Gare d'Austerlitz. This hospital was then and had been for a century one of the most respected in Europe.*

---

* At the end of the nineteenth century, it was known especially for its neurological institute, the place where Jean-Martin Charcot, the creator of modern psychiatric research, practiced and where Freud studied as a young man. It is known today as the hospital in which Princess Diana died after being rushed there from her accident, which took place farther west, on the Seine *autoroute*. Josephine Baker also died there of a stroke in 1975.

The Germans, knowing a good thing when they found it, had already appropriated the Salpêtrière as a major emergency and convalescent hospital for their military. Wehrmacht banners and the German swastika were everywhere evident when Bruller arrived; dozens of uniformed German officials were scurrying through the campus. What are we doing here? the author must have wondered. But just across the street was a small printing shop where invitations, announcements, and calling cards were produced. Its clackety-clack activity was barely heard over the constant comings and goings of German ambulances and sirens, and it was here where the most famous story to come out of Occupied Paris was printed. Bruller still had to find glue and cardboard for the book's covers and men and women to sew together the printed fascicles. He did. The result was the first book published by a clandestine press in Paris, a press he named Éditions de Minuit (Midnight Publications), which would go on to publish about twenty-five works during the Occupation. After the war, it would publish the writings of luminaries such as Samuel Beckett, Marguerite Duras, Alain Robbe-Grillet, and others. (It continues to publish today.)

But some felt that more aggressive measures should be taken against the Occupier. On a hot August day in 1941, in the Barbès-Rochechouart Métro stop, not far from the Gare du Nord, a group of young partisans were trying to be inconspicuous while waiting—not for a train but for a German military officer, any German officer. Finally a naval ensign, dressed in the whites of the Kriegsmarine, arrived, and as a train pulled in and came to rest he started to step into the center, first-class car, reserved for him and his companions. As he placed his foot on the threshold of the car, a twenty-two-year-old Frenchman—who would be later known all over Paris as Fabien (the code name of Pierre Georges) and, subsequently, as Colonel Fabien, leader of the Resistance—pulled out a pistol and fired two shots into the back and head of the young officer, Alfons Moser.* Both names would soon be known throughout Paris. Moser was the first German officer to be shot

---

* The young French "colonel" would be killed in a mine-clearing accident in Alsace-Lorraine in 1945.

publicly, in daylight, in France, and with his killing resistance against the Occupation had taken a decisive turn: the result would be a much more oppressive surveillance in the large cities of the Unoccupied Zone and more vigorous punishment, including executions of hostages, meted out by the Germans.

Such violence against the Germans became almost commonplace beginning in 1942. A *résistant* remembers a late spring night, probably that year, along the Quai d'Orsay, on the Left Bank. This was the upper-class area near the Ministry of Foreign Affairs where many German officers worked diligently at keeping the city calm. Undiscovered, two young men had been walking along the quay at the same time for a week, trying to discern a pattern of comings and goings as the Germans left their offices for their apartments or hotel rooms. On this evening, the two were sauntering along, glancing from time to time at the river, talking loudly, nonconspiratorially. Their mission: to obtain a firearm, the most precious and rarest possession of any resistance group. Soon, as they had expected, they heard the assertive sound of a booted officer coming up behind them. They kept walking beside the swift-moving river. The boots approached and then passed them. Pulling a blackjack and a hammer from their pockets, they leaped on the unsuspecting officer, beat him down, took his pistol and two ammo magazines, pocketed them, and ran down a side street, not stopping until they were blocks away. It would be, if they were lucky, hours before the German's body—for he must have died from the double blows—would be found.

Such events had unpredictable and predictable consequences. One never knew how the German authorities would react. Would they shoot a dozen hostages? Would they change the curfew? Would they close down the neighborhood in which the attack had occurred and arrest all Jews and immigrants they could find in a roundup? For the sake of one pistol, an entire area and the many lives within it might be disrupted. On the other hand, the Germans would feel more vulnerable, less willing to go out alone when armed and in uniform. Not a few Parisians would be pleased that such efforts, though small in the scheme of major events, would remind the Occupiers that they were never going to be comfortable in the City of Light. Weighing ethically and practically the consequences of violent action became common practice as the war dragged on.

Bébés Terroristes

Harrassment of the Germans began almost the day they arrived. For the most part, the perpetrators—pacifists, anti-fascists, pro-Communists, Catholics, Jews—were in their teens or early twenties. This makes sense in a way, since youth do not have jobs to protect or families to provide for. The German-Soviet Pact, signed in 1939, right before Hitler attacked Poland, had hamstrung the most organized anti-fascist political group, the French Communist Party.* All members of the party had strict instructions not to attack the Germans, which gave the latter a year in which to set up an effective policing strategy with their Vichy allies and to concentrate on other challenges to their new order. By the late fall of 1940, de Gaulle's message—about "continuing the struggle" and reminding the French that a battle may have been lost but the war continued—was getting through, especially to the most ungovernable of Parisian residents, high school and university students. The graffiti that promptly appeared on the walls, the whistling and hooting at German soldiers, the papers and tracts that were published and distributed—these activities were almost all the work of adolescent Parisians. Beginning in the winter of 1940–41, the first "battle" was initiated between the Occupier and Parisians: the Germans referred to it as the *V-aktion;* the French as "the war of the *V*s." Scrawled in chalk over walls, café chairs and tables, official posters, Wehrmacht directional signs, and especially on Métro walls—indeed, on almost any flat surface—were *V*s for *victoire,* often appearing with de Gaulle's

---

* This was an especially trying time for the party, founded in France in 1920. It had gained support during the 1920s and early 1930s and was an important and an active participant in the leftist *Front populaire* government (1936). Many of its members had gone to Spain to fight alongside the Republicans against Franco's coup d'état. They were well organized, many with battle experience, but Stalin's Machiavellian pact with Hitler had sidelined them during the early days of the Occupation.

Cross of Lorraine. German propaganda offices immediately appropriated the angular letter as an abbreviation of *Victoria,* a sign of German success on all fronts. (The Germans appropriated the Latin term, since "victory" in their language, *Sieg,* begins with an *S.*)

As Adolf Hitler looked down on Paris from his perch on Montmartre during his brief visit in June of 1940, he would have seen a large casernlike building to his right, visible in photographs of that moment. That structure would be one of the most vibrant centers of resistance during his army's occupation of the city: it was the Lycée Rollin. With more than two thousand young male students, including those in middle school (*collégiens*) and high school (*lycéens*), it was one of the largest schools in Paris,* located in a neighborhood filled with the "degenerates" that Nazi propaganda had been fulminating against for almost a decade:

Almost a third of the inhabitants were of foreign extraction: Poles, Ukrainians, Russians, Romanians, Armenians, North African Arabs, and Berbers...Among the refugees, the Jewish community from eastern Europe was the largest. Paris was a sort of "new Jerusalem." As a consequence of the dismantling of the Ottoman Empire, Sephardic merchants from Turkey and Greece had established themselves in Montmartre. Tailors, furriers, cloth merchants had created the Saint-Pierre market at the base of Sacré Coeur, just a few meters from the Lycée Rollin. German Jews began to arrive in the early thirties.[16]

Nevertheless, thousands of German soldiers visited the nearby Boulevard de Clichy, Place Pigalle, and Rue Lepic every weekend for four years, so the youngsters of the neighborhoods knew well and close up the *haricots verts* (green beans).

The political complexion of the Lycée Rollin ranged politically

---

* Its sister lycée for girls, Jules-Ferry (where the diarist Berthe Auroy had taught), was a few blocks away. The kids would meet midway, on the Boulevard de Clichy, for their rendezvous.

from the right to the left, but it earnestly leaned more leftward. The politicization of the student body, and of many of the one hundred or so professors, had begun well before the defeat of 1940 and the Occupation itself. The 1930s in Paris had seen street riots between supporters of neo-fascism, and the right in general, and young Communists and Socialists, especially after the election, in 1936, of the first leftist government since the nineteenth century, the *Front populaire,* led by the Jewish politician Léon Blum. And then there had been the Spanish Civil War, between the elected Republicans and the right-wing rebel Nationalists under Francisco Franco, a war that divided French political opinion deeply. When asked when she had joined the French resistance, one young Frenchwoman answered:

In 1937, when I saw on the walls of Paris photos of children massacred by Nazi aviators; when my parents took into their home little Pilar, five years old, whose parents had been killed in Bilbao and who hid under a table whenever she heard a plane over Paris. We were a group of young *lycéens,* and we founded Lycéens de Paris, an anti-fascist movement that demonstrated against the French government's refusal to come to the aid of the Republicans.... Our entry into the Resistance was for us the consequence of this earlier engagement. The same struggle was continuing.[17]

The civil war in Spain, which had ended in mid-1939, had sent thousands of Republican refugees to France. Many of them were former fighters, and they provided a ready-made cadre for military resistance to authority. They had experience in the preparation and distribution of propaganda, in sabotage, in military excursions, and were adept at forming clandestine networks. Their children wound up in the lycées and universities of Paris. So it was to no one's surprise that the attack on Poland, the defeat of the Allied armies in 1940, and the massive occupation of France's capital would serve as motivation for these youngsters to let the Germans know that they were not welcome in Paris. And they were often encouraged by the outspokenness and courage of their professors. Both the Germans and the Vichyists kept a close watch on these youngsters.

The Lycée Rollin was the only high school to change its name after the war; it is now known as the Lycée Jacques-Decour, the nom de guerre of a teacher of German, Daniel Decourdemanche. One day, as his students prepared for their professor's arrival in the classroom, the door opened, and in walked the school's principal. The students stood immediately. The room, filled with fourteen- and fifteen-year-old boys, was still; the principal almost never visited classrooms in session. One alumnus remembers what happened next:

> The principal stood on the podium. Gravely, a piece of paper in his hand, he told us: "Your German professor has been executed by the army that occupies our city. He asked me to read this letter to you." Almost seventy years later, I can't remember the exact details, but I do remember their general sense and the letter's last words. He wrote us that when we heard this letter, he, Daniel Decourdemanche, would no longer be alive. That he was dying so that one day we would be free men. The principal slowly folded the letter and, after casting a glance over the whole class, left the room. Our temporary professor had to ask us to be seated. In that class, students had many different political views. Some were Pétainistes, others Gaullists; there was even a collaborationist who, later, would sign up with the Legion of French Volunteers against Bolshevism. Many were just preoccupied with their continuing hunger. Silence followed the principal's remarks. How could that professor, whom we had seen just a few days ago chatting with his colleagues, no longer be alive? For the first time, all of us, in a state of disbelief, were suddenly and forever aware of the horror of war. Amazingly, not one of the students denounced the principal to the authorities! Courageously, he had risked his own life to give us students a lesson in dignity, in patriotism.[18]

Adolescence is a telling filter through which to analyze the Occupation. The unpredictability of adolescent judgment, actions, and responses must be the bane of any authority endeavoring to enforce order and predictability on a populace. A typical narcissism imposes itself on the adolescent, an almost compulsive need to separate oneself from a comfortable environment—an urge, if not a desire, to create a more personal and private world. The result can often devolve into secrecy vis-à-vis one's parents; impatience with curfews and other limitations on time, space, and forms of amusement; and a commensurate disregard for even the most anodyne authority figures. There is a thirst for an attenuation of dependence yet an almost erotic need to form new affective relationships—often quasisecretive—as counterweights to the parental and familial ones weakening. In addition, there is an intellectual awakening, a moving away from the imposed teachings and beliefs of one's parents and mentors, and often a simultaneous search for other, nonparental adults to fill in for those psychologically rejected. This makes adolescents especially susceptible to recruitment for "adult" enterprises. A new confidence in physical energy and ability emerges, too, accompanied by an urge to progress into new public and private spaces. It is no wonder, then, that an urban adolescent, finding himself under the thumb of a foreign occupier, is confused, resentful, and exhilarated all at once—or intermittently.

It was not too long before various organizations began assertively appearing in opposition to the Occupier. Eventually they would be unified under the umbrella of *Forces unies de la jeunesse patriotique.* But before that attempt at unification, the teenagers of occupied France called themselves the *Jeunes chrétiens combattants,* the *Bataillons de la jeunesse,* the *Jeunes protestants patriotes,* the *Fédération des jeunesses communistes,* the *Front patriotique de la jeunesse,* and on and on. There was often tension between these groups and those organized by more mature *résistants,* as the latter felt that lack of coordination, enthusiasm, and independence were detrimental to an organized resistance. Yet the adolescents were everywhere, and they kept up the spirits of those against the Occupation, especially in its early years.

One of the most extraordinary of these youngsters was a boy named Jacques Lusseyran. A student in the prestigious Lycée Louis-le-Grand, situated on the Left Bank near the Collège de France and the Sorbonne, Jacques realized, at the age of sixteen, that unlike his placid parents and their friends he was not ready to acquiesce to this new "normality": "I was no longer a child. My body told me so.... What attracted me and terrified me on the German radio was the fact that it was in the process of destroying my childhood.... To live in the fumes of poison gas on the roads in Abyssinia, at Guernica, on the Ebro front, in Vienna, at Nuremberg, in Munich, the Sudetenland and then Prague. What a prospect!"[19] Jacques's "uneasiness was more intense than the uneasiness of people full grown," so he and a small group of friends began meeting to figure out how they could "resist." The group named themselves the *Volontaires de la Liberté* and selected Jacques as their leader. It was his job to decide who could be trusted to join their group. But Jacques Lusseyran *had been blind since the age of eight.* The confidence that his school chums had in him was based in part on the way that he had handled that handicap as a schoolboy; they were also confident that the Germans would never suspect that a blind boy would be a *chef de la Résistance.*

For almost two years, until they were betrayed by another school chum, the group's membership grew from a dozen to more than five hundred, and at one time Lusseyran could call on five thousand Parisian youngsters to distribute tracts, hide printing presses, compose copy, act as lookouts, and support other resistance groups. The tenacity of this group of youngsters, their clear-eyed belief in liberty, their hatred of the Germans and their acolytes the Vichy supporters, stood as a model for other resistance groups, though as Lusseyran estimates in his memoir: "Four-fifths of the resistance in France was the work of men less than thirty years old."[20] One of the main tasks of this group of youngsters was to encourage those other French citizens too hesitant to take a stand against the Occupation. Lusseyran insisted that his newspaper was not a political document but rather a "way of spreading passive resistance. Most of all we made it clear that there was an active Resistance at work, one that was growing from day to day. [Our membership] was invisible to our readers...The only sign it could give at that stage was our two-page printed sheet."★ [21]

A little-known novel by Roger Boussinot, *Les Guichets du Louvre* (The Louvre's Portals), takes as its subject perhaps the most familiar and despairing event of the Occupation, the massive arrest of Jews on July 16–17, 1942, primarily by French police. Boussinot's autobiographical fiction reminds us that Paris had acquired a new topography for *all* its citizens (not just those especially sensitive to German presence, e.g., Jews and political refugees). A Gentile French student, packing up to return to his home near Bordeaux for summer vacation, learns from a friend on the fringe of the resistance that there will be a roundup of Jews on the Right Bank that very day, the infamous July 16, 1942. His friend suggests that if the young man and others like him were immediately to go to the targeted neighborhoods, they might each save someone by leading him or her to and through the *guichets* (the small gates through which one enters the Louvre complex from the Rue de Rivoli) onto the Pont du Carrousel and then across the river to the Left Bank, which was felt to be safer, less "German," and more open to refugees than the Right Bank. The implication is that the river has demarcated what had become in effect two Cities of Light. Says the narrator: "On July 16, at about 4:00 a.m. in a Paris still asleep, buses with their bluish headlights left barracks, military camps, and depots and, under the curfew, started toward the neighborhoods of Belleville, Saint-Paul, Popincourt, Poissonnière, and the Temple."[22] All these neighborhoods were filled with Jewish families and businesses. Young policemen had been brought into Paris from the provinces to do the dirty work of rounding up Jewish families, and Boussinot depicts them as innocent tourists, visiting Paris for the first time: "The glances of the gendarmes...seemed to see nothing and only lit up when they recognized a public monument: then the kepi-covered heads would almost all lean forward together, trying to catch a glimpse of the top of the

---

★ Jacques Lusseyran was finally arrested in 1943 and sent to Buchenwald. He survived there mainly because of his knowledge of the German language and, strangely enough, his blindness, which separated him from the harsher sections of the camp. He was liberated in 1945.

Eiffel Tower, or the Obelisk, or to follow the passing of the elevated Métro above the trees."[23] Yet as with Hitler's tour that had preceded theirs by two years, their apparently innocent gaze hid a devastating project. Jews were in danger because the French, not the Germans, were on the hunt.

The young student decides, impulsively, to take up his friend's challenge and sets out to cross the river:

> I don't know why, but crossing the Seine was disorienting for me.... From the Latin Quarter to Montparnasse, the Left Bank was as familiar to me as the streets of Bordeaux, or almost, but the Right Bank seemed to me the true capital, immense; I barely knew the big boulevards over there. Alone, immobile under the narrow and cool vault of the Louvre's central portal, I was suddenly aware of a new feeling—of throwing myself into an adventure for which I was not prepared—a feeling of nervousness, of danger, even of anticipated failure.... I am still a bit away from where the roundup was supposed to be taking place, but perhaps because I'm alone, because everything is so quiet, the whole area seems to be a cunning trap, covering the occupied city like a hostile chill.[24]

Once "over the river," he finds a Jewish girl a few years younger than he and saves her from being caught up in the pitiless dragnet. Soon, to avoid capture, the two youths are forced, as they move surreptitiously through a sinister environment, to find new uses for previously innocuous doorways, cafés, stairways, Métro entrances, concierges' loges, shops, and the narrow streets of the Marais.

> It was like a game of cat and mouse that lasted almost three hours in a labyrinth of streets that I did not know and where we often lost our way; in courtyards, rear courtyards, at the entrances, and especially on the staircases of apartment houses, always accompanied by this agonizing sense that we were alone in the world and

that the police were everywhere—but with one advantage: the cats did not know that we were mice.[25]

On that sad day, most of the city's buses (the familiar green-and-cream vehicles Jews had ridden every day to work and back) had been commandeered to take them to the Vélodrome d'Hiver, a massive indoor bicycle-racing track on the Left Bank, and thence to Drancy and other concentration camps near Paris—a very cynical trick. The city's transportation systems are essentially closed to our two protagonists, for the Métro has become dangerous as well, their entrances guarded by the police and used as traps to capture unsuspecting Jewish travelers. So the youths have to walk from the Marais to the Louvre, and with care. They use public subway maps, posted outside stations, to find their way, but these maps are essentially useless for clandestine movement through the city. Ultimately they have to rely on their spontaneous and cunning use of the available spaces of the Parisian streets to make their way eventually to the *guichets* of the Louvre and from there to the Pont du Carrousel, bringing them to the Left Bank and some safety. Despite the fact that they have become emotionally close during their three-hour escapade, the girl decides to turn back, to find her family, and the boy, disappointed, gets on the train that takes him home to Bordeaux. This is a quite remarkable historical novel, one in which the very restrictions that the Germans used to keep people apart provide a nearly erotic atmosphere that inexorably pulls two of them close to each other. The absence of a happy ending only underlines the sorrow that pervaded the city of lovers during the Occupation.

Boussinot did not have an easy time getting his novel published in 1960, fifteen years after the war. In an afterword that he wrote to the 1999 edition, he places the blame for this initial censorship on the sensitivity of French memory. Few wanted to think about the Occupation and its embarrassing moral compromises. Another reason for the hesitancy to publish was the book's ambiguous ending. The Jewish girl decides to return to the Right Bank, to seek succor from the Union générale des Israélites de France (the UGIF), an organization approved by the Vichy government and the German Occupation bureaucracy. We now know that this organization partially served as camouflage for an insidious attempt at separating immigrant Jews from French Jews, and often, purposely or not, served the racial policies of the government. But perhaps more significant to the unofficial censors of Boussinot's work was the response of the unwittingly courageous young Gentile after his offer to accompany the girl to the Left Bank is politely refused: "I said nothing. And yes, I admitted it: let her leave now, go wherever she wanted, and leave me alone. I was tired of the whole thing. Tired of her. Tired of having to decide, to walk, to argue, tired of being afraid. Tired of the heat, of the police, of still being in Paris, of not being comfortable in my own skin. Tired of the Jews.... Don't forget how young we were!"[26] This honest memory would have touched the nerves of French readers in the early 1960s. Being in the underground, even for a day, was not a game. Everyone who made that decision had to consider his career as a student or an employee; he or she had to think of the effect on his or her family. The Germans soon put up posters that warned that any arrested "terrorist" would be responsible for having all male members of his family arrested, deported, or sent to work for the Germans.

One man remembers what it was like to be an adolescent in such a troubling environment:

The reasons for being afraid and of being apprehensive every time we went out into the city were numerous. In the streets, ID checks and roundups were continuous, even more so because we were all old enough to be recruited for the STO [Service du travail obligatoire, the conscription of young men for work in Germany]. Once we put a foot outside, we were at risk of being stopped at any point. To make matters worse, our false documents were so obviously forged that they would barely pass even the most casual scrutiny.[27]

And another is even more succinct:

> Fear never abated; fear for oneself; fear of being denounced, fear of being followed without knowing it, fear that it will be "them" when, at dawn, one hears, or thinks one hears, a door slam shut or someone coming up the stairs. Fear, too, for one's family, from whom, having no address, we received no news and who perhaps had been betrayed and were taken hostage. Fear, finally, of being afraid and of not being able to surmount it.[28]

Such feelings of wanting to do something yet being afraid of painful consequences, meant living in constant anxiety; that is probably why, at the end of his novel, Boussinot's adolescent protagonist, when asked at home in Bordeaux, "What's going on in Paris?" responds: "Nothing."[29] Perhaps best just to lie low and, if one had to confront the authorities, try to forget it.

The Red Poster

The Vichy government and German censors controlled all the official press—daily, weekly, and monthly. Radio signals from London were successfully—but not completely—scrambled, and the strong signals from Radio Paris (the official station) sent continuous and biased information to a populace thirsty for news of any kind. Newsreels emphasized German advances and minimized the results of Russian, British, and American successes. The underground did not have access to these outlets, though the BBC did get on the air for a few minutes every night, and the Allies did drop millions of leaflets across France with messages of hope. Still, many independent and organized resistance groups risked imprisonment and worse to spread a counternarrative. One young Jewish boy would take his six-year-old sister with him all over Paris to distribute tracts that described how Jews were being treated; they passed right before the eyes of their wary enemies. And we have seen how paper, ink, and printing apparatuses were as sought after as arms. The underground groups still were able to print one-page newspapers or tracts in almost a dozen languages in addition to French: Spanish, Polish, Russian, Czech, Armenian, German, Romanian, and Yiddish. Yet the Communist Party believed that louder, more consequential actions would not only enhance their own reputation but also keep up the spirits of an increasingly tired, hungry, and depressed Paris. "Loud" and "consequential" meant violent action, coordinated and effective.

With the Grande Rafle (the Big Roundup) in July of 1942, attitudes changed radically for all those concerned—Germans, Parisian police, Jews (foreign and immigrant), Parisians in general, and resistance groups. We will in the following chapter learn more details of this giant dragnet, but one thing can be said now: the raid not only confirmed that no Jew was safe in Paris, it also made evident to other Parisians that the Nazi racist ideology, and its cynical support by the French police, could no longer be ignored. Finally, it radically changed the more hesitant immigrant resistance groups, who concluded that only force could meet force. A new "generation of anger" among young Jews and their Gentile friends was born overnight. And, at the same time, the costs paid by more aggressive *résistants* could no longer be ignored.

For Parisian passersby reading a garish *affiche rouge* (red poster), pasted everywhere on public walls, some names were almost unpronounceable, and certainly not "French": Fingercwajg, Manouchian, Grzywacz, Wajsbrot. Unlike other posters that listed only the names of those executed by the Germans, this one had photographs of the alleged perpetrators, a first for the German propagandists. Against a dull red background, the poster showed portraits—mug shots, really—of shadowy, solemn, hirsute, "foreign-looking" faces. Also listed were their national origins: Polish, Italian, Hungarian, Armenian, Spanish, Romanian, and French. The bottom third of the sheet was covered with photographs of derailed trains, a bullet-pierced torso, a dead soldier, and a collection of small arms. The poster, printed in red and black, appeared on walls all over France in February of 1944. The terms *Libérateurs?* and *Libérations?* were written in very large fonts, implying that these "jobless bandits," "terrorists," "foreigners," and "criminals"

The Red Poster. *(Mémorial de la Shoah)*

were unworthy of patriotic respect. The propaganda campaign was carefully organized; booklets were liberally distributed along with the posters. The accompanying single-page tract was even blunter than the *affiche*:

HERE'S THE PROOF:

If some Frenchmen pillage, steal, sabotage, and kill...

It is always foreigners who command them.

It is always the unemployed and professional criminals who do the jobs.

It is always Jews who inspire them.

IT IS THE ARMY OF CRIME AGAINST FRANCE!

Banditry is not the expression of a wounded patriotism, it's a
foreign plot against the daily lives of the French and against
the sovereignty of France.

It's an anti-France plot!

It's the world dream of Jewish sadism!

*Strangle it before it strangles you, your wives,
and your children![30]*

Who were these "foreign bandits" who had seemed to unleash all
the paranoid fury of an occupying army and bureacracy that, by late
1943 and early 1944, were realizing that Germany was losing the war?
The so-called Manouchian Group was an armed, Communist-supported
team of urban guerrillas, part of the FTP-MOI (Franc-tireurs et
partisans–main d'oeuvre immigrée, or Irregulars and Partisans–
Immigrant Labor Force), which had been formed from mostly young
Jewish independent operators who had been attacking Germans in
Paris since the fall of 1942.★ The Communist Party had decided that it
would be more effective, and would bring more publicity to their own
anti-German resistance, if these young men—and a few women—
were organized in the manner of a military commando force, or a
small, mobile combat unit.

Over the first six months [of 1943], the teams of the MOI carried
out ninety-two attacks in Paris, which was under especially high
surveillance at the time.... on April 23, grenades were thrown at
a hotel near the Havre-Caumartin Métro station [in the heavily
German-populated 9th arrondissement]; on May 26, a restaurant

---

★ After Germany attacked the USSR in June of 1941, the French Communist Party no
longer felt bound by the German-Soviet Pact of August 1939; in fact, Moscow ordered
their French comrades to set up an armed resistance to the German Occupation of France.
And they were ready and eager to do so.

reserved for German officers was attacked at the Porte d'Asnières...
On May 27 at 7:00 a.m., a grenade was thrown at a German patrol
crossing the Rue de Courcelles...On June 3, on the Rue Mira-
beau...a grenade was tossed at a car carrying officers of the
Kriegsmarine....The months of July, August, and September saw
an upsurge of derailments of trains leaving the Gare de l'Est on
their way to Germany.[31]

Finally, a coup de théâtre: on September 23, a small team managed
to assassinate, in the cozy, German-preferred 16th arrondissement,
General Dr. Julius Ritter, the head in Paris of the hated STO, which
identified and drafted young French men between the ages of eighteen
and twenty-two for forced work in Germany.

The Germans were caught off guard by this surge of violent attacks,
and their troops were more and more demoralized as they watched
"safe" Paris become a site for both discriminate and indiscriminate
attacks against the Occupier. Enormous pressure was put on the French
police, who created their infamous Brigades spéciales—about two
hundred especially xenophobic and anti-Communist officers who volunteered to track down "terrorists" in the streets and neighborhoods of
Paris. This office developed quite sophisticated means of following and
setting up surveillance on suspected members of the underground.
They were patient, even to the point of not stopping some attacks if
they knew that bigger fish were still to be caught. They were experts in
following their suspects, always working in twos and sometimes putting as many as four such teams on the heels of only one *résistant*. They
disguised themselves as postal workers, bus drivers, even priests; one
person caught in their snare reported that the team following him had
even worn yellow stars! Once they arrested their suspects, they used
the most brutal methods of interrogation, often to the embarrassment
of their colleagues in other departments. After the war, many members
of the Brigade spéciale were arrested, tried, found guilty, and put
away for years, if not executed. In just a year, they managed to capture
more than 1,500 young members of the Resistance, severely weakening the MOI.

When the MOI group was finally captured in November of 1943, after having been betrayed from within their ranks, they numbered twenty-three men and one woman. Interrogated and tortured for more than three months, they faced a hurried military trial, were found guilty, and were shot at the Mont-Valérien prison, outside Paris, in February of 1944. The one woman, Golda Bancic, a Romanian, was not allowed to die with her companions but was shipped to Germany, where she was decapitated in May of 1944.

Besides its Armenian leader, Missak Manouchian, perhaps the best known of the *armée du crime* was the Jewish teenager, Tommy Elek. In photos, his boldly blond hair and direct gaze grasp one's attention if only because of the effort made by the photographers to present the group as a bunch of unshaven, darkly hirsute, menacing foreigners.

Tommy Elek. (*Mémorial de la Shoah*)

His mother, Hélène, kept a restaurant on the Rue de la Montagne-Sainte-Geneviève, in the 5th arrondissement, right behind the Panthéon and in the middle of the Latin Quarter. The restaurant, Fer à Cheval (The Horseshoe), was a favorite haunt for Tommy's leftist friends and for students in general—and for the Germans. (The restaurant had three entrances and thus three exits—the Jews, as well as their antagonists the Germans—sought with care residences and places of work with more than one exit, so it was a perfect place for the transfer of weapons, tracts, and so forth.) Hélène knew German (she had been born and raised in Budapest, where German had been a second language for many), so the Germans felt welcome in a restaurant whose proprietor spoke their tongue with such skill. They marveled at how handsome her seventeen-year-old son was, how much he was the perfect example of an Aryan, with his blond hair and blue eyes. Of course they did not know that Tommy had been active in the Communist resistance for about a year. Imagine their surprise when he was arrested along with the rest of the Manouchian Group in November of 1943.

In fact, one of the best-known resistance acts in Paris had been devised and carried out by Tommy before the Manouchian Group brought him under their quasicontrol. He had taken a large book—his father's copy of Marx's *Das Kapital*—carved out its pages, and settled a dynamite bomb into it. He fearlessly took it to the prominent German bookstore Librairie Rive Gauche, on the Place de la Sorbonne. Placing the book on a table, he left and waited to watch it explode through the store's plate-glass window, behind which were displayed works by German and collaborationist authors; an exultant smile creased his young face as customers left, coughing, trying to escape the fire that was raging. The attack was bold and very public; on the other hand, it was an example of what the Communist underground feared most: acts carried out by independent operators that would force the Germans and the French police to be more alert while having little effect on the war machine itself. Still, Tommy's bomb drew much attention to the vulnerability of the Occupation forces in his city.

Hélène's restaurant stayed open until 1943, when she finally had to put up a JEWISH ENTERPRISE sign. In her memoir, Tommy's mother recounts how she came to learn of her son's arrest. Tommy's young brother, Bela, burst breathlessly into their apartment. Tears streaming down his face, all he could say was

"Tommy, Tommy."

"What about Tommy, Bela? What about him?!"

Sobbing, he stammered: "They've put up a poster every-where...with Tommy on it...and Joseph [Boczov, Elek's friend and fellow *résistant*]...I saw it in the Métro, but here, too, in the street, they are everywhere.... They are all there, Maman...with horrible photos, cadavers, derailed trains.... For Tommy they've written ELEK, HUNGARIAN JEW, EIGHT DERAILMENTS.... They call them the army of crime."[32]

Hélène Elek knew that Tommy's fate was sealed, that he was dead or soon would be. She ran down her building's stairs and outside to see the fateful poster for herself.

Tommy Elek's last notes to his family, sent via the concierges of the buildings in which he had been hiding, were written a few hours before he was shot at Mont-Valérien in February of 1944. The poignant brevity of the notes, written by a barely nineteen-year-old youth, speaks not only to his courage but also to his confidence that he will have died for something larger than himself:

Monday 21/2/44

Dear Madame Verrier,

I am sending this letter of adieu to you in the hope that you will one day find my family again. If you see them one day, tell them that I did not suffer and that I died without suffering, thinking a great deal of them and especially of my brothers, who will have a happier youth than mine. I die, but I insist [they] live, for we will all be together again one day. Good-bye; may my memory remain in the hearts of those who knew me. May all my friends live, and my last wish is that they not be sad about my fate, for I die so that they will always live happily. Good-bye, and may life be sweet for you.

Tommy Elek[33]

In a second, even shorter letter to his friends, again addressed in care of a concierge (probably to avoid giving away addresses), he writes, again with laconic sensitiveness:

Dear friends,

I write you this letter of adieu to confirm, if need be, that I was pure in all my intentions. I don't have time here to write long, empty phrases. All I have to say to you is that you mustn't be sad, but rather happy, for better days are soon to come [*car pour vous (viennent) les lendemains qui chantent,* a very clear Communist innuendo]. Adieu; keep me in your hearts, and speak about me sometimes to your children.

Thomas Elek[34]

Hélène Elek was an extraordinary mother. She knew from the time he was sixteen that her elder son was resisting the presence of the Germans in Paris. She had worried but decided that the more she helped him and his leftist friends the more control she could have over his actions. Like any young teenager, Tommy was impulsive, naive, and often incorrigible, and his mother's presence had given him some stability. He was proud of his Jewishness. Wrote Hélène: "Thomas knew perfectly that he was Jewish. He had learned it by looking at his thing. He was circumcised; I had had it done when we were in Hungary. Not to be religious, but because I thought it was healthier. And then, when he was five, he was in kindergarten in Budapest, and he had to announce his religion. He knew it well."[35] Hélène's son told her almost everything, stories to make a mother faint. Street stops were becoming more frequent; anyone who looked like a foreigner would be searched even down to his genitals, but not Tommy—he just looked too Aryan. Elek recounted another story in which he and a fellow underground member were stopped on the Métro by a French cop. His friend was carrying a satchel containing ten grenades. "What do you have in that bag?" demanded the policeman. "Grenades," answered the young man. "Smartass," retorted the cop. "Be careful what you say; someone else would've arrested you." Then he let them go.

Once Tommy's photo appeared on the Red Poster and the name Elek became known to everyone, his mother had to go even deeper into hiding, especially because she began to work more diligently for the Resistance. In her memoir, published thirty years after the events, Hélène pulled no punches. Had it not been for the enthusiasm, as clumsy as it might have been, of her young son and his leftist friends, early resistance would have amounted to nothing: "And I can assure you that it was the left that resisted. I'm not saying that de Gaulle's call to arms meant nothing; it was a good trick, in effect. But the Resistance was here, right here in Paris, thousands of young seventeen-to-twenty-year-olds who risked their skins every day."[36]

For about a year after her restaurant was closed she managed to keep on the move (she wrote that she had found sixteen different hiding places for her family and was about to look for another when the Germans left Paris). She lived almost invisibly in Paris, thanks to the support of friends, Gentile and Jewish, and to her extraordinary sangfroid. She and her family were among those forty thousand Jews who were living in Paris, many with their yellow stars still affixed to their clothes, at the end of the Occupation. Given the zeal of the combined police forces of the Reich and of Vichy, this is an extraordinary number. Much of the credit for their survival is due to the courage of those people, Jews or not, who stayed with, went to the barricades for, and never gave hope up for the Resistance. But what we learn as we study this period and its unknown actors more closely is how diligently, imaginatively, courageously, and successfully young Jews resisted. As a fine historian concludes in her history of Jews in France during the Second World War: "The proportion of Jews in the Resistance was greater than that for the French population as a whole.... [The underground] remained an alternative society that had taken in Jews on an equal basis and offered them a chance to act without changing any part of their identity."[37]

Why had the Manouchian Group rattled the Vichy and German Occupation authorities so much that they worked diligently to paste thousands of copies of the Red Poster in large and small cities across the whole of France, almost overnight? How did a team of about twenty-five persons, most in their twenties, become literal poster children for a defiant resistance to increasingly uneasy Germans? The group was in effect a carefully planned effort by the Communist Party and other leftist resistance groups convinced that there had to be a relentless campaign not only of propaganda but also of organized violence if the Nazi propaganda machine were to be neutralized. The Germans took stark notice.

A Female Resistance

Of those arrested by the Brigades spéciales, we must note and remember that there were dozens of young women. Without the help of women and girls, the Parisian resistance, no matter its ideology, could not have been as successful as it was. We have already noted that Paris had become a city where many, many young and middle-aged men were in prison, concentration camps, in hiding, or in the underground. Women were holding together households, in many of which there were several children, with string and baling wire. They were often outspoken about the deficiencies in the distribution of food and consumer goods, sometimes taking to the streets to voice their concerns, Germans or no Germans. And they were especially active in underground movements:

> They despised the Germans, who had sent them on the road during the exodus of June, 1940; who kept their husbands, brothers, and sons in prison camps; who made their daily life so difficult with so many interdictions, shortages of food, of clothing, of coal; with constant ID checks in the street, with hostages shot, and with the roundups of Jews.... Women were indispensable in

all domains. It was they who typed and coded messages; there was no word processing in those days, and typists were always women. They served as liaisons between groups and individuals; they were the ones who accompanied a *résistant* or an Allied pilot on the run, because couples were less often stopped than a man alone. They lodged all these men in hiding, openheartedly, washed their clothes, fed them, and took care of their wounds.... Many went to prison and were tortured. Sometimes it takes more courage to do laundry...than to use a machine gun.[38]

Hundreds of women took in Jewish children during the most oppressive years, 1942–44. Pretty French girls would flirt with the Occupier while carrying forbidden stencils in their bicycle pumps; they would smile brightly as they passed the French police with tracts, or even munitions, hidden in their prams under their babies' bodies or under skirts that made them look pregnant.

Girls were often the boldest when confronted directly, as they were in the matter of the imposition of the yellow star. Many of the Gentiles who confronted the Germans with their own stars, making fun of this ukase, were young women. And they were arrested and incarcerated for months. Françoise Siefridt's recently published memoir, *J'ai voulu porter l'étoile jaune* (I Wanted to Wear the Yellow Star), reveals the honesty and passion of a nineteen-year-old. On the Sunday morning following the mandated deadline for wearing the bright yellow stars, she and a fellow Christian friend proudly walked down the Boul' Mich' (an age-old popular abbreviation for the Boulevard Saint-Michel, which cuts right through the Latin Quarter, on the Left Bank of Paris). She wrote that they were insolently displaying "a magnificent yellow star that we had crafted. I had written on mine PAPOU [from Papua New Guinea]. Passersby said 'Bravo' or gave us an approving smile. But a [French] policeman whom we had just passed made a sign to us: 'What if I took you to the station?' Another in civilian clothes who was behind us added: 'Take them to jail'; and, as if he feared that the uniformed officer would let us go: 'I'll go with you.'... I followed them without any concern, convinced that after a good talking-to we would be let go."[39]

The young women soon found themselves sitting on benches in the precinct's waiting room, imagining their punishment. A young Jewish girl was brought in with a male African friend who had been insulted by a German.* The girl had insulted the German in return, and she was immediately locked up; the black man was sitting there waiting to see what would happen to him. Françoise's father immediately appeared at the station; he was allowed to embrace her but not to speak. By his look, though, she knew that she was in more trouble than she had imagined.

Soon the girls were transported in a Black Maria (police van; the French call them *paniers à salade:* salad baskets) to Tourelles prison, in the northeastern part of Paris, then the official jail where Gentiles who publicly supported Jews were interned. Françoise saw a few other young Gentiles there, too, because they had made fun of the yellow star. Put into cells at first with Jewish girls, Françoise noticed that these latter did not remain long in the cells; they were being separated from their Gentile friends and sent off in convoys to Drancy. On June 20, "the ten Aryans who are in the camp for having worn the yellow star on June 7 are ordered to wear [in prison] the Jewish star, plus an armband inscribed FRIEND OF JEWS."[40]

Two weeks later, a German officer appeared in the camp; concluding that their armbands were not big enough, he ordered them enlarged. At the same time that she was being punished for having mocked the Occupation authorities Françoise watched as Jews were being brought in for not having obeyed the yellow star edict, witnessing firsthand what many Parisians were ignoring or refusing to see:

---

* There were a substantial number of black residents in Paris at the time. Some were American veterans of World War I who had stayed on rather than return to the Jim Crow atmosphere in the United States. And there were many West Africans coming from French colonies on that continent. The Germans despised people of African descent; they casually shot African members of the French army and initiated regulations against them even before they got around to doing the same against the Jews.

namely, that their fellow citizens were being reported, picked up, and imprisoned for ethnic reasons. If Françoise had been a casual "friend of the Jews" before, she was a formal one now.

In prison for two months, Françoise was never told when she would be released; on August 13, she and her Aryan friends were also transported to Drancy. It is unclear why the Germans—or the French—treated French teens this way; after all, they did not want to upset the French bourgeoisie unnecessarily. Perhaps it was just a bureaucratic mistake, but it must have been terrifying, not only for Françoise and her comrades but also for her parents and relatives.

Here we are at Drancy. It is a type of American village with gigantic cement buildings and skyscrapers of fifteen stories. Barbed wire, searchlights, machine guns, and sentinels surround the camp. We get off the bus. Jews carry our packages and welcome us warmly.... Then a Jew leads us to our new dormitory. By German order, one "friend of the Jews" is put in each dormitory.[41]

Finally, on August 31, Françoise was freed, after almost three months in captivity: "I look through the windows [of the bus]. Passersby are freely walking. The sky is blue. I'm free! How beautiful liberty is! My God, thank you."[42] So ends her brief memoir. We do not hear another word from her and are left to wonder how her experience affected the rest of her life as a young woman in Paris. We also wonder how her parents and their friends felt.

Obviously, many of the German Occupiers had no sense of humor, which put adolescents at a special disadvantage when they played their careless games; they had no patience with adolescent rebellion, for they were petrified that the shenanigans of young Parisians would infect the apparent complacency of the city's population. Yet their intolerance only exacerbated the Parisian's sense of humiliation. Adolescents were doing what more seasoned adults should have been doing, an opinion that only added to the then moribund sensibility of French honor.

In late October of 1944, after Paris had been liberated but before the war was over, the surrealist poet and editor Lise Deharme wrote in a Communist literary magazine about the role of young women during the Occupation. She deftly describes one of their subtlest tactics, which was to remind the Germans that though they may be in Paris they did not control it. She describes those Parisiennes who, with

> a tear in the eye but a smile on their lips, beautiful, made up, discreet, and perfectly insolent in their impeccable outfits... really exasperated the Germans. The beauty of their hair, their complexions, their teeth, their thinness compared to the fat hideousness of their own little birds dressed in gray [German typists, nurses, and others] — yes, that bothered them. These Parisians were *résistantes*. Rich or poor, their adorable presences disinfected the streets and the stinking Métros. Young as flowers, fresh as fruit, these bike fiends with their acrobatics brought smiles to many disenchanted men.[43]

Who Got the Credit?

After the war, many longtime members of the Resistance, and quite a few who had joined only much later, rushed to get out their stories of sacrifice for France during its darkest period. At the same time, former Resistance groups were fighting among themselves about who had done the most, or had been the most courageous, or had visited the most effective damage upon the German and Vichy occupations. The Communist Party, referring erroneously to itself as the "party of the executed seventy-five thousand," was riven by internal debates over who had followed the party line and who had deviated. As a result, the stories of the Resistance immediately following the liberation of French territory were muddled. Efforts were made by postwar governments, institutions, media, and politicians to attenuate these divisions; the result was instant "legendification" that was not troubled again until the 1970s, when, in order to understand more deeply what had happened, filmmakers, historians, and novelists began evaluating the contradictory stories of resistance and of collaboration. Doubtlessly there was intimacy, trust, and honor among those who fought the Germans, armed or not. Fear of failing was stronger glue for the group than blood; the death of a comrade demanded that his memory be engraved indelibly in that of his surviving brothers. But such utopian recollections covered errors and compromises, so the myth of a solidified, fraternal, and eminently successful resistance against the German occupation and its Vichy servants lasted a very long time.

If we stop to think what it took to resist an implacable, insecure, yet ideologically certain foe, we wonder why anyone would not just wait it out. Yet the historian Adam Rayski has written: "On History's clock, the hands moved faster for Jews than for the other populations of occupied Europe. Time for others was not exactly our time."[44] We have seen how the Berliners set Paris on Prussian time, and even on Prussian summer time, thus bringing the French into the temporal current of Nazism. But the historian Alya Aglan and others have argued that one of the major objectives of the Resistance, perhaps even without the participants' knowing or understanding it, was to bring France—and Paris—back into their temporal normalcy: "The Occupation was lived as a waiting period, a timeless time, and the Resistance was a desire to exist beyond this blocked period. Totalitarianism negates time, but Resistance creates it. . . . The Occupation generated a fragmented [and thus ersatz] time, with its own temporal density." One could then read this period—with its constantly manipulated curfews, its inconsistent train, Métro, and bus schedules, and especially its constantly revised daily timetables governing when Jews could shop, go out, and conduct their business—as a struggle over time. The Occupier may have had rules and have been able to enforce them efficiently, but somewhere and somehow alternative temporal avenues had been discovered, and, for a brief moment, some Parisians experienced, through a type of resistance, the liberty that would not be theirs for another few years.

Later, as we sit comfortably in our armchairs, trying to understand why anyone would resist rather than just wait for liberation, it seems unseemly to gauge the responses of those who lived through those awful years. Once we realize how disrupted and ruined was Parisians' daily existence; how much they suddenly, almost overnight, had to worry more immediately about those they needed to protect; how much they had to bow before an implacable foe; then who are we to judge? Yet as with any human endeavor, both victims and witnesses of violence want their voices heard. They call for some sort of judgment from us. This is the tension created for any student of this era. The question, then, is not who "gets credit" but rather whether *you* (living in a world that I can only begin to fathom) interrupted or enabled what happened. How comfortable did *you* feel with your excuses? For we, more than seventy years later, hesitate to judge.

Chapter Seven

⊹⇒◯⇐⊹

The Most Narrowed
Lives — The Hunt for Jews

"Maman, qu'est-ce que c'est: juif?" *(Mama, what does "Jew"*
mean?)

— Hélène Elek[1]

Being Jewish in Paris

How often was the above question asked by Jewish children aware of
how anxious, protective, and suspicious their parents had become after
June of 1940? At this time, there were about three hundred thousand
self-identified Jews in France. About half of them, at least at first, lived
in the northern, Occupied Zone, but soon tens of thousands began
immigrating to the southern, Unoccupied Zone. European, North
African, and Middle Eastern Jews had seen the capital of France as a
"new Jerusalem" since 1791, when the Assemblée nationale had given
them full civil rights, later confirmed, though with occasional bureaucratic hiccups, by Napoleon I. Beginning with the enormous political
upheavals of the mid-nineteenth century across Europe, Jews from eastern Europe, and many from the Ottoman Empire and later Turkey and
the Levant, sought France as a refuge. Some came because they tired of
the official anti-Semitism, the pogroms, and the lack of economic
opportunity in their homelands. Others came because of their progressive political beliefs. Of course, millions had to remain in Poland and
Russia, in ancestral shtetls, villages, small towns, and large cities.

240

By 1939, two-thirds of the Jews in France lived in or around Paris.[2] They were not a homogeneous group. Some had become so assimilated that they barely remembered they were Jewish. These generally lived in the western part of Paris, in the 8th, 16th, and 17th arrondissements; if they practiced Judaism at all, it was only on the high holidays. Others were highly observant and tended to settle in the Saint-Paul quarter, a quite poor area of the Marais, just a few blocks from the city hall. Jews all over Europe knew of this neighborhood, called the Pletzl, Yiddish for "little place." Soon the 1st, 2nd, 3rd, and 4th arrondissements were chock-full of small, artisanal businesses, many operating from the owners' own apartments. Those Jews who were more politically than religiously active—consisting mostly of leftists (but not necessarily Communists), Zionists, and others who were strongly anti-fascist—tended to congregate in the 11th and 20th arrondissements, in the former villages of Belleville and Ménilmontant. Cloth merchants and clothiers set up shop in the northern 18th arrondissement, near the enormous flea market at Clignancourt (which is still there today). The Russian Jews generally chose the 19th arrondissement, near Montmartre. All these districts, with the exception of those in the richer western quarters, were centers of low-rent, decaying, badly serviced buildings, where large families shared small apartments and where each ethnic group could hear the languages that it had brought from home: among them Ukrainian, Russian, Armenian, Polish, Yiddish, Czech, Hungarian, and German. Dozens of newspapers were available in these languages as well. Sixty percent of Jewish immigrants were artisans and craftsmen who worked from their homes and who often had carts that they pushed or pulled throughout the city.

By the late 1930s, Jews knew to keep their heads down, even before the Germans had arrived. "If we keep quiet," they seemed to intuit, "we may just be ignored." In November of 1938, a year before the invasion of Poland, a young Polish-German illegal immigrant blew apart the shield of anonymity that French Jews were using to hide under. Angry that Germany had deported his parents back to Poland, where they were put into camps, seventeen-year-old Herschel

Grynszpan walked into the elegant German embassy on the Rue de Lille, right behind the Gare d'Orsay, on the Left Bank. Surprisingly, he was not stopped or searched. Entering the building with confidence, he was shown upstairs to talk with one of the three legation secretaries, the young Ernst vom Rath. Vom Rath asked how he could help, at which point Grynszpan pulled from his pocket a small pistol, which he had purchased that day, and fired five times. Grynszpan was immediately grabbed by German diplomats and brought to the street, where he was handed over to the French police without a struggle. In the car on the way to their station, he calmly offered: "I have just shot a man in his office. I do not regret it. I did it to avenge my parents, who are miserable in Germany."★ ³

As vom Rath lay dying in a Paris hospital (he would pass away two days later), Hitler and Goebbels talked about how to react, beyond making the usual diplomatic complaints. Their response was the largest organized pogrom in Germany before the war, what has become known as Kristallnacht (Night of the Crystal, in reference to the sounds and sights of broken glass). Jews throughout Germany were arrested in large numbers; many were beaten and some killed by Gestapo and brownshirt hooligans; signs were displayed on Jewish-owned shops that declared REVENGE FOR THE MURDER OF VOM RATH; thousands of establishments branded as Jewish were looted and vandalized; hundreds of synagogues desecrated; whole neighborhoods ransacked. On November 17, Vom Rath was honored with an elaborate state funeral in Düsseldorf, which Hitler attended. The death of this middling young diplomat had provided the Reich with the excuse to send the strongest possible message to Jews throughout Europe that they would

---

★ The young assassin almost escaped German incarceration after June of 1940. French police spirited him off to the Unoccupied Zone, but he was betrayed by a Vichy sympathizer, turned over to the Germans, and taken to Berlin, where a show trial was prepared. For reasons that are still unclear, the trial was forgone, and Grynszpan disappeared into the "night and fog" of the Reich's bureaucracy. Some think he survived the war, but that is most likely a myth. An informative book by Jonathan Kirsch, *The Short, Strange Life of Herschel Grynszpan*, gives a formidable narrative history of this complex and important episode.

not be safe under German occupation should war break out, which it did only ten months later.

Parisian Jews were appalled that this murder had taken place in the midst of their city. The event brought attention, especially through the right-wing press, to the fact that there was a large Jewish population in Paris, many thousands of whom stateless, all waiting to create confusion and havoc at the slightest provocation. (One of the ironies of the Second World War is that had the Jews of Europe actually had the economic, social, and institutional power imputed to them by raving anti-Semites, they could have easily thwarted their sworn enemies.) Another tension, too, was evident in Paris, and that was the cultural, religious, educational, and even ethnic differences among Jews themselves. When the first ukases began coming down from the Vichy government and the Occupation authorities, many French Jews did not believe that these edicts applied to them. Impatient, even angry, toward their coreligionists, they would gradually discover that, in fact, to the Germans and many anti-Semitic Vichy officials, all Jews were the same.

With the outbreak of war in September of 1939, Germans and Austrians who had fled to Paris were rounded up by French authorities and put into concentration camps. They were sitting ducks when the Nazis took over and began roundups of their own recalcitrant German compatriots—e.g., Communists, Socialists, labor leaders, and Jews.* The Vichy government, before the Germans had unpacked their bags, began to issue edicts aimed at putting Jews in their place. Between July of 1940 (only a month after the Occupation) and October of that year, they passed edicts that repealed naturalizations granted after 1927 (thereby depriving thousands of immigrants of citizenship). They regulated medical professions (a foreshadowing of the delicensing of Jewish

---

* Increasingly studied, these French camps played important roles during the late 1930s, when they were used for Spanish refugees, and during the war, when they were used first for German nationals and then for enemies of the Vichy regime, including Jews. Some of the best-known camps were at Beaune-la-Rolande, not far from Paris, and in the south, at Gurs, Rivesaltes, and Les Milles. The most notorious was at Drancy, outside Paris, which was eventually requisitioned by the Germans.

doctors), repealed a law against racial defamation, and passed legislation that limited membership in the legal profession.

There was also a law passed in October that defined what a Jew was; another permitted departmental prefects to lock up Jewish immigrants so as to reduce the "excess of workers in the French economy"; yet another removed citizenship from French Jews of Algeria, up to then considered French. In September of 1940, the German authorities (still controlled by the Wehrmacht) published an ordinance defining a Jew as "a person belonging to the Jewish religion or having more than two Jewish grandparents (in other words, who also belonged to the Jewish religion)."[4] The Vichy government a few days later published a similar ordinance; for the first time since the Revolution, the French government was officially identifying ethnic groups. Though Vichy took care not to speak of Judaism per se but rather of lineage, the difference was barely noticed by the Jews themselves or, for that matter, by most French people. The German ordinance also instructed that all Jews in the Occupied Zone must report to their local police station and register as Jews before October 20; by October 31 all Jewish stores were to have affixed to their businesses a sign in German and French: JÜDISCHES GESCHÄFT and ENTREPRISE JUIVE (Jewish business). Between October of 1940 and September of 1941, the Vichy government had published twenty-six laws and thirty decrees concerning Jews.[5] The drip, drip, drip of these edicts, accompanied by officially approved radio programs and newspaper editorials excoriating the smothering effect of the Jewish race on French culture, religion, and the economy, immediately divided most Jews into two camps: those who tried to leave, and soon, and those (the majority) who had to stay or could not believe that they were personally in danger if they just followed the rules.

It may surprise us today that by the end of October in 1940 about 150,000 Parisians had docilely trooped to Parisian police stations and registered as Jews. (Remember that these were only those residing in the Occupied Zone, for the Vichy politicos had not agreed to the German request that they do the same in the Unoccupied Zone.) But it is understandable if we put ourselves in their shoes: What other options did they have but to follow the laws of their own government and the powerful Occupier? The repression was relentless, and escape was far more complicated than it might seem today. Soon Jews were forbidden to serve in positions where they would have to meet the public (which meant that no Jew could be a concierge); Jewish bank accounts were frozen and lockboxes opened. Apartments were seized, requisitioned, and looted, either by the police or by their neighbors. Writes one historian, "By the summer of 1941, according to [an] estimate made at the time, almost 50 percent of Jews found themselves cut off from all means of earning a living."[6] For every injunction or law or requirement Jews followed, another was introduced.

The propaganda campaign against Jews and Judaism raced toward an apogee of hatred. Taking clues from ten years of anti-Semitic vitriol in Nazi rhetoric, the Vichyists produced their own campaign of misinformation: cartoons, posters, photographs, and newspaper diatribes unencumbered by any sense of decency. Jews who at first thought that France would protect them from the Nazi ideology discovered the opposite. In September of 1941, on every Parisian kiosk appeared huge posters that announced a massive exhibition at the Palais Berlitz, in the city's 2nd arrondissement: *Le Juif et la France* (The Jew and France). This exhibition's raison d'être was to show the French how to recognize the "racial" characteristics of Jews: they had already heard that the Jews were behind Bolshevism, capitalism, and the British Empire, but now they had to know how to discover those who had changed their names (forbidden by edict in February of 1942) and those who were otherwise trying to "pass" as Aryans. Professor Georges Montandon, author of *Comment reconnaître le Juif?* (How to Recognize the Jew, 1940), curated the exhibition and would be appointed in 1943 the director of the Institute for the Study of Jewish and Ethno-Racial Questions. A hit, the show attracted more than two hundred thousand Parisians (among them, quite probably, were many Jews fascinated with the depiction of their "race" by the Nazis).★

Just a few months earlier, French movie screens had begun showing

---

★ After his name had been published in a clandestine newspaper, Montandon was attacked by *résistants* in his home in early August of 1944. Wounded, he was transferred to Germany, where he most likely died of a combination of cancer and the wounds.

The Jew in France: Vichy Propaganda. (Bundesarchiv)

Veit Harlan's film *Le Juif Süss* (The Jew Süss), produced by Goebbels and his propaganda ministry. It depicts a famous Jewish courtier of eighteenth-century Germany as a conniving, manipulative, greedy, and sexually obsessed paragon of his race. More than a million French citizens would view this juggernaut of anti-Semitism by 1944. However, many who went to see it were appalled, and small, unplanned demonstrations, especially among students, occurred throughout France wherever it was shown. Nevertheless, events such as the exhibition and the film continued the deadly drumbeat of anti-Semitism that became part of the weave of French society during the Occupation.

The level of anxiety rose as families argued about whether to leave for the Unoccupied Zone or the Italian Occupied Zone, known for its more casual attitude about bureaucratic control of Jews. Should they send the children into hiding? Should they find a hiding place in Paris? Whom could they trust? One of the main problems was that these families were often large; not only did they have children to worry about, they also had their fathers and mothers and aunts and uncles, who were not as easily moved. There is one story of a grandfather who took his own life so that his family would not be encumbered and could slip south into the Unoccupied Zone. For a time, the richest Jews could pay their way into Switzerland, Spain, or Portugal (not all had enough foresight to do so). But what about those without comparable resources? Perhaps they could find a cheaper way, such as someone who could get them over the Demarcation Line, in the center of France, between the Occupied and Unoccupied Zones. But the Germans soon closed off that option, too: Jews were not allowed to move, period.

At first, as Jacques Biélinky noted in his journal, German soldiers occasionally protected Jews against their anti-Semitic French neighbors if they were harassed while standing in lines or at soup kitchens. At one point, "in order to prevent attacks against the Jewish population of the 4th arrondissement, patrols of [French] gendarmes began to move about the streets. . . . This impresses visibly the Jewish population, obviously worried."[7] Yet such events were the exception. Jews soon began to realize that with general restrictions on foodstuffs, fuel, and clothing, it would only be a matter of time before they would be at the end of every line. Still, despite the weekly beat of anti-Semitic edicts and laws, life in the Jewish quarters proceeded quasinormally. But Biélinky noticed that he was hearing more frequently about Jewish suicides, about companies asking employees to sign a statement saying that they were indeed Aryan. At the same time, he noticed a "war of the walls," in which anti-German graffiti and the defacement of German posters reminded the Jews that they were not alone in their disdain for the Occupier. Biélinky optimistically, and perhaps somewhat naively, noted that, after the November 11, 1940, demonstration on the Champs-Élysées, "the anti-Semitism that had existed in the Latin Quarter before the war has totally disappeared today, and the relations between Jewish and Catholic students (even those on the right) are cordial."[8] Reading between his lines, we see the contradiction: he wanted to be an objective journalist, but he was a fearful Jew, too. He was searching desperately for evidence of an anodyne relationship between Jews and their state enemies. This was a common state of mind for even the worldliest Jews.

Displacement of Jewish residents took place regularly, often without arrests. Claims were put on apartments, especially large, well-furnished ones. The Germans had lists of private libraries, galleries, and art collections owned by Jews. They knew about safe-deposit boxes and items in warehouse storage, and had traced the movement of collections from Paris to private châteaus in the nearby countryside. Large mansions were immediately confiscated. A Rothschild mansion across the street from the Élysée Palace was one of the first.* When a less prominent Jewish home was raided, it most often was sealed and the keys given to the concierge or a neighbor. Later, movers would come to take away everything in that apartment if the neighbor or concierge had not beaten them to it. When arrested, Jews were permitted to carry away almost nothing; even toys were taken from deported children and left behind, an especially cruel act.

Serge Klarsfeld, the indefatigable historian and agitator for the rights of those taken away as well as those left behind, published in 2005 a small collection of letters and memoirs that contains the woeful depiction of what happened when a man who had escaped the roundup returned to find his home empty. "My throat closed like a watertight door; I ran up the streets, looking only straight ahead; I saw no cops or Germans. Arriving in my street, French [i.e., non-Jewish] women stopped me with compassionate faces: 'Poor man, they took your wife

---

* On his return to Paris after the war, the Baron Élie de Rothschild asked his maître d'hôtel (chief butler) who had visited the German residents of his home while he was a prisoner of war: "The same ones who came when you were here, monsieur le Baron."

and your son. You, you're probably a French citizen, that's why you are still free.' I said nothing; I could not speak."[9] Other Jewish fathers and husbands, who had thought they could outsmart the French police and their German accomplices by staying away from home, would return to their buildings for belongings or a few clothes only to be told by recalcitrant concierges that the apartments had been sealed or that they were forbidden to let them in. Some, coming back a week later, would see large trucks emblazoned with GIFTS FROM THE FRENCH PEOPLE TO HOME-WRECKED GERMANS parked at the curb; workers were emptying the Jews' apartments and loading their belongings onto the trucks. What was left soon disappeared into the concierge's loge or neighbors' apartments.

The first large roundups began a year after the Occupation, in the spring of 1941. As we observed earlier, Jews in France lived in or near large cities — Paris (with the most Jewish residents, by a large majority), Lyon, Marseille, Bordeaux, and Toulouse. The first significant raid occurred in Paris in May of 1941 (and netted about four thousand Jewish men, mostly Polish immigrants); the second was in August (especially in the 11th arrondissement), and there was another, in December of 1941 — this was the first and only time that a raid was led solely by Germans. Most of the raids, as would be the case for the largest one, in July of 1942, would be organized and carried out by the French police, closely monitored by the Commissariat Général aux Questions Juives. In fact, members of the French, not the German, police performed more than 90 percent of the arrests of Jews during the Occupation. Those arrested in these raids were boys and men ages sixteen to fifty-five, and for the most part they were foreign-born, unnaturalized. (There was always a handful of French-born Jews in these early roundups, though the Vichy government resisted German demands that they be arrested en masse. As the war proceeded, the distinction between foreign-born and French Jews would slowly evaporate.) In general, the detainees were sent to concentration camps spread all over France, in the Occupied and the Unoccupied Zones. Each of these raids, too, had specific Jewish nationalities as targets, identified according to their home country's relationship with the Reich. For example, Hungarian Jews were generally ignored until Hitler invaded that country in 1944.

And then, in late March of 1942, the Germans, with the close support of the French police, began putting Jews (and some Communists and underground members) onto trains and shipping them from Bobigny and Drancy to an "unknown" destination in Germany or Poland.* For the next two and a half years, thousands of Jewish women, children, and men would be sent primarily to Auschwitz but also to Buchenwald, Bergen-Belsen, and Ravensbrück. Until then, Drancy had been a transitional prison camp for those who were to be transported to French camps. Detainees might be released from time to time (after they pulled strings or paid or argued for their liberty); letters and packages could be sent and received, and even visits were permitted. But after the arrival of SS officer Alois Brunner in June of 1943, "a wind of anguish blew into the camp."† 10 A protégé of Adolf Eichmann, Brunner was there to prepare the German appropriation of Drancy, which took place on July 2. Brunner forbade the wearing of sunglasses and beards and the receipt of individual food packages (all such deliveries had to go to the central kitchen). Jews were not to look directly at German soldiers or officers and were to push themselves flat against the wall if they met any in a stairwell. Unpredictable violence against internees was the norm. Prisoners who had relatives still "at large" were forced to write them, begging them to join the prisoners at Drancy—or else.

Drancy fast became known not as a final destination but a temporary transfer station until enough cattle cars could be found to load between eighty and one hundred human beings into a space for eight horses. Last letters were sent from the camp or thrown from the trains as they passed through stations on the way. Many began: "We are on

---

* At first they were put into third-class cars with seats. This did not last long, and cattle cars soon replaced those.

† Brunner has been the target of Nazi hunters ever since the war. Like Eichmann, he escaped from the Allies and wound up in Damascus, Syria, where he was afforded protection until his (putative) death.

our way to an unknown destination." It would take months, but soon the word began to come back — from camp escapees, even from some sympathetic German soldiers — that many of the deportees were being gassed right after they arrived at Auschwitz. Disbelief abounded, but soon the immensity of their fellows' fate did sink in, and though they often refused to talk about it, even among themselves, more Parisian Jews searched for places to hide.

How did news of the camps, and eventually of the death camps, seep into the Jewish community? In the summer of 1941, Jews had been ordered to turn in their radios; as of August of 1942, they were forbidden to have telephone accounts. All newspapers remained under strict German and Vichy censorship, but there were many underground tracts distributed. One that appeared right after the Grande Rafle of July 1942 baldly stated: "We know that 1,100 Dutch JEWS, taken to the concentration camp at Dachau, in Germany, underwent experiments with TOXIC GAS and that almost all died."[11] And the grapevine was strikingly efficient, primarily because many Gentiles, and not a few policemen, helped create it. But who knew what the truth would turn out to be?

Jewish men knew that the police and the Germans were arresting males — rarely women and never children. This demographic selection probably helped to undercut those who had news of death camps in Eastern Europe. Why would the Germans go to all the trouble to round up, imprison, and transport healthy Jewish men just to kill them? They might work them to death, but that could take years, and "years" meant that anything could happen. The Germans cleverly kept the Jewish population off balance, using their roundups to identify certain national groups, e.g., the Czechs or the Poles, and the Jews themselves found a thousand excuses that would permit them to avoid thinking of the worst: "They were recent immigrants." "They were Communists." "They were Germans." "They didn't have the correct identification." "They lived in dangerous neighborhoods." "They didn't have families." The excuses served to calm, and many remained, protected at least for a while by luck and their own savvy.[12] Lazy or sympathetic policemen, Gentile neighbors who were as alert as they, money to buy off bureaucrats, superbly forged papers, and even certificates that stated that the carrier did not belong to the Jewish race saved many from arrest and deportation.

Three Girls on the Move

Three tales give us an intimate picture of the ways in which young Jewish girls, from three different communities, learned to accommodate themselves to a city under occupation by officials who despised them. In 1988, doing archival research for one of his fictions, the French novelist Patrick Modiano noticed an advertisement that appeared in late 1941 in *Paris-Soir,* Paris's most popular newspaper. It read: "Missing: a young girl, Dora Bruder, age fifteen, height 1m 55cm, oval-shaped face, gray-brown eyes, gray sport jacket, maroon pullover, navy blue skirt and hat, brown gym shoes. Address all information to M. and Mme. Bruder, 41 Boulevard Ornano, Paris."[13] There in laconic prose lies a sad tale, which Modiano turns into his documentary fiction, *Dora Bruder.* A Jewish adolescent had run away from home, and her desperate parents, already lying low, had to go public to find her, thereby drawing attention to their presence in Occupied Paris.

Modiano imagines Paris as it must have appeared to Dora, an unhappy teenager in a city that no longer provided the cocoon of familiarity and that was threatening to her and her family. The familiar Métro lines might have comforted Dora. When all else is mystery or danger, the predictable Métro might offer a sort of mental emollient. The labyrinthine city beckoned this teenager with its promise of experimentation in anonymity. Not even the stark fear of being discovered by an implacable police force daunted young Dora, or raised the idea, had she entertained it, that her parents' concern could lead them to danger. It does not take much for a youngster to explore, even irresponsibly: "The sudden urge to escape can be prompted by one of those cold, gray days that makes you more than ever aware of your solitude and intensifies your feeling that a trap is about to close."[14] But this freedom is nothing but a seductive lure, and Dora must have at least intuited that she had been "placed in bizarre categories [she] had never heard of and with no relation to who [she] really [was]....If only [she] could understand why."[15] We never learn where she spent the months she went missing, but we are moved by the fact that, possibly, she finally might have met her concerned parents again at Drancy, where they all waited for deportation.

In another memoir of the Occupation, the philosopher Sarah Kofman's *Rue Ordener, Rue Labat* (1994), we read of a young girl, as she grows from the age of about eight to ten, who has to deracinate herself, geographically, ethically, and relationally, in order to survive.* When her father, a rabbi, is hauled off to the Vélodrome d'Hiver in the infamous roundup of July 1942, Sarah's mother has to find a new apartment, at least temporarily, until she can get to the Unoccupied Zone (perhaps because there was a two-year-old at home, she and her six children were not arrested). Fortunately, a Catholic friend who lives only a few blocks away invites her and her children to stay there. Soon, though, other arrangements must be made, and little Sarah is left alone with this woman, who lives on Rue Labat and whom she calls Mémé.

The memoir recounts young Sarah's move from "Rue Ordinaire," as she called her former home on Rue Ordener, to "Rue Là-bas," her name for the home on Rue Labat.† Though only a street or two apart, this distance is psychologically enormous: "One Métro stop separates the Rue Ordener from the Rue Labat. Between the two, Rue Marcadet; it seemed endless to me, and I vomited the whole way."[16] At the cusp of adolescence, Kofman is bewildered, bereft, and frightened, unprepared for the "liberty" that is being forced on her. Immediately, she is thrown into conflict: she comes to love her new "mother" as much or more than her birth mother. She becomes a perfect little Gentile disciple, eating pork and horse meat and breaking Shabbat decorum while listening to Mémé casually reprove the Jews. This sudden, new

---

* Kofman's memoir is all the more poignant because she took her own life at the age of sixty, soon after having written it. A brilliant teacher and philosopher, she most likely still felt deep guilt at having survived by rejecting her birth mother and the traditions of her rabbi father.

† The street names are, coincidentally, quasihomonyms of *ordinaire* (ordinary) and *là-bas* (over there).

freedom, at first scary, then exhilarating, soon becomes suffocating, for now she has two mothers, each asking that she choose between identities: a Catholic or a Jew, French or foreign, young woman or child.

The only times that she feels free are when she walks the streets of the 19th arrondissement or takes the Métro. There is scarcely a page of this memoir that does not have a geographical reference—the name of a street, an impasse, a boulevard, a Métro stop, a *quartier*, a monument. Kofman, remembering a traumatic adolescence, literally "renames" Paris as she tries to buttress, as an adult, her own continuing sense of namelessness, her loss of a stabilizing identity. The names of Paris have not changed; clinging to them helped dilute her unease at having to live in a city under occupation, either by Germans or irrepressible memories.

In 2008, there appeared on the shelves of French bookstores a book whose title was simple—*Journal*—and whose cover featured the

Hélène Berr, college student. (*Mémorial de la Shoah*)

photograph of a beautiful young girl, the sort of photo that one would give a close friend. The author was Hélène Berr, and through her, we receive yet another new geography of the occupied city. Indeed, her diary entries are so specific about topographical data that one can map easily "her" Paris. There are well over two hundred specific site references in her work — streets, bridges, Métro stations and lines, buildings — which emphasizes how much her sense of freedom depended on her constant comings and goings, marked by familiar names and places. Her diary covers but two years — from the spring of 1942 until the spring of 1944, with a ten-month break — yet it offers its readers a glimpse of how a young person attempted to lead a normal

Hélène Berr's home in Paris

life in an increasingly threatening environment. Hélène was searching, through writing, to transform the threats of occupied Paris into an imagined city, one where she had once been secure and free. It was in the Latin Quarter, among her fellow students, that she felt the safest, even after the imposition of the yellow star. There she intuited that the neighborhood's intellectual cosmopolitanism could somehow protect her from the tacky provincialism of the Occupation. In the Sorbonne's amphitheaters, she was just another student. In the courtyards of the Sorbonne, she fell in love. In the library of the English studies department, she answered polite questions of German soldiers. Her friends had conspired to create ersatz "stars" to show their solidarity. She copies verses of Keats to push the Occupation from her thoughts.

Yet she had daily to return home, to an apartment where her father was constantly in danger of being arrested, where the phone rang regularly to inform her mother of another Jewish family caught up in the sticky web of Nazi and Vichy anti-Semitism. The mundane doorbell was no longer a harbinger of pleasant visits; it could announce, heart-stoppingly, the police. "If they ring the bell, what do we do?"[17] About a month before the imposition of the "star" in late May of 1942, Hélène came to terms with the knowledge that she was being identified as a pariah.

Saturday, April 11. This evening I've a mad desire to throw it all over. I am fed up with not being normal. I am fed up with no longer feeling as free as air, as I did last year. I am fed up with feeling I do not have the right to be as I was. It seems that I have become attached to something invisible and that I cannot move away from it as I wish to, and it makes me hate this thing and deform it. . . . I am obliged to act a part. . . . As time passes, the gulf between inside and outside grows ever deeper.[18]

She is still a Parisian, still a student, still a young woman in love, but she no longer completely belongs to the changed cityscape. After the star edict she notices how people look at her as she walks through the streets wearing her emblem: some are sympathetic and give her a thumbs-up sign of solidarity; others turn away; others look at her in disdain. She is proud; she is resolute; she is still French, but "out of place." She has been exiled while remaining in her city.

The Occupation authorities tried mightily to restrict movement in the city of Paris—for everyone. Walking freely might have been the only form of resistance available to those living in a tightly controlled city, and Berr walks everywhere. She also takes the Métro, but there she is reminded constantly of the Jewish laws (once "starred," she is unable to ride anywhere but in the last car) or of the possibility of identity checks at the exits. Berr not only describes where she goes and why, she details how she gets there, as if she is using Ariadne's thread to keep her connected to her family and to the security of the apartment. The young girl analyzes her affective relations, but she also hints at something more sinister, a time where all Jews will be caught in the web of self-deceit, of deceiving others, and of feeling less free, "attached" by invisible cords to a plan of movement that will limit their physical and psychological liberties.

Berr lived on the Left Bank, close by the Seine, and she often refers to the river as a place of solace and contemplation. Its continuous, inexorable movement toward the sea attracts her. Its bridges give a weak promise of escape from an Occupied land, though she knows that the Germans are "over there" as well as "over here." The street—Avenue Élisée Reclus—where her family resided is in one of Paris's most coveted neighborhoods. Named for a French geographer, the name also suggests the safety that many French Jews sought immediately after the Occupation—a "hidden Elysium." Quiet and shaded, the road runs along the side of the Champ de Mars, almost under the Eiffel Tower. Its neighborhood is about as far away as one could get imaginatively, if not geographically, from the teeming Marais or the 20th arrondissement, where so many foreign and poor Jews lived. When one walks the street today it is hard to believe that such a peaceful place would not have protected a family from the Occupiers.* The Left Bank did seem to be less "Occupied" than the Right, primarily because of the large number of

---

* As fortune would have it, the short avenue was the address also of the famous playwright, actor, and director Sacha Guitry, who was among those French artists, including Jean Cocteau, closely associated with the Germans and their Vichy collaborators.

offices of the Occupation bureaucrats in the latter. And, of course, it seemed that way because there was still some security to be found or at least dreamed of in the Latin Quarter: "I walked down Boulevard Saint-Michel beneath the glorious sun among the milling throng, and by the time I got to Rue Soufflot all my usual marvelous joy had returned. From Rue Soufflot to Boulevard Saint-Germain I am in an enchanted land."[19] Berr creates an imaginary map of the Latin Quarter, and as she writes those familiar street names in her diary, she reassures herself that there is some overlap between this imagined view of an unbeaten Paris and the real one, between a "safe" and an "occupied" city, that her "own" map is more real than the actual one. She senses that the heart of the Latin Quarter protects her with its intellectual armature and history, even though Jews had been forbidden to register officially for classes at the Sorbonne since June of 1941. Seeing her friends provided "the only glimmer of peace in the hell in which I live, the only way to hang on to real life, to escape."[20] There, her mind is not Jewish or "occupied" as she sits in class; the Sorbonne is a temporary but ultimately illusory haven of freedom. Berr walks, walks, walks through Paris, as if to imprint her body on the city, ensuring that it remain the same despite the threats that increasingly cloud her life and that of her family. She sits in the Jardin du Luxembourg and the Jardin des Tuileries, soon to be closed to Jews. She runs errands all over Paris, on both Right and Left Banks; she returns almost obsessively to the Sorbonne; she rides the Métro, though she finds it smelly and stuffy.

Her final letter, written from a detention camp on the day she and her family were arrested, is to her sister Denise (who was safe) and says that the event they had feared had finally occurred. It returns to the image of a threatening doorbell:

March 8, 1944, 7:20 p.m. This morning at 7:30, *dring!* I thought it was a telegram!! You know the rest. Tailor-made arrest. [Papa] was the target, it seems, for having had too many exceptions made for him [he was an important chemical executive] over the last eighteen months. A little trip in a private car to the police station.

Remain in the car. And then here, the holding place in the 8th [arrondissement]...The French police were rude this morning. Here, they are nice. We are waiting.[21]

She warns her sister not to return home until they return. She had given her journal to the family cook, who would keep it for years. Hélène Berr and her mother and father were deported three weeks later from Drancy to Auschwitz, only five months before the Liberation of Paris.

These three stories of courageous, naive, frightened, and resourceful Jewish girls have come down to us by way of chance and sorrowful memory. They reflect the psychological confusion that dominates when one's surroundings are suddenly, relentlessly made sinister. Each of them imagined a freer, more protective Paris than they found themselves in. Each of the three, though not at the same time, discovered that her imagination, in the end, could not protect her from the pernicious efficiency of a focused hatred.

Low-cost housing: Drancy transit camp. (© *Roger-Viollet / The Image Works*)

A Gold Star

In May of 1942, the German authorities imposed the wearing of a yellow star (the Magen David—ironically, "the shield of David") on all Jews over the age of six. As we have seen in Hélène Berr's account, no emblem "narrowed" lives more than the gold star, the invidious symbol of German racial policy. This imposition was more vividly and poignantly remembered (by Gentiles as well as Jews) than any other regulation during the Occupation, and it continues to be among survivors. Neither Gentile Parisians nor Germans could ignore the garish pieces of cloth affixed to coats, sweaters, and dresses: "For the last eight days, the Jews have had to wear a yellow star, thereby calling public disdain onto their heads," wrote Jean Guéhenno in 1942.[22] Ernst Jünger, our "better" German, noted with asperity:

On the Rue Royale, I came into contact, for the first time in my life, with the yellow star, worn by three girls who passed by me, arm in arm. These markers had been distributed yesterday. . . . I saw the

Worn proudly. (Ghetto Fighter's House Museum)

star much more frequently later that afternoon. I consider that event as deeply affecting.... Such a sight cannot but provoke a reaction, and immediately I was embarrassed to find myself in uniform.[23]

Of course, having to wear the yellow star gave rise to a devastating realization for the Jews: they were definitely the intended targets of an anti-Semitism that was to be much more vigorous from that point on.

The star was an awkward, if not clumsy, Nazi adaptation of a centuries-old European tradition that was intended to distinguish Christians from Jews in some visible manner. Using the same rationale, starting in Poland in 1939, and then in Germany itself in 1941, the Nazis hoped to use these obnoxious little badges not only to humiliate but also to encourage non-Jews to avoid the despised "other." The bright yellow badge removed all attempts at anonymity—one of the advantages of living in a large city. Yet the bureaucratic apparatus needed to enforce this law often led to confusion and unintended consequences for both the Occupier and the citizen of Paris.[24] Immediately there were exceptions demanded and approved. Would only immigrant Jews wear the star? Or French Jews as well? What about Jewish citizens from other Axis or neutral nations? What if one were only half Jewish, or married to a French Gentile? Why did French Jews have to wear the stars and Turkish and Bulgarian Jews (from countries allied with the Reich) not have to do so? And there were distribution problems. The short span between publication of the law (on May 29) and its implementation (on June 7) meant that a herculean effort had to be mounted in order to produce enough of the badges to be effective. "In France, this meant four hundred thousand yellow stars needing five thousand meters of cloth to be manufactured hastily under orders from the occupier.... For certain messier professions (butchers, those working with children...), stars were specially made in celluloid."[25] We know the names of the French companies that found and prepared the cloth, manufactured the stamps that printed JUIF in bold, quasi-Hebraic lettering, and that produced the stars. One wonders, as artisans employed by these companies worked overtime to prepare these odious markers, what went through their minds.

The order also insisted that: "The badge must be worn about the level of the heart, firmly sewn to the garment, and must always be visible. It is forbidden to hide [*cacher*] the star in any manner whatsoever. One must take care of the insignias. In sewing the star onto the garment, one must turn under the border that extends past the star."[26] (Stars were delivered in squares and had to be cut or sewn as described; one reason given by the police for the arrest of Hélène Berr's father was that his star had not been firmly sewn onto his jacket.) The macabre precision of detail, the insistence that the "star of David" be dominant, the assumption that one would easily remove the star under certain circumstances, even the use of the word *heart* rather than "left side of the chest" and the unintended similarity between *cacher* (to hide) with *kascher* (kosher): all this language bespoke the oblivious obsessions that subtended Nazi racial policy.

The Parisian public's reaction to the yellow star was varied and still fascinates. The injunction had a palpable effect on those who did not wear the star, who looked away when a Jew passed—in the apartment building, on the street, in the shop, in the Métro—thereby making an ethical decision that had been unnecessary up until then. Everything from eye contact to physical intimacies had to be recalibrated. The star created a mobile ghetto, one where Jews were identified publicly for the first time. Overheard were such snide remarks as "Imagine! Such a nice, polite man; when I saw his star I was truly shocked." Jews (and blacks) had been relegated to the last car on the Métro since 1940, but then there was no way of telling who was and who was not Jewish. Now conductors and ticket takers were instructed to make sure those wearing stars rode in the rear. One Nazi, offended that a Jewish lady confidently wearing her starred sweater had entered the first-class coach of a Métro train, pulled the emergency cord and ordered her out. She was followed by all the Gentiles, leaving the red-faced thug alone in his newly "cleansed" coach.

By then everyone had heard, or had read, of the laws that deprived Jews of property and rights; many Parisians had Jewish acquaintances who had been rounded up, or they had noticed empty and emptied apartments. Yet the overwhelmingly general response had been to half

Waiting in line with a star. (© *Roger Schall / Musée Carnavalet / Roger-Viollet /*
The Image Works)

believe Nazi propaganda, which said that those arrested were Communists or foreign terrorists or black marketers. (One of my sources told
me exactly this: as a fifteen-year-old boy, he was only interested in girls
and bikes; the posters announcing the executions of "terrorists" barely
interested him.) Before the star, Jews could "pass" as Aryans (though
their official identity papers were stamped with a red JUIF or JUIVE).
Now no such shelter remained. For the first few days, groups of young
anti-Semitic rowdies would slap Jews in the street or force them inside
if they were having coffee on an outdoor terrace. The French police,
strangely enough, patrolled the streets to stop this harassment (probably

to prevent retaliation), briefly protecting the very Jews who had been humiliated by having to wear the star in the first place. But as noted earlier, there are also many anecdotes about Gentiles saluting, winking at, or otherwise showing solidarity toward Jewish strangers having to wear the yellow badge. During one of her walks, Hélène Berr came across a couple at the Métro stop at the Place de l'Étoile: "There were a young man and woman in the line, and I saw the girl point me out to her companion.... Instinctively I raised my head—in full sunlight—and heard them say: 'It's disgusting.'"[27] The ambiguity of the Gentile girl's remark emphasizes how daily engagement among citizens had been altered by the appearance of the stars.

The Germans were understandably nervous about the public's reaction to the gold stars, as memoranda circulated among them indicate; they commented on the complications of the recent introduction of stars in the Netherlands and in Belgium.* Their responses to infractions were swift and draconian, too. The badges worn by some young Gentiles eager to show solidarity, emblazoned with words such as SWING or GOI or INRI, did not amuse the Occupation authorities—or, for that matter, their allies. One woman had put a paper star around the neck of her dog; when stopped by the police, she grabbed it and ate it, according to the police report, but she was arrested anyway. (The Vichy government had forbidden the law's enactment in the Unoccupied Zone for exactly this reason: fear of public criticism.) Just a few days after the stars began appearing on the streets of Paris, a German police official wrote: "According to intelligence arriving hourly, Gaullist and Communist groups are making propaganda for trouble this coming Sunday [the first since the law's imposition]. Directives have been given that Parisians sympathetically salute Jews wearing stars on the *grands boulevards*."[28] The bureaucrat had also heard that many Gentile Parisians were planning to wear their own yellow stars, either blank or with something else written on them, and suggested these individuals should immediately be arrested and put on trains to the east. Perhaps, he mused, Jews should even be forbidden to

---

* In order to avoid distribution problems, the Germans in Belgium had used a *J* for both the French *Juif* and the Flemish *Jood*, thereby having to print only one model of star. One is always amazed at the German knack for bureaucratic precision and efficiency.

A star in solidarity with Jews. (Préfecture de la Police de Paris)

walk along the Champs-Élysées, the Rue de Rivoli, and other large boulevards the following Sunday. And the chauffeur of a Gestapo official even reported that he had seen Jews appearing *proud* of their stars, pointing them out with humor and irony to their French compatriots. These latter were saluting them, shaking their hands, expressing regrets. One was overheard saying, "Just wait a bit more. Today they are forcing you to wear the star. But that will not last much longer, and the few Germans who will survive this war will be obliged to wear the swastika for all eternity."[29] Another German wrote indignantly: "Especially surprising was the effrontery with which Jews circulated in groups on the large avenues and paraded in the cafés and restaurants."[30] Some of the more courageous Jews actually sat at tables next to German officers, to the amusement of other patrons. But this would not last long, for on July 15 (just a day before the largest roundup of this period), the Germans published an ordinance that forbade Jews to frequent any public establishment or attend public events, e.g., "restaurants, cafés, cinemas, theaters, concerts, music halls, swimming pools, beaches, museums, libraries, expositions, châteaus, historic monuments, sporting events, racecourses, parks, campgrounds, and even phone booths, fairs, etc."[31]

The star was especially burdensome for children. In fact, Parisians seemed most upset by seeing six-, seven-, and eight-year-olds wearing the huge badges (everyone over six years old had to wear one; there were no children's sizes) pinned and sewn to their school clothes.

Closed to Jewish children. (*Mémorial de la Shoah*)

Annette Muller remembered how it was. Her mother sewed the stars on her four children's garments and then marched them down the streets of the 20th arrondissement, ordering them to walk with heads high. "Her arrogant gaze seemed to defy those who looked at us silently," Annette recalled. "She wanted to show to everyone that she was a young Jewish mother, proud of her Jewish children."★ [32]

But what was worse than being paraded by offended parents was having to go to school. We all know that children, after a certain age, want to fit in, not to stand out, so it is not hard to imagine what happened when a child appeared in class (especially in a class with few Jewish children) wearing a huge yellow star. The Gentile parents of many children had not prepared them for seeing their Jewish friends so distinguished, and their first reactions were often humorous, teasing, and occasionally bullying. At school, Muller noticed that her non-Jewish friends stopped asking her for playdates; more significantly, she remembered a very

---

★ Annette's thirty-four-year-old mother would be deported and killed before two months had passed.

Even the children. *(Mémorial de la Shoah)*

pretty, blond, blue-eyed girl from a very well-off family, a young icon for all the other kids, who showed up the same day with a bright star on her chest. Even Annette was surprised. This was not the only eyebrow-raising event: many folks were surprised to see so many stars on people who did not "look Jewish." Noted Biélinky:

> Thanks to the stars, [an objective observer] could see that the large majority of Parisian Jews did not carry the classically assumed characteristics of the "race." Without the stars one could never take for Jews this multitude of young men and women with agreeable, normal characteristics, similar to those the indigenous French population itself would like to have.[33]

The caricatures that the Germans had been promulgating for more than two years, that Jews were all quasi-Semitic, with pendulous lips, large hands, hooked noses, frizzy hair, and small, greedy eyes, were seen as just that: exaggerations.

Despite this upending of stereotypes, her mother's courage, and her pride in being Jewish, Annette Muller concluded at that young age that "to be Jewish meant to be dirty, disgraceful, shameful. That shame—I felt it in the street when people turned away at the sight of the star, which marked us like a hateful and stinking stain. Was this what it meant to be Jewish? That's what I was, and I was ashamed. I wanted so much to be like the others, good people, clean and proper."[34] The attention that the new edicts were increasingly directing toward children also made Jewish youngsters feel uncomfortably "special." Parks were closed to them; fairs, festivals, puppet theaters, sailing ponds, athletic teams similarly denied them. They had to stay close to home, and be there after 6:00 p.m.

Another French Jew, seventy-year-old Edgar Sée, left us a much more oblique memoir—only recently published, a short notebook of the last year of his life in Paris—which helps us understand why so many star-wearing Jews did not leave the city and even managed to survive, though not he. Sée was an eminent attorney, teacher of law, and active member of his Jewish community. His family had deep roots in the Alsatian community and had been French for at least two centuries. In his diary, he describes a day just after the imposition of the star when he met an elderly Gentile couple on a walk along the Seine: "[They] questioned me about the star, assuring me of their respect and sympathy, just as had previously numerous ecclesiastics, individuals, [and] working-class people especially; [some] would get up to give me their seat in the Métro, or allow me to advance in line because of the restrictions put on our shopping times, etc."[35] He was arrested along with other Jews on his street, the elegant Avenue Victor-Hugo, in a roundup occasioned by the assassination of a German official in his neighborhood. The detained were promptly sent to Drancy. Sée had thought he might be safe from such scrutiny, for he had a friend in the German embassy with whom he had worked for more than ten years when he was younger, but even though that colleague wrote a letter the day after his arrest ("Although he is a Jew, and seventy years old, for years [he] has defended German interests [and] merits the protection of Germany"[36]), it was ignored by higher-ups, and Sée was deported two weeks later. He did not return.

Sée was caught up in the self-deception of many French Jews, especially wealthy and well-connected ones, such as Hélène Berr's father, that somehow they could ride out the disaster that was surrounding them, encroaching daily on their lives. If they gave up their arms and radios, if they renewed their IDs, if they wore punctiliously the yellow star, if they rode the last car of the Métro train, they would be fine. "[These French Jews] could not bring themselves to believe that the same men would commit in France the same infamies [they were carrying out in the east]. The country of the rights of man had its traditions and would preserve them."[37]

In his unpublished manuscript, the late Berkeley historian Gerard Caspary, a Jewish survivor, annotated an extensive correspondence between his mother, Sophie, and her mother, Martha, who had been living in Sweden since the early 1930s. The letters were written in the early 1940s, as the Germans focused their attention on the Jews of Paris, and he wrote in his introduction that there was a distinct disconnection between what was happening to Jews in the city and in France and the daily lives of the Casparys in Sèvres, just beyond the limits of the capital. On the one hand, mother and daughter, now separated from each other not only by distance but by war, were writing as if the separation were only temporary and could be resolved by either emigration or good luck. On the other hand, the letters speak of the daily problems of living in an occupied environment; but slowly the persecution of Jews, especially the limitations placed on their daily lives, seeps into the correspondence.* Knowledge of what was going

---

* It is just plain luck that the correspondence exists. First, Sophie's mother fortunately kept copies of her own letters to France as well as her daughter's originals. Sophie's older brother wanted the whole correspondence destroyed after the war in order to prevent young Gerard, who had escaped arrest and immigrated to the United States, from being wounded by the memory of his ordeal. But Sophie's younger sister, living in Sweden, intervened, and Caspary, an accomplished medieval historian, spent the last years of his life annotating the correspondence, which proved to be a consolation to him as a survivor. I am grateful to Robert Weil for offering me this remarkable manuscript, and for encouraging me to write about it.

on around them gives an aura of solemnity to even the most mundane observations. There is much discussion about cost of living, money transfers, clothing for a fast-growing teenager, cold, and foodstuffs. His mother is proud that Gerard can take the Métro to Paris to go to movies or to accompany his classmates on field trips. Little by little, though, coded terms begin to appear in the letters between mother and daughter that signal deportations, plans for escape, and war news. The yellow star legislation receives only an oblique mention, yet it is obvious that every trip far from their abode, especially into Paris, was fraught with danger. Parisian friends were disappearing, and roundup news was passing fast through the innumerable grapevines that connected Jewish households. Caspary wrote of a "mad sort of normality," a description of Jews' efforts to avoid trouble and act as if everything were fine. It remains impossible to know whether Sophie's letters were written this way because of censors who were reading them, or because she was making a doomed effort to find normality in an upturned world.

Caspary had been born in Frankfurt and came to France with his parents around the age of four. He kept his Jewish origins to himself and only told a French friend or two about his ethnic heritage. He was surprised one day when his teacher told him that he had come in first in a competition but was going to be awarded second prize because he was Jewish. It was the first time the outside world had made a point of his Jewishness. Then came the day when he had to wear the yellow star to class for the first time. His mother told him to be proud, to hold his head up; but he wanted to do that for her sake, not because he was proud: "I was absolutely terrified. Previously I had told only one boy in school that I was a Jew. . . . When I knew that the Jewish star was coming I told no one of my fears except Claude [his friend], who swore that though all the other kids would turn against me he would stick with me...no matter what." To his surprise, the school principal had announced to all his students that anyone bullying or otherwise making fun of a Jewish boy would never receive a recommendation from him; in fact, he would be sure that others would not write recommendations for them, either. This did not really mollify poor Caspary.

Unbeknownst to him, his mother, "hating and fearing authority figures as much as she did, but knowing how scared I was, must, on her own and without telling me...have gone to the principal and asked him to do something."*

Caspary described the arrest of his parents by French police succinctly, but quite effectively:

Very early in the morning of October 23 [1943] they finally came for us. We had of course been expecting them since summer. What I remember is that in the middle of the night I came up like a diver out of a very deep sleep with my mother bending over me with one hand over my mouth and the other pointing toward the window, from which there came the shrill sound of the bell ringing, ringing, and ringing. It was pitch dark....What I remember...is the constant sound of the bell that just went on and on. (They must have inserted a matchstick into the mechanism.)...I started arguing with my father [about escaping out the back door, but he] objected and said that they probably had posted some people in the back. My mother took my father's side. Finally at 8:00 a.m. precisely (they later told us that they were legally not allowed to break in before that time, something that today I do not believe...), we heard them break down the front door.

Caspary thinks that the police might have been giving his parents a warning, but he never found out, and they were taken like squirrels in a trap. The police offered to let the teenager go (he was only fourteen) if his parents could find a place for him. Sophie called a friend; Caspary embraced his parents and left the house in tears, on his way to a new, safer, and lonelier life. He never saw them again.

---

* Caspary also remembered that two years later, after the war, before he left for exile in the States, he returned to thank the principal for having stood by him. But "he was quite angry with me that I was leaving France"—that Caspary was not returning a patriotic Frenchman's kindness with loyalty to the nation. Such a country and such an accusation must have seemed strange to that sixteen-year-old boy.

The Big Roundup

Just six weeks after Jews had been ordered to wear the yellow star came the Grande Rafle. Over two days and in dozens of Parisian neighborhoods, thirteen thousand foreign and French Jews were taken from their homes, from their hiding places, from hospitals, from schools, retirement homes, even asylums. As a result of this enormous dragnet, more Jews with French citizenship were caught than ever before. Finally, and most poignantly, more than four thousand children, ranging in age from about two to fourteen, were collected and deported. Many children were abducted from their classrooms, from their kindergartens, and from their nurseries before the eyes of their classmates and teachers. A casual walk through the Marais and other sections of Paris today will reveal plaques that commemorate those events and the numbers involved. Some children were not taken, but when they returned home they found their parents gone and the apartment doors sealed. Or they found the seals broken because neighbors and the concierge had broken in to take possession of objects or the

ARRÊTÉS PAR LA POLICE DU GOUVERNEMENT DE VICHY, COMPLICE DE L'OCCUPANT NAZI, PLUS DE 11000 ENFANTS FURENT DÉPORTÉS DE FRANCE DE 1942 A 1944 ET ASSASSINÉS A AUSCHWITZ PARCE QU'ILS ÉTAIENT NÉS JUIFS.

PLUS DE 500 ENFANTS VIVAIENT DANS LE 4ème ARRONDISSEMENT, PARMI EUX LES ÉLÈVES DE CETTE ECOLE

Le 15 décembre 2001   NE LES OUBLIONS JAMAIS

The French finally remember: Vichy police arrested Jewish children.

space itself. One police record reports a Gentile neighbor asking, on behalf of a Jewish girl, if she could go into her parents' apartment to collect a change of clothes.[38]

Some mothers had left their babies in their cribs, unnoticed by the police because they were not on any list; some had hidden them in closets or in hideaways prepared months in advance. One father kept repeating to his friends: "My ten-month-old is all alone; I didn't have time to give a key to the concierge, and I don't know where my wife is!" Sympathetic Gentiles had, fortunately, carried off a few youngsters before the Grande Rafle; and many had been grabbed out of lines, ready to mount buses for Drancy and the Vélodrome d'Hiver. But many more were roaming around a dreadfully quiet neighborhood after the buses had taken away their parents. The neighbors they knew had been carried away, too; most of the children did not know the area around their quarter well at all, for their parents had forbidden them to leave the street or block. They had no money, though we do know that some prescient parents had sewn francs into the hems of their clothing just in case. Fortunately, they did have one organized group of saviors: the Éclaireurs israélites de France, the Jewish scouting organization, similar to the Boy Scouts in Great Britain and the United States. (There were female members, too, and later the name of the organization was changed to include "Éclaireuses.") These teenagers, who themselves had escaped arrest because they had been living in other areas, were well organized, and their leaders sent them out immediately on July 17 to search the streets for wandering children. They found hundreds of them and took them first to temporary orphanages in Paris, then later, when they could, to the countryside. In this way, thousands of youngsters were saved and survived the war, generally in hiding. Occasionally, groups of children would be denounced by anti-Semitic French citizens and deported, but overall the French people can look with pride at their active participation in being among the "Justes" and in saving these young Jews.*

---

* In 2012, the city of Paris organized an exhibition, with the help of the Mémorial de la Shoah, called *C'étaient des enfants* (They Were Children). The stunning thoroughness of the Occupier at rounding up, imprisoning, transporting, and murdering French and

Nevertheless, the toll was horrific, as was the complicity. The pressure on the Vichy government from the Germans, who felt that the Parisian police and the Vichy masters were dragging their feet on arresting and deporting all Jews living in France, had been enormous. They knew, too, that the Italians were not as fanatic as they were, and that as a result many Jews were living in relative safety both in the Unoccupied Zone and in the zone controlled by the Italians in the far southeastern part of the country. This situation especially offended the Commissariat Général aux Questions Juives, that their allies were protecting so many Jews.

Wishing to palliate the German Reich, with which he was still hoping to establish some sort of alliance, the ever canny Pierre Laval, who had returned to head the Vichy government in April of that year, knew that he had to win over (and outmaneuver) a hesitant Pétain, assuring the old Maréchal that only foreign Jews would be rounded up in this massive action. Pétain, it appears, was concerned that his own integrity would be besmirched should word spread (which it did) that the French government was in effect doing the Nazis' bidding regarding deportation. It is unclear who decided that "families should not be separated," a decision that would permit the roundup of children with their parents. The blame most often goes to Laval; Pétain always denied knowledge of this decision. We do know that it was not originally a German priority; why would they want to be responsible for the imprisonment and transport of thousands of children? They had even suggested that churches and Jewish orphanages take care of the young ones. But an offhand suggestion by Laval was finally sent to Berlin, and the word came back to the Commissariat Général aux Questions Juives that children "could" join their arrested parents. The children were sent to Auschwitz a few months after their parents, a story that spread like wildfire throughout France, and was the death knell that rang out for a corrupt regime.

---

non-French Jewish children (and many had been born in France, though of foreign parents) made the exhibition mesmerizing and completely dispiriting. Some of the anecdotes I recount come from the catalog for the exhibition, edited by Sarah Gensburger (see bibliography for details).

The French police were deadly efficient. There had been warnings that a massive roundup was about to take place. The Jewish Communists were especially attuned to the plan to make a major sweep across Paris; most likely this information was garnered from their own spies among the Parisian police. A few days before the roundup, a tract appeared in Jewish neighborhoods:

> Do not wait for these bandits in your home. Take all necessary measures to hide, and hide first of all your children with aid of sympathetic French people. . . . If you fall into the hands of these bandits, resist in any way you can. Barricade the doors, call for help, fight the police. You have nothing to lose. You can only save your life. Seek to flee at every moment. We will not allow ourselves to be exterminated.[39]

And yet.

The collection of files (*fichiers*) gathered over the previous two years by the Occupiers and their Vichy functionaries provided names, addresses, occupations, ages, and numbers of family members, from which smaller lists were made and handed to each arresting group so that not one registered Jew would be missed. Though the French police have spent years trying to dodge their reputation as enablers, there is no doubt, now that the archives are almost all freely open, that the French forces of order were active, not reluctant, collaborators with the Germans. Indeed, there is no way the Germans could have succeeded as well as they did in rounding up these "illegals" if it had not been for the help of the local police forces. The Germans quite simply did not have enough personnel to track and keep files on Jews or plan and carry out raids, arrests, and incarcerations. Nor did they know as intimately the labyrinth that was the city of Paris.

The effect of this massive roundup was devastating. It ended for once and all the myth that some Jews were protected from the arm of the law. It established without any doubt that the French police were a major, unsympathetic force. There exists no record of even a single French policeman having refused to participate in his assignment.

Filed lives.

However, quiet subterfuges did occur, and many Jews did escape under the turned gaze of a sympathetic officer, but much of that information is primarily anecdotal, just as is the information concerning the courage of some concierges and the jealous hatefulness of others.*

About 4,500 French policemen organized and participated in the operation. The Germans were nowhere to be seen—this of course particularly infuriated both the Jews and their Gentile neighbors. Despite the initial successes of the roundup, which began at 3:00 a.m., the German authorities, surreptitiously evaluating the results, were apoplectic. Hoping to round up 27,500 Jews, the great majority of them during the early hours of July 16, the police had only, by mid-

---

* Perhaps as many as ten thousand Jews, especially children, escaped this roundup; they just happened to be out or were hidden by Gentile Parisians or other Jews and later moved out of Paris into the countryside. Also, those who had children less than a year old or who were pregnant, were, strangely enough, exempted.

morning, been able to find about 13,000, and the action was threatening to take a day or more. What was the problem? A note from a French police bureaucrat, written at 8:00 a.m. on July 16, cites excuses for the roundup's slowness:

> The operation against the Jews has been going on since 4:00 this morning. It has been slowed up by many special cases: many men left their homes yesterday. Women remain with a very young child or several children; others refuse to open their doors; we have to call a locksmith. In the 20th and the 11th [arrondissements] there are several thousand Jews; the operation is slow. [Nevertheless] by 7:30, ten buses have arrived at the Vél d'Hiv.[40]

This roundup collected primarily women and children. The police had reserved about fifty public buses for transport. In retrospect, it was clear that seeing police officers in recognizable uniforms, as well as the familiar green-and-cream buses, helped to calm the hunted. Men composed only about 30 percent of the detainees, for they had by now learned to sleep away from home at night or to hide out; no one thought that women and children were in danger. Most of those rounded up were taken either to the Vélodrome d'Hiver, in the 15th arrondissement, or to the railhead at Drancy. The Vélodrome d'Hiver (Winter Bicycle Track) was a huge covered meeting hall and racing venue. Over 17,000 spectators could watch a variety of events: rallies, boxing, even a bullfight, and the track could be used for roller-skating, even ice-skating. Everyone knew where the Vél d'Hiv was — right near the Eiffel Tower, on the Left Bank. It was a place for screaming throngs of fans, entertainment, and healthy competition. But it would become synonymous with the cruelty of Paris's acquiescence to the German desire to rid the city of all Jews. Finally torn down in 1959 (after having been used as a holding center for anitcolonialist Algerians in 1958), there is now a Place des Martyrs Juifs du Vélodrome d'Hiver in memory of those incarcerated there for a week during the hot month of July in 1942.

Buses that brought Jews to the Vél d'Hiv. *(© BHVP / Roger-Viollet / The Image Works)*

Vélodrome d'Hiver at a happier time. (© *Roger-Viollet / The Image Works*)

The descriptions of conditions in this huge bicycling-rink-cum-concentration-camp were later recounted on film, in memoirs, and in firsthand accounts (several dozen victims were able to escape during the commotion of trying to direct eight thousand people into the building). One example from an eyewitness:

> It was like hell, like something that takes you by the throat and keeps you from crying out. I will try to describe this spectacle, but multiply by a thousand what you imagine, and then you will only have part of the truth. On entering, your breath is cut by the stinking air,

279

and you find before you an arena black with people crowded next to each other, clasping small packages [of clothes, belongings, food]. The scarce toilets are blocked. No one can fix them. Each is obliged to do his or her business along the walls, in public. On the ground floor are the ill, with full waste containers next to them, for there aren't enough people to empty them. And no water....[41]

Hundreds of rapidly scribbled and notes and letters from detainees were sneaked out of the Vélodrome, but only about two dozen of them have made their way to the archives of the Mémorial de la Shoah in Paris.★ They ask friends, relatives, concierges to send them packages; they have no idea how long they will be in the arena or where they will be taken afterward. One Polish woman even thinks she will be released because her two daughters had been born in France, and she asks her concierge if they can stay with her when they return. The letters provide confirmation of what archival research has shown since: there were no uniformed German soldiers at the Vél d'Hiv, only French police; there were thousands of babies and very young children; most of the detained thought they would be sent to French concentration camps permanently; others thought they might be released because they were mothers of small children; some few—e.g., furriers and leather workers—were released because the Germans needed their services (for Eastern Front uniforms).

Among the thousands waiting in the Vél d'Hiv to find out their fate, some committed suicide—these were Jews who knew that the roundup was not just for the purpose of taking names. Perhaps the most moving testimony of this awful week in this awful place comes from a fireman, part of a cohort brought in to check—unbelievably—for fire hazards caused by overcrowding. In 2007, one of those Parisian firemen,

---

★ The Mémorial de la Shoah in Paris is found on the Rue Geoffroy l'Asnier, in the Right Bank area known as the Marais. On entering the memorial, one passes by marble slabs engraved with the names of all those Parisian Jews who were deported between 1942 and 1944. Running your fingers across those marks, it is impossible to avoid seeing the birth dates of the victims: 1936, 1937, 1939, 1940, and 1941. For the extant letters of those who wrote from the arena, see Taieb and Rosnay, *Je vous écris du Vél d'hiv*.

JACH 1909 • Renée DEBITON 1909 • Eugénie DEBRE 1864 • Adèle DECLERCQ 1909 • Dwojra DEGENSZ/
1899 • Mowsza DEJCZ 1889 • Abraham DEJONG 1875 • Rosalie DEJONG 1868 • Lucien DEL POR
IELVAILLE 1921 • Marcel DELVAILLE 1894 • Mardoche DELVAILLE 1926 • Renée DELVAILLE
IBINSKA 1886 • Anna DEMBO 1895 • Schneier DEMBO 1886 • Erwin DENHOF 1925 • Paula DE
1918 • Adrienne DERKAUTZAN 1886 • Gaston DERMAT 1892 • Aziza DERROUAZ 1894 • Otto DERSCH
SSEGNO 1889 • André DEUTCH 1909 • Daniel DEUTCH 1923 • Isidore DEUTCH 1892 • Julia DI
1878 • Adalbert DEUTSCH 1905 • Georges DEUTSCH 1929 • Gisèle DEUTSCH 1886 • Hersz DEU
5CH 1932 • Maurice DEUTSCH 1872 • Paula DEUTSCH 1883 • Pepi DEUTSCH 1878 • Pierre DEU1
le DEUTSCH 1873 • Towja DEUTSCH 1920 • Yolande DEUTSCH 1909 • Alf DEUTSCH-GERM/
EDE 1900 • Ente DIAMAND 1878 • Hélène DIAMAND 1941 • Jeannette DIAMAND 1938 • Rywka DIA
IANT 1919 • ⬛⬛⬛⬛⬛⬛⬛⬛ • Henri DIAMANT 1943 • Marthe DIAMANT 1918 • Maurice DIAN
IMENT 1891 • Laja DIAMENT 1903 • Maurice DIAMENT 1907 • Perl DIAMENT 1926 • Joseph DI
1908 • Sigmund DICKMAN 1909 • Mordko DIDITCHE 1877 • Chaja DIENER 1897 • Israël [
919 • Bernard DIMAND 1896 • David DIMENT 1899 • Joseph DINAR 1908 • Alice DINESM
IL 1889 • Ester DITMAN 1894 • Sarina DJAHON 1897 • Szlama DJAMENT 1892 • Estera DJI-TCHANC
• Massoenda DJIAN 1887 • Hélène DJIAN-BENGUIGUI 1905 • Mentech DJIBRE 1882 • Elie DJOUR
BELSKAIA 1879 • Jankel DOBIN 1906 • Mordehay DOBIN 1880 • Paul DOBLIN 1878 • Jean DOB
IUK 1889 • Rose DOHERN 1887 • Kalman DOLBERG 1885 • Samuel DOLINER 1890 • Jack

Some were so young. (Names inscribed at the Shoah Memorial.)

F. Baudvin, recounted his story for the archives of the Mémorial de la Shoah in Paris. One can still feel his distress sixty-five years later. On entering the forecourt of the arena, he noticed that there were no Germans, only gendarmes and municipal police, but on one side, he glimpsed a few men in civilian clothes — "gabardine," he wrote. Were they the Gestapo? He did not know or have the leisure to further consider the possibility. As soon as he and his fellow firemen went inside, detainees ran up to them, begging for help, stuffing their potential saviors' pockets with notes and letters for the outside while pleading for something to drink. Against orders from the police, the firemen turned on the hoses, mercifully spraying the arena and the crowd. They tried to separate themselves from the anxious detainees, afraid that they would be searched, or worse, by the police or the "gabardines" when they left. When they finally returned to their caserne, their chief gathered the five young men:

> You agreed to do some favors during your recent assignment. You must honor them. What you collected should be sent to their

addressees, but you should use only the most public mailboxes. Avoid the 7th, 15th, and 16th arrondissements [the wealthiest, where many Germans lived or worked], and be careful. I'm giving each of you liberty for a day; the desk sergeant will give you the permissions as well as some Métro tickets when you leave. Finally, if one of you has a problem, say that you are acting on your own. You received no order or suggestion from me. I won't be able to help you; leave and do your best.[42]

Baudvin tells us that he had collected 144 notes and letters. He spent the morning finding envelopes and stamps and trying to decipher addresses before he and his colleagues spread out across Paris to mail what was, for many, the last word received from their imprisoned relatives or friends.*

Next to the assignment of the yellow star, the decision to arrest children between the ages of two and sixteen, then separate them from their parents, was probably the most significant public relations mistake of the Vichy government and their German partners. It is impossible in such a compact city to arrest and move around more than thirteen thousand people, especially when most are women and children, without that information becoming known. The sight of youngsters in buses, roaming the streets alone, or holding their mothers' hands as they mounted police vehicles made an impression on Gentile Parisians. Police reports following the roundup were especially sensitive to public opinion. Excerpts from two such reports reveal this concern:

> The measures taken against the *Israélites* have rather profoundly troubled public opinion. Though the French population is generally anti-Semitic, it nonetheless judges these specific measures as inhumane.... It is the separation of children from their parents that most affects the French population and that provokes...

---

* A quite melodramatic film about the Grande Rafle by Roselyne Bosch was made in 2010. *La Rafle* has some startling improvised sequences filmed at a re-created Vélodrome d'Hiver.

strong criticism of the government and of the occupying authority.

The arrests of foreign Jews on July 16 and 17 have occasioned numerous reactions among the public. The great majority believed that the operations were aimed at French as well as foreign Jews. In general, our measures would have been well received if they had only been aimed at foreign adults, but many were moved at the fate of the children; rumors are still circulating that they were separated from their parents.[43]

The French, much more than the Germans, realized that support for the État français depended on the continuing credibility of the Vichy leaders, especially Maréchal Pétain. Already, food shortages, the snail-slow release of French prisoners of war, and declining living conditions had made criticism of Pétain's "contract with the devil" come under much more incisive criticism from the public. Indeed, the plight of French prisoners was one of the recurring obsessions of Pétain's government, and the Germans played bait-and-switch games with them for four years. The Vichy administration put a huge emphasis on *Famille, Travail, Patrie,* but you cannot have a *famille* without a *père,* at least according to the government's own (conservative Catholic) dogma. Thousands of letters written to prison camps from desperate wives must have lowered the already basement-level morale of the French men in the stalags in eastern France and in Germany. And the Vichy government found itself awkwardly caught between the demands of a "new order" based on traditional ideas of family and a recalcitrant German authority that was using the prisoners as a token for blackmail. Once the Unoccupied Zone had been invaded and militarily occupied by the Germans in November of 1942 (the invasion of North Africa by the Allies had convinced them they should protect more closely their Mediterranean flank), Parisians and other French citizens came to see the embarrassing ineffectiveness and political impotence of the État français. Beginning in early 1943, many supporters of Pétain and Vichy would begin to hedge their bets, quietly joining or supporting the Resistance, which was finally coalescing around de Gaulle by this time.*

If we define a city in part by its institutions and its history, Paris will never be able to erase its responsibility for the roundups, especially the "big" one. These events revealed clearly the truth behind the German and Vichy French policy toward the Jews, and they did more to undermine the Occupation's goals—those of the Wehrmacht, the SS, the Gestapo, the foreign service, and the propaganda machine—than any others. That is one reason why the German reaction to the breakup of the Manouchian Group in late 1943 was so furious: the Germans wanted to prove that France was in more danger from all these foreigners than from them.

In his most famous speech, on the fiftieth anniversary of the Grande Rafle, President Jacques Chirac was the first French head of state to assume responsibility on behalf of all the French and of the republic itself for what had happened; "Oui, la folie criminelle de l'occupant a été secondée par des Français, par l'État français" (Yes, criminal madness was assisted by the French people and by the French state"). It had taken fifty years for such a direct acknowledgment of guilt to have been formally offered, but this, of course, did not put to rest the major questions that continue to harass the French consciousness. How much had a deeply anti-Semitic vein, dating back to the Middle Ages, enabled the Vichy government in their efforts, not to mention the efforts of the Germans? Many French Gentiles put their livelihoods, families, and lives in danger to help their Jewish compatriots and Jewish immigrants, but how widespread was this phenomenon? Why did not more complain to their religious leaders or the government about what they could no longer avoid seeing as the deportations begun in early 1942 and after children were separated from their parents? What could they have done? Why were more than a million letters written to authorities in the five years of the Occupation denouncing

---

* The best-known Vichy official who went over to the other side was, of course, the fourth president of the French Republic, François Mitterrand, whose "confession" of his Vichy activities (he was minister of prisoners of war) cast a shadow over the last years of his presidency.

neighbors, especially Jewish neighbors? What options did the French police have to resist German authority? When the French saw the first edicts targeting Jews, why was there not more of an uproar? Was it because the French Gentiles, too, had been traumatized by the defeat and the sudden appearance of German soldiers at their thresholds? Did they have their own concerns that prevented an active counter-voice? Their new living conditions, and the pressures they were under, forced the occupied to be selfishly preoccupied. Eyes were cast downward, and not toward others too far from their circle. "Why not leave it to the Communists and others to handle this? I have enough on my plate." "The Allies will probably win." "You can't trust everything you hear."*

These questions can never find complete answers, but in a way that is not something to regret. Pierre Laborie, in his little essays on what certain terms and concepts meant in 1939–40, warns us against being anachronistic, that is, in thinking that we, today, can understand what it was like to live in an occupied city in the 1940s. He warns, too, against thinking that just because it was "only" seventy years ago when all this happened, temporal proximity allows us to assume knowledge of such a different time, culture, and spirit.[44] Yet asking these questions is what any society must do once it slips from the path it has set as its purest way. Many French — politicians, bureaucrats, historians — tried for a quarter of a century after the war to erase the memory of Vichy collusion in the Occupation; they failed, and in the almost half century since then they have addressed, straight on, their failures and their successes, trenchantly, effectively, and apologetically. A sense of historical, collective guilt can be seen as the sign of a healthy society, one that does not turn from self-criticism.

The story of the 1,500 nights of the Occupation lends itself to the most clichéd metaphors of nooses tightening, walls closing in, traps being laid, lights dimming, and so forth. Yet the strategy of the Germans

---

* One of France's most engaging social critics, Pierre Bayard, has written a fascinating analysis of what might have been necessary for the average Gentile Frenchman to begin immediately resisting the Germans: *Aurais-je été résistant ou bourreau?* (Would I Have Been in the Resistance or an Executioner?, 2012).

and their French police cohort was stealthy, predictable, and almost successful. Until mid-1942, when anti-Jewish operations became more violent and the rumors of a Nazi "final solution" had finally reached Paris, most well-meaning and generous Parisians were aware, in general, of the laws restricting the lives of their Jewish cohabitants but had convinced themselves that the government was only trying to control immigration and "terrorism." They certainly did not know of the plans to deport them to their deaths, but to their deaths they went: the last, sad convoy to carry children, three hundred of them, left Drancy for Auschwitz on July 31, 1944, at the orders of Alois Brunner. The final transport of adult deportees left on August 17, a week before Paris would be liberated.[45]

Chapter Eight

-◦-══❍══-◦-

How Much Longer?
(1942–1944)

All the prisoners of the town realized [they had been aban-
doned], and each was thinking that something—no matter
what—must be done to hasten their deliverance.

—Albert Camus[1]

"You Can Come Over Now!"

The Grande Rafle and its fallout had made everyone—not just
Jews—tenser and more concerned about when the war would end.
The Gestapo had taken over the security apparatus from the Wehrmacht, and though the latter had not been gentle in their repressions,
the idea that the honor and traditions of the Germany army would not
serve as a moral brake on the Occupation authorities' actions frightened even the most uninvolved citizen. Increasingly, it was the turn of
non-Jewish citizens to be the focus of a stupendously hungry war
machine. In the late spring of 1942, Hitler demanded that some 350,000
French workers be assigned to the Nazi effort. So many German men
had been needed for the Eastern Front that almost overnight Germany
found itself without enough workers for factories and agriculture. In
order to make Hitler's demand more politically palatable, the Vichy
government, under the newly reinstated Pierre Laval's urging, made
what it thought was a brilliant move: to "swap" three voluntary workers for every freed prisoner of war. But the French population's response

287

to requests to go work in war-ravaged Germany was tepid, embarrassing both Laval and the Germans, who had agreed to the deal. Estimates suggest that by August of 1942 only about seventeen thousand workers, mostly unemployed laborers and not the technically specialized workers Germany needed, had signed up. It remains unclear how many prisoners were liberated under this scheme, but its failure led to another piece of legislation in late 1942 that would further undermine the Vichy regime's legitimacy, and would noticeably increase active resistance against the Germans: the establishment of the Service du travail obligatoire (required labor service). The STO, as it was commonly referred to, was in effect a national draft—imposed not by the Germans, who had enacted similar measures in other occupied countries, but by the French themselves. Every male between the ages of eighteen and fifty—and, in an even bolder move, every unmarried woman between the ages of twenty-one and thirty-five—was required to give two years' service to the Nazi (and French) war effort. The French families affected schemed to prevent the census necessary to identify eligible workers. Whole families with boys in *collèges* (middle schools) and lycées had left Paris for the imagined safety of the countryside, and many young people left on their own to join the *maquis,* the quasiguerrilla groups living off the land. In 1939, there had been more than thirty-five thousand university students in Paris and its environs; that number was cut in half or more by 1942. Hundreds of educators had been fired because they were Jews, Freemasons, or troublemakers, or they had been deported for the STO or had gone into hiding. As a result, the school population of the city had fallen from nearly two hundred thousand in 1938–39 to only about fifty thousand in the spring of 1944. Paris was becoming soulless.

Trains for the east often left Parisian stations half empty. Still, between March of 1942 and March of 1944, more than six hundred thousand French men and women were put on them—not to death camps but to factories, farms, and public utilities in the greater German Reich (which then included Austria and parts of Poland and Czechoslovakia). Many perished while abroad, killed by bombing raids or felled by malnutrition and exhaustion, but most returned to France after the war.

To take away fathers and sons, many of whom were the only bread-winners for their families, was considered abominably "antifamily" and thus deeply stupid of the Vichy government, which had based much of its "renaissance" of French social culture on "family values." Not unlike the imposition of the yellow star, this decision forced Parisians of all political colors to consider that the Occupation was no longer to be endured but to be ended. "The time of homilies, [patriotic] appeals, threats mixed with seduction was over; the unruly had become rebellious, [passive] resisters [turned into] insurgents."[2] And hope sparked, albeit amid an increasing darkness. In his journal, Jean Guéhenno wrote:

> June 26 [1942]. We are doubtlessly in the most somber weeks. Germany will have new victories, in Egypt, in Russia, [and] will conquer perhaps all of the Near East. We must have steady nerves. But these victories will resolve nothing. Germany can construct nothing on this immense hatred that it has awakened everywhere. Hitler does not attract, as did Napoleon, even a bit of admiration from those he enslaves. Europe is not bewitched. She watches the increase in the power of an infernal machine that she knows will break.[3]

Daily life in Paris was increasingly difficult. Rationing had been introduced early, and the availability of *cartes de rationnement* became a daily obsession. There were coupons for meat, bread, eggs, and other necessities that could be used only on certain days or by certain categories of citizens—children, workers, or nursing mothers. Use of these "coupons" was not optional; they were almost as valuable as gold itself. Just obtaining enough food for one's growing children, not to mention oneself, could take all day, as parents went from store to store, waited in interminable lines, and often paid people to hold their places while they followed another rumor about fresh eggs, butter, or meat. Parisian babies were being born smaller and sicklier than they had been before the war. Children's physical development was slowed, and even ordinary diseases played harsh havoc with their young bodies. For example, doctors reported many cases of chilblains because of the absence of wool and leather for winter clothing. One woman told me of her desperation to obtain some citrus fruit—and thus vitamin C—for her infant. The markets certainly had none, and prices on the black market were exorbitant. Fortunately, she had a relative who was forced to do business with collaborators and other well-connected Parisians, so whenever they invited him to a restaurant, he always ordered tea so he could slip the lemon in his pocket for his nephew. The less connected or less entrepreneurial citizen just prayed that a sudden illness—unthreatening in better times—would not be fatal for their weakened children.

In her memoir, published in 1945, the American writer Gertrude Stein (who spent the war hiding in the *département* of Ain, in the Rhône Valley, for she and her partner, Alice B. Toklas, were Jewish) describes, in her unabashedly inimitable style, the mind-set of the French at mid-Occupation:

And now it is the first of December 1943 and everybody is cross just as cross as they can be and there is a reason why. Everybody well they did not think it but it was possible and they did hope it that the war would be over. Oh dear they say another winter, well but it is always winter in December yes but we did not think that this December would be another winter, we did not think there could be another winter and now it is December and there is another winter of war. And certainly there is another winter, everybody is so tired of having wood and not coal, of eating quite well [in the countryside at least] but always worried of having it all be such a bother and not being able to go out and buy something if you have the money and worst of all well of course it is the worst of all, that it is the worst of all, the worst of all.[4]

Newspapers, including the German *Pariser Zeitung* (Paris Times), were read more often for announcements about the availability of food than for any war news, which by then was considered by nearly everyone as suspect.* German soldiers, and those French people with available cash or connections, continued to eat well, but the average citizen had to do with less than 1,200 calories a day; as one German reporter noticed early in 1941, "The entire Occupation was [already] 'a question of the stomach' [*Magenfrage*]."[5] Writing immediately after the war, the journalist Pierre Audiat described the state of the Parisian body in late 1943:

> Finally, the wheat harvest having been very abundant in 1943...
> the daily ration of bread was augmented by 25 grams per day.
> This "improvement" in provisions appeared derisory given that
> the situation was getting worse from month to month. The lack
> of food combined with the nervous tension brought on by [the
> Occupation] caused serious loss of weight; tuberculosis was dev-
> astatingly rampant (30 percent more [reported] cases than in
> 1939); a general debility was evident in different forms among the
> population, accompanied often by depression, which expressed
> itself through conversational pessimism.[6]

Counterfeit *cartes de rationnement* became, along with the black market, an important source of foodstuffs. The same children who were the most affected by these penuries were often called upon to help cheat or outsmart the system. Besides the continued use of children to cut in lines, adults found that children were becoming increasingly adept at handing over phony food tickets to unsuspecting merchants — and even, on occasion, at forging them. One boy remembered using small pieces of chewed bread to fill the holes in Métro tickets so they could be reused. Another man remembered that, as a ten-year-old, he was always hungry or cold. Fortunately his parents encouraged him to "get by in another way":

---

* As early as March of 1941, the Occupation authorities had set substantial fines, followed by death sentences, for anyone caught or reported listening to broadcasts from the BBC and Swiss radio. Still, Parisians tuned in.

There is almost nothing to eat, and it's bad. . . . We are so hungry. We can still buy some food with tickets or on the black market, [where] you can get forged IDs for tickets. They look the same, but the paper and the color are of bad quality. We are afraid to use them. . . . [But] I am becoming a great artist. I am a specialist in painting the number 7. On the bread tickets, there are tickets for 50 [grams] and tickets for 750. . . . All you have to do is put a 7 in front of the 50! [Et voilà!] It's not good to cheat. But we aren't ashamed. We are cheating cheaters and thieves.[7]

A generation of children learned that to lie or fool people under certain circumstances would be excused by their parents and, most likely, by their confessors.

But the lack of nourishment was not the only imposition by the Germans. The latter continued their efficient looting up until the last German left in August of 1944. (In fact, many of the escaping motorcycles, trucks, automobiles, and tanks in those last days were piled high with French belongings, last-minute "retribution" for having chased out the enemy.) In 1943, in order to organize, pack, and ship off the loot from more than forty thousand apartments, the Germans, with the help of the Vichy government and Paris police, had set up three huge warehouses: one near the Gare d'Austerlitz, because of its accessibility to trains going east; one in a luxurious (Jewish-owned) mansion on the Rue Bassano, just a few blocks from the Avenue Champs-Élysées; and one in the former Jewish-owned Lévitan furniture store, in the middle-class 10th arrondissement, on the Boulevard Saint-Martin. The "clerks" they used to do the work of receiving, logging in, and organizing the looted items were Jews married to Aryans who had, for the most part, come from the Drancy concentration camp on the outskirts of Paris. There are reports that they occasionally saw their own belongings pass before them; they had to pack up their own picture frames, tchotchkes, and children's toys as if they belonged to someone else.

A team from [Operation Furniture] would meet the removal [van] at the appointed time. . . . The *Préfecture de la Police* in Paris . . .

was informed of each removal in order to take charge of the apartments that were left empty. There were up to eighteen teams working at any one time. The vans' contents arrived at the [warehouses]—each more or less specialising in particular types of objects—where they were sorted and packed into crates. These then left by the trainful for the Reich. When an apartment belonging to a Jew was opened, it would be thoroughly looted by the [Department of Operation Furniture], who would take away virtually everything it contained, from the largest pieces of furniture to the smallest, most everyday objects, from kitchen dressers to school exercise books, from stoves to books and ashtrays.[8]

Years ago, a Parisian Jew who had immigrated to New York City showed me the smaller pieces he had recuperated after the war, still with the cataloging marks the efficient Germans had used to record their massive appropriation of even the most mundane loot.

A rich novel by W. G. Sebald, *Austerlitz* (2001), implies that present-day Paris forgets what still lies beneath its placid surface. The new, futuristic Bibliothèque nationale de France on the Left Bank, in the 13th arrondissement, he suggests, sits confidently but obliteratively over one of these infamous depots:

On the waste land between the marshaling yard of the Gare d'Austerlitz and the pont de Tolbiac where this Babylonian library now rises, there stood until the end of the war an extensive warehousing complex to which the Germans brought all the loot they had taken from the homes of the Jews of Paris.... For the most part the valuables, the bank deposits, the shares and the houses and business premises ruthlessly seized at the time...remain in the hands of the city and the state to this day.[*][9]

The cityscape was also changing. Years of neglecting the facades of

---

* Recent research has suggested that the warehouse was a bit farther west of where the Bibliothèque is located, closer to the Salpêtrière hospital. But Sebald's point remains well taken: Paris has forgotten aspects of its sordid past.

public buildings had given them a dull look; shuttered private mansions and deserted, emptied museums suffered from a lack of personnel to keep these massive buildings in good shape. The use of gardens as parking lots, vegetable plots, and sites for guardhouses had removed much of the traditional joy of seeing another spring beat out a doleful winter. The Germans continued to build massive concrete blockhouses and bunkers throughout the city as well as put grilles and bars in the windows of the hotels they used for headquarters. The city was taking on more and more the affect of a fortress. This did not calm the minds of Parisians, who began to wonder whether, should the Allies make their way to the capital, their Occupiers would declare Paris an "open city" or whether they would defend it down to the last Nazi. Métro stations were closed with more frequency, sometimes for security reasons but also because of the absence of personnel, the lack of repair parts, and sporadic electricity. This meant that the trains that did run were filled to the brim with Parisians and Germans, increasing an intimacy unwanted by both. There were fewer motorized vehicles, including public buses, on the street; bicycles continued to be essential and thus everywhere, though their owners suffered from a paucity of tire rubber and oil. A flat tire or stripped gears could be a major event in the life of a worker or a mother responsible for her children's welfare.

As food vanished, so did unfortunate Parisians: the German authorities were taking larger numbers of hostages; more and more posters were appearing that announced their executions in prisons near and within Paris. Jean Guéhenno noticed that in late 1943, he began hearing more frequently on his walks through the city the playing or singing of "La Marseillaise," forbidden by both the Vichy government and the Germans. One day a paddy wagon of French prisoners drove by him and other passersby on the Boulevard Saint-Michel; from inside the van, they could hear the voices of the likely doomed prisoners, going who knows where, while belting out the world's best-known anthem against the invader. The witnesses of this moving event dared not look at each other as they stopped and listened, but Guéhenno hoped that at least they had their fists clenched in their pockets.

How Much Longer? (1942–1944)

In his high school classes at the elite Lycée Louis-le-Grand, Professor Guéhenno also began to notice that nerves were fraying among his young charges. There were no draft exemptions for students once they turned eighteen, but there was hope that the reputation of this excellent institution would protect them. But what would happen if they turned eighteen in the middle of the school year? Some of Guéhenno's students would come by his home for his advice; others left surreptitiously to join the underground, returning secretly to talk over with their prof their activities and covert plans. On the other hand, there was a more obvious assertiveness from the young men who supported the Vichy regime. In early 1943, the État français had established a paramilitary force, the Milice française (French militia), which many young, unemployed, and/or strongly anti-Gaullist men had joined. It would count more than thirty thousand members by June of 1944, of whom only about half were active and armed. Guéhenno suspected that there were a few such right-wing *mouchards* (sneaks, or spies) in his class, too young still to join the Milice but obvious sympathizers. Guéhenno was eventually reported for his lack of respect for the Occupier and their French comrades, and was sent to teach middle-school as a punishment. Scenes like this must have been repeated throughout Paris as the German authorities and the Vichy government became increasingly nervous.

Parisians began to remark, too, that the "blond warriors," who had become their ideal of the perfectly drilled and accoutred German soldier, had, for the most part, disappeared. Increasingly, very young and middle-aged reservists had replaced them. Less disciplined and fearful that they might be sent off to the Eastern Front, they tended to hang out in larger groups, to drink publicly and to excess, and be more physically impolite to Parisians. The "correctness" of the first year of the Occupation had been replaced with a surly apprehension that added to the city's discomfiting atmosphere. One youngster remembered being on an overcrowded Métro train when three rather bedraggled soldiers, perhaps on leave from the front, entered the car he was in. One of his friends incautiously said in a loud voice: "Boy, they must have scraped the bottom of the barrel for these guys!" Everyone laughed, and the Germans, abashed because they knew no French, joined them. The discipline, focus, and pride of the great Wehrmacht had begun to crack as the massive war on the Russian and Italian fronts and the devastating bombings of German cities took their toll on Nazi morale.

In the first half of 1943, the Wehrmacht's surrender at Stalingrad, the final defeat in May of Rommel's Afrika Korps in North Africa, the invasion of Italy by the Allies in July, and the relentlessness of Allied bombers targeting the factories and rail yards on the outskirts of Paris, all combined to raise both hope and anxiety in the capital. The liberation of Corsica in October of 1943 only made the anticipation more intense for those waiting for the continent to be invaded from the west. Where were the Allies? A repeated joke made the rounds: Stalin's army finally crosses Germany, then France, until it reaches the English Channel. Taking up a loudspeaker, the leader of the USSR bellows across the Channel to the British and Americans: "You can come over now!"

That year—1943—may have been the most psychologically debilitating and demoralizing of the Occupation, for it offered hope that the war might end soon without diminishing the mystery of *how* the war would end. After intensive negotiations among the Communists, the Gaullists, and independent French patriot groups, the Resistance had finally been officially unified in May of 1943 under de Gaulle's administrative umbrella as the Conseil national de la Résistance. The result was that resistance to German authority became bolder.* This was of course a factor that might lead to eventual victory, but it was no boon for those caught in the gears of an increasingly violent guerrilla war. More and more hostages—the innocent and the unlucky as well as the perpetrators—were being arrested, tortured, and shot. And, French Jews—not just their immigrant coreligionists—were increasingly vulnerable to arbitrary roundups.

---

* Earlier called the Mouvements unis de la Résistance (United Resistance Movements), this new configuration finally gave an official name and recognition to the uncoordinated resistance activities—both passive and direct—that had been going on at least since the first Germans had entered France in May of 1940.

The Plague

Albert Camus had left Paris, where he was a journalist for *Paris-Soir,* in 1940, just a few days before the Germans arrived. Following his colleagues first to Clermont-Ferrand, then to Bordeaux, he searched for a means to get back to his native Algeria, away from a France where "life had become hell for the mind."[10] Eventually, in January of 1941, he caught a ship from Marseille to North Africa, where he would remain until July of 1942, when he returned to France. During his stay in Algeria, he thought about "doing something" to resist the Vichy government then in control of Algeria, but mostly he wrote his great trilogy: *Caligula* (a play), *L'Étranger* (*The Stranger,* a novel), and *Le Mythe de Sisyphe* (*The Myth of Sisyphus,* a philosophical essay). The novel had passed German censorship (it was read and approved by Gerhard Heller,

Albert Camus. *(© Roger-Viollet / The Image Works)*

who found the work apolitical and asocial and therefore of no interest to Nazi sensibilities). It was published openly in 1942, along with *The Myth of Sisyphus,* a treatise on the metaphysical absurdity of existence, specifically, the moral uselessness of suicide.* Postwar, we can read these two morally rigorous books as excursuses on the war itself and the moral decisions it forced on even the most neutral citizen.

In July of 1942, on his doctor's orders that he spend time in the mountains of France, Camus left for the mother country. He traveled immediately to the Vivarais region's high plateaus, south of Lyon, where he could breathe more easily and where he and his wife could find healthier food than had been available in Algeria. In January of 1943, the twenty-nine-year-old author finally reached France's publishing capital, where he was feted. Both *The Stranger* and *The Myth of Sisyphus* had drawn much attention—some negative, but mostly positive—and made Camus a star on the French literary scene. Suffering from recurrent tuberculosis, however, he soon left the city and spent much time in the mountains, where he worked on several versions of his major novel, *The Plague* (*La Peste*), finally published in 1947. Later in 1943, Camus returned to Paris, where he would remain until the Liberation. This time, he actively joined the Resistance (although, as he emphasized then and after the war, he never carried a gun) and edited the most influential clandestine newspaper, *Combat,* until after the end of the war.†

In Paris, he took up residence in the Rue Chomel off the Boulevard Raspail, in the 6th arrondissement, just a block or two from the Lutétia hotel, headquarters of the Wehrmacht's intelligence service, the Abwehr. From that small apartment, he stayed in contact with a host of acquaintances from Picasso to Simone de Beauvoir, wrote stunning editorials for *Combat,* and completed the final version of *The Plague.*

---

* Some references to Franz Kafka in *The Myth of Sisyphus* had to be excised. Of course, no Jewish writer or thinker could be cited in a Vichy- or German-approved work.

† The staff also included Jean-Paul Sartre, Pascal Pia, Raymond Aron, and André Malraux. The newspaper would continue publication for two decades after the war. It had taken its name for the Resistance group Combat, which had its origins in northern France.

The novel is presented to the reader as a diary kept by a medical doctor as he lives through the sudden arrival—and, eventually, the sudden departure—of bubonic plague in Oran, a major port city in Algeria. Through this allegory, Camus analyzes what it is like to live in a beloved familiar city that has become unfamiliar by virtue of the massive presence of a foreign host—in this case, rats carrying a devastating bacillus. It would be too simplistic to merely equate the gray vermin that spread the plague in Oran with the gray-uniformed Germans who occupied Paris—Camus's vision of occupation and of the quarantined citizens' reaction to that situation is much more subtle—but that has not kept generations of French readers and others from using it as a convenient fable for a morally complicated time.

In the novel, Camus repeatedly suggests that there are two major sentiments shared by those living through a plague and those under military occupation in a city: notions of exile and solitude. At first, after the shock of a deadly invasion, some residents seek to flee their theretofore comfortable environment. Those who stay soon find the city quarantined, cut off from the rest of the world; consequently there develops a fear of being forgotten by the outside, healthier world. As more of their fellow citizens die, survivors identify a variety of causes for what is happening to them and invent the most flimsy reasons why they will not succumb, too. Confidence in the medical profession weakens, as does belief in religion and social relationships, all previously trusted means of confronting and vanquishing an unexpected imposition on one's life. Death and illness make few exceptions among a wary, then terrified, city, and in silent persistence, a notion of being out of place crawls deeply into the thoughts and actions of the residents of Oran:

> It was undoubtedly the feeling of exile—that sensation of a void within [that] never left us, that irrational longing to hark back to the past or else to speed up the march of time, and those keen shafts of memory that stung like fire. Sometimes we toyed with our imagination, composing ourselves to wait for a ring of the

bell announcing somebody's return, or for the sound of a familiar footstep on the stairs, but...that game of make-believe could not last....We realized that the separation was destined to continue, we had no choice but to come to terms with the days ahead. In short, we returned to our prison-house, we had nothing left us but the past, and even if some were tempted to live in the future, they had speedily to abandon the idea...once they felt the wounds that the imagination inflicts on those who yield themselves to it.[11]

Camus's sensitivity to what it must feel like to make a life under enemy occupation is uncannily perceptive—especially for someone who did not live in Paris during most of the war.

In Oran, Camus describes a mundane, boring, unattractive city, even though it is situated beside one of the most beautiful seas of the world; a city that is French, but not really; Arab, yet not quite; sophisticated, but only in its own eyes; caught amid many cultures, histories, religions, ethnic groups, and classes:

> The town itself, let us admit, is ugly. It has a smug, placid air and you need time to discover what it is that makes it different from so many business centers in other parts of the world. How to conjure up a picture, for instance, of a town without pigeons, without any trees or gardens, where you never hear the beat of wings or the rustle of leaves—a thoroughly negative place, in short.[12]

Oran might be passionless, banal, and modern—the antithesis of Paris—yet Camus understands how the mundane and the exceptional are bound together when a foreign host invades.

> The plague forced inactivity on [our townsfolk], limiting their movements to the same dull round inside the town, and throwing them, day after day, on the illusive solace of their memories. For in their aimless walks they kept on coming back to the same streets and usually, owing to the smallness of the town, these were

streets in which, in happier days, they had walked with those who now were absent.★ [13]

The longer the "plague" lasts, the more solitary, the more "exiled," the citizens feel. Who will help us? Where are they? Parisians had given up on their spiritual mentors—bishops, priests, preachers—who only mouthed platitudes; they had given up on the Resistance, which was, if anything, making things more difficult (ten hostages for every German killed). They had given up on the Allies. When, for God's sake, would they open the second front? Had France been overlooked or forgotten because of its attachment to the Vichy regime? Like the citizens of Oran, Parisians felt that such uncertainty had become almost as harmful as the plague itself.

Camus worried in his notes about what to call his novel, and at one point he almost threw away its present one: "Don't put 'the plague' in the title. Something like 'the prisoners.'" [14] Further on, he considers titling the book "Journal of the Separation" and "Diary of the Separated Man," for he wanted to present a topography of apprehension, where helpless citizens of a vibrant city are threatened with the loss of solidarity. Camus was almost certainly thinking of occupied Paris as he wrote, both when he lived in the provinces and in the city itself. He was fascinated with the ways in which individuals react morally to sudden or swift changes in their environments and to moments when the comfort of habit is taken away. For him, the new philosophical response to the horrors of an absurd world, Existentialism, was indeed about situational ethics: we are placed in situations—physical and psychological—that force us to act or compel us not to act, both of which are inescapably moral choices. There is no such thing as an "innocent" choice, or, for that matter, *not choosing*, which was itself a

---

★ Unknown to Camus, Jean Guéhenno was writing similarly in his private journal, refer-ring to Paris after years of Occupation: "Air raids are constant. Five or six per day...The railroad stations around Paris are one after the other destroyed. From now on we feel almost completely isolated" (Guéhenno, 410). Time had become long and short at the same time, he continued, as signs proliferated that the Germans would leave soon, but still they stayed.

choice. Using the plague as his dominant metaphor, Camus exquisitely suggested that a nation needs a firmer commitment to justice and fraternity than France had had in 1940 to withstand such an attack.

"No longer were there individual destinies; only a collective destiny, made up of plague and the emotions shared by all. Strongest of these emotions was the sense of exile and of deprivation, with all the crosscurrents of revolt and fear set up by these."[15] The phrase "exile and deprivation" sums up not only Camus's major theme—the effects of a "plague"—but also the general psychological and physical situation of most Parisians by the third year of the Occupation. Paris was, after all, still their city, but the Occupiers' wear and tear on its environment and on the residents' bodies and minds had made it less a place of solace than an unreadable facade. Were Parisians having the same reaction to a changed Paris that Hitler had felt when he first met its stony indifference? Though Camus was actively engaged in the Resistance for the rest of the war, his sense of solitude and loneliness in an Occupied Paris never completely abated; he, too, despite his assertive philosophy, felt himself an outsider in the damp grayness of northern France.

Observers from the Palace

"Plague had killed all colors, vetoed pleasure," wrote Camus's fictional diarist.[16] And in her cramped apartment in the Palais-Royal, that protected bubble within a bubble in the center of Paris, the indomitable Colette added a last chapter to her earlier newspaper articles, giving us another subtle analysis of what Paris had become after four years of military occupation. Not unlike the sleepwalkers that Camus describes, Parisians seemed to be going through the motions of life without living at all. Colette had early on decided not to leave Paris for the country; the city, even in anxiety, continued to provide inspiration for her work, giving her insight into how people love and live under depressing circumstances. "What a trail it leaves in our hearts, four years of war," she intoned.[17] From her window she had noticed that children had lost a good part of their youth; benumbed by hunger and constant, unconsummated threats, they laughed and mimicked the sounds of the air alerts rather than leave the gardens. They used indecorous language, for which they would have been slapped before the war, but who could blame them, when so many adults were likewise accommodating themselves to disruptive circumstances? Those on the cusp of adolescence, she noticed, did not try to hide their clumsy sexual groping and passionate kisses; in the Métro, Colette sees them pressed up against each other, oblivious to those around them. Girls try to dress like women, women like girls. The war has scratched away at the veneer of decorum, so important to a society's stability. It was not prudishness that inspired Colette to describe a changed Paris but rather a desire to record, as a journalist, signs of the wearing down that war had caused. And it was literal:

> New and sad signs are becoming more common: the right elbow of a man's jacket is [a shade lighter] than the left. Almost all the handles of overused shopping bags are threadbare, covered with string. You can still see, covering women's svelteness, many dark blue "suits." But don't be put off that the skirt was not dipped into the same blue as the jacket.[18]

And there was the new sound of the wooden-soled shoes of a group of girls running through the Palais-Royal's arcades on their way to stand and giddily scream "Jeannot" under the window of the apartment where Jean Marais, the brilliantly handsome movie actor, lived with his lover, Jean Cocteau, Colette's neighbor.

A flirtatious playwright, artist, and novelist, Cocteau produced his own journal after the war. In it he reveals another view of the tired, dejected, suspicious Paris that most memorialists depict. In his rather superficial jottings, he unapologetically describes the life of one of the most successful occasional collaborators during the Occupation—his own. There is no mention of the penury that afflicted so many of his urban compatriots; he ate, drank, and partied continuously for four years. Nor is there any of the self-flagellation, retrospective guilt, or apology one finds in the postwar memoir of another "fellow traveler," the theatrical actor and film director Sacha Guitry. Openly and comfortably gay, Cocteau moved in all the best circles, always in motion in a Paris noted for the absence of easy transportation. (He mentions a bicycle only once.) His need for attention and his easy morals probably got him rides in the limousines of many wealthy Parisians and Occupiers who found him amusing. At the same time, he kept in close touch with his less obnoxious artistic colleagues, signing, for instance, a letter to the Occupation authorities asking for the release of his friend the poet Max Jacob from Drancy. (Jacob would die of ill health before that release could be effected.) Cocteau fretted about air raids, but only because they kept him from parties; he panicked when *Life* magazine listed him among collaborators who must be chastised after the war. But he could not help himself. The Paris he maps in his journal is a sort of ego map, one that enables us to see how distant collaborationist Paris was from the rest of the city. At the end of the war, many thought he would be "purged" along with other artists who had flown too close to the flame of Nazi fascism. Yet his extraordinary naïveté most likely protected him, and he was barely touched by the postwar "purification" trials. He died in 1963, a few hours after having learned of the death of his friend Edith Piaf.

As one reads these memoirs, it becomes clearer how many strategies were used, especially among those influential enough to protect themselves through their own notoriety, to effect a modus operandi during a period of social upheaval and inconsistent alliances. There were a handful of important Parisians who, unlike Camus's diseased Oranians, were not ethically troubled by their comparative freedom to continue living their lives under the Occupation. Celebrities such as the chameleon dramatist and actor Sacha Guitry; Serge Lifar, head of the Opéra ballet; the movie star Arletty (who famously said, "My heart is French, but my ass is international!"); Coco Chanel; and Maurice Chevalier, who, along with Cocteau and many others, skirted these ethical difficulties by repeatedly assuring all who would listen that they were French patriots and that their best moral choice was to continue to entertain all those French citizens less fortunate than they, keeping their spirits high.[19]

Signs of Defeat

Memorialists, diarists, and other witnesses had noticed for the last few months of 1943 and early 1944 that the soldiers of the Wehrmacht were certainly not of the same quality as those who had invaded the city in 1940. The best had suddenly been shipped off to the Eastern Front. (Even bordello madams noticed the change.) Some Parisians remember the sadness on the faces of the departing young men who had felt so keenly their luck at having been assigned to Paris. Their apprehension touched even those who were happy to see them leave and even happier that the Soviet Union was demanding so much from the arrogant Occupier. Germany needed even more than before the wealth of France, especially its food production, its manpower, and its still not inconsiderable industry, but for the Eastern Front there was no substitute for German bodies. Sadly, the Gestapo stayed and took more brutal control—in the form of increased arrests, confiscations, torture, and executions—of a city that had become restive. The distinction between a military occupation and a police occupation became sharper. As Allied bombs fell with more frequency and regularity, and as their troops came closer and closer to Paris, the Nazis dug in, resisting anyone who would challenge their authority. The orders from Berlin were clear: keep Paris as long as you can; its rail centers, its industries, and its large population were still important assets to the Reich.

Beginning in mid-1943, the Occupation authorities changed how they addressed the increasing number of attacks against its personnel. Rather than blatantly reporting attacks and their consequences through newspapers, radio, and by plastering posters across the city, it toned down the rhetoric. The Germans had realized that rather than being cowed by the taking of hostages and the other repercussions of resistant activity, the population was, rather, paying closer attention to the actual disruptions. German anxiety increased as, for the first time since they had arrived in 1940, the idea of an urban insurrection seemed less theoretical. It would not take much, they surmised, for a housewives' strike to grow into a series of violent street riots.

305

The occupier manifested a noteworthy nervousness and anxiety... [it] took security measures that appeared so extreme as to be laughable to Parisians; the sites where Germans assembled, previously lightly guarded, now were transformed into redoubts, even fortresses. Not only were barriers raised around even the smallest hotel, a special cadre of French police guarded them day and night; the detours that pedestrians had to take around these improvised bastions were wider.[20]

Parisians were also amused that the combination of less experienced troops, many not battle-hardened, and this ambience of trepidation would sometimes manifest itself in the very behavior of the patrols that still marched through the city. The more nervous they became, and as the distressing news of German reversals on the front increased, the louder the marching platoons would sing, as if they were whistling past the graveyard. After three-plus years of Occupation, Parisians had become fine-tuned analysts of any change in their previously arrogant, carefree wardens. The Parisians were not the only ones who were feeling exiled and solitary: as the news of Germany's defeats in Africa and Stalingrad, of their reversals in Sicily and Italy, percolated through the ranks, the proud flanks of the Wehrmacht begin to feel more defensive, more threatened, and less cocky than before. Just a smirk or two from a local a day or two after a Nazi reversal would be enough to tell those assigned to Paris that although the city might have been "without a face" it was not without an opinion. Casual contact between the Occupier and the occupied, already tense, became a minefield.

One tongue-in-cheek anecdote describes just such an encounter. A crowded city bus swerves unexpectedly, and a booted Wehrmacht soldier inadvertently steps on a Frenchman's foot. Instantly, the Frenchman slaps the soldier in the face. The bus passengers become very quiet, but from the other end of the vehicle, a small, elegantly dressed gentleman pushes his way toward the antagonists, and he, too, slaps the German. The passengers gasp; the conductor calls for the bus to stop; the police come to take the three men to the police station. The German soldier complains that both gentlemen had slapped him in front of the other passengers. He demands justice. Impressed that the soldier would come to the French police rather than report the event immediately to his own superiors, the captain moves immediately to resolve the issue. Turning to the first man, he demands: "What possessed you to slap this soldier? Don't you know that's against the law?"

"Oui, monsieur le commissionaire," answered the nervous man. "But, you see, I have very sensitive feet, and when the bus turned abruptly, the soldier stepped on one of them. The pain was intense, and I spontaneously slapped him. I apologize sincerely for my action." The German agrees that it was an accident and accepts the man's apology. The commissioner turns to the prim elderly man and asks: "But why did you walk all the way to the front of the bus to slap this soldier? He didn't step on *your* foot!"

"No, indeed he did not, but when I saw this gentleman slap a German soldier, I wanted to do the same, for I thought that meant the Allies had landed!"

One of the most difficult things to understand about this period is why the Germans, anxious about the impending loss of Paris, continued their roundups of Jews and why they continued to execute hostages. Not only were convoys leaving Drancy and Bobigny for Auschwitz up until the last minute, the Gestapo, the Wehrmacht, and the Vichy Milice continued to track down those preparing for the inevitable fall of Paris. In his book *Nazi Paris,* Allan Mitchell has an interesting theory about this obsession to keep maintaining protocol and order. Up until the moment when the last German truck and the last motorcycle would leave Paris, it was important for the authorities to show that they were still in charge so that the populace would not dare to rise up. Given the fact that the city had been controlled rather successfully by a powerful bureaucracy for more than four years, given the number of false alarms that Parisians had already had about an impending liberation, this theory makes sense. The German fear of showing weakness or debilitated commitment to the Reich's successes reinforced their strategies of occupation until the very end.

Nine days before the city would be free of its nemesis, one of the worst antiresistance actions occurred. Three groups of young *résistants* were anxious to get their hands on weapons, the greatest need of underground fighters. (The Germans had been stunningly efficient and effective at controlling access to arms heavier than pistols and grenades.) But the teams broke one of the cardinal rules of clandestine groups: they moved too fast, bringing into their confidence others who turned out to be spies for the Abwehr, German military intelligence. Betrayed, the would-be fighters were arrested en masse, interrogated, then loaded into trucks that took them deep into the Bois de Boulogne, the large wooded park on the western border of Paris. There the thirty-five young men were ordered out of the vehicles, and as they descended they were machine-gunned. After the fusillade, three grenades were thrown into the pile of bodies as a clumsy coup de grâce. The gory scene took place near an artificial waterfall (*cascade*) in the park, not far from the famous Longchamp racecourse. Ten years later, a member of another group described the way in which the crime was discovered: park personnel had heard machine-gun fire the night of August 16 but had waited until daylight to find out what had happened. The pile of bodies told the macabre story. "A few cadavers were still warm that morning, which suggested how long and painful their agony had been. We found no papers or IDs on the victims."[21] A memorial plaque now looks over the site of this massacre of unarmed potential liberators. Once the city had been freed, other sites— including the Jardin du Luxembourg, in the center of Paris, as well as quickly emptied prisons—would reveal the hastily buried bodies of those the Germans and the Milice had considered "terrorists," and whom they executed as they left town.

Memoirs, letters, novels—they at best present a broken mosaic, and when one tries to piece it together there is always a tendency to give coherence when there was none. Contemporary journals and diaries are perforce focused on the daily lives of their writers and the happenstance of those lives; there is often much depth, but from a narrowly focused personality. Official documents—of the Resistance, of the Germans, and of the Allies—are disparate, and often reflect the confusion that is the handmaiden of war. Uncertainty reigned on both sides—or all three sides—of the major players in Occupied Paris. The city was an island of relative peace in a continent being torn apart; yet there were many within the city who challenged the authority of the Occupiers. It was a city where Jews were being hunted down daily, but in July of 1943, a bureaucrat from the Vichy Commissariat Général aux Questions Juives had complained to his German partners that "there were thirty-two Jewish pharmacies still operating in the Paris region [and] dozens of Jewish physicians still practicing."[22] There was a continuing effective control of resistance efforts by the police, but there was, too, an increasing number of attacks against the Occupier. Even Allan Mitchell, a very precise historian, hesitates when describing the atmosphere of Paris in 1942–44. In his concluding pages, he writes, "Until the very last days of the Occupation, Paris was remarkably quiet, occasional bomb attacks and assassinations notwithstanding."[23] These inconsistencies reveal how complex daily life was, both for the Parisians and for those directly involved in the repression that defined the Occupation.

Chapter Nine

Liberation — A Whodunit

Paris is like a beautiful woman; when she slaps you, you don't slap her back.
> — *General Dietrich von Choltitz, a few days*
> *before he surrendered the city*

Is Paris Worth a Detour?

In his memoir, Raoul Nordling, the Swedish consul in Paris who played a capital role in formulating the surrender of the city by the Germans in late August of 1944, wrote about the news of the disembarkation in Normandy: "Paris was still relatively far from the new front, and life went on as before, but there were many signs of an increasing nervousness. Troop transports toward the west [the Normandy front] grew day by day, while in the circles of German leaders [of the Occupation authorities], great efforts were made to remain optimistic."[1] A former Parisian remembered that, as a young girl, she used to watch these trucks from her windows and hear their sonorous rumbling as they passed her on the way to school. Other witnesses wrote of the changed atmosphere following the unbelievable news of June 6: fast-moving transports and tanks were passing through and around Paris as the Wehrmacht, under the manic control of a deeply paranoid Adolf Hitler, tried with some early success to push the Allied forces back into the English Channel. Beginning in late June and early July, however, signs of the enormous cost to the Reich of the D-day invasion became more visible. (Hundreds of thousands of German troops would die in the three months between the invasion and the collapse of the Wehrmacht in France in late 1944.) Ambulances, trucks, tanks, even staff cars filled with wounded, frightened soldiers, were increasingly seen heading eastward toward the Rhine; camouflaged panzer units were retreating. One French wag covered his rickshaw-like *vélo-taxi* with dead branches as he rode around Paris, mocking the German attempts at evading Allied bombers.

For purely military reasons, the Germans were desperate to keep Paris in their hands. "From a strategic perspective, the transportation network of Paris and its suburbs was the single most important military asset of the capital."[2] The symbolic reasons that had earlier dominated so much of their policy were much less important now. All French railroads and major highways passed through Paris; geographically, the city also provided a generous redoubt to allow the Wehrmacht to "regroup," because Hitler had forbidden his armies to retreat. They also hoped that keeping Paris would give their armies retreating from Normandy time to reach Germany before being surrounded. *Festung Paris* (Fortress Paris) was the keystone in what was left of the German Occupation of France, for on August 15, the Allies had invaded the nation from the Mediterranean and were rushing northward to cut off the Germans trying either to reinforce the Atlantic Wall in Normandy or move eastward to the Rhine. Yet to defend and hold Paris would have taken, as the French themselves had estimated in 1940, at least three corps (anywhere between sixty thousand and 135,000 first-line troops). And where was the *General von Gross Paris* to get those numbers and the materiel necessary to support them? On top of this, they still had to feed the Parisian population, if for no other reason than to prevent uprisings.

The Germans did have one advantage, though it was unknown to them at that moment. Allied generals Dwight Eisenhower and Omar Bradley did not regard "Paris itself [either] as a major Allied objective [or] a German strongpoint."[3] In fact, Ike would not decide to march into Paris until August 22, three days after the Parisians themselves had begun their insurrection. Given the significance that the city had had for Germany's propagandistic aims just four years earlier, and given the amount of attention the major branches of the Reich's government had lavished on the French capital, it might come as a surprise that the Allies did not consider its liberation strategically crucial. This conundrum—if we set aside the military reasons for such a hesitancy—brings us back to Albert Camus's description of how deeply the inhabitants of an occupied city feel about being abandoned, or forgotten, or overlooked. The hole such anxiety leaves in a population's psyche takes much time to fill, especially after the hardships endured seem to call for some sort of closure.

Was Paris worth less to the Allies than it was to the Germans? For one military commander, at least, it remained symbolic: soon after the Allies broke through the Wehrmacht's defensive front in Normandy, Adolf Hitler began plotting to use the city as a means of slowing the enemy's advances. At first his attention turned to the region's railway depots, major highways, airports, and the Seine bridges, which he was planning to disable well before the Allies reached Paris. But soon his instructions took on a more hysterical tone: to some of his subordinates, he appeared to want to raze the City of Light, to make it permanently dark. His obsession with Paris was fueled by the fact that he did not trust his commanders in the west (i.e., the Normandy front). Many of the German senior staff in Paris and nearby had been implicated in the assassination plot of July 20, and he was suspicious that his orders were only being dilatorily carried out.* In part, he was right. A German historian remarks that

---

* An almost successful attempt had been made on Hitler's life on July 20, 1944, at Wolf's Lair, his headquarters in East Prussia. Carried out by anti-Nazi but still pro-victory Wehrmacht officers, the attack succeeded in only lightly wounding the Reich's leader. Officers died around him, but he survived, thus feeding his megalomania. Searching for disloyal Wehrmacht staff officers severely disrupted military operations in the middle of a two-front war and led to Hitler's decision to micromanage even more carefully the Reich's war plans, including the defense of Paris. Several major officers stationed in Paris were later charged with treason; consequently the Occupation went through a very unsettling—for the Germans, at least—period of confusion.

the commanders in charge in the west occasionally found themselves forced to adapt a rather odd rhetoric to conceal the disparity [between such orders and what was militarily justifiable at any given point]. These commanders formally complied with the contents of such orders, but in the final analysis they executed only those elements that seemed absolutely necessary.[4]

Paris had become a military conundrum for both sides.

We have seen how tired of living close together both the Occupier and Parisians had become by the summer of 1944. Hope for liberation became almost palpable in the streets of the capital. Yet on the other hand, there was the concern that Paris, like Stalingrad and Warsaw, would become a battleground and that perhaps it would be best for the Allies to skirt the city, isolating a weakened German garrison as they pushed on toward the Rhine and an end to the war.

From the first discussions of an invasion of France, de Gaulle had had the liberation of his nation's capital at the forefront of his strategy. Did the persistent resistance from both the Americans (Roosevelt never trusted the French general's political ambitions) and the British (Churchill referred to de Gaulle as his "Cross of Lorraine to bear") reveal a lack of understanding of what Paris meant to the French psyche? This would have been a strange notion, given the fascination that both nations had for France and her capital. But de Gaulle, along with his supporters as well as those French who were still ambivalent about him, seemed to have best grasped that without Paris, no French government would have the credibility needed to salve the nation's wounds.* De Gaulle never caved on his demand that Paris be liberated as soon as possible and, at least in part, that it be liberated by French troops.

His problem was that he did not command the French troops necessary to do the job, nor were there enough of them. He *had* to rely on the Allies, on General Eisenhower and General Bradley, for materiel,

---

* Pétain himself had from day one in Vichy pestered the Germans about moving the capital of the État français at least to Versailles, right outside Paris, if not to the capital itself. They of course refused; Paris was too rich a prize for them to.

support, and men. And, as we have noted, the Allies, taking signals from their forceful leaders, Roosevelt and Churchill, were not overly impressed with the leader of the Free French. They had not even told de Gaulle the date of the Normandy invasion until a few hours before dawn on June 6; they tried to stop him from flying to France on June 14, when he received a rapturous welcome from the citizens of Bayeux, the first major French town liberated. And they made every effort to hamper communications between him and General Philippe Leclerc, the commander of the Second Armored Division, the best equipped Free French unit in the Allied army. At the same time, de Gaulle was worried about the strength of the Communist Party's resistance movement and about the independence of the FFI, the Forces françaises de l'intérieur, who were acting only partially in concert with him and the Free French stationed in Algiers. He thought it quite possible that the internal resistance movements might assert a moral right to an equal status with the Gaullist initiative or, worse, that the well-organized and well-armed French Communist Party could effect a coup d'état, as the left had in 1871, when Paris refused to accept the French surrender to the Prussians.

Unlike his most impulsive commanders, the British Bernard Montgomery and the American George Patton, Eisenhower believed that a massive push toward the Rhine and then Berlin would be much more effective than the strictly targeted strikes both men preferred. Ike knew that coming behind the establishment of beachheads in Normandy would be enormous loads of materiel and hundreds of thousands of troops. He wanted to beat the Wehrmacht into the ground; a feint to take over a huge city, with all the logistical demands that would ensue, was not practical. If there were a massive uprising, Ike feared he might have to deploy thousands of men to protect a severely underarmed civilian populace. Add to this the fact that President Roosevelt did not want de Gaulle installed in Paris before an interim American occupation authority could be set up and Ike's belief that liberating Paris in August had to be avoided took on more weight.

As it turned out, in terms of strategy, Ike was right, but de Gaulle outmaneuvered him, as de Gaulle himself had been outmaneuvered by important elements of the consolidated Resistance army he had established earlier. The French leader's postwar plan for governing the country relied on the premise that the Parisians, with assistance from his Free France government, must liberate their capital. But as we have learned, de Gaulle, too, was concerned that political and ideological parties other than his provisional government might attempt to establish a new French state, or at least demand a large voice in France's future. A civilian-led insurrection, acting in isolation of Allied plans, would threaten his leadership. To de Gaulle's chagrin, Colonel Rol (whose real name was Henri Tanguy), leader of the Resistance in Paris and an important Communist partisan, had threatened to order such an uprising (which he would do later in the month) to force the Germans to leave the city. On the other hand, the Germans were desperate to keep the city's massive transport systems open for reinforcements and strategic retreats, though they did not have the troops to do this effectively while fighting on two fronts—an urban insurrection and the Allies encroaching from the West.* So leaders on both sides, within and without Paris, were on tenterhooks, watching carefully to see how the drama would play out and what the other side was going to do.

As for their control of Paris, the Germans had not been reassured by the celebrations of July 14, Bastille Day. An archivist and member of the Communist underground, Edith Thomas, describes in a pamphlet she wrote right after the war how surprised she was when she walked outside that July morning. She noticed first that the colors blue, red, and white seemed to be everywhere. Every store window had decorations in those hues; many passersby were wearing the colors either in their lapels or in their hair, or they were wearing blue, white, and red clothing. "La Marseillaise," it seemed, was being sung on every street corner. Accordionists who played it were surrounded to the point where they feared

---

* Estimates vary, as always, but there were about twenty thousand German troops of varying quality around Paris and perhaps only about five thousand within the city itself, a paltry number to defend a major metropolis against the Allies while protecting retreat paths for the Wehrmacht reeling from the Normandy breakout.

being overwhelmed by their compatriots. Pedestrians coalesced into crowds that walked boldly up and down the broad boulevards, still empty of all vehicles except for those carrying German soldiers to and from the Normandy front. Their wait for liberation seemed to be over, yet there was no news about the Allied advance (at this point, the Germans were still mounting a vigorous attempt to keep the Allies locked in pockets only a few miles from their disembarkation points; it would be two more weeks before their defenses broke and the Americans would begin their rapid march through north-central France). That memorable July 14, more than a thousand Parisians loudly gathered in the Place Maubert, a well-known site for massive popular political demonstrations before the war, just down the Boulevard Saint-Germain from the Sorbonne, singing and waving improvised French flags. "The [Parisian] police arrive. Someone cries: 'They are ten; we are ten thousand!' Faced with such resolve, the officers pulled back.... At the Porte de Vanves, a bonfire was built, and Hitler was burned in effigy."[5] Thomas surmised that there was not a strong reaction from either the Vichy police or the Occupation authorities because they were cautious about touching off an insurrection in an increasingly moody city. In fact, the insurrection that would break out a month later, on August 19, was still in preparation, and those who would lead it were far from capable of taking on even the less formidable German military still in the city. There may have been thousands of FFI and independent guerrillas in Paris in late July and early August, but they had few arms and other materiel for sustained street fighting. The insurgents had stolen, and would continue to steal, arms from isolated German units, but their harvest was composed mostly of pistols; they had some caches hidden underground all over the city, but their armaments were certainly insufficient to stand against the light and heavy machine guns, artillery, and armored vehicles of their Occupiers, regardless of the latter's diminishing morale. The Allies had refused to parachute armaments into such a labyrinth, fearful, of course, that they would fall into wrong or—perhaps worse—untrained hands.

On the surface Paris remained surprisingly calm in late July and early August of 1944. But still, Parisians could sense a building tension.

The Beast of Sevastopol Arrives

The Siege of Sevastopol, in the USSR's Crimea, had been murderous for both sides. Dietrich von Choltitz, scion of an old Prussian family, had led troops that had finally broken the siege in July of 1942. The city had been bombed and shelled mercilessly, and when Paris learned that Hitler had personally selected the "Beast of Sevastopol" as the new general in charge of the defense of Paris, a collective chill could be felt. As it turned out, von Choltitz had only a fortnight to keep the city open for the military, to contain the still disorganized French Resistance, to obstruct the Nazis who wanted the city razed, and—as if that

The Beast of Sevastopol. *(© Roger-Viollet / The Image Works)*

were not enough—to effect an armistice with the Allies, especially the de Gaulle government. In his memoirs, he describes his first and only meeting with Hitler, who had decided to appoint him to this prestigious position. The Führer, still recovering from the attempt on his life, was almost incoherent, his body shaking, his spittle spraying the nonplussed general's face and uniform, as he demanded that Paris be saved from the Allies at any cost. Rather than feeling gratified that, after long and successful service to the war effort, he had been awarded a major position, von Choltitz soon knew that the job was only temporary, for the Reich was on its way to destruction. Nevertheless, this assignment was still in theory the culmination of any general officer's career, a chance to show the world that only the Germans could protect the "capital of Europe."

Unaware of how tenuous the German position in Paris was, he was surprised on his arrival on August 9 to find that a partial evacuation of the city had already been quietly prepared. Nonmilitary personnel, especially the women who served as assistants, would be the first to return to Germany; any man who was minimally qualified to carry arms would be dragooned into service. The experienced commander could see that only hollow defenses stood between his command and the Allied onslaught. Extensive Allied bombing had also stopped the import of foodstuffs to the city; the Germans had large warehouses filled with food, and von Choltitz did release some of it for the population to keep them from rioting. But Paris would be starving well before the Allies arrived if something was not done to clear the Seine and the roads so that more supplies could get through. Less concerned with an insurrection than with the massive Allied advance from Normandy—and with keeping Paris from being surrounded so that German troops, including his own, could not retreat—von Choltitz sought to buy as much time as he could. One of his first acts was to gather all uniformed men, vehicles, and artillery and march them down the Avenue de l'Opéra to impress on the Parisians that the Wehrmacht was still there, still ready to defend itself and Paris. He arranged for the first lines of troops to loop back and march again down the avenue so that Resistance spies and Parisians would think he had a larger force than in fact he did. The Swedish consul at the time, Raoul Nordling, tells us that von Choltitz sat in a café on the Place de l'Opéra to watch the reactions of the Parisians to this last German parade in their city.[6]

Von Choltitz's orders had been clear: "Paris must lose in a minimum of time its character as a port of call with its unhealthy symptoms. The city must not be a reservoir for refugees and cowards but an object of fear for those who are not loyal citizens, ready to help our troops who fight at the front."[7] But on his arrival, the Prussian general had recognized immediately that his demoralized, badly disciplined, under-trained, and underarmed cohort of troops, many of them aging reservists, was a straw force at best, even with the support of a massive antiaircraft armory. (The Germans had always overprotected Paris from air attack, though no major bombing was ever unleashed on the city.) Hitler's rabid orders would be easier given than carried out. Desperate looting had by now become standard procedure among his command; almost immediately he had to send out officers to stop retreating Germans from commandeering French vehicles and using them to escape from the city with their stolen goods. The evacuation of the hundreds of women auxiliaries—the *souris grises* (gray mice)—was an early and encouraging sign to the Parisians that the Occupation was winding down.*

The French railway workers went on strike on August 10, the day following von Choltitz's arrival, and the French police, finally, did the same on August 14. At this point, von Choltitz asked through intermediaries such as Nordling that there be a "live and let live" policy as his troops evacuated the city. In other words, if not fired on, the Germans would not retaliate. Simpler said than done. The order that von Choltitz could still demand of his own troops was not mirrored in a fundamentally disorganized Resistance. For a bit, von Choltitz's truce held; one witness noticed that German trucks would pass others filled with

---

* When the last handful of women auxiliaries had to be evacuated from Paris, von Choltitz asked Nordling and the Red Cross to round them up and give them safe passage. Many carried heavy luggage that, when opened and searched, revealed linen, silver, and other fine goods that had been lifted from the luxurious hotels in which they had been working and living.

Resistance fighters, neither glancing at the other for fear that a firefight might explode into a major conflagration. Rather incredibly, and certainly suddenly, it seemed that the Occupation was ending quickly and more peacefully than had been hoped.

But significant numbers of young Parisians, with little or no leadership or coordination, were stealing arms, erecting barricades, making Molotov cocktails, and physically harassing a beleaguered, very frightened German military. The police had taken control of their own mammoth headquarters on the Île de la Cité, ejecting their collaborating brothers and Nazi bureaucrats; they began sending forays out regularly to test the will of the nervous Germans. Suddenly emboldened citizens began throwing objects down onto German patrols, whose anxious soldiers fired at apartments where French flags were dangling from balconies. Increasingly, Germans in uniform went out or patrolled only in groups. Here and there on isolated city streets dead and wounded civilians and Wehrmacht recruits began to appear. Radio communications among the German troops were spotty because of Resistance interference; von Choltitz and the German strongpoints around the city had to resort increasingly to insecure telephone lines. (Miraculously, the Parisian telephone system, soon to be known by generations of study-abroad students as the worst in Europe, continued to function up to and after the battle for the city.)

To his chagrin and disgust, the new commander was told that the SS troops and police under General Carl Oberg were already preparing to leave. When confronted by von Choltitz, Oberg only shrugged, implying that his superb troops were needed elsewhere to defend the Reich, not to hold an already lost city. In an understatement, von Choltitz wrote in his memoirs, "One must not think that playing with the destiny of Paris was an easy job for me. Circumstances had constrained me to a role that, in fact, I was unprepared for."[8] His nearby Wehrmacht colleagues had offered him reinforcements to defend the city, which he deftly refused, recognizing more clearly than they that it would be a useless loss of men and materiel needed for a more important mission: defending the borders of the Fatherland.

Adding of course to the burden of "defending" Paris was Hitler's demand that von Choltitz destroy much of the city rather than leave it as he had found it. (The Germans derisively referred to such policies as "Rubble Field orders.") On August 22, general headquarters had sent him orders signed by Hitler: "Paris is to be transformed into a pile of rubble. The commanding general must defend the city to the last man, and should die, if necessary, under the ruins."[9] In his memoir, von Choltitz remembered a telephone conversation he had with General Hans Speidel, chief of staff to the general commanding the defense of France. He had just received the aforementioned order to destroy Paris:

"I thank you for your excellent order."

"Which order, General?"

"The demolition order, of course. Here's what I've done: I've had three tons of explosives brought into Notre-Dame, two tons into the Invalides, a ton into the Chambre des députés. I'm just about to order that the Arc de Triomphe be blown up to provide a clear field of fire." (I heard Speidel breathe deeply on the line.) "I'm acting under your orders, correct, my dear Speidel?"

(After hesitating, Speidel answers:) "Yes, General."

"It was you who gave the order, right?"

(Speidel, angry:) "It isn't I but the Führer who ordered it!"

(I screamed back:) "Listen, it was you who transmitted this order and who will have to answer to History!" (I calmed down and continued:) "I'll tell you what else I've ordered. The [Église de la] Madeleine and the Opéra [to Hitler's horror?] will be destroyed." (And now, getting even more excited:) "As for the Eiffel Tower, I'll knock it down in such a manner that it can serve as an antitank barrier in front of the destroyed bridges." It was then that Speidel realized that I was not being serious, that my words were only to show how ridiculous the situation was. . . .

Speidel breathed a sigh of relief and said: "Ah! General, how fortunate we are that you are in Paris!"* [10]

---

* For not having ordered the air bombardment of Paris, General Hans Speidel was arrested by the Gestapo a week after the Liberation. He had refused to use either the Luftwaffe or the V-1 and V-2 rockets that were being loosed on London — though later his

The Reich's occupation of Paris ended on August 25, 1944, as the last bedraggled German units pulled out or surrendered. Early that morning, before von Choltitz's surrender, a Luftwaffe plane had dropped thousands of leaflets onto the increasingly confident city, still in the midst of forcefully "liberating" itself from Nazi control. The text of this leaflet reveals a first attempt for the Germans to craft the history of their Occupation of Paris, one that Charles de Gaulle would soon try to rewrite. The tone of this text is both exculpatory and pathetic:

FRENCHMEN!

Paris is living through an especially critical time, whether we hold the city or the Americans or the English occupy it soon!

It is a time when the populace is trying to take power, an event that each citizen fears with panic.

Rowdy crowds are guessing when the German troops will leave Paris and how much time there will be before the Allies arrive! A relatively short lapse of time, but long enough to threaten the life of each citizen.

Paris is still in the hands of the Germans!

It is possible that the city will not be evacuated!

It is under our protection; it has known four years of relative peace. It remains for us one of the most beautiful cities of that Europe for which we fight; we will preserve it from the chaos that it has itself created.

Gunshots are trying to terrorize the city! Blood has flowed, French blood as well as German! False nationalist or surely Communist rhetoric seeks to incite the street to riot or to pit citizens against each other.

---

orders would be countermanded, and about a dozen rockets did fall on and around Paris, but to little effect. He was also questioned about his role in the July 20 assassination attempt against Hitler. Miraculously, he survived these contretemps and would later return to Paris as NATO commander in chief from 1957 to 1963. French eyebrows were raised at this appointment.

So far the sources of this discord are controllable, but the limits of the humanity of German troops in Paris are being pushed.

It would not be difficult to bring a brutal end to all this!

Stalin would have already set the city on fire.

It would be easy for us to leave Paris after having blown up all the depots, all the factories, all the bridges, and all the train stations and to close up the suburbs so tightly they would believe themselves under siege.

Given the absence of food, water, and electricity, a terrible catastrophe would occur in less than 24 hours!

It is not to your usurpers or your Red committees that you should turn to in order to avoid such a calamity, or to the American and English troops that are only advancing step by step and who might arrive too late to help you.

It is rather to the humanity of the German troops that you should turn, but you should not push them beyond their patience.

You owe your loyalty to [the German nation], this marvelous source of European culture, and to your respect for reasonable Frenchmen, for the women and children of Paris.

If all this were not sacred to the population, we would have no reason to remain so tolerant.

We warn the criminal elements for the last time. We demand the immediate and unconditional cessation of all acts of hostility toward us as well as between citizens.

We demand that Parisians defend themselves against the terrorists and support their own demands for order and calm so that they can go about their daily affairs.

That and that alone can guarantee the life of the city, its provisioning, and its preservation.

—Commandant of the Wehrmacht of Greater Paris[11]

I cite this document in its entirety, for it reveals an amazing narrative: the history of the Occupation through German eyes. Doubtlessly it was written to bring about some calm as the Germans were evacuating before the Allied advance. But it also speaks to some of the points raised earlier about how the Germans perceived Paris—repeating, for example, the claim that the Germans had, in their magnanimity, saved Paris from the ravages of the war. The text also sings the familiar song about current troubles coming from the "terrorists"—the Communists—and the power-hungry, thus playing up the real fear of a civil war that might follow a German retreat. As much as the French may have hated their Occupiers, it says, the Germans were better than chaos (especially Bolshevism) and the slow disintegration of Christian civilization. (We should take note that it makes no mention of the regime's racial policies.)

The flyer's rhetoric pleads for recognition that the Germans had been valiant stewards of Paris since 1940, that they still have the best interests of the beautiful capital at heart, and that, should chaos ensue, Parisians will regret the absence of such a strict but respectful authority. Few readers of this flyer knew the drama that was then ensuing among General von Choltitz, diplomats, Resistance leaders, and an adamant Hitler, who was insisting that the city's bridges and other architectural monuments be destroyed. One order from Berlin demanded that "the severest measures [be used] upon the first indication of an uprising, such as demolition of residential housing blocks [and] public executions."★ [12] The Parisian answer had been to barricade the streets and snipe at the retreating enemy, something that had definitely not occurred in the confused days of June 1940. The Occupation had come a long way from Hitler's parting monologue on the steps of Sacré-Coeur, just four years previously.

★ Von Choltitz was caught between two unruly forces—the FFI and his Führer—neither of which fully comprehended what was happening on the ground in Paris. Indeed, one historian reminds us that "[von] Choltitz…saw himself and his army not as oppressing Paris but as protecting it from the gang of violent thugs he believed the Resistance to be" (Neiberg, 148)—an argument von Choltitz would make for years after the war, to the point where many Parisians hailed him as the hero who had saved their capital.

"Tous aux barricades!"

"They are getting nearer, those dear 'they,'" wrote young Benoîte Groult in her diary on August 15, 1944, and later on August 19: "'They' are still here, but the other 'they' still haven't arrived." She noticed a wary anticipation as Parisians walked through the late daylight: "An operetta atmosphere, with a foretaste of tragedy."[13] For the Parisian, these must have been deeply harrowing days. Transportation was interrupted, as was electricity. People still lined up at food stores, but shipments to and through the city were almost ended. Young armed strangers were appearing in every neighborhood; tracts were being glued to walls; the Germans themselves seemed in constant movement, though at the same time directionless. Rumor was becoming — tentatively — fact.

The most serious threat for the Germans was the combined Anglo-American force moving quickly from the Normandy front toward Paris. Von Choltitz had arranged a brief truce with some leaders of the Resistance while the Germans sped up their plans to evacuate the city. But when Colonel Rol asked for an insurrection to begin on August 19, Parisians turned to their historical memory to call *"Tous aux barricades!"* (Everyone to the barricades!). For the first time since 1871, streets and intersections were blocked by Parisians. Colonel Rol had distributed a new call to arms: "Organize yourselves neighborhood by neighborhood. Overwhelm the Germans and take their arms. Free Great Paris, the cradle of France! Avenge your martyred sons and brothers. Avenge the heroes who have fallen for...the freedom of our Fatherland....Choose as your motto: A BOCHE [Kraut] FOR EACH OF US. No quarter for these murderers! Forward! Vive la France!"[14]

Hundreds of barricades popped up almost overnight, manned — and womanned — by neighborhood residents, played on by children, and generally left abandoned at night, during blackouts. Everything was used for the barricades: kiosks, cobblestones, downed trees, burned-out automobiles, old bicycles, street urinals, benches, and tree grilles. Films show women and men and children digging up cobblestones and

"To the barricades!" *(© LAPI / Roger-Viollet / The Image Works)*

macadam and relaying them to each other in long lines to build an improvised rampart across the wide boulevards that Napoleon III's Paris prefect, Baron Haussmann, had created in the nineteenth century in order to make such structures difficult to construct. Thousands of sandbags, likely taken from former German strongpoints and protected monuments, served to close bridges across the Seine. Those who were at the barricades were dressed in street clothes, uniforms, and even shorts. Some had red scarves around their necks, reminding each other of the color worn by the Communards in 1870. They were armed, barely, with pistols or old rifles; some had helmets, but most did not.

Other curious Parisians—observers, not participants—surrounded the barricades; there was a general sense of novelty, even gaiety, until the rattle of a machine gun or the appearance of a German tank or armored car chased everyone into a nearby apartment building or café. Children were everywhere; school was out, and nothing was more fun than seeing one's parents act like youngsters at play. "Public buildings, the Sorbonne, hospitals enthusiastically raised the tricolor. Telephone calls spread the marvelous news from one end of Paris to the other; Champagne was brought out...saved for this wonderful day."[15] The military effectiveness of the barricades was rudimentary, but their presence was a sign to everyone, including the tense Wehrmacht troops, that control of the city was changing hands.

The major questions then became which of the anti-German forces would take over the city and how quickly and effectively the Wehrmacht could evacuate from Paris. The Germans still maintained order, even directing traffic at major crossroads and making threatening gestures at those who booed them or brandished a French flag. But the bloodiest forty-eight hours remained to be played out. Raoul Nordling, the Swedish consul, was desperately visiting prisons, trying to save thousands of French political prisoners from being deported or, worse, just shot. Already news had reached Paris that the Nazi commander of the major prison in Caen had executed all his prisoners, even those held for minor infractions or still under investigation. At the same time, von Choltitz was attempting to put up the strongest possible resistance so that he could retire from the city with honor. And both sides were undisciplined, with communications constantly interrupted and everyone hoping to have the last shot at saving the honor of the city or that of the German army. Chaos had to prevail, bloody chaos, and it did, until the morning of August 25. Soon the holiday air that had first surrounded the establishment of the barricades dissipated; defenders began to fall as the Germans finally reacted with deadly force. Groups of the FFI began to appear less cocky as more combatants and passersby fell under the crossfire of the undisciplined opponents. Brave citizens put on Red Cross armbands and ran under fire to rescue those who had fallen. Confusion reigned as Resistance newspapers began to appear with contradictory headlines: PARIS IS FREE OF GERMAN FILTH!; PARIS IS NOT YET LIBERATED!

Still, thousands of retreating, disoriented, frightened, and angry Germans remained within and just outside Paris. Many were isolated from their units, standing guard over an installation or a building that their headquarters had long forgotten. Without uninterrupted communication, they were targets for roving bands of insurgents. Jean Guéhenno remarked in his journal:

Yesterday morning in the Rue Manin [in the northeast 19th arrondissement of the city, near the Parc des Buttes Chaumont]...I noticed two German guards who seemed quite venturesome. Only an imbecile would have put them there, out in the open. There was no mistaking that they sensed danger. With grenades on their belts, their machine guns in their hands, they were terrified, waiting for their imminent death at the hands of a casual passerby who would pull a pistol from his pocket and shoot them point-blank. At quiet moments, they thought of their Saxon or Thuringian homes, of their wife, their children, their fields. What were they doing there, in Rue Manin, in the middle of that crowd that neither loved nor hated them but only wanted to kill them? By eight o'clock that evening, they were dead.[16]

A documentary made from moving images shot clandestinely during the last days of the Occupation shows the strange atmosphere that reigned during these last two weeks.[17] Pedestrians and Parisians on their bikes nonchalantly pass roving tanks, armored cars, and troop carriers as the Germans appear to be deciding how to defend the city. We see a beautiful city, under bright August skies, indulgently waiting for the moment of liberation. Astute editing suddenly introduces gunfire and scenes of the haphazard fighting that goes on in neighborhood after neighborhood. Every type of French citizen appears to participate: teenagers, men, women, poor and wealthy, old and young. But it is especially the moment of the young—sometimes the too young. Jacques Yonnet, in his memoir, described a corpse he glimpsed on the street: "I saw a body [picked] up at Les Halles—a kid in short [pants], fifteen years old at most. He'd attacked a *Boche* truck that was flying a white flag. The kid was armed with a...pistol with a mother-of-pearl grip, a 1924 ladies' handbag accessory. The real criminals weren't in the [German] truck."[18] The real criminals, Yonnet implied, were those who had ordered this *mobilisation générale* of civilians to confront a still venomous German presence. Debate would continue well after the war about whether the insurrection had been foolhardy or even necessary.

The film shows in detail the arrival of the French Second Armored Division and its US-uniformed soldiers, American-made tanks, and Jeeps. (For some viewers around the world, it appeared that the Americans were the first to enter Paris, but it was a French division, outfitted in American gear.) Images reveal a strange combination of slowly advancing troops surrounded by applauding Parisians in their everyday clothes. It is as if they are at some theme park where the insurrection of Paris is being reenacted; shots are heard, but smiles are everywhere. Soldiers are crouching, checking out apartment windows and balconies, while residents are casually leaning in doorways, smoking, gossiping, and watching. One old gentleman actually claps his hands in applause as soldiers dodge sniper fire. Had Parisians become inured to the sounds of battle and commotion over the past week of the insurrection, or were they just oblivious to the dangers of urban street fighting? What remains unclear is how much of the continuing violence was a result of the actions of French people who were still pro-Vichy and anti-Resistance and how much was the response of German regulars. The so-called Radio Concierge network (concierges passing along news and gossip) continued to function, and word of the advancing Allies was shouted from loge to loge along the streets of both banks of the Seine. Loudspeakers, mounted on trucks and cars, passed by announcing the cease-fire that von Choltitz had agreed to, but it appeared that neither side was willing to stop firing, at least intermittently, on the other.

Erratic activities by both the FFI and the Wehrmacht made walking to work or going to the hospital or even going to church a dangerous activity. In her short history of the Liberation, the archivist Edith Thomas said that going from the Left Bank to the Right Bank for a meeting was like a trek to a remote land. She felt like "a Sioux" moving cautiously in an unfamiliar forest as she passed FFI barricades and roving German tanks. When she ran from doorway to doorway, apartment residents asked if she had news from up the street or around the corner, "as if I had just come from a long voyage."[19]

Thomas would eventually get access to the many orders that Colonel Rol had distributed throughout the city—through radio broadcasts, posters on thousands of walls, loudspeakers, and leaflets thrown from fast-moving cars—and they would reveal how well organized, finally, the Resistance had become. Seeking to unite the irregulars with his own well-led cadres, Rol even sent out runners—especially teenage girls and boys—to stand in the crowds that surrounded the posters and listen for those who expressed an interest in joining the fighting. After the gawkers had moved on, the youngsters would follow them around the corner to tell them how they might join up.

Still, most of the fighting was dispersed and only intermittently planned:

> It's impossible to give a description of the battle as a whole. Now it's a series of local actions, but all aimed at the same goal: to annihilate the enemy. Automobiles against tanks, Boulevard de la Chapelle, Boulevard des Batignolles, Avenue Jean-Jaurès, Rue de Crimée...; arms taken from the enemy: a Renault tank, two Tigers, a truck, munitions, two little autos in the 17th arrondissement. Here and there, Germans are taken prisoner and are astonished that they are not shot by the "terrorists," [astonished] to see these men without uniforms, these civilians, respecting the laws of war that they themselves had so badly followed.[20]

Our nervous friend Pablo Picasso ventured out of his apartment in the 6th arrondissement, after the insurrection had begun, and took up residence on the Île Saint-Louis with his former mistress, Marie-Thérèse Walter, and her daughter by him, Maya. His then companion, Françoise Gilot, described his anxiety:

> In the last few days before the Liberation, I talked with Pablo by telephone, but it was next to impossible to get to see him. People were already beginning to bring out the cobblestones to build the barricades. Even children were working at the job, especially in

the 6th arrondissement, where Pablo lived...where there was a great deal of fighting....German snipers were everywhere. The last time I talked to Pablo before the Liberation he told me he had been looking out the window that morning and a bullet had passed just a few inches from his head and embedded itself in the wall.[21]

While waiting for the city to be liberated, Picasso painted a joyously liberating work, *The Triumph of Pan,* which he told friends he worked on as he listened to the battle going on around him. It depicts a Dionysian festival, one that might celebrate the joy of freedom from want and fear. The work is small and done in watercolor and gouache, but its exuberance belies all the somber work that had preceded it during Picasso's volitional exile in Paris during the war years. In the words of one critic, "Picasso seems to have equated the reappearance of Dionysus, 'his epiphany as a bringer of happiness after [a] dark period

Picasso celebrates the Liberation. (Photograph by Francis Lee)

of hunting and sacrifice,' with the deliverance of Paris and, by extension, the world after the great sacrifice symbolized by the war."[22]

While painting, Picasso must have wondered: What is going on? Who is winning? Are the Germans regrouping? Where are the other Allies? Jean Guéhenno gives a tersely vivid account of trying to cross the Seine and finding himself trapped near Les Halles, the great marketplace on the Right Bank: "German tanks were patrolling. As I was trying to get across the Boulevard de Sébastopol, one of them began firing only thirty meters from me, decapitating a woman and gutting a man. On side streets fifty meters from that scene, strangely enough, people were sitting on their stoops gossiping. Curiosity and joy are at their strongest."[23]

The city had become a patchwork of violence mixed with celebration, both sides firing indiscriminately not just at each other but also into crowds. The passions of the last four years had created an explosion of fury, misdirected and unable to distinguish combatants from tired and frightened citizens. Many Parisian civilians were fearless. Running openly into crossroads, they would tear down the innumerable German-language signs that had decorated their city for more than four years. Film clips show that not all the panels were destroyed; some were taken off as trophies and are probably still in attics and wine cellars across Paris.★

Such small dramas filled the forty-eight hours that separated the erection of the first barricades, the first openly defiant insurgency against the Occupation, from the late-night arrival of the first French-manned tanks of the Second Armored Division, which had rolled through the city's Porte d'Orléans. Carrying the first French soldiers in Paris since June of 1940, this small tank force, under Captain Raymond Dronne, had sped along the side roads and backstreets of the suburbs, crossed the Seine by the Pont d'Austerlitz, and driven along the quays on the Right Bank to reach the Hôtel de Ville just before midnight on August 24. Few Parisians knew this, for curfews had prevented them

---

★ Among the most prized must have been the ones that had been put up only a few months before: ZUR NORMANDIE FRONT (To the Normandy front).

from leaving their homes, and the still Nazi-controlled radio only reported what seemed to be repeated instances of successful German defense against the victors of Normandy, who were trying to reach the city. But everyone heard the giant bells of Notre-Dame begin to ring, something they had not heard since the Occupation had begun.

Even after the Germans had surrendered or left, small battles still were occurring throughout Paris. By then the fights were part of a civil war between the FFI and remnants of the Vichy Milice. Uniforms did not distinguish the combatants; the Milice had changed into civilian clothes, some even putting on FFI armbands as a disguise. Among the latter were not only last-ditch supporters of the Vichy regime but also young men trying to escape Paris alive, to return to their homes in the countryside. No one knew whom to trust, and despite de Gaulle's appointment of General Pierre Koenig, Gaullist commander in chief of the FFI, as military commander of Paris, disorder would rule the streets for a few more days.

On Saturday, August 26, Berthe Auroy, our schoolteacher who lived in Montmartre, had gone to the Champs-Élysées to watch de Gaulle strut in victory down the grand avenue.* Everyone was excited, laughing, dressed as if for Bastille Day in all sorts of blue, white, and red regalia. On her way back along the Rue de Rivoli, she and her sister heard machine-gun fire and the whistle of bullets. The FFI irregulars yelled at everyone to lie on the sidewalk, to keep their heads down. Then, at a break in the firing, they urged the frightened crowd to run for the Jardin des Tuileries. But inside the garden's gates, the firing continued, and Auroy and her sister again ran, fell to the ground, got up, and ran a few more yards, until they reached the Louvre. There they saw a group of people in a line, seeking refuge, with the aid of a ladder, via a service entrance; someone had broken a large windowpane, and the civilians

---

* A few days earlier, de Gaulle had landed at Saint-Lô, in Normandy, making his way through that region and Brittany as the liberated French wildly celebrated his arrival. Driving from Le Mans to Chartres, and then to Rambouillet, right outside Paris, he awaited news of the insurrection and prepared his triumphant victory march down the Champs-Élysées.

were climbing into the museum. Berthe and her sister ascended to find themselves

> before one of the grand staircases of the museum. We sat down on the steps. It was calm there, and we were comfortable on the beautiful carpet. We stayed there a good bit of time, then we risked going outside, and hid next under a grand entry arch of the Louvre. We couldn't leave before we were carefully searched.... We climbed over the benches that had served as barriers, and we went back up to Montmartre using narrow side streets, where, now, nothing bothered us but a few isolated gunshots.[24]

With the arrival of Leclerc's division, there were touching scenes of French men and women being reunited after long separations. The soldiers and officers who were Parisians themselves jumped off their motorbikes and tanks to run into the nearest café to call home: "Mom, I'm coming; I'm almost in Paris." One writer described a scene in which a young tanker sees his father in the crowd of Parisians yelling their pleasure at seeing their liberators. "That's my papa," he screamed; jumping from his vehicle, he ran up to the stunned elder man. The father just stared, then grabbed his son's cheeks with both hands and pulled him so close and so tight that bystanders had to separate them. Scenes like this, often filmed and photographed, justified de Gaulle's canny insistence that the first Allied troops to enter the capital be French.*

Von Choltitz surrendered three times on August 25 before he was spirited off to England, then to a prison camp in Mississippi, of all places. The first time was at the Hôtel Meurice, on the Rue de Rivoli, where the military commander of Paris had been installed since June of

---

* And yet dozens if not more in the Second Armored Division were from Spain, veterans of the Republican war against Franco's fascist regime. Spaniards also played important early roles in the armed resistance, since most French soldiers were away in prison camps. In 2004, the city of Paris recognized the part these men from south of the Pyrenees played in the liberation of Paris. There is a memorial plaque now on the Seine side of the Hôtel de Ville, the city hall.

French soldiers are first into a liberated Paris. (Musée du général Leclerc de Hauteclocque et de la Libération de Paris / Musée Jean Moulin EPPM)

1940. Von Choltitz had ordered his guards to put up a modest resistance before giving up the building; when French irregulars burst into his office, one demanded awkwardly: "Sprechen Deutsch?" Von Choltitz, who had laid his arms on his desk, answered suavely: "Yes. A bit better than you." He was taken by a French tank commander to the Préfecture de police, where he officially surrendered to General Philippe Leclerc, commander of the Free French Second Armored

Division. Von Choltitz knew he had lost the city when, the evening before, he had heard the great bells of Notre-Dame Cathedral ringing for the first time since the Occupation began, signaling a new day in Paris. Soon every church bell in the city was vigorously pealing. The general had picked up his phone and called General Speidel at the Wehrmacht headquarters near Soissons, some fifty miles north of Paris; putting the receiver up to the window, he said: "Please, listen. Did you hear?" Speidel replied, "Yes; I hear bells." Said von Choltitz, "You heard well: the French-American army is entering Paris."[25] Finally, von Choltitz was taken to the Gare Montparnasse, the major railway station on the Left Bank, to sign official papers and an order that all German resistance cease. That order had to be transmitted by means of loudspeakers mounted in Jeeps that went to all the strongpoints left in the city. The last fortress, at the Palais du Luxembourg, finally surrendered at midday on August 25. Paris was liberated.

Von Choltitz came out of all of this with shining colors, more than any other German leader of Paris during the Occupation. Though he manufactured much of his legend ("I saved Paris for the Allies!"), his patience and sangfroid most certainly kept France's capital from being severely damaged during those hectic two weeks. Nevertheless, he had approved the deportation of more than three thousand political prisoners just a week before the surrender, and members of the Gestapo, at least those who had stayed until the last minute, were still tailing, arresting, and torturing "terrorists," including those they would massacre in the Bois de Boulogne. In addition, among the reasons why Paris was not demolished were that General Speidel had refused to order the Luftwaffe to bomb it, and, fortuitously, perhaps, that von Choltitz did not have the personnel or the materiel to do the massive destruction demanded by Hitler.★

★ The Germans could not leave without one last measure of defiance toward the city that had defeated them. German planes flying in from Holland and Germany dropped more than a thousand bombs on the capital, primarily in the eastern sections, on the evening of August 26; there were hundreds of civilian casualties in this, the last bombing of the city.

Why Do Americans Smile So Much?

The anonymous authors of the United States Army's *Pocket Guide to France* were quite aware that Paris would be one of the major attractions for the soon-to-be-victorious GIs. "If you get to Paris, the first thing to do is to buy a guide book, if there are any left after the Nazi tourists' departure. Paris is in a sense the capital of Europe and regarded as one of the most beautiful and interesting cities in the world. We don't know just what the war has done to Paris. These notes will assume that there'll still be lots to see."[26]

By the time the Americans had arrived in the almost German-free Paris, most of the street fighting had ended. Most of the Germans and their Vichy Milice supporters had been captured, wounded, or killed. Many of the captured were the bureaucrats who had overseen the Occupation, pouring out of the elegant Meurice, Majestic, Lutétia, and Raphael hotels at the first sign of the FFI or French soldiers entering their lobbies. There are reports that some patriotic Nazis fired on their more pusillanimous fellows as they crowded through doors, hands raised. Anywhere from one thousand to 1,500 *résistants* and Parisian citizens died, and about 3,500 were wounded. About 130–150 members of the Second Armored Division were killed or died from wounds after the Liberation; they also lost a large number of tanks, half-tracks, and materiel, which shows that the Germans were not totally ineffective. Estimates of the number of Germans killed range from 2,500 to three thousand. The battle for Paris was not one of the major urban confrontations of the war, but it was not a skirmish, either.[27]

De Gaulle had insisted that the first Allied forces to enter Paris be French, and they were, as noted, the legendary Second Armored Division (Deuxième Division Blindée).* They had been heavily

---

* This unit was a part of the American First Army's V Corps, under the command of Major General Leonard Gerow, with whom General Leclerc would have serious command issues. At one point, Gerow wanted to court-martial Leclerc for having taken the initiative against Paris on the orders of General de Gaulle rather than defer to Allied command.

outfitted by the Americans and were driving American tanks and trucks, wearing American uniforms and helmets, and carrying American gear. Thus, for the first time, Parisians saw close-up not only their victorious soldiers but also the significant role that the Americans were playing in the liberation of their nation. One of the most meaningful filmed events of the liberation of Paris occurred a day after de Gaulle had marched triumphantly down the Champs-Élysées: the American Twenty-Eighth Infantry Division and Fifth Armored Division, trooping the same path.* This American show of force drew huge crowds;

And then came the Americans. (Creative Commons)

---

* De Gaulle, worried that his sparse Free French forces could not pacify the capital alone, had begged Eisenhower to leave behind enough Allied troops to supplement his. Ike refused, but he did agree to this grand victory parade, larger even than the one organized by the Germans four years earlier.

their enthusiasm brought smiles to the faces of the soldiers who had just endured the rigorous Normandy campaign and who would be involved in major battles for the next eight months as they made their way to the Rhine and into Germany. Grins and grit, the air of confident vigor, sent a clear message to the world: the Americans were in Europe to stay, not because they were imperialists but because without them Europe would have disintegrated.

All the same, there was distrust on both sides of the ledger. Had not French soldiers let the Wehrmacht roll over them in just a few weeks in 1940—and then sheepishly gone off to prison camps? Had they not left their wives and children behind to fend for themselves during the harsh Occupation? The Americans still did not have much respect for a country that had been so docile in defeat, and most viewed French culture as immoral. Officers reminded their men constantly that French girls were "too easy" and that they should be careful to avoid catching something. In return, the French still remembered the World War I American doughboys' rough impatience with their mores. And almost immediately, the presence of American soldiers in Paris brought tension between them and the FFI irregulars. There appeared, in the opinion of the latter, to be a masculine entitlement on the part of the GIs, a strong hint that Paris and France now needed to be "remasculinized" in the image of a virile, conquering, confident, and smiling army. More important, the news brought to Paris by refugees from the Normandy front, where thousands of civilians had been hurt or killed and where whole city centers had disappeared, suggested the Americans had been rather careless in their bombing. Finally, stories—true and exaggerated—of the exuberant Yanks in their Jeeps, looting anything not nailed down, and their rough treatment of French women, including multiple episodes of rape, attenuated some of the joy at seeing these sons and grandsons of the First World War doughboys, who themselves had been especially rambunctious. Yet for the most part, the appearance of this new, powerful army temporarily overcame these differences as the French joyfully jumped on tanks and trucks to kiss, embrace, and give gifts to the Yanks. And after all, weren't they "sexy," an erotic observation enhanced by their apparent innocence?★[28]

"Le peuple français est bon et joli!" (The French people is good and pretty [sic]), yelled an American soldier awkwardly when a French microphone was put before him as he entered Paris. The American army only spent a few days in Paris after its liberation, but the memory of those healthy, young, and always grinning men, marching with a certain nonchalance in contrast to the memory of the rigidly disciplined Wehrmacht, would have a lasting effect on Paris's collective memory of those joyful days. One of the Groult sisters wrote amusingly about seeing her first "liberator," a blond, blue-eyed architecture student named Willis. Flora watched him from her balcony as he asked her neighbors in broken French for a place to get a bite to eat. She rushed down and in perfect English asked him up for a meal. Her mother and sister found him casual, intelligent, charming, and, for the first time in years, they felt comfortable talking to a man in uniform. Having been given permission to wash up, he casually removed his shirt in front of the women, all of whom noticed his white complexion, sunburned neck, and gently muscled chest. "[After his ablutions], we sat down to supper, and he ate without knowing it one of our last eggs. How could he have guessed, this little conqueror, that we only had four left?"[29] Obviously, Willis had not read, or had forgotten, the admonition that could be found in the *Pocket Guide to France,* distributed by the millions to young Americans at the time of D-day:

> If the French at home or in public try to show you any hospitality, big or little — a home cooked meal or a glass of wine — it means a lot to them. Be sure you thank them and show your appreciation. If madame invites you to a meal with the family, go slow. She'll do her best to make it delicious. But what is on the table may be

---

★ The American army estimated that 85 percent of GIs were virgins when they joined up or were drafted. (One wonders how the survey gathered that information.)

all they have, and what they must use as leftovers for tomorrow or the rest of the week.[30]

After dinner, the sisters delightedly climbed into his Jeep, and the proud GI drove them around a Paris still delirious with the scent of freedom. The next day Willis came back with packages of bacon and stewed beef, but then he suddenly left Paris, and for good, off to continue the fight against a retreating but still dangerous Wehrmacht. "They are different, these free men, with their sun-browned skin, their innocent looks, rolled-up sleeves, who fight, kill, spend a little time with you, then leave."[31] Many of her contemporaries would wonder how an army so casually disciplined could have been so successful against the rigorously disciplined Germans. And they smiled so often and so spontaneously!

Berthe Auroy wrote about meeting her first Americans in early September, well after the "war of the rooftops" between the FFI and the remnants of Vichy resistance was over. Walking down to the Place de Clichy (then, as now, a center for nightclubs, sex shops, and open prostitution), she met three American GIs. "I asked them to climb up the Butte [Montmartre] with me. Two were pink and chubby-cheeked, like babies, and the third had big, very American teeth and glasses."[32] Not unlike the young German soldiers who saw Paris on leave in July of 1940, these Yanks had a day pass to visit the city, which they had found stunning. In fact, many American soldiers, having marched through dozens of towns and villages damaged by the war, were surprised at how "whole" Paris was, how few were the signs of the conflagration that was going on around it. The next day, Auroy went to the Champs-Élysées to see an American encampment; there she was struck by how friendly these "giants" were and embarrassed at the sight of her countrymen reaching to grasp the cigarette and gum packages thrown to the crowd. Yet, she remarked how nice it was to see the cafés filled with the (yes) smiling, laughing, friendly young men in khaki and how relaxed the French patrons sitting near them were, a state of affairs that Paris had not experienced for more than four years.

Much younger than Berthe Auroy, and much more interested in flirting, the Groult girls were also astute analysts of what it was that made the Americans so different. First was the endless supply of canned goods, condensed milk, chocolate, and cigarettes they distributed with abandon. Every American invited into a Parisian home brought with him evidence of the wealth of that faraway country. An enormous war machine most likely bolstered their naive self-confidence. And indeed, the Yanks were patronizing; after all, the United States was once again rescuing Europe from its own excessive incompetence. Yet the GIs were touched and amused by the generosity of those they had "liberated." Civilian and army journalists were expansive in their coverage of how the GIs had been embraced by the delirious French. Flora Groult attempted to explain:

Tall, big men, we are relieved of every vain worry in your presence. You climb the stairs to our apartment, our doors are open, you bring packages, all as it should be. That's it, the overwhelming advantages behind which you hide your weaknesses. And what are they? No inferiority complex about their inferiority. They say: "I don't much like that!" (Literature, music, art...).... They manage so well the immensity of their ignorance, as if it were a light feather....[33]

The Parisians were bedazzled, but still held on to an old European view: Americans are strong and rich, but without the culture that Parisians still treasure. The images that immediately came back to the United States via the great magazines *Look* and *Life,* plus the newsreels shown weekly in American movie houses, emphasized the affectionate response of French women and girls to the arrival of Americans. The rapturous delight of children reaching out their hands for chocolate and chewing gum were also a photographic staple. Americans were not only liberating; they were showing the expansiveness of the culture and mores of the United States.

One of the first Americans into a liberated Paris was the incorrigible Ernest Hemingway, officially there as a correspondent for *Collier's* magazine.* Hemingway had finagled himself onto one of the LSTs (landing craft able to carry men and large machinery, including tanks) that were in the first wave approaching the Normandy beaches on June 6, but the Allied command did not allow him to land with the troops. (His wife, Martha Gellhorn, had been able to land on that day from a hospital ship, a feat for which Ernest never forgave her.) Returned to the mother ship, he had to wait before finally setting his boots on French soil. For the next two and a half months, the macho author acted as correspondent, morale officer, combatant, and overall pest as the Allies broke out of the invasion beachheads and made their way to Paris. Because he was such a well-known writer, and because he was reporting for a massively popular American publication, his version of what happened as the Second Armored Division was mopping up still resonates and, for many, left a definitive record of the emotion that enveloped those who had helped to liberate the capital. We know that Hemingway had already had an emotional relationship with the city; *A Moveable Feast,* published after his suicide, in 1961, tells us that. His almost valiant attempt at being among the first Americans into the quasiliberated capital speaks to the sentimental value that the capital had for him. "I had a funny choke in my throat and I had to clean my glasses because there now, below us, gray and always beautiful, was spread the city I love best in all the world."[34] There he had been a beginner, a newlywed, an impecunious writer; now he was a famous author, a hero, and he could return to—and in his own way help liberate—the place that had given him the independence every writer needs.

The Americans brought more than military liberation. Their casual acceptance of French enthusiasm, their obvious pleasure in being kissed and hugged by thousands of French girls, their distribution of candy, cigarettes, and chewing gum (still the term used by the French for this delicacy), their lack of ideological fervor, their protection of German soldiers and bureaucrats who had fallen under their authority, their

---

* For years afterward he would brag, with a palpable wistfulness, that he had "liberated the Ritz Hotel," where German elites (and Coco Chanel) had lived in cosseted style for more than four years.

obvious joy at being victorious: all these signs created an image of a nation ready to help its wounded cousin recover, efforts that would continue after the war with loans, reconstruction funds, and eventually the very generous Marshall Plan. On the other hand, American soldiers did loot; they did attack women; they often showed little respect for French custom, but at the same time they reminded the French of what absolute and unquestioned freedom could be. It was as if they were saying: "We're free. It's fun. Come along. We'll help you get there again."

And then there was the Jeep, first produced in 1942—the emblem of American industrial ingenuity. One of the most memorable photographs of Americans in a liberated Paris shows two soldiers in a Jeep coming up the stairs from a Métro stop. They had obviously backed the Jeep down the steep steps so that they looked as if they were emerging from the underground. They have huge smiles on their faces as they tease the Parisians into believing for a moment that they had done the impossible. Paris suddenly found itself under a new version of occupation, much more benign but ultimately more influential and long-lasting.

Whodunit?

On April 26, 1944, only four months before the liberation of the city, Maréchal Philippe Pétain had visited Paris for the first and only time as chief of state of the Vichy government. The crowds had been moderate but enthusiastic, as contemporary photographs reveal. (Schoolchildren had been given the day off.) Speaking at a lavish dinner in the Hôtel de Ville that evening, the elderly statesman offered, "This is the first visit I have paid to you. I hope that I will be able to return soon to Paris without being obliged to inform my [German] guardians...I will be without them, and we will all be much more at ease."[35] Even at this late date, there had been many who were still confident in the doughty old man's leadership. Indeed, until the Liberation, there were those who seriously believed that he and de Gaulle would eventually meet, shake hands, and together bring France back from the destitution and division of four years of war and the Occupation. Pétain himself had wanted to go to Paris once it was liberated, but his German handlers forbade it, spiriting him and his close cadre off to a castle in Germany, where they remained until the end of the war. On August 26, only four months after this triumphant visit, a determined Charles de Gaulle would enter the Hôtel de Ville and stand in the same spot as his former commander to declare that Paris once again belonged to its citizens.

The Liberation of Paris had filled the world with exultation. Spontaneously, "La Marseillaise" would be sung around the world in plazas, on avenues, in offices, in movie houses, even in legislatures. No event, except the end of the war itself, would receive such widespread notice and occasion such joyous expressions of relief and happiness. Their capture of Paris had given the Nazis a great propaganda victory and had convinced the world that the Third Reich was a force that would last—if not a thousand years, then at least a few decades. Their subsequent loss of Paris, as the Allied armies streaked across northern France and wended their way vigorously up from the south, seemed to put the imprint of final and total victory on a horrific conflict that had lasted for five years. But the liberation of the city had come at a cost to the plans of the Allied command. Generals Eisenhower and Bradley had been correct: taking the capital of France had slowed the advance of their motorized armies. Precious fuel supplies had been depleted; diverting troops to encircle and take the city had weakened their advance units. As a result, the Germans were able to retreat in some order to the Siegfried Line (a major series of fortifications on the border of France and Germany) and hold off the invasion of their homeland for another six months. Was Paris worth the Battle of the Bulge and the other major last-ditch efforts of the Reich that caused hundreds of thousands of military and civilian deaths? This unanswerable question is almost never asked, for the Liberation of Paris was such a major symbolic victory of the forces of good against the legions of evil.

Yes, in the end, de Gaulle took most of the credit for having saved Paris on behalf of the "French people." The *Pocket Guide to France* sustains this myth. We should admire the French, it admonishes its naive readers: "The French underground—composed of millions of French workers, patriots, college professors, printers, women, school children, people in all walks of life of the real true-hearted French—has worked courageously at sabotage of Nazi occupation plans."[36]

"Millions" is a strong exaggeration, but more important than the number is the idea that *most* French people had withstood the blandishments of the Vichy regime (which is mentioned only once, glancingly, in the brochure) and, more important, the propaganda and brutality of the Reich. Charles de Gaulle himself could not have written a better history. (Who knows? Maybe he did write it, since the "authors" of this document have remained anonymous, listed simply as the "War and Navy Departments, Washington, D.C.")

For years after the Liberation, arguments over memorials, laws and edicts, reparations, and political representation would divide the political classes of France. The Communist Party of France would lead one of its largest propaganda campaigns in an attempt to accumulate as much recognition for the Liberation as they could. Former Vichy supporters, a resurgent Catholic Church, and former *résistants* with all sorts of ideologies—including those who had followed de Gaulle into exile and those who had stayed on the soil of France—would vie for the right to call themselves liberators of the City of Light and maneuver to capture for themselves the glorious residue of that great symbolic event.

All this commotion raises the question: Who *did* liberate Paris? The Allies, the Communists, the ragtag FFI, de Gaulle's Free French troops, and even the insurgent citizens of Paris wanted a stake in the answer. As we have seen, even the German commander of *Gross Paris* wanted some recognition for his role in "liberating" the city. The liberation of Paris was made possible by an overlapping combination of events, military and political decisions by a formidable mix of personalities, and the spontaneous participation of a long-repressed population. Train and transport workers went on strike; the police gave up their loyalty to the Vichy regime and its German supporters; armed irregulars of the FFI, strongly supported by the Communists but comprising many ideologies, united; Leclerc's eager Second Armored Division fought bravely through German defenses to reach the crown jewel of French nationhood; and the massive support of the American army provided an invaluable backstop.★

For a few brief days, as one historian has pointed out, "La Marseillaise" and "The Internationale" were joined together as the liberated Parisians celebrated not only the departure of the Germans but also the end of the Vichy regime, and perhaps, just perhaps, a truly radical break with the past, one not unlike the great Revolution of 1789.[37] Gertrude Stein described the euphoria:

> And now at half past twelve to-day on the radio a voice said attention attention attention and the Frenchman's voice cracked with excitement and he said Paris is free. Glory hallelujah Paris is free, imagine it less than three months since the landing and Paris is free. All these days I did not dare to mention the prediction of Saint Odile [patron saint of Alsace], she said Paris would not be burned the devotion of her people would save Paris and it has vive la France. I cant tell you how excited we all are and now if I can only see the Americans come to Culoz [the tiny village where she was living] I think all this about war will be finished yes I do.[38]

Soon the optimism dissipated as the factionalism that had torn France apart for years, both preceding and during the war, began again to dominate. Most of the world, though, was unaware of these dissensions; what counted for all who loved Paris was that the city was back

---

★ The British took a backseat in the Liberation, primarily because of the lingering antipathy of many Frenchmen toward their erstwhile allies. The aforementioned *Pocket Guide to France* took notice of this rift. In the section called "A Few Pages of French History," after explaining the 1940 defeat, the narrator addresses his readers directly: "Some citizens of France in defeat have harbored bitter feelings toward their British allies. Don't you help anybody to dig up past history in arguments. This is a war to fight the Nazis, not a debating society."

in the hands of the French, who had risen up to wrest their capital from an evil empire. And, miraculously, the city on the Seine seemed to have suffered very little, especially when compared to the terrific desolation of so many of Europe's capitals. What the world did not see was the economic, social, and psychological damage wrought by the Occupation, which would take years to repair.

Chapter Ten

◦⊱═◉═⊰◦

Angry Aftermath — Back on Paris Time

The putting right of France, [spiritually and] economically, did not happen as rapidly as we would have hoped.
— *Jacques Spitz*[1]

Rediscovering Purity

The immediate responses to the liberation of Paris from its heavy-handed Occupiers were not pretty. At least temporarily, Parisians of all classes and political ideologies took on the same demeanor as their former oppressors. What happened during the few weeks following the hasty departure of the Germans does no honor to the liberators or to the liberated. The hysteria — there is no other term that comes to mind — that took over the crowds of Parisians as they saw the tanks, Jeeps, and uniforms, first of Leclerc's Second Armored Division and then of the American divisions that followed them, was uncontrollable. Along with joyful release, there was a much darker side of uncontrolled mob behavior. Soon large cohorts of German soldiers, still in uniform, hands raised, were being paraded around the city. Protected by French irregulars, American troops, and French soldiers, they were still jeered at, spat on, targeted with rotten vegetables (though not many; Paris was still hungry), and harder objects. Suddenly, the excitement was invaded by a sense of paranoia and hatred that could not wait for the new authorities to calm. For a few weeks, there was literally blood in the streets, as episodes of violence became more unpredictable, more public, and more arbitrary than they had even been while the Germans were running the city.

No one knows exactly how the disorganized violence began, but this much is clear: there was a convulsion, almost an orgasm (the word was used often to describe the phenomenon) of retribution that took over the city in those first few weeks of "freedom." Again, estimates vary, but perhaps in the vicinity of ten thousand Parisians, mostly men and some women, were victims of rapid and frequently fatal justice in the year following the D-day invasion. These judgments and executions were carried out by members of the FFI, the official Resistance army, and members of the informal, self-appointed resistance as well as by vengeful neighbors and competitors. The last gasps of the Vichy Milice were responsible as well for sudden retributive murders until they were finally eradicated a few days after the Germans had escaped. Even before the last Germans had left the city, gangs of official and unofficial armed men began to knock on doors, seeking someone to punish—anyone—even, in a few cases, those who had themselves resisted the German Occupier.

With the signs of liberation finally appearing, the desire to find scapegoats to remove the feelings of guilt and anger that had dominated the four years of Occupation and the five years of the nation's military humiliation was too strong to repress. The first *public* victims of this effort to "recreate a patriotic virginity"[2] were women suspected of having consorted in some inappropriately intimate way with German personnel. But men were vulnerable as well, for the newly dominant forces for order sought to exculpate themselves and their city from blame for their failure to expel the enemy over the course of four years. The difference was that men were often shot behind closed doors, or off in the woods, or even in their homes, while women had their heads shaved in public. The shaving of women's heads—which was often accompanied by the defilement of their bodies—was immediately photographed and distributed by most of the world's primary news organizations.

A generally held belief is that more than twenty thousand women throughout France, ages sixteen and older, were so "shorn" between late 1943 and early 1946 in retaliation for *collaboration horizontale* with members of the German forces. But recent studies have corrected this assumption; archival research has revealed that only about 47 percent of the punished were specifically accused of sleeping with the enemy. The rest were women betrayed, more often than not, by their female peers because they had worked with or served the Germans, because they had ended the war a bit better off than their compatriots, or because they had in other ways insulted common mores, affective and otherwise. Local jealousies and attempts at redirecting attention from some who were guiltier were often behind accusations of lack of fidelity to imprisoned husbands and other excuses for punishment.

Women and girls were dragged from their homes and places of work; sometimes a "trial" would be held, but generally crowd justice was immediately inflicted. Rarely did relatives try to stop the violence to their aunts, cousins, sisters, and even mothers. Frequently children

Scapegoats. (Bundesarchiv)

would be made to stand by as their mothers were shorn and branded (generally with ink or charcoal, but occasionally actual torture was used to make them pay for their purported crimes, e.g., *all* body hair would be cut or even burned off). After being shorn, they were marched through the streets of their communities, some even carrying the babies that might have been the result of their *collaboration horizontale*. We should remember that hairstyles in those days featured long tresses, not bobbed cuts; the sight of piles of hair lying at the feet of women who had had no defenders was the result.

The furor of a hysterical and still apprehensive population did not waste time or energy on details. On the gates leading to the city hall of the 18th arrondissement, dozens of "scalps" were hung, sending a message to all who might have even thought about collaborating that their turn might be next. Of course, "collaboration" was then and would remain a nebulous designator; where did "accommodation" end and "collaboration" begin? As we have seen, men suffered as well but were not as publicly humiliated. (One writer has suggested that the shorn women should not have complained: better to have your hair cut off than to be shot in the back in a dark alley.)

Women may have been denounced for the most part by other women, but it was mainly men who did the "shearing" (though women did participate here and there).* There is no record of a man having been publicly shaved. No one has ever cited a case of a man who slept with one of the *souris grises,* the German women who had accompanied the Occupation bureaucracy. That most of these punishments were done in public spoke to the community's felt need to exorcise the *souillure* (filthy stain) that had besmirched French honor. In fact it was the very publicity of the event that was a major desideratum of those who were doing the punishing. Thousands of photographs were taken, posted, printed in newly liberated newspapers, and shared among friends. One cannot but think of similar publications and postcards of

---

* *Tondre* is the French term for "shearing" and refers mainly, as does the English word, to the shaving of wool from sheep. It can also mean "mowing," as a lawn. Those shaved are called the *tondues,* or "sheared women."

the lynchings that took place in the United States, especially in the South, in the 1910s, 1920s, and 1930s.

We have seen throughout this work how prominent Parisiennes were in daily life during the Occupation of their city. Throughout it all, many of them had tried to maintain an aura of self-possession in their dress and comportment. Germans remarked on the style these citizens maintained, even amid shortages of fabric, leather, and other fashion material. Shortages in chemicals meant that the exquisite attention they had given to their hair was also limited, so many began wearing turbans, with a few locks showing, in order to cover the listless tresses that shortages had forced on them. Then the poor women who had their heads shorn began to wear turbans, too, and that more benign fashion statement quickly disappeared from the streets of Europe's fashion capital. But a terrible coincidence soon occurred: women returning from Ravensbrück and other detention camps, or from work in Germany, appeared with *their* heads shaved, a common remedy for removing typhus-carrying lice. Soon they adopted the turban, not knowing at first that the headpiece had become the sign of a "shorn" woman. Many, many incidents of misidentification further confused the Parisians as they tried to put upright a world that had been turned upside down and inside out. (One person who kept wearing the turban as a fashion statement was Simone de Beauvoir, but we do not know whether she did so in solidarity with her sisters or for convenience.) Women had worked bravely in the Resistance; they had kept the home front in some sort of order; they, for the most part, had stayed faithful to their imprisoned husbands and lovers. But none of these activities was enough to protect many from a blindly vengeful public during the impossibly chaotic months after the liberation of their city and their nation.

To add insult to injury, prostitutes who had provided their services to the Germans were not, in most cases, shorn. Another piece of masculine sophistry protected them: they were, after all, only doing what they were intended to do. Prostitution was legal in France, and during the Occupation there were more than thirty bordellos designated for Germans; it is further estimated that there were about one hundred thousand "underground" women and girls who regularly sold their favors to French and to Germans, the aura of commerce protecting them from accusation and retribution.* They had not "betrayed" French men. This sort of ethical parsing defined the events, along with a sense that some sort of spectacle, of communal bonding, was needed immediately to end the potential civil war that threatened France. The fact that this bonding had to occur around the humiliation of women continues to embarrass French collective memory.

Without delving too deeply into communal psychology, one can venture that these events were definitely aimed at putting women "back in their place." The Vichy government had tried imposing a system of "family values" on French women, but without much success, given the need the country had for female labor and ingenuity during the Occupation. True, as the war wound down, Colonel Rol had offered that without women in the Resistance as many as half its accomplishments would have been impossible. His adjutant, Albert Ouzoulias, wrote in his history of the *Bataillons de la jeunesse* that "during the insurrection, just as during much of the Resistance, [women] played an irreplaceable role."[3] They were brilliant administrators and exceptional liaisons between separated groups; they rode bicycles for hundreds of kilometers, often under fire. They helped build barricades, worked as nurses, and coordinated efforts to assist those who were fighting.

> They organized the new life born of the insurrection; they concentrated their attention on the most difficult problems, such as the nourishment of children and of those unable to fend for themselves.... Their civil rights [e.g., the right to vote] were not given to them; they won them in the Resistance and in the

---

* Immediately after the war, in 1946, the Fourth Republic voted to outlaw prostitution. *Maisons closes*, or bordellos, disappeared from the Parisian cityscape. The explanations for this act range all over the political and moral spectrum, but the effect, of course, was predictable: legal prostitution just became illegal prostitution. Coincidentally, French women won the right to vote from the provisional government in the spring of 1944 and were first able to exercise it in 1945. These two "positive," pro-women initiatives fell on either side of the *tontes,* that is, the public haircuttings.

struggles for Liberation. No one can take away what we owe them for the Liberation.[4]

The FFI itself tried to stop the *tontes,* calling them illegal. Yet France needed to reassume, and quickly, its virility, and the most symbolic way of doing that was to remind everyone that the disasters it had undergone had been the fault of women who had had sexual relations with the Occupier. Paris, the center of fashion, feminine style, and beauty, became for a brief period a center of misogynist scapegoating.

American, Canadian, and British soldiers, especially, found the practice repugnant, and at times they would interfere to protect the victims; we have reports, letters, and interviews with them in which they show how much respect they had lost for the French. All this soon pushed the practice and its recording onto a back burner as the French tried to regain the moral upper hand by reminding the world that Paris was free and was putting itself back together with special attention to a resuscitated joie de vivre. The vehemence that had appeared in newspaper reports, gleefully accompanied by photographs of embarrassed women, began to fade into a general list of excuses, a common response during those chaotic days. Once the visceral need for some sort of justice had been sated, there generally followed an immediate feeling of guilt or embarrassment.

Despite de Gaulle's very serious efforts to bring order quickly to the city, chaos was unavoidable, for the civil war that had been smoldering persistently just below the surface of the French polity needed only a spark to become a conflagration. Numbers are contradictory, but we know that hundreds of summary executions were carried out in Paris, while the same sort of denunciations that had peppered the years of the Occupation continued. Based often on surmise, or personal jealousy, or bad information, these accusations nonetheless served to bring many French men and women to "justice" before kangaroo courts that were set up on street corners, on truck beds, on specially built platforms, in public gardens, in cafés, in back rooms, and in quickly emptied offices throughout the city. No one knows exactly how many were involved in these countless expressions of repressed anger, guilt, and a deep belief that justice must be had. The effects of this period of *épuration* (purification), which had begun in October of 1943 in Corsica, the first French *département* to be liberated, still resonate in Parisian memory. Memoirs, fiction, and essays that appeared right after the Liberation often describe a disoriented population caught up in the social and political dislocation that defines any postwar society.

That this urge to rehabilitate French virility and honor was visited on the bodies of women has been much studied by sociologists and historians. Despite the successes the Free French forces enjoyed on the battlefield up until the final defeat of Germany, and despite their participation in the liberation of Paris and other towns, many who had lived through the debacle of 1940 had not forgotten their army's pathetic defeat. More than a million French soldiers were still in the hands of the Germans, and though they would begin trickling home soon, their neutralization by a more powerful army still rankled. One historian has referred to these embarrassing events as a "rite of passage," necessary when a society moves violently from a period of forced quiescence to find itself immediately free to express years of repressed anger.[5] Yet it was only around the turn of the twenty-first century that major analyses of the events began to correct hoary assumptions — assumptions that tended to protect those who acted illegally, vindictively, and spontaneously after the evacuation of the Germans from French cities and eventually from French soil.

One of the earliest rumors that took hold in Paris while the tanks were rolling in to liberate the city was that members of the Vichy Milice and die-hard German defenders were firing on civilians as well as on armed troops from the rooftops. Looking for marksmen, the city's eyes were turned to the typically low and uneven roofs and high windows of apartment houses. Though there were definitely examples of such activity, *la guerre des toits* (the rooftop war) became a formidable myth that persisted for a month after the liberation of the city. The first civilians targeted by vengeful "liberators" were often those suspected of being on the rooftops taking shots at the celebrants. There are a few eyewitness accounts of what happened at first to those who, for whatever reason, were seen as having not been celebratory enough in welcoming the city's liberators or who had the misfortune to live on one of a building's top floors, especially in southern Paris, where the first French soldiers were welcomed.

A witness tells a tale that matches in horror all that had happened in the city during the Occupation: an innocent man went to his balcony with a telescope to look across the rooftops and down at the victorious Allied troops. All of a sudden, someone in the street looked up and yelled: "There's one of them, with a rifle. He's shooting at us!" Quickly, young armed men, wearing their FFI armbands, rushed up to the building's top floor, burst in, but found no weapons. No matter. They forced the bystander down the stairs; he, and some of his neighbors, pleaded with the gang, telling them that he had hidden Jews as well as downed pilots and had been active in his neighborhood resistance, but the lust to find enemies to bring to justice prevailed. When the group reached the street, other neighbors and bystanders grabbed the poor man, lifted him, and threw him under the treads of the advancing Sherman tanks. The smear of his carcass on the pavement caused a combination of revulsion and a perverse sense of retribution. Embarrassed, the crowd turned and walked away.

The Conseil national de la Résistance, under the general standard of the loosely Gaullist FFI, had been coordinating resistance activities since mid-1943. Coordination was the order of the day. The Communist militant Henri Tanguy (Colonel Rol) was in fact the commander of the FFI in the *département* of the Seine, which included Paris and its immediate environs.★ He had been selected by the Gaullist forces to lead the Parisian secret army because of his extensive combat experience in Spain and during the war. A leader respected by all sides, he nonetheless could not stop the freewheeling, unpredictable, and violent acts of retribution that took over the city for about a month after the Liberation. What made his job more difficult was that many young hoodlums, looters, and even pro-fascists had taken on the aura of being "freedom fighters." Gangs quickly formed all over the city, and for a variety of often contradictory reasons—ideological, personal,

---

★ In the early 1970s, Tanguy would legally change his name to Rol-Tanguy.

pecuniary, and to create camouflage for previous sins of collaboration—there was "blood in the city" for the two months following the departure of the Germans.[6] Among the first to "purify" their ranks were the police, who used accusations, quick judgments, and executions—as well as frequent attempts at hiding their own members' histories of cooperation and collaboration—as acts of retribution. Soon the camaraderie that had defined the Resistance began to fray, then tear, as Communists, Gaullists, and even some former Vichy supporters began to struggle for power in the new government. Not only did these groups quarrel with each other, they often had internecine disputes as everyone sought political purity. Communist turned on Communist; former Vichy bureaucrats denounced each other; and Gaullists who had spent the war abroad nervously watched those who had been fighting on French soil. The FFI and Gaullist leadership immediately tried to compel these groups to cooperate, to surrender arms, to stop the arbitrary arrests, punishments, and executions. But they were initially unsuccessful, and the "false FFI" men continued to engage in blackmail, armed robbery, swindles, and other "normal" crimes.

"Kill All the Bastards!"

With the Liberation, the most innocuous places in Paris became, as they had under the Occupation, sinister. A commandeered dental school in a lower-middle-class arrondissement is one example. There, for about two weeks, the Franc-tireurs et partisans (FTP), an armed branch of the Communist Party, mirrored what the Gestapo had done for the previous four years. Individuals were arrested—or, rather, rounded up—for a variety of unclear reasons: being in the wrong place at the wrong time, being suspected collaborators (whatever that meant at the time), being on the wrong side of the Communist Party, or being on the wrong side *within* the party. Whatever. A further manifestation of the scapegoating was even more violent, though it remains one of the least understood events in histories of the period after the Liberation. No photographs were taken; public humiliation was not part of the terror; all was done in private, and the evidence, the cadavers of the victims, was thrown into the Seine, which threw them back on shore over the course of the following two months.

The Institut dentaire George-Eastman, in the 13th arrondissement, had served as a German hospital for the entire Occupation. Once evacuated by Hitler's troops, it provided an excellent, well-protected building in which acts of retribution against one's enemies could be carried out without public knowledge. FTP members tied the hands of each victim with the same type of cord they used to hang a large limestone cobblestone around the murdered victim's neck before disposing of them in the Seine. It turns out that these stones would not be heavy enough to keep the corpses under water; most of the cadavers, fished from the Seine by the police, had signs of having been tortured before being shot. At first officials thought these were among the final victims of the Gestapo, furious at having to give up Paris. But soon the word spread that they were considered to be enemies of the Communist Party. Old scores had been settled; retributive vengeance had been imposed; an appropriation of judgment had given the party members a sense of ethical superiority over those who were already negotiating with collaborators to remake the city. Up until late December of 1944, bodies would be found, with the signature method of disposal, as if those who did the deed wanted their actions to be recognized and thought about. The whole story is still not known, though recently historians have provided us with much more information about this month of terror: dozens of individuals were picked up, brought to the Institut dentaire, and tortured. More than two dozen of them were so murdered.[7] The victims seemed to have been chosen at random — subjects of rumor, envy, personal grudges, and differing views of what constituted collaboration. Concierges who had been seen scrubbing off anti-Vichy and anti-German graffiti (which they were required to do), café owners and waiters who some thought too close to the Occupier, anti-Communists, pacifists, reputed mistresses of Germans: no one seemed safe once the attention of a vengeful FTP eye was turned on him or her.*

---

* Later, halfhearted efforts were made to find out exactly which specific group was responsible for the murders at the Institut dentaire, but to little avail. The FFI insisted it had never given orders to the FTP for this sort of *rafle* and imposition of casual justice; the

One of the most touching stories concerns a park monitor in late middle age who had been caught up in an FTP assassination attempt a year earlier. In August of 1943, an FTP team had plotted to kill an important German officer in the Parc Monceau, beautifully situated in the heart of the luxurious 8th arrondissement. A partisan fired and hit the major in the thigh, who immediately started to yell in excellent French that he had been attacked. A fifty-one-year-old park guard, Gustave Trabis, having use of only his left hand because of a World War I injury, ran to the wounded German's aid and grabbed at the assailant's bicycle; the shooter managed to escape without having finished the job of killing the major. Sadly for the unfortunate park monitor, the Vichy-controlled press made a big deal of his effort, something he later regretted when he learned that a Paris resistance group had carried out the attack. Nevertheless, he was arrested a year later by the outlier group of *résistants,* tortured, and killed with a blow to the head. His body, like those of the others, was thrown into the Seine. The FTP and other groups were especially diligent at finding Parisians who had impeded *résistants* while carrying out their missions. Instinctively, many bystanders would help police officers apprehend those whom they thought were common thieves. But their names were often written down, and many paid with severe punishments during this interregnum of terror that besmirched the exultation and relief of the Liberation.

But those actions against those seen to have collaborated with, or at least cooperated with, the Occupier were carried out haphazardly. Marcel Jouhandeau was a minor author and a minor collaborator who had written a few anti-Semitic pieces and one pro-Vichy article early in the war. He left a diary that describes the anxiety with which he lived for about six months after the Liberation. Jouhandeau, like many others considered to have been too cozy with the Occupiers (and we must keep in mind that the French had not yet decided exactly what

---

FTP, supported by the Communist Party, insisted that it had had authority from the FFI—though Colonel Rol always denied it. Besides, the FTP asserted, the ones who were killed deserved it, all of them being unpatriotic Frenchmen—that is, *salauds* (bastards).

collaboration entailed, so almost any interaction with the Germans could have been so designated), had already received little coffins in the mail as well as ominous telephone calls ("We know who you are and where you live"). His wife, Elise, was always on the verge of hysteria, and these insistent reminders that they had been perhaps living too well during the Occupation only added to the couple's fright. The Jouhandeaus did live in one of the most chic quarters, the 17th arrondissement, near the Bois de Boulogne and the Porte Maillot, a major German strongpoint. As the citizens of Paris became more emboldened, and as the Germans were obviously abandoning the city, Jouhandeau noticed that he was being watched more and more by passersby. He had friends in the literary world who were in the Resistance, and many promised to protect him, but on a day-by-day basis he felt increasingly vulnerable.

One morning during the Liberation, he learned that his name had been put on a list of collaborators who were to be rounded up. For more than thirty days after the Germans had left, Jouhandeau and his wife moved from friend to friend, from acquaintance to acquaintance, only occasionally sneaking back to their apartment. They kept waiting for a knock at the door, especially since friends were telling them repeatedly that they had been inquired about. They had to learn which concierges they could trust, which ones they should ignore. There seemed to be a fever of counter-denunciation going on in Paris; for every denunciation of a Jew or a Gaullist that took place during the Occupation there appeared to be a corresponding denunciation of a collaborator after the Liberation — even someone who had done something as innocuous as talk with a German. One day, as he was crossing a busy street, a car marked with the large white letters FFI stopped beside him. A young man called out: "Professor Jouhandeau." It was one of his mediocre students, who remembered him well and who offered to take care of him during this period of retribution. Did he now need such help? Were they that close to arresting him? Jouhandeau's fears were enhanced when he heard that many political prisoners were being held and being mistreated at Drancy by the FFI. Another source told him about the acts of humiliation being visited on women who had fraternized with Germans and on *collabos* who had looked down their noses at the Occupied: they were being beaten, tattooed, shorn, and otherwise tormented. One young man, in Jouhandeau's presence, asked a member of the literary resistance if there was any newspaper that would publish his article about how political prisoners were being treated by the FFI. "None," answered the sympathetic publisher. "But it's just as it was before," said the debutant journalist. "Yes," answered the publisher, "just backwards." Jouhandeau soon began to whine—to himself, to others, to his readers—that he was like Christ, a persecuted but innocent man. He refused to admit that the opinions of those who found him repulsive might have had any validity whatsoever. "After the Liberation," he brilliantly observed, "formalities are infinitely more complex than under the Occupation."[8] Well, yes. . . . Jouhandeau ultimately escaped any chastisement for his happy cooperation with the Germans after the war, except for his panic during those months. His case was closed, and he continued to teach in Paris.*

These and other recollections of the way justice was arbitrarily assigned in the months after the Liberation use the same metaphors and images of those who recall what it was like to live under the Germans and their Vichy servants: stomachs knotting when a heavy tread is heard on the stairs; doorbells ringing at odd hours; suspicion of one's neighbors; anonymous letters appearing in one's mailbox, threatening some violent action; clandestine phone calls to friends to find out the latest news; reading with apprehension the newspapers to see who had been arrested and for what; fear of any interaction with official authority—the syndrome of fearful anticipation did not disappear with the disappearance of the Occupier. Almost like a mirror reflection, behavior was the same, only the objects of punishment had changed. If

---

* Another well-known fascist and anti-Semitic French journalist, Robert Brasillach, was not so fortunate. Arrested after the Liberation, he was tried for treason and quickly found guilty. Despite having received a letter signed by such literary and artistic figures as Colette, Camus, Aymé, and Cocteau, General de Gaulle refused to commute his sentence; he was executed—shot—in early 1945.

the Occupation affected Parisians, if the memory of their own and others' actions haunted them, the same could be said for the immediate period following those events. For years, decisions made and actions taken during those terrible months would have the same befuddling impact on Parisian collective memory as had the Occupation itself.

The Return of Lost Souls

In April of 1945, a well-dressed middle-aged woman was sitting comfortably on a bus when she looked up to see a startling apparition: a walking skeleton had just mounted the steps to board. The other passengers were silent, some staring, others looking away. The man, whose age was difficult to determine, was wearing clean clothes, but they swallowed him. What passengers noticed first were his shaved head and his baleful eyes, staring into the middle distance. Moving with caution, holding on to the bus's poles, he shuffled rather than walked. Immediately the woman rose to offer him her seat, which he took with a slight smile and a *merci*. Prisoners of war were making their way back home. As well those who had been deported for political, racial, or economic reasons were, almost overnight, revisiting liberated Paris. Now explanations had to be heard, excuses given, dramas relived, and lives begun again.

On a corner opposite the Gare de Lyon, as trains and trucks dropped off hundreds of returning Parisians and other French citizens, crowds would gather to gape. Janet Flanner (writing as Genêt), the inimitable Paris correspondent for *The New Yorker*, described in a cable dated April 1945 one especially moving arrival:

> The first contingent of women prisoners arrived by train, bringing with them as very nearly their only baggage the proof, on their faces and their bodies and in their weakly spoken reports, of the atrocities that had been their lot and the lot of hundreds of thousands of others in the numerous concentration camps our armies are liberating, almost too late. They arrived at the Gare de

Lyon at eleven in the morning and were met by a nearly speech-less crowd ready with welcoming bouquets of lilacs and other spring flowers, and General de Gaulle, who wept.[9]

One of those waiting was Marguerite Duras, the novelist (Americans know her best as the author of *The Lover*) and member of the Resistance. Her husband, Robert Antelme, had been arrested by the Gestapo in a trap from which she had escaped with the help of her resistance group's leader, François Mitterrand, future president of France. Antelme had been deported to Buchenwald, then Dachau, and she had heard no word of him. Her memoir, *La Douleur* (Painful Sorrow), recounts the anxiety that had taken over the City of Light as the deported began coming back. Surviving Jews, political prisoners, captured soldiers (most of whom had been in prison since surrendering in the spring of 1940), and other men and women were being dropped off at railroad stations, such as the Gare de Lyon or d'Orsay, and especially at the Lutétia (still the only major grand hotel on the Left Bank), the just-vacated site of the Abwehr, the Wehrmacht's intelligence service. Like Duras, many had waited days and weeks and months to see who had come back, bearing photographs of missing relatives, begging for information. When they did find their loved ones, they were often unrecognizable, for their trauma had lasted for so long. The city offered little solace to the waiting. Writes Duras in her memoir:

> No one has anything in common with me....At this moment there are people in Paris who are laughing, especially the young. I have nothing left but enemies. It's evening. I must go home and wait by the phone. A slow red sun over Paris. Six years of war ending....Everything is at an end. I can't stop walking. I'm thin, spare as stone.[10]

She wandered in melancholy from train station to train station, from the Lutétia back to her apartment in Saint-Germain-des-Prés; she was regularly phoned or stopped on the street by friends who asked, "Any news?" And she returned compulsively to the Gare d'Orsay to watch in apprehension and pity as "old men" were helped off trains and trucks by Boy Scouts. But they were not old; they were exhausted, ill, starved. Many were still in their twenties, and many of those would die before they got home, weakened irreparably. No matter how hungry Paris had been, there had been no scenes like this in its streets; for the first time, Parisians had an inkling of how fortunate they had been, in their bubble, as the rest of Europe had turned into a charnel house. The scenes were emotionally draining as well as morally agonizing: How could humans do this to one another? How could the French have supported this Nazi insanity?

Duras was disgusted with Charles de Gaulle's haste to forgive and forget. Forgiveness accompanied a refusal to know, to remember:

> On April 3 [1945] he uttered these criminal words: "The days of weeping are over. The days of glory have returned." We shall never forgive.... De Gaulle doesn't talk about the concentration camps; it's blatant the way he doesn't talk about them, the way he's clearly reluctant to credit the people's suffering with a share in the victory for fear of lessening his own role and the influence that derives from it.[11]

De Gaulle was far from alone in feeling a sense of ownership of the tragedy; many groups claimed their story in the resolution of and the costs of the war and of the Occupation. But Duras touches on perhaps a major legacy of the Occupation and the war, namely, that institutions, no matter how much they will try, cannot forgive, forget, or remember on behalf of affected populations: only those who suffered have that right.

In one of the most remarkable stories that come from this period, François Mitterrand was visiting officially the newly liberated Dachau concentration camp when, from a pile of cadavers and dying inmates, he heard a weak "François, François, c'est moi!" The voice was that of Robert Antelme, ill with typhus, starved, and dying. Quickly, Mitterrand had him transported home to Paris, expecting at any moment that he would pass away before Marguerite Duras saw him. Telephoned by another friend with this news, she waited at the apartment door to see the man for whom she had been waiting, searching, and dreaming of for months. She rushed down the stairs and witnessed Robert being helped to the first landing. "I can't remember exactly what happened. He must have looked at me and recognized me and smiled. I shrieked no, that I didn't want to see. I started to run again, up the stairs this time. I was shrieking, I remember that. The war emerged in my shrieks. Six years without uttering a cry."[12] I know of no more devastating scene as the imagined world of war's horrors confronts the actual. Duras had studied photographs and had watched as "old men" arrived at the train stations; she knew what to expect. But when looking directly into the eyes of her husband, then at his ravished body, she had to let all imagined horrors be replaced by a very intimate one. Such reactions were occurring daily in Paris after August of 1944 and, especially, after the end of the European war, in May of 1945, as those coming home were suddenly, insistently there, or as the idea sank in that others would never be returning. The joy of the Liberation had been replaced by, or at least had to stand side by side with, the reality of a still barely perceived Holocaust.

In her descriptions of the anticipated legacies of the war and the Occupation on her beloved city, Duras envisioned a mass grave, a "black ditch" that had inscribed itself on the Paris cityscape. "Beside the ditch is the parapet of the Pont des Arts, the Seine. To be exact, it's to the right of the ditch. They're separated by the dark. Nothing in the world belongs to me now except that corpse [of my missing husband] in a ditch," she wrote. Later: "No one can know my struggle against visions of the black ditch."[13] A personal image, yes, but a powerful one for the city of Paris itself as it crawled out from under the devastations of the Occupation. It is as if there were a dark line drawn across the memory of the city, separating *gai* Paris (if it ever were truly so) from a metropolis hollowed out by fear, guilt, regrets, and anger. The events that had immediately followed the departure of the Germans would mark the city and its residents as indelibly as had the black years of the Occupation itself.

Chapter Eleven

Is Paris Still Occupied?

Peace is visible already. It's like a great darkness falling; it's the beginning of forgetting.

— Marguerite Duras[1]

De Gaulle Creates a Script

Paris had been made a martyr, had been crushed, and had, against all odds, risen to liberate itself both militarily and morally from the Nazi yoke and Vichy ignominy. France was once again a whole nation, ready to reassume its position as one of the great powers. In perhaps the most significant speech he ever made, at least in terms of its historical resonance, Charles de Gaulle established the myths that would define the Occupation of Paris and the resistance of Parisians for the next quarter of a century.

> Why should we hide the emotion that now clutches us in its grip, men and women here, at home, in Paris, resolute and ready to liberate itself, and by its own hands? No! We will not hide this deep and sacred emotion. There are times that are larger than our own poor lives. Paris! Paris offended! Paris broken! Paris martyred! But Paris liberated! Liberated by itself, liberated by its people with the aid of the armies of France, with the help and support of all of France, of the battling France, the only France, the true France, the eternal France. So it is, now that the enemy that held

Paris has capitulated to us, that France reenters Paris, home again. She returns bloodied, but with resolve. She returns, enlightened by an immense lesson she has learned, but more assured than ever of her duties and of her rights. I mention duties first, and I reduce them to their essence by saying that, for now, these are duties of war. The enemy is weakening, but he has not yet been beaten. He is still on our soil. It will not be enough once we have, with the support of our dear and admirable allies, chased him from our land that we are satisfied, especially after what has transpired. We want to enter his territory, as we should, as victors. It is for that reason that the French avant-garde entered Paris with cannons firing. It is for that reason that the great French army of Italy has landed in the south and is moving rapidly up the Rhône Valley. It is for that reason that our brave and cherished interior forces will now have modern arms. It is to have that revenge, that vengeance, and that justice that we will continue to fight until the last day, up to the day of total and complete victory. This duty of continued war—all men who are here present and all those who hear us throughout France know that it demands national unity. All of us who will have lived through the grandest hours of our history want nothing but to show ourselves, up to the end, worthy of France. Vive la France!"*

De Gaulle had multiple goals in mind, and in this short speech, he addressed them all. Films of the remarks show a self-assured, uniformed general towering over those around him, speaking fluently and confidently. Obviously, he wanted to anticipate others' definitions of the French reaction to the Occupation, especially that of the Communists, who were already describing themselves as the "party of the executed seventy-five thousand."† He wanted to end the civil war—which was

---

* This is my somewhat free translation, in which I emphasize the blatant emotion of a masterful speaker and writer as he composes the first French history of the Occupation. The original French may be found in an appendix.

† Most historians set the bar at sixteen thousand Communists shot or deported to their deaths by the Germans—not a measly number, but not seventy-five thousand, either.

still going on, and threatening to escalate—by uniting the French in a common cause: the total defeat of Nazi Germany. He sought to renew confidence in the French armed forces, deeply diminished since May of 1940, and to ask for wide support of their efforts. He reminded the French that the war was not over, that their sacrifices would have to continue for months more. Cleverly, he wanted to build the myth that the French alone had liberated Paris, though with essential aid from the Allies, to whom he only glancingly refers. Finally, he intended to ensure that the Vichy experiment would soon be forgotten (he refused to declare a new republic, because, he argued, the old republic had not ended—though it had, and legally) and, perhaps most cynically, that the Resistance, courageous as it had been, was no longer essential to the liberation of France.

Parisians and the rest of France accepted these myths immediately and with some confidence. Fortunately for de Gaulle and this version of history, the État français, the Pétainist government, had remained in Vichy, in the middle of the provinces, during the Occupation and had not established residence in Paris or even in Versailles, for which Pétain had petitioned. Paris had thus remained "pure" though occupied, unsullied by the Vichy experiment.

Most of those watching the joyous newsreels, especially the Americans, could not fathom the complications of French politics, but everyone knew that the liberation of the world's most famous city meant an almost fatal blow to the Third Reich's control of the rest of Europe. Warsaw had been razed, twice; a besieged Leningrad had been bombed and shelled for three years; Budapest would be stubbornly defended by the Germans and severely damaged; Vienna and Berlin, especially, had been regularly and mercilessly bombed; but Paris, the jewel of the continent, had remained whole, effectively untouched (though it did not totally escape paying the costs of warfare). The Germans had not succeeded in leveling it—if they had ever had that intention, Hitler's apocryphal "Is Paris burning?" notwithstanding—and the French (with a bit of help) had liberated it with little damage to its monuments and landmarks. An aura of optimism about the impending end of a terrible war spread across continents, and Charles de Gaulle's speech cemented this optimism to his own plan to control post–Occupation France.

De Gaulle was as sensitive to the symbolism of memorials, national celebrations, and public sites as he was to language. In the year and a half he would spend as head of the provisional government (from August of 1944 to January of 1946), he would steadily reappropriate the sites that the Vichy government and the Germans had used to impose their legitimacy—for example, the gold-painted bronze statue of an equestrian Joan of Arc on the Rue de Rivoli, at its intersection with the Rue des Pyramides. The deeply Catholic young woman who had fought the perfidious English, and who had been tortured and burned by them, was a perfect symbol for the Anglophobic, hyper-Catholic, militaristic État français and had been given exemplary attention by the Vichy government. Groups of Vichy supporters and other rightists had gathered at the statue to express their nativist confidence in a resurgent France. (The statue remains today a rallying point for right-wing groups in Paris.) But Joan of Arc had been born in a village in Lorraine, in eastern France, and de Gaulle had adopted the Cross of Lorraine as the emblem of the Free French. It had been scribbled on walls of occupied France for more than four years. On May 16, 1945, de Gaulle organized a massive event around the statue, taking her back, so to speak, reclaiming her as a symbol of the resolve, courage, and liberty of the true France: "By paying homage to Joan, de Gaulle recovered a heroine whose vibrant patriotism, deep faith, and humble origin could at bottom sum up the Gaullism of the war, while playing on two symbols, 'the birth in Lorraine of one and the Croix de Lorraine of the other.'"[2] This process of recuperating sites of collective French memory continued—often with ferocious opposition from the Communists, who had their own sites of memory—well after de Gaulle left the government in 1946.

De Gaulle returned to power in 1958, called to address the horrible mess that the Algerian revolution was creating for the Fourth Republic. After being the midwife for a new, Fifth Republic, one that made the presidency of France much more than an honorific position, he continued to impose his memory of the Occupation and its precedents on French history. With the rhetorical help of his comrade in arms André Malraux—the novelist, Resistance figure, and French army officer who was then his minister of culture—he made a major decision that would, he hoped, close and seal the book of memory: the transfer in 1964 of the remains of Jean Moulin to the Panthéon, the national mausoleum that sits atop the tallest hill in the Latin Quarter. Here the *grands hommes* of France (and Marie Curie) are interred in honor of their service to *la France éternelle*.★

Jean Moulin had been de Gaulle's emissary, charged with uniting the fractious resistance groups that had formed the *armée secrète* that had so worried the general. Moulin succeeded in his mission in mid-1943. But betrayed by still-unknown colleagues, he was tortured so severely that he died on a Gestapo prison train taking him to Germany. In choosing to honor Moulin, de Gaulle hoped, in an ironic move, to put the ashes of the Resistance to rest permanently as well. And, by choosing his own man to represent the Resistance (and not a Communist, of course, or any non- or anti-Gaullist), he also appropriated the Resistance as part of the great Gaullist initiative that had saved France. In a magnificent oration, Malraux powerfully augmented this narrative of the Resistance. Referring to Moulin as the leader of "a people of the night" and "the people of the shadows," he repeatedly invoked nocturnal and supernatural images not only to remind his audience of the glories of the Resistance two decades after the events of these sacrifices but also to recall that it had been General Charles de Gaulle—now president—who had enabled their successes.

> Each group of *résistants* could gain legitimacy from whichever ally [Britain, America, Russia] armed them, or indeed by their own courage; only General de Gaulle was able to bring the Resistance movements together among themselves and with all other combatants, for it was through him only that France conducted one [unified] struggle.... To see in the unity of the Resistance the

---

★ In February of 2014, President François Hollande announced that two more women would join Marie Curie in the Panthéon. Both Geneviève de Gaulle-Anthonioz (a niece of Charles de Gaulle) and Germaine Tillion participated actively in the Resistance.

most important means of struggling for the unity of the nation was perhaps to [create] what has been called, since, Gaullism. It was definitely the means that attested to the survival of France.[3]

But it is not easy to assign new causes to events repressed in collective memory, nor are their effects so easily controlled. For the next fifty years de Gaulle's Fifth Republic would find itself continuously addressing the legacies of France's unique World War II history, and much of this debate would occur in Paris, where so many efforts were made to invoke the city's history in various claims of authenticity.

Stumbling Through Memory

The political fractionalization of the new postwar Fourth Republic (1946–58) permitted the blossoming of dozens of organizations that thought they should at least be part of, if not write the history of, the Occupation and the Resistance. Labor and political deportees, former prisoners of war, Jewish organizations, groups of still influential ex-Vichy officials, Communists, anti-Gaullists, the many and various resistance groups—the list seemed endless—all demanded formal recognition, either in terms of memorialization or official recognition or financial compensation (pensions). Plaques began to appear on Parisian buildings as each society or association remembered its own. The Cold War, which began almost immediately after the end of World War II, further divided the country between those who were staunchly anti-Communist and those who supported a still vibrant French Communist Party and the left in general; and then there were the colonial wars in Indochina and Algeria. One would think that these important events, plus the massive rebuilding of France that was being financed by the Marshall Plan, would push the memory of the Occupation into the background. So did the presidents who followed de Gaulle in the Fifth Republic (1958–), hoping that his efforts at tying, once again, the success of the French during the war to his own person would neutralize the persistence of this collective memory. No such luck. Georges Pompidou (president from 1969 to 1972) was criticized for defending his pardon of Paul Touvier, a notorious Vichy and Nazi sympathizer and leader of the despised Milice, the Vichy paramilitary arm. He implored his critics and others to get on with the work of modernizing France: "Are we going to keep the wounds of our national discord bleeding eternally? Has the time not come to draw a veil over the past, to forget a time when Frenchmen disliked one another, attacked one another, and even killed one another?"[4] The answer, in 1972, was "not yet."

The next two presidents of the Fifth Republic — Valéry Giscard d'Estaing (1974–81) and François Mitterrand (1981–95) — both burned their political fingers whenever they endeavored to put memories to rest about the defeat of 1940 or the Vichy experiment or the Occupation or the Liberation. Who was to be remembered? Who had suffered the most? Who had been unjustly unmemorialized? Were the Gaullists more effective than the Communists at national union? What about the Vichy supporters who were patriots and anti-German? What was owed them? And the interrogation went on and on. Amnesties, the establishment of public holidays marking those years, constructions of memorials: all brought grief to French presidents who wanted to move into a new future, unburdened by a sordid past. The fact that the center-right — Gaullists — remained in executive and legislative power until 1981 exacerbated the divisions that still prevailed in French politics and culture. However, President François Mitterrand, the first leftist leader of France since the *Front populaire* of the 1930s, also was pierced by the arrows of those who still had grievances. To make matters worse for him (and for the resolution of the differences), before joining the Resistance Mitterrand had been a low-level member of the Pétain government. He was still friends with some former Vichy servants, and he insisted, until he left office in 1995, that a wreath in his name be laid annually at Pétain's grave on the Île d'Yeu.* When the full story of Mitterrand's Vichy engagements became more widely

---

* Since Pétain's death, at the age of ninety-five, in 1951, his supporters have been petitioning that his remains be moved from this isolated island off the Atlantic coast of France to join his World War I comrades in arms at Verdun, the site of his great victory. They remain on the Île d'Yeu.

known with the publication in 1994 of a book approved by him, he would argue that he was a *maréchaliste,* not a *Pétainiste,* one of those exquisite distinctions that had become the hallmark of self-definition after the war, referring to the difference between those who admired the "victor of Verdun" for having saved France in 1917–18 (the "marshalists") and those who had bought into being the principles of the "New Order," created under the persona of Philippe Pétain.

Jacques Chirac became Paris's first popularly elected mayor.* He was a classic French pol, integrated fully into the Gaullist ideology, and not known as an imaginative or especially articulate representative of French ideals. But between July 18, 1986 (he was mayor of Paris from 1977 to 1995), and January 18, 2007 (he was the Fifth's Republic's fifth president from 1995 to 2007), he made eleven major speeches about Paris during the Occupation, about the French responsibility for Vichy excesses, and about France having forgotten, for a brief period, its traditions as the nation of *Liberté, Égalité, Fraternité.* We have seen how, in 1986, as mayor of Paris, at the site of the Vélodrome d'Hiver (which had been razed in 1959), he insisted that "in that summer of 1942, our capital knew the weight and the straits of a foreign occupation but had not yet taken the complete measure of the horrible ideology that subtended it....France had still not completely sensed to what point the Nazi order was perversely and insanely criminal."[5] Still seeking forgiveness for the nation for its irresponsibility in failing to protect the most vulnerable of its citizens and residents, Chirac nonetheless was forthright in remembering the horror of the Grande Rafle. After he assumed the presidency, Chirac brought a clear and focused light to the rhetorical and political obfuscation that had attenuated Parisian memory of the excesses of the Vichy government. On Sunday, July 16, 1995, fifty years after the end of World War II, President Chirac spoke with a vigor that shattered the Gaullist legend, which had sought to subsume all requited suffering and courageous resistance under the Cross of Lorraine. The scene was again the

---

* In 1871, as a result of the civil war that had produced the government known as the Commune, Paris had been stripped of much of its autonomy. The prefect of the city had been appointed by the state, but in 1976 substantial administrative autonomy was returned to the city.

Jacques Chirac. *(Jean-Régis Roustan / Roger-Viollet / The Image Works)*

former site of the Vélodrome d'Hiver, where a statue was being dedicated that represented the thousands of Jews who had been temporarily imprisoned within its walls. Chirac began his remarks with his major theme: "There are, in the life of a nation, moments that wound its memory as well as the idea that one has of one's country."[6] For those who had fought with each other for a half century over the ownership of the legacies of 1940–45 France, these words must have brought a sudden silence. Reassuring not only the Jewish members of the audience but also, by extension, many of the immigrants who had arrived since the war, Chirac insisted that Parisians—in fact, all French citizens—must "recognize the mistakes of the past—and especially those committed by the [Vichy] state. Nothing must block out the dismal hours of our history if we are to defend a certain idea of humanity, of liberty, and of dignity. In so doing, we struggle against those dark forces that are constantly at work. This ceaseless combat is mine as much as it is yours."[7] No other speech by a French politician did more to erase the ambiguity of the Mitterrand years and, in effect, undermine the internecine squabbles that were still going on (many of the *résistants* and Vichy supporters were still alive and quite active; we must not forget how young they were in the 1940s). In one of the most important addresses given by a French statesman in the twentieth century, Chirac resurrected the ghost of the Occupation in order to put it to rest. His speech did not bring complete closure to the continuing confusion and arguments about who was responsible for the worst excesses of the Occupation, but it did move the debate toward more trenchant, and thus more transparent, arguments.

Nicolas Sarkozy was born in 1955, the first Fifth Republic president to have been born after the war. Insensitive to, because he was essentially ignorant of, the querulous arguments about the Occupation that had bedeviled his Fifth Republic predecessors, Sarkozy nonetheless chose, as early as 2006, to use in his campaign the example of a youth named Guy Môquet—"a young man of seventeen who gave his life to France; this is an example not of the past but for our future."[8] Immediately, leftist politicians, including former Communists, attacked the arrogance of a politician from the right using a Communist youth to support his run for office. But more significant is that Sarkozy and his staff did not appear to be aware of the complicated story of this young man from the 17th arrondissement. He had been caught up, at the age of sixteen, in the Nazi frenzy following the assassination in broad daylight of two German officers, one in the Métro station at Barbès-Rochechouart in August of 1941 and the other, a *Feldkommandant,* in the streets of Nantes in October of that year. Immediately, Hitler had ordered fifty hostages shot for each German killed; after much negotiation between the Vichy government and the Germans, the ratio of ten hostages per assassinated German was agreed upon. Soon after this agreement, at a camp run by the French government near the Breton town of Châteaubriant, twenty-seven young men, Communists, for the most part, were executed. The Germans felt that the execution of Communists would send a clear signal to the French that their most important enemy was internal and not the Occupiers.

For reasons that are still unclear, among the selected victims was the youngster from Paris, barely seventeen. It was his letter home a few hours before his execution that Sarkozy would read in his campaign. The problem is that though Môquet had certainly "resisted," it was not against the Germans but against the Vichy government. In fact, the *lycéen* had been arrested in October of 1940, while the Communist Party was following orders from the USSR not to fight the German Occupiers, for they were allies. Guy and his young Communist buddies had been posting tags and stickers all over his neighborhood demanding that his father, a Communist deputy arrested after the Soviet-German treaty, be released from prison; the Vichy government, dead set against Communism, had arrested not only deputies but also many party members. Earlier, too, even under the Third Republic, Guy and his friends had been protesting against French support for Finland in its short war with Russia (during the fall and winter of 1939–40). The point is that Guy was not demonstrating against the German authorities but against the governments of his own country.

But Minister Sarkozy, later President Sarkozy, persisted. His first edict as president, aimed at marking his commitment to unite France under the banner of collective patriotism and duty to the Republic, instructed high school teachers in France to recite Môquet's last letter to his mother in their classrooms on October 22. Ridicule, political correctness, old memories, and partisan opposition combined not only to revive memories that many thought had been put to rest, but also to remind everyone that those memories would never stay buried. Slowly, the edict was forgotten.*

---

* Ever since his execution, the Communist Party had insisted that Môquet was one of theirs, a valiant example of the "party of seventy thousand," who had died in opposition to the German Occupier.

François Hollande, the current president of France, paid attention to his predecessors' *faux* pas. He has returned to the less divisive memories of the Occupation, those surrounding the rounding up, imprisonment, deportation, and murder of Jews. Speaking at two Parisian sites early in his presidency—at the place where the Vélodrome d'Hiver once stood and at a new museum at the Cité de la Muette, in Drancy—he took up Jacques Chirac's charge to the French nation to take responsibility for what happened: the État français had been a major player in the French Shoah. On July 22, 2012, he emphasized that "this crime took place here, in our capital, in our streets, in the courtyards of our buildings, in our stairways, on our school playgrounds." The French government had betrayed Jewish confidence that "the country of the great Revolution and City of Light would be a safe haven for them."[9] At Drancy two months later, he stated that "our work is no longer about establishing the truth. Today, our work is to transmit.... Transmission: there resides the future of remembering."[10] Even if one has to insist on how treacherously the French government had acted against those seeking protection in France, it was better than trying to figure out who was most responsible for the crimes and for their punishment.

Should We Blame Paris?

In his second essay on the Occupation, "Paris Under the Occupation" (1945), Jean-Paul Sartre, the twentieth century's most famous philosopher, tried to capture what it was like to live cheek by jowl with one's oppressor.* "A thousand times in these last four years, French have seen serried rows of bottles of Saint-Emilion or Meursault in the grocers' windows. Approaching, tantalized, they found a notice saying 'dummy display.' So it was with Paris: it was merely a dummy display."[11] He offers that Parisians had lived only in the past or present in the early 1940s, for their future had been stolen from them. Camus's

---

* His first essay, "The Republic of Silence," was composed and published only a month after the city's liberation and contains the existentially ambiguous phrase "Never were we freer than under the German occupation" (Sartre, *Aftermath of War*, 3).

The Plague would echo another of his themes: "France . . . had forgotten Paris. . . . Paris was no longer the capital of France."[12] But the Occupation had done more than diminish the spirit of the city's citizens; the very nature of the built environment had changed: "Everything was hollow and empty: the Louvre had no paintings, the Chamber no deputies, the Senate no senators and the Lycée Montaigne no pupils." Earlier, Sartre describes even more specifically the architecture of the city:

> There was nothing but ruins: shuttered, uninhabited houses in the 16th arrondissement, requisitioned hotels and cinemas, indicated by white barriers which you suddenly bumped up against, shops and bars closed for the duration . . . plinths with no statues, parks partly barricaded off or disfigured by reinforced concrete pillboxes, and all these big dusty letters on the tops of the buildings, neon signs that no longer light up.[13]

In the spring of 2008, the estimable Bibliothèque historique de la Ville de Paris (BHVP), located in the Marais, announced and opened an exhibition entitled *Les Parisiens sous l'Occupation: Photographies en couleurs d'André Zucca*. Few who saw the handsome posters recognized the name of Zucca, a somewhat talented Italian-Frenchman who had passed away in 1973. But what did strike Parisians and tourists were the vibrant photographs featured in the show, depicting a colorful Paris basking in the light of the Occupation. The BHVP had bought from the Zucca family the thousands of photographs that he had taken between the 1930s and his death. Included in that collection were about six thousand shots, mostly of Paris under the Occupation; of those, about one thousand were in color. Color film was still a nascent technology and a rare commercial commodity in the early 1940s; it was an expensive and delicate technology, used primarily by the military and the propaganda ministry to project the actions of the Wehrmacht and other arms of the military. That a French photographer, André Zucca, had had access to it was exceptional.

Zucca, a Germanophile probably on the right wing of French politics, had been the only French person hired by the German magazine *Signal* as its photographic correspondent.* None of the images in the 2008 exhibition ever appeared in the magazine, but the fact that Zucca had been given a press pass, access to a supply of film, and freedom to snap away wherever he wanted meant that he was able to provide us with a rich record of certain aspects of daily life in occupied Paris. Not surprisingly, the exhibition immediately brought back into the open the same questions that had been bedeviling Parisian politics since the Liberation. Whose view of the Occupation is the correct one? Were not those fifteen hundred nights of Paris's agony the *années noires* (the dark years), a period that it had valiantly emerged from? The colored brilliance of hundreds of photographs showing Paris as a tourist site in the 1940s, with Germans and Parisians in casual contact, was immediately criticized in the media. One city official referred to the "indecency" of the photographs, arguing that they represented "mundane revisionism."[14] Pierre Assouline, novelist and biographer, wrote in *Le Monde:* "In this exhibition, it is never made clear…that all these photos are a matter of propaganda."[15] Editorials appeared on the right and on the left; Zucca's descendants argued with each other in public (the son referring to his father as a collaborator and anti-Semite); the librarians and curators at the BHVP went public with their own internecine squabbles; bureaucrats working for the city of Paris spoke publicly about their dissensions. Finally a compromise was reached: the title of the exhibition (but not the catalog, which had already been printed[†])

---

* *Signal* was an illustrated biweekly, much like *Life,* that featured home-front news as well as German military escapades. Controlled by the Wehrmacht rather than Goebbels's ministry of propaganda, it was published at its height in more than twenty-five languages and had well over two million subscribers. Available in the United States until January of 1942, it never appeared in Germany itself. It was distributed in occupied territories, countries allied with the Reich, and in Portugal, Spain, and Switzerland.

† In his preface to the catalog, the historian Jean-Pierre Azéma does draw attention to the contradiction between the "black and white" Occupation and the Occupation "in color": "What catches Zucca's lens is the Paris of the good life, where pleasures continue as if nothing had happened…The Paris of Zucca is a bit empty, but serene, without a serious problem, almost existing out of time (Baronnet, ed., *Les Parisiens Sous l'Occupation,* 10)."

would be changed from *Les Parisiens...* to *Des Parisiens sous l'Occupation*. Changing one letter enabled the offensive direct article to become a partitive one, from "[The] Parisians" to "*Some* Parisians." And a separate flyer was handed out to all viewers at the entry booth stating that these photographs had been shot by a man with strong connections to and some ideological agreement with the Occupier. The show was quite successful, but the brouhaha over its interpretation, sixty-four years after the Germans had left, revealed how sensitive Paris and Parisians remain about the role of the city and its citizens in its most humiliating moment of the twentieth century.

"The Landscape of Our Confusions"[16]

Our engagement with the urban landscape is persistently one of interpretation. The history of a city resides in a combination of its architectural evidence *and* the present and past activities of those who have lived within that built environment. This is important: physical, mental, and spiritual engagements with a planned and unplanned architectural environment, not its geopolitical location, define the essence of any metropolis. And that essence changes with the knowledge that we as inhabitants, tourists, temporary residents, filmgoers, readers, and artists garner as we learn about the upheavals that powerful cities such as Paris have undergone.

Imaginative essayists and writers of fiction as well as historians and cultural critics have plumbed the psyche of those disoriented by the disappearance of liberty in a city known for that freedom. In his *Invisible Cities,* Italo Calvino, the Italian essayist, imaginatively wrote about how urban dwellers, both physically and in their dreams, adapt their city to their desires and vice versa—about their desires "constructing" their cities. "The city...does not tell its past, but contains it like the lines of a hand, written in the corners of the streets, the gratings of the windows, the banisters of the steps...the antennae of the lightning rods, the poles of the flags, every segment marked in turn with scratches, indentations, scrolls."[17] Paris was physically marked during the Occupation, and many of those marks remain. A military occupation leaves as well traces on the "invisible" history of a city, but its inhabitants make a daily effort to ignore them, to forget them. "We can keep only 'one' city in our mind verbally, though others are there [always], visually, experientially."[18] Once the occupier has gone, the evidence of his presence diminishes; although, just as memory protected the invested city, memory also never quite allows the occupier to disappear completely. In our master example, Paris has yet to be "liberated" totally from the Occupation of 1940–1944.

"Paris" is not just a set of GPS coordinates but also, and maybe mostly, an imagined city; its special genius has always been based on this fabulous definition. We are far from the Terror of 1793–94, but many of the buildings where its executions and tortures took place are still standing. We are much closer to the 1940s. Some historians do not want us to forget what happened in the buildings occupied by the Germans and their Vichy accomplices. But in the end, what will remain of the memories of that period? What will be the equivalent of the tumbrel and the guillotine? Will de Gaulle be compared to Napoleon, who brought the nation out of the Revolution with his assertion in 1799 that "It is finished"? Will the memory of the Occupation and the Liberation be whitewashed? Do we really have to know about the Occupation in order to understand and "feel" contemporary Paris? When our children pass those little pieces of marble that say so-and-so died here, do they really care? Should they? Will these memorials eventually fall to the ground, forgotten? And if they do, if there is no written record on the walls of Paris, where will the memory of the Occupation and its legacies go?

Yes, the lights came back on, and Paris was no longer darkened, either by war or by the presence of its enemies. But as we have seen, the city has remained haunted by this period. "We'll always have Paris" means that we will always have the memories of how we felt at some past moment—but *that* Paris is gone.

If reading this book has made you more curious about Paris and its violent midcentury history, and if you can still admire her almost unreal self-confidence, then I am pleased. If, on the other hand, the information in these pages has made you more suspicious of her charms, more critical of her adaptation to the "plague," then that, too, would please me. For either way, or both ways, you would have thickened your knowledge so that the next time you confront Paris, either in person or imaginatively, you will have more respect for her resiliency as well as for the hope that she still offers those seeking to escape the depravations of ignorance and cultural violence.

Appendix

De Gaulle's Speech
on the Liberation of Paris

Pourquoi voulez-vous que nous dissimulions l'émotion qui nous étreint tous, hommes et femmes, qui sommes ici, chez nous, dans Paris debout pour se libérer et qui a su le faire de ses mains? Non! nous ne dissimulerons pas cette émotion profonde et sacrée. Il y a là des minutes qui dépassent chacune de nos pauvres vies. Paris! Paris outragé! Paris brisé! Paris martyrisé! mais Paris libéré! libéré par lui-même, libéré par son peuple avec le concours des armées de la France, avec l'appui et le concours de la France tout entière, de la France qui se bat, de la seule France, de la vraie France, de la France éternelle. Eh bien! puisque l'ennemi qui tenait Paris a capitulé dans nos mains, la France rentre à Paris, chez elle. Elle y rentre sanglante, mais bien résolue. Elle y rentre, éclairée par l'immense leçon, mais plus certaine que jamais, de ses devoirs et de ses droits. Je dis d'abord de ses devoirs, et je les résumerai tous en disant que, pour le moment, il s'agit de devoirs de guerre. L'ennemi chancelle mais il n'est pas encore battu. Il reste sur notre sol. Il ne suffira même pas que nous l'ayons, avec le concours de nos chers et admirables alliés, chassé de chez nous pour que nous nous tenions pour satisfaits après ce qui s'est passé. Nous voulons entrer sur son territoire comme il se doit, en vainqueurs. C'est pour cela que l'avant-garde française est entrée à Paris à coups de canon. C'est pour cela que la

Given at the Hôtel de Ville, August 25, 1944.

grande armée française d'Italie a débarqué dans le Midi! et remonte rapidement la vallée du Rhône. C'est pour cela que nos braves et chères forces de l'intérieur vont s'armer d'armes modernes. C'est pour cette revanche, cette vengeance et cette justice, que nous continuerons de nous battre jusqu'au dernier jour, jusqu'au jour de la victoire totale et complète. Ce devoir de guerre, tous les hommes qui sont ici et tous ceux qui nous entendent en France savent qu'il exige l'unité nationale. Nous autres, qui aurons vécu les plus grandes heures de notre Histoire, nous n'avons pas à vouloir autre chose que de nous montrer, jusqu'à la fin, dignes de la France. Vive la France!

Acknowledgments

This list is long, for the project has been long. Venturing into a field that has been so deeply studied, and from a perspective that has been underemphasized, especially in English, took encouragement from many, good critics all of them, and all faithful to the idea that the path of narrative is the best means to find one's way through the underbrush of history.

I have dedicated this book to my family, but it must also be dedicated in part to two friends whose help and encouragement kept me steadily and confidently on target. Stacy Schiff recognized early that my project was larger than my timid aspirations for it. She explained the world of trade publishing to someone who had only published with academic presses; she found my agent; she made me sit up straight when I slumped; she checked in regularly with sisterly encouragement. (I'd say "motherly," but I'm much older than she.) Her generosity and friendship define those terms, and are equaled only by her brilliance as a writer.

And I take special pleasure in thanking my *pote* Philippe Rochefort, a French friend of more than four decades, and one of the most widely read, critically astute, and deeply generous men I know. Philippe served as my touchstone on all facts concerning his beloved France, especially the complexities of its history. He volunteered as chauffeur to sites of the Occupation (including a re-creation of Hitler's own tour of Paris), sent me books and articles, suggested directions that I had ignored, and generally supported my efforts with wit and intelligence. In the end, his comment—"You have been fair to the French"—meant more to me than he knows.

Later to the game, but just in time, was my editor at Little, Brown— Geoff Shandler. When I described to writer friends how Geoff edited my manuscript, they all offered a version of the same theme: "I didn't know editors like that still existed." Geoff believed in this project from the beginning, even before I was sure about its shape. And he has read several versions of it, several times — cutting, editing, reorganizing, and gently suggesting. The result has his fingerprints all over it.

Catherine Lafarge and English Showalter were early evaluators of my first forays into Hitler's tour of Paris. Their firm analyses structured my earliest attempts at organizing the complexity of the project. Catherine regularly offered advice, information, and more books than I was able to read. English has been calmly and supportively at my side since we first met almost fifty years ago.

Two fellow scholars of the Occupation and its representations in film and literature, Judith Mayne and Leah Hewitt, were essential readers, deepening my focus when it might have been superficial, and unselfishly offering perspectives from their own work.

Finding an agent as a first-time trade author was an adventure. I benefited from long discussions with Ike Williams, and his colleague, Katherine Flynn, and especially with Michael Carlisle and his assistant, Lauren Smythe, both of whom got me off to a good start. But being adopted by Geri Thoma, now of Writers House, was the opening I needed. Geri took me on after only an hour's conversation, and it has been a perfect match. Her warmth, intelligence, uncanny knowledge of the ever-changing world of publishing, and her generous sense of humor (which has gotten me through many panicky phone calls) have all made this book better.

The Little, Brown editing, design, production, and marketing teams have built a remarkable safety net. As long as there are teams this gifted, publishing in the United States has a healthy future indeed. I extend my warm gratitude to Michael Pietsch, Reagan Arthur, Allie Sommer, Pamela Marshall, Miriam Parker, Lisa Erickson, Amanda Brown, Amanda Lang, and Keith Hayes. Liese Mayer was an early and enthusiastic guide. Many authors complain about the hard-heartedness of copyeditors, but this author was fortunate enough to have Barbara Clark, an intelligent and sensitive reader. My estimable publisher in the United Kingdom, John Murray, Ltd., through the persons of Roland Phillips and his aide,

Becky Walsh, have reminded me that this book is being read by those who know intimately the period it covers.

At key points in the writing of this narrative, I have benefited from the wise criticism and encouragement of Joseph Ellis, Dennis Porter, Elaine Showalter, William O. Goode, and Drake McFeely. Scholars and amateurs in this and ancillary fields have also offered suggestions and advice: Melanie Krob, Stanley Burns, Roger Hahn, Alan Marty, Allan Mitchell, Bert Gordon, Robert Paxton, Alan Riding, Anthony Grayling, and Robert Weil.

Friends old and new have shown polite interest as I rambled on about Germans in Paris. Just being there meant a lot to me: Harriet Welty Rochefort, Maggie and Bob Pearson, Nicola Courtright, Jason Rosenblatt, Marc de la Bruyère, Roger and Gayle Mandle, Hope Glidden, Laurent Gargaillo, Sidne Koenigsberg, and Rob Dumitreseu.

Closer to home, colleagues in the "Valley"—that is, at Amherst College and its nearby Five-College sisters—listened and debated and suggested: Polina Barskova, Marietta Pritchard, Lucia Suarez, Clark Dougan, Mark Kesselman, Christian Rogowski, Tom Dumm, Sara Brenneis, Sigi Schutz, Lawrence Douglas, Chris Benfey, Ute Brandes, the late Don Pitkin, Bill Taubman, Judy Frank, Heidi Gilpin, Scott Turow, and especially Catherine Epstein. Others will certainly remind me that I forgot to mention their generous help. Sigh. The world of social media is an unruly one, but Julia Hanley's calm savvy made me sociable.

Amherst College has been extraordinarily generous in supporting this project—financially and morally, through sabbaticals, extensive financial support for travel and research, and student research assistants. *When Paris Went Dark* took shape under its aegis. Deans of the Faculty Lisa Raskin and Gregory Call always answered my requests for support. Their leadership has ensured that the faculty of our college are not impeded in their work by a paucity of funding. I am also grateful for the generous support of alumni and trustees, especially the selfless generosity of Axel Schupf, who repay the College faithfully for the memorable educations they received here.

Among the staff at Amherst who made this project so much easier, I would like to thank John Kunhardt, Susan Sheridan, Jayne Lovett, Megan Morey, Betsy Cannon-Smith, Ellie Ballard, and the staff at Amherst's Frost Library and its Center for Informational Technology. The Mead Art Museum at Amherst, and its director, Elizabeth Barker, deserve thanks as well for their generous support. In the French Department office, Liz Eddy and Bobbie Helinski effortlessly (it appeared) eased me through even the modest bureaucracy of this college.

Other institutions have provided me with the space, the resources, the aid, and the comforts that every writer who ventures over much-traveled ground needs. Allow me to thank the staffs at the Mémorial de la Shoah and its Centre de documentation juive contemporaine in Paris, the Archives nationales de France, the Musée de la Résistance nationale in Champigny-sur-Marne, the United States Holocaust Memorial Museum (especially Michael Grunberger, director of collections), the Cinémathèque française, the Musée du Général Leclerc de Hauteclocque et de la Libération de Paris/Musée Jean Moulin, the archives of the Préfecture de la police de Paris, the Bibliothèque historique de la Ville de Paris, the Bibliothèque de nationale France, the New York Public Library, and the libraries of Smith College, Hampshire College, and Mount Holyoke College, the W. E. B. Du Bois Library at the University of Massachusetts, Amherst, and especially the archivists at the Imperial War Museum, London.

I have talked to many, many citizens of France and Paris who either lived through these events as adults, as teenagers, or as youngsters. Some did not want to be identified, so I must thank them anonymously but no less deeply. Others may — and should — be named, for they give heft to a story slowly disappearing into cloudy history: Marie-Jeanne Rochefort, Brigitte and Guy Bizot, Arnaud de Bontin, France Batoua, Madeleine and René Boccara, Pierre-Élie de Borone, Anne-Marie Chouillet, Jean and Denise Dréno, Roger and Ellie Hahn, Viviane Lemaire, and Hessy Taft.

Finally, and with the honors that such placement brings, there is an army of young people, all students of mine, who have listened to me for years as I carved this tale from the history of twentieth-century France. In courses on the history of Paris and France, on the urban imagination, on World War II in film and literature, and others, they have followed as I taught new texts and let my enthusiasm for the history of the Occupation hijack the syllabus. Most important, they worked for me as research assistants, fitting my own demands into their already busy schedules, for they were all serious students. I acknowledge here their diligence, their imagination, and their friendship: Ethan Katz, himself now a historian of the period and prominently mentioned in my bibliography; Chris Chang and Sam Huneke, both currently PhD students in history, and David Crane, Jesse McCarthy, and Brian Thayer. Kane Haffey gave freely his time to photograph this author, almost succeeding in making him look authoritative. And special thanks must go to a patient and punctilious trio who were crucial during the especially chaotic final months of preparations: Michael Harmon, Elizabeth Mardeuz, and the almost unbelievably competent, perceptive, and imaginative Lu Yi. This young scholar from Shanghai has worked with me longer than anyone. I've asked my wife if we can adopt him so that he won't leave after he graduates from Amherst, but clearly he has other plans: yes, a PhD in history.

Collaboration has bad connotations in a book about the Occupation, but in this case, I could not have succeeded, if indeed I have, without the generous collaboration of these supportive institutions, and especially these thoughtful people who have accompanied me on this narrative journey.

Notes

Preface

1 Janet Malcolm, *Two Lives: Gertrude and Alice* (New Haven, CT: Yale University Press, 2004), 186.
2 Philippe Burrin, "Writing the History of Military Occupations," in *France at War: Vichy and the Historians,* ed. Sarah Fishman (Oxford: Berg, 2000), 80–81.
3 Cédric Gruat, *Hitler à Paris: June 1940* (Paris: Tirésias, 2010), 17. Unless otherwise noted, all translations from the French are mine. I have also slightly modified some existing translations of selected works.
4 Pierre Audiat, *Paris pendant la guerre, 1940–1945* (Paris: Hachette, 1946), 6.
5 Jacques Lusseyran, *And There Was Light: Autobiography of Jacques Lusseyran, Blind Hero of the French Resistance* (Sandpoint, ID: Morning Light Press, 2006), 137.
6 Jerome Kern with Oscar Hammerstein (New York: Chappell, 1940). "The Last Time I Saw Paris" was an immediate hit. It was sung by Kate Smith and, later, performed by Ann Sothern in the 1941 film *Lady Be Good.*

Introduction

1 Henry W. Miller, *The Paris Gun: The Bombardment of Paris by the German Long Range Guns and the Great German Offensives of 1918* (New York: Jonathan Cape and Harrison Smith, 1930), 59.
2 G. I. Steer, "Historic Basque Town Wiped Out; Rebel Fliers Machine-Gun Civilians," *The New York Times,* April 28, 1937.
3 See Lynn H. Nicholas, *The Rape of Europa: The Fate of Europe's Treasures in the Third Reich and the Second World War* (New York: Knopf, 1994). This study tells us that every sort of artwork was stolen, hidden, and destroyed during this war; her research taught us a great deal about what can be characterized as the mobility of national patrimonies.
4 Michel Schneider, *Un Rêve de pierre: Le "Radeau de la Méduse," Géricault* (Paris: Gallimard, 1991), 14.
5 Laurent Lemire, ed., *1940–1944 Der Deutsche Wegleiter* (Paris: Alma, 2013), 26.
6 Ibid.
7 Allan Mitchell, *Nazi Paris: The History of an Occupation, 1940–1944* (New York: Berghahn Books, 2008), 3–4.
8 Jean Dutourd, *Au Bon Beurre: Scènes de la vie sous l'Occupation* (Paris: Gallimard, 1952), 48.
9 Irène Némirovsky, *Suite Française* (New York: Knopf, 2006), 198–99.
10 Vercors, *The Silence of the Sea,* ed. James W. Brown and Lawrence D. Stokes (Oxford: Berg, 1991), 51.
11 A. J. Liebling, *World War II Writings* (New York: Library of America, 2008), 654.

Chapter One: A Nation Disintegrates

1 From a radio address made by Pétain on June 18, 1940. In French: "C'est le coeur serré que je vous dis qu'il faut cesser notre combat."

2 Simone de Beauvoir, *Wartime Diary* (Champaign, IL: University of Illinois Press, 2009), 38–39.

3 Ibid., 49.

4 Ibid., 135.

5 Edith Thomas, *Pages de journal, 1939–1944,* ed. Dorothy Kaufmann (Paris: Viviane Hamy, 1995), 59.

6 Pierre Bourget, *Histoires secrètes de l'Occupation de Paris (1940–1944),* vol. 1, *Le Joug* (Paris: Hachette, 1970), 47.

7 William L. Shirer, *The Collapse of the Third Republic: An Inquiry into the Fall of France, June 1940* (New York: Simon and Schuster, 1969), 772.

8 Jean-Marc de Foville, *L'Entrée des Allemands à Paris, 14 juin 1940* (Paris: Calmann-Lévy, 1965), 69.

9 Ibid., 93.

10 Ibid., 99.

11 Guy de Maupassant, *Boule de suif* (Paris: Albin Michel, 1999), 19–20.

12 Irène Némirovsky, *Suite Française* (New York: Knopf, 2006), 3.

13 Foville, *L'Entrée des Allemands à Paris,* 57.

14 Némirovsky, *Suite Française,* 49.

15 Jean de La Hire, *Les Crimes de l'évacuation: Les Horreurs qu'on a vues* (Paris: Tallandier, 1940), 32.

16 Shirer, *The Collapse of the Third Republic,* 775.

17 Hanna Diamond, *Fleeing Hitler: France 1940* (New York: Oxford University Press, 2007), 13.

18 La Hire, *Les Crimes de l'évacuation,* 79–80.

19 Shirer, *The Collapse of the Third Republic,* 825–26.

20 Ibid., 862.

21 Ian Kershaw, *Hitler, 1936–45: Nemesis* (New York: W. W. Norton, 2000), 299.

22 Shirer, *The Collapse of the Third Republic,* 939.

Chapter Two: Waiting for Hitler

1 August von Kageneck, *La France occupée,* préf. Jean-Paul Bled (Paris: Librairie Académique Perrin, 2012), 49.

2 Omer Bartov, *Hitler's Army: Soldiers, Nazis, and War in the Third Reich* (New York: Oxford University Press, 1991), 13.

3 Kageneck, *La France occupée,* 59.

4 Clara Longworth Chambrun, *Sans jeter l'ancre (1873–1948)* (Paris: Plon, 1953), 223.

5 Rosalind E. Krauss, *The Picasso Papers* (New York: Farrar, Straus and Giroux, 1998), 111.

6 Harriet and Sidney Janis, "Picasso's Studio," in Marilyn McCully, ed., *A Picasso Anthology: Documents, Criticisms, Reminiscences* (Princeton, NJ: Princeton University Press, 1982), 224.

7 Alexander Werth, *The Last Days of Paris: A Journalist's Diary* (London: Hamish Hamilton, 1940), 28.

8 Brassaï, *Conversations avec Picasso* (Paris: Gallimard, 1964), 76, 89.

9 Bryan Hammond and Patrick O'Connor, *Josephine Baker* (London: Jonathan Cape, 1988), 19–20.

10 Irène Némirovsky, *Suite Française* (New York: Knopf, 2006), 194.

11 Simone de Beauvoir, *Wartime Diary* (Champaign, IL: University of Illinois Press, 2009), 284–85.

12 Jean Guéhenno, *Journal des années noires, 1940–1944* (Paris: Gallimard, 1947), 17.

13 Berthe Auroy, *Jours de guerre: Ma vie sous l'Occupation* (Montrouge, France: Bayard, 2008), 70.

14 Benoîte and Flora Groult, *Journal à quatre mains* (Paris: Denoël, 2002), 38.

15 Ibid., 54.

16 Ninetta Jucker, *Curfew in Paris: A Record of the German Occupation* (London: Hogarth, 1960), 51.

17 Pierre Bourget, *Histoires secrètes de l'Occupation de Paris (1940–1944),* vol. 1, *Le Joug* (Paris: Hachette, 1970), 59.

18 Ibid., 63.

19 Adolf Hitler and H. R. Trevor-Roper, *Hitler's Table Talk, 1941–1944: His Private Conversations,* trans. Norman Cameron and R. H. Stevens (New York: Enigma Books, 2000), 98–99.

20 Bourget, *Histoires secrètes,* 81–82.

21 Mabel Bayliss, Private Papers. Catalog number 5527, Imperial War Museum, London.

22 Ibid.

23 Némirovsky, *Suite Française,* 344–45.

24 René Mathot, *Au Ravin du loup: Hitler en Belgique et en France, mai–juin 1940* (Brussels: Racine, 2000), 74.

25 Arno Breker, *Paris, Hitler et moi* (Paris: Presses de la Cité, 1970), 10. This remains the most authoritative account we have of Hitler's visit.

26 A meticulous analysis of the images of this visit can be found in Cédric Gruat, *Hitler à Paris: Juin 1940* (Paris: Tirésias, 2010).

27 Albert Speer, *Spandau: The Secret Diaries* (New York: Macmillan, 1976), 102.

28 Frederic Spotts, *Hitler and the Power of Aesthetics* (New York: Overlook Press, 2002), 280.

29 Ibid., 286–87.

30 Breker, *Paris, Hitler et moi,* 102.

31 Albert Speer, *Inside the Third Reich: Memoirs* (New York: Macmillan, 1970), 172.

32 Breker, *Paris, Hitler et moi,* 97.

33 Tobin Siebers, "Hitler and the Tyranny of the Aesthetic," *Philosophy and Literature* 24, no. 1 (April 1, 2000): 99, 108.

34 Friedrich Sieburg, *Who Are the French?* (New York: Macmillan, 1932), 188–89.

35 Thomas Weyr, *The Setting of the Pearl: Vienna Under Hitler* (New York: Oxford University Press, 2005), 36.

36 Ibid., 170.

37 Adolf Hitler, *Mein Kampf,* trans. Ralph Manheim (Boston: Houghton Mifflin, 1971), 261.

38 Ibid., 265.

Chapter Three: Minuet (1940–1941)

1 Pierre Sansot, *Poétique de la ville* (Paris: Éditions Payot-Rivages, 2004), 22.

2 Eyal Benvenisti, *The International Law of Occupation* (Princeton, NJ: Princeton University Press, 1993), 8.

3 Pierre-Louis Basse, *Guy Môquet: Une enfance fusillée* (Paris: Stock, 2000), 20.

4 Dominique Jamet, *Un petit Parisien, 1941–1945* (Paris: Flammarion, 2000), 109.

5 Francis Carco, preface to Colette's *Oeuvres,* vol. 4 (Paris: Gallimard, 2004), 569.

6 Liliane Schroeder, *Journal d'Occupation: Paris, 1940–1944. Chronique au jour le jour d'une époque oubliée* (Paris: Guibert, 2001).

7 Pierre Audiat, *Paris pendant la guerre, 1940–1945* (Paris: Hachette, 1946), 52.

8 Ibid., 24.

9 Max Hastings, "The Most Terrible of Hitler's Creatures," *The New York Review of Books* 59, no. 2 (February 9, 2012), 38.

10 Cécile Desprairies, *Ville lumière, années noires: Les lieux du Paris de la Collaboration* (Paris: Denoël, 2008), 22.

11 Gaël Eismann, *Hôtel Majestic: Ordre et sécurité en France occupée (1940–1944)* (Paris: Tallandier, 2010), 28.

12 Arno Breker, *Paris, Hitler et moi* (Paris: Presses de la Cité, 1970), 105–6.

13 Georges Poisson, *Le Retour des cendres de l'Aiglon* (Paris: Nouveau Monde, 2006), 80–81.

14 Renée Poznanski, *Jews in France during World War II* (Waltham, MA: Brandeis University Press in association with the United States Holocaust Memorial Museum, 2001), 25.

15 Jacques Biélinky, *Journal, 1940–1942: Un journaliste juif à Paris sous l'Occupation* (Paris: Cerf, 1992), 113.

16 Colette, *Paris de ma fenêtre,* in *Oeuvres,* vol. 4 (Paris: Gallimard, 2001), 1258.

17 Ibid., 605.

18 Eric Alary, *Les Français au quotidien: 1939–1949* (Paris: Librairie Académique Perrin, 2009), 18.

19 Christine Levisse-Touzé et al., eds., *1940: l'Année de tous les destins* (Paris: Paris-Musées, 2000), 124; exhibition catalog.

Chapter Four: City Without a Face — The Occupier's Lament

1 Felix Hartlaub, *Paris 1941: Journal et correspondance* (extraits) (Arles: Actes Sud, 1999), 117.

2 Karen Fiss, *Grand Illusion: The Third Reich, the Paris Exposition, and the Cultural Seduction of France* (Chicago: University of Chicago Press, 2009).

3 Jean Guéhenno, *Journal des années noires, 1940–1944* (Paris: Gallimard, 1947), 110–11.

4 Patrick Buisson, *1940–1945: Années érotiques* (Paris: Albin Michel, 2011), 89.

5 Hélie de Saint Marc and August von Kageneck, *Notre histoire, 1922–1945: Conversations avec Étienne de Montety* (Paris: Arènes, 2002), 159–60.

6 Hartlaub disappeared during the defense of Berlin in April–May of 1945. His sister published some of his disparate writings under the title *Von unten gesehen* (View from Below) in 1950, and five years later his journal as we have it was published in his *Gesamtwerk* (Complete Works). In 1999, a French translation of the journal was published as *Paris 1941*. The latter is the edition I have used.

7 Hartlaub, *Paris 1941,* 113.

8   Ibid., 114–15.

9   For very detailed information on sexual mores during this period, see Patrick Buisson, *1940–1945: Années érotiques* (2 vols.), Insa Meinen, *Wehrmacht et prostitution sous l'Occupation (1940–1945),* and Jean-Paul Picaper and Ludwig Norz, *Enfants maudits.*

10 Buisson, *Années érotiques,* vol. 1, *Vichy, ou Les infortunes de la vertu,* 85.

11 Buisson, *Années érotiques,* vol. 2, *De la grande prostituée à la revanche des mâles,* 294.

12 For an extensive study of this phenomenon, see Jean-Paul Picaper and Ludwig Norz, *Enfants maudits: Ils sont 200,000; On les appelait les "enfants de Boches"* (Paris: Syrtes, 2004).

13 Colette, *Paris de ma fenêtre,* in *Oeuvres,* vol. 4 (Paris: Gallimard, 2001), 692.

14 Insa Meinen, *Wehrmacht et prostitution sous l'Occupation (1940–1945)* (Paris: Payot, 2006), 10.

15 Fabienne Jamet, *One two two* (Paris: Presses Pocket, 1979), 107.

16 Ibid., 111.

17 Ibid.

18 Allan Mitchell, *The Devil's Captain: Ernst Jünger in Nazi Paris, 1941–1944* (New York: Berghahn Books, 2011), 68.

19 Ernst Jünger, *Journaux de guerre,* vol. 2, *1939–1948* (Paris: Gallimard, 2008), 322.

20 Gerhard Heller, *Un Allemand à Paris: 1940–1944* (Paris: Éditions du Seuil, 1981), 34. (209)

21 Ibid., 201.

22 Ibid., 199.

23 Ibid., 201–2.

24 Ibid., 203–4.

25 Ibid., 206.

26 Charles-Louis Foulon, Christine Levisse-Touzé, and Grégoire Kauffmann, *Les Résistants,* vol. 2, *Lucie Aubrac et l'armée des ombres* (Paris: Société Éditrice du Monde, 2012), 120.

Chapter Five: Narrowed Lives

1   Michèle Cointet and Jean-Paul Cointet, *Paris 40–44* (Paris: Librairie Académique Perrin, 2001), 10.

2   Tatiana de Rosnay, *Sarah's Key* (New York: St. Martin's Press, 2007).

3   Gaston Bachelard, *The Poetics of Space* (New York: Orion Press, 1964).

4   Otto Friedrich Bollnow, *Human Space* (London: Hyphen, 2011), 87.

5   Marcel Aymé, *Le Passe-muraille: nouvelles* (Paris: Gallimard, 1943), 18–19.

6   Ibid., 19.

7   Edith Thomas, *Pages de journal, 1939–1944,* ed. Dorothy Kaufmann (Paris: Viviane Hamy, 1995), 154.

8   Victoria Kent, *Quatre ans à Paris* (Paris: Éditions le Livre du jour, 1947), 78.

9   Dominique Jamet, *Un petit Parisien, 1941–1945* (Paris: Flammarion, 2000), 89.

10 Ibid., 85.

11 Ibid., 99.

12 Sharon Marcus, *Apartment Stories: City and Home in Nineteenth-Century Paris and London* (Berkeley: University of California Press, 1999), 2.

13 Ibid., 24.

14 This and the previous episode are described in Anne Thoraval, *Paris, les lieux de la Résistance* (Paris: Parigramme, 2007).

15 Berthe Auroy, *Jours de guerre: Ma vie sous l'Occupation* (Montrouge, France: Bayard, 2008), 181.

16 Ibid., 96–97.

17 Private papers of Mabel Bayliss, catalog number 5527, Imperial War Museum, London.

18 Jacques Yonnet, *Paris Noir: The Secret History of a City,* trans. Christine Donougher (Sawtry, UK: Dedalus, 2006), 22.

19 Kent, *Quatre ans à Paris,* 192.

20 Pascale Moisson, *Anecdotes... sous La Botte* (Paris: Harmattan, 1998), 91.

21 Auroy, *Jours de guerre,* 122–23.

22 Laurent Lemire, ed., *1940–1944 Der Deutsche Wegleiter* (Paris: Alma, 2013), 121.

23 Edmond Dubois, *Paris sans lumière, 1939–1945: Témoignages* (Lausanne: Payot, 1946), 122.

24 Ibid.

25 André Halimi, *La Délation sous l'Occupation* (Paris: Edition 1, 1998), 89. Halimi also filmed a very fine documentary, *Délation pendant l'Occupation,* that cites many such letters and analyzes the characteristics of people who sent them.

26 Paul Achard, *La Queue: Ce qui s'y disait, ce qu'on y pensait* (Paris: Mille et une nuits, 2011), 95.

27 Elsa Triolet, *Quatre récits de l'Occupation* (Brussels: Société des amis de Louis Aragon et Elsa Triolet/Aden, 2010), 33.

28 Achard, *La Queue,* 79.

29 Jean Galtier-Boissière, *Mon journal pendant l'Occupation* (Paris: La Jeune parque, 1944), 55.

Chapter Six: The Dilemmas of Resistance

1 Clemenceau's aphorism was used as the motto of the widely distributed Resistance journal *Combat.*

2 Jean Texcier, "Conseils à l'occupé," available on the Musée Virtuel de la Résistance website (http://www.museedelaresistanceenligne.org/doc/flash/texte/2616.pdf).

3 Robert Paxton's *Vichy France: Old Guard and New Order, 1940–1944* (New York: Knopf, 1972) and Henry Rousso's *The Vichy Syndrome: History and Memory in France Since 1944* (Cambridge, MA: Harvard University Press, 1991) are thorough, clear, and definitive studies about the Vichy regime and the detritus it left behind in France's collective memory.

4 The best recent historians of the idea of French resistance to the Occupation are Philippe Burrin, Matthew Cobb, Olivier Wieviorka, Jean-Pierre Azéma, Alya Aglan, and Jean-François Muracciole.

5 Jean-François Muracciole, *Histoire de la Résistance en France* (Paris: Presses universitaires de France, 1993), 29.

6 Jean-Pierre Azéma, *1940: L'Année noire* (Paris: Fayard, 2010), 417.

7 Ibid.

8 Jean-Louis Crémieux-Brilhac, *La France Libre: De l'Appel du 18 juin à la Libération* (Paris: Gallimard, 1996), 89.

9 Ibid., 98, 101.

10 Dwight D. Eisenhower, *Crusade in Europe* (Baltimore: Johns Hopkins University Press, 1997), 296.

11 Matthew Cobb, *The Resistance: The French Fight Against the Nazis* (London: Simon & Schuster, 2009), 3.

12 Jean-François Muracciole, *Histoire de la Résistance en France,* 103.

13 Gaël Eismann, *Hôtel Majestic: Ordre et sécurité en France occupée (1940–1944)* (Paris: Tallandier, 2010), 134. Eismann's book is the most thorough analysis of the structure and actions of the MBF in Paris during the Occupation.

14 Ibid., 161–62.

15 Charles-Louis Foulon, Christine Levisse-Touzé, and Grégoire Kauffmann, *Les Résistants,* vol. 1, *Jean Moulin et les soutiers de la gloire* (Paris: Société Éditrice du Monde, 2012), 182.

16 Bertrand Matot, *La Guerre des cancres: Un lycée au coeur de la Résistance et de la collaboration* (Paris: Librairie Académique Perrin, 2010), 24. Matot presents an excellent sociological study of the school. In his preface to this book, the novelist Patrick Modiano writes that this was "l'école de la Résistance" (the school of the Resistance; 10). *Cancre* is a familiar term for dunce, or lazy student.

17 Marie Granet, *Les Jeunes dans la Résistance: 20 ans en 1940* (Paris: Editions France-Empire, 1985), 184.

18 Matot, *La Guerre des cancres,* 146–47.

19 Jacques Lusseyran, *And There Was Light: Autobiography of Jacques Lusseyran, Blind Hero of the French Resistance* (Sandpoint, ID: Morning Light Press, 2006), 110.

20 Ibid., 173.

21 Ibid., 112.

22 Roger Boussinot, *Les Guichets du Louvre* (Paris: Denoël, 1960), 11. In 1974, Michel Mitrani made an excellent film adaptation of this novel with the same title.

23 Ibid., 12.

24 Ibid., 27–28.

25 Ibid., 109.

26 Ibid., 148.

27 Musée de la Résistance, "Résistance," *Notre Musée* 11 (2001).

28 Cited in Charles-Louis Foulon, Christine Levisse-Touzé, and Grégoire Kauffmann, *Les Résistants,* vol. 2, *Lucie Aubrac et l'armée des ombres,* 34.

29 Boussinot, *Les Guichets du Louvre,* 151.

30 Adam Rayski, *L'Affiche rouge: Une victoire posthume* (Paris: Délégation à la Mémoire et à l'Information Historique, 1999), 16–17.

31 Ibid., 27–28.

32 Alain Blottière, *Le Tombeau de Tommy* (Paris: Gallimard, 2011), 216–17.

33 Thomas Elek, Letter to Hélène Elek, February 21, 1944, available on the *L'Affiche rouge* blog (http://lafficherouge.skyrock.com/2841967794-Thomas-Elek.html).

34 Thomas Elek, Letter of good-bye to his friends, February 21, 1944, available on the *L'Affiche rouge* blog (http://lafficherouge.skyrock.com/2841967794-Thomas-Elek.html).

35 Hélène Elek, *La Mémoire d'Hélène* (Paris: F. Maspero, 1977), 189.

36 Ibid., 177.

37 Renée Poznanski, *Jews in France during World War II* (Waltham, MA: Brandeis University Press in association with the United States Holocaust Memorial Museum, 2001), 164.

38 Lucie Aubrac, *La Résistance expliquée à mes petits-enfants* (Paris: Éditions du Seuil, 2000), 29.

39 Françoise Siefridt, *J'ai voulu porter l'étoile jaune: Journal de Françoise Siefridt, chrétienne et résistante* (Paris: Robert Laffont, 2010), 81.

40 Ibid., 112.

41 Ibid., 131, 133.

42 Ibid., 148.

43 Cited in Jean-Pierre Arthur Bernard, *Le Goût de Paris*, vol. 2, *L'Espace* (Paris: Mercure de France, 2004), 38.

44 Rayski, *L'Affiche rouge*, 8.

Chapter Seven: The Most Narrowed Lives

1 Hélène Elek, *La Mémoire d'Hélène* (Paris: F. Maspero, 1977), 189.

2 For an encyclopedic yet clear analysis of their plight, see Renée Poznanski, *Jews in France during World War II* (Waltham, MA: Brandeis University Press in association with the United States Holocaust Memorial Museum, 2001).

3 Jonathan Kirsch, *The Short, Strange Life of Herschel Grynszpan: A Boy Avenger, a Nazi Diplomat, and a Murder in Paris* (New York: Liveright, 2013), 11.

4 Poznanski, *Jews in France during World War II*, 31.

5 Antoine Sabbagh, ed., *Lettres de Drancy* (Paris: Éditions Tallandier, 2002), 44n1.

6 Poznanski, *Jews in France during World War II*, 42.

7 Jacques Biélinky, *Journal, 1940–1942: Un journaliste juif à Paris sous l'Occupation* (Paris: Cerf, 1992), 46.

8 Ibid., 76.

9 Serge Klarsfeld, *Adieu les enfants (1942–1944)* (Paris: Mille et une nuits, 2005), 30. Klarsfeld's monumental *Le Calendrier de la persécution des Juifs en France, 1940–1944* is the lifetime work of a man dedicated to the memory of those who disappeared. It is indispensable to those who study the French Shoah.

10 Poznanski, *Jews in France during World War II*, 314.

11 Sarah Gensburger, *C'étaient des enfants: Déportation et sauvetage des enfants juifs à Paris* (Paris: Skira-Flammarion, 2012), 93.

12 One historian has convincingly estimated that at the end of the Occupation in Paris, about forty thousand Jews, many with yellow stars sewn onto their nicest clothes, continued to live in Paris. See Jacques Semelin, *Persécutions et entraides dans la France occupée: Comment 75 percent des Juifs en France ont échappé à la mort* (Paris: Éditions du Seuil/Éditions des Arènes, 2013), 23.

13 Patrick Modiano, *Dora Bruder* (Paris: Gallimard, 1997), 3.

14 Ibid., 46–47.

15 Ibid., 31.

16 Sarah Kofman, *Rue Ordener, Rue Labat* (Lincoln, NE: University of Nebraska Press, 1994), 31.

17 Hélène Berr, *The Journal of Hélène Berr*, trans. David Bellos (New York: Weinstein Books, 2008), 245.

18 Ibid., 19.

19 Ibid., 27.

20 Ibid., 28.

21 Ibid., 263.

22 Jean Guéhenno, *Journal des années noires, 1940–1944* (Paris: Gallimard, 1947), 26.

23 Ernst Jünger, *Journaux de guerre*, vol. 2, *1939–1948* (Paris: Gallimard, 2008), 146.

24 About the yellow star and its ramifications, see Léon Poliakov, *L'Étoile jaune* (Paris: Grancher, 1999), Cédric Gruat and Cécile Leblanc, *Amis des Juifs: Les Résistants aux*

étoiles (Paris: Tirésias, 2005), and Serge Klarsfeld, *L'Étoile des Juifs: Témoignages et documents* (Paris: l'Archipel, 1992).

25 Gruat and Leblanc, *Amis des Juifs,* 45.

26 Ibid., 47.

27 Berr, *The Journal of Hélène Berr,* 54.

28 Klarsfeld, *L'Étoile des Juifs,* 64–65.

29 Ibid., 66.

30 Ibid., 90.

31 Biélinky, *Journal, 1940–1942,* 232.

32 Klarsfeld, *L'Étoile des Juifs,* 96.

33 Biélinky, *Journal, 1940–1942,* 217.

34 Klarsfeld, *L'Étoile des Juifs,* 97

35 Michèle Feldman, *Le Carnet noir: Un notable "israélite" à Paris sous l'Occupation (1er novembre 1942–12 octobre 1943)* (Paris: Harmattan, 2012), 45.

36 Ibid., 99.

37 Ibid., 62.

38 Many of these memories have been collated, taped, and transcribed by the remarkable archivists at the Centre de Documentation Juive Contemporaine, now sited in the Mémorial de la Shoah in Paris.

39 Maurice Rajsfus, *La Rafle du Vél d'Hiv* (Paris: Presses universitaires de France, 2002), 67.

40 Ibid., 50.

41 Karen Taieb and Tatiana de Rosnay, *Je vous écris du Vél' d'hiv: Les lettres retrouvées* (Paris: Robert Laffont, 2011), 191.

42 Gensburger, *C'étaient des enfants,* 80–81.

43 Rajsfus, *La Rafle du Vél d'Hiv,* 54, 55.

44 See Pierre Laborie, "Anachronismes," in his *Les Mots de 39–45* (Toulouse: Presses universitaires du Mirail, 2006), 14–16.

45 Klarsfeld, *Adieu les enfants,* 155.

Chapter Eight: How Much Longer? (1942–1944)

1 Albert Camus, *The Plague,* trans. Stuart Gilbert (New York: Modern Library, 1948), 12.

2 Pierre Audiat, *Paris pendant la guerre, 1940–1945* (Paris: Hachette, 1946), 194.

3 Jean Guéhenno, *Journal des années noires, 1940–1944* (Paris: Gallimard, 1947), 268.

4 Gertrude Stein, *Wars I Have Seen* (London: Brilliance Books, 1984), 105.

5 Allan Mitchell, *Nazi Paris: The History of an Occupation, 1940–1944* (New York: Berghahn Books, 2008), 24.

6 Audiat, *Paris pendant la guerre,* 241.

7 Jean-Pierre Guéno and Jérôme Pecnard, *Paroles de l'ombre: Lettres et carnets des Français sous l'Occupation, 1939–1945* (Paris: Arènes, 2009), 48–49.

8 Jean-Marc Dreyfus and Sarah Gensburger, *Nazi Labour Camps in Paris: Austerlitz, Lévitan, Bassano, July 1943–August 1944* (New York: Berghahn Books, 2011), 25.

9 W. G. Sebald, *Austerlitz* (New York: Random House, 2001), 288.

10 Olivier Todd, *Albert Camus: A Life* (New York: Alfred A. Knopf, 1997), 114.

11 Camus, *The Plague,* 71–72.

12 Ibid., 3.

13 Ibid., 71.

14 Albert Camus, *Notebooks, 1942–1951,* trans. and ed. Justin O'Brien (New York: Knopf, 1965), 28.

15 Camus, *The Plague,* 167.

16 Ibid., 113.

17 Colette, *Paris de ma fenêtre,* in *Oeuvres,* vol. 4 (Paris: Gallimard, 2001), 687.

18 Ibid., 680.

19 See Alan Riding, *And the Show Went On: Cultural Life in Nazi-Occupied Paris* (New York: Knopf, 2010), and Frederic Spotts, *The Shameful Peace: How French Artists and Intellectuals Survived the Nazi Occupation* (New Haven, CT: Yale University Press, 2008), for full histories of this moral embarrassment during and after the Occupation.

20 Audiat, *Paris pendant la guerre,* 205.

21 Guy Krivopisco, *Les Fusillés de la Cascade du Bois de Boulogne, 16 août 1944* (Paris: Mairie de Paris, 2000), 10.

22 Mitchell, *Nazi Paris,* 131. Mitchell's book is a gold mine of information on the bureaucratic operations of the Occupiers.

23 Ibid., 155.

Chapter Nine: Liberation—A Whodunit

1 Raoul Nordling with Victor Vinde and Fabrice Virgili, *Sauver Paris: Mémoires du consul de Suède (1905–1944),* ed. Fabrice Virgili (Brussels: Éditions Complexe, 2002), 118.

2 Michael S. Neiberg, *The Blood of Free Men: The Liberation of Paris, 1944* (New York: Basic Books, 2012), 11.

3 Steve Zaloga, *Liberation of Paris 1944: Patton's Race for the Seine* (New York: Osprey, 2008), 7.

4 Joachim Ludewig, *Rückzug: The German Retreat from France, 1944,* ed. David T. Zabecki (Lexington, KY: University Press of Kentucky, 2012), 142.

5 Edith Thomas, *La Libération de Paris* (Paris: Mellottée, 1945), 14.

6 The two fullest eyewitness accounts we have of these last few days of the Occupation are those of Nordling, *Sauver Paris* (Saving Paris) and von Choltitz's own self-serving but fascinating memoir, *De Sébastopol à Paris: Un soldat parmi des soldats* (Paris: Aubanel, 1964). Two more informative histories are the well-known *Is Paris Burning?* by Larry Collins and Dominique Lapierre (New York: Simon and Schuster, 1965) and two recent histories of the Liberation by Neiberg, *The Blood of Free Men,* and Matthew Cobb, *Eleven Days in August: The Liberation of Paris in 1944* (New York: Simon and Schuster, 2013).

7 Choltitz, *De Sébastopol à Paris,* 207.

8 Ibid., 247.

9 Ibid., 239.

10 Ibid., 240–41.

11 Cited in Edmond Dubois, *Paris sans lumière, 1939–1945: Témoignages* (Lausanne: Payot, 1946), 210–11. The leaflet was distributed by air over Paris on August 25, 1944; late the night before, the first Allied tanks, led by the French, had entered the city.

12 Cited in Ludewig, *Rückzug,* 145.

13 Benoîte and Flora Groult, *Journal à quatre mains* (Paris: Denoël, 1962), 459, 460.

14 Pierre Audiat, *Paris pendant la guerre, 1940–1945* (Paris: Hachette, 1946), 298.

15 Ibid., 296.

16 Jean Guéhenno, *Journal des années noires, 1940–1944* (Paris: Gallimard, 1947), 433–34.

17 Institut national de l'audiovisuel, *Journal de la résistance: La Libération de Paris* (video), available at the INA website (http://www.ina.fr/video/AFE99000038).

18 Jacques Yonnet, *Paris Noir: The Secret History of a City,* trans. Christine Donougher (Sawtry, UK: Dedalus, 2006), 171.

19 Thomas, *La Libération de Paris,* 69.

20 Ibid., 71.

21 Françoise Gilot and Carlton Lake, *Life with Picasso* (New York: McGraw-Hill, 1964), 53.

22 Victoria Beck Newman, "*The Triumph of Pan:* Picasso and the Liberation," *Zeitschrift für Kunstgeschichte* 62, no. 1 (January 1, 1999), 115.

23 Guéhenno, *Journal des années noires,* 436.

24 Berthe Auroy, *Jours de guerre: Ma vie sous l'Occupation* (Montrouge, France: Bayard, 2008), 337.

25 Choltitz, *De Sébastopol à Paris,* 249.

26 United States Army, *Instructions for American Servicemen in France during World War II,* with a new introduction by Rick Atkinson (Chicago: University of Chicago Press, 2008), 50–51.

27 Writes Matthew Cobb in his book on the Liberation, *Eleven Days in August:* "Figures given by historians vary substantially, and can rarely be traced back to any original source." He gives the range of variants on page 509, note 30. See also Neiberg, *The Blood of Free Men,* page 246, for more information—and confusion.

28 Mary Louis Roberts's *What Soldiers Do: Sex and the American GI in World War II France* (Chicago: University of Chicago Press, 2013) gives embarrassing details of US soldiers' sexual behavior during the Liberation. She extensively describes the ways in which sexuality and the American character were on display during these few months.

29 Groult and Groult, *Journal à quatre mains,* 468.

30 Ibid., 18–19.

31 Ibid., 469.

32 Auroy, *Jours de guerre,* 344.

33 Groult and Groult, *Journal à quatre mains,* 479.

34 Cited by Seymour I. Toll in "Liebling Covers Paris, Hemingway Liberates It," *Sewanee Review* 112, no. 1 (2004): 49.

35 Michèle Cointet and Jean-Paul Cointet, *Paris 40–44* (Paris: Librairie Académique Perrin, 2001), 269.

36 *Instructions for American Servicemen,* 24.

37 H. R. Kedward and Nancy Wood, eds., *The Liberation of France: Image and Event* (Oxford: Berg, 1995), 4.

38 Gertrude Stein, *Wars I Have Seen* (London: Brilliance Books, 1984), 237.

Chapter Ten: Angry Aftermath—Back on Paris Time

1 Jacques Spitz and Clément Pieyre, *La Situation culturelle en France pendant l'Occupation et depuis la Libération: Notes rédigées en 1945 pour la Section historique de l'Armée américaine* (Nantes: Joseph K., 2010), 72.

2 Patrick Buisson, *1940–1945, Années érotiques,* vol. 2, *De la grande prostituée à la revanche des mâles* (Paris: Librairie générale française, 2011), 337.

3 Albert Ouzoulias, *Les Bataillons de la jeunesse* (Paris: Éditions sociales, 1967), 443.

4 Ibid., 443–44.

5 Corran Laurens, "'La femme au turban:' Les femmes tondues," in H. R. Kedward and Nancy Wood, eds., *The Liberation of France: Image and Event* (Oxford: Berg, 1995), 176–77.

6 The title of a book by Richard D. E. Burton that details the history of violent revolts in Paris since the Middle Ages.

7 See especially Jean-Marc Berlière and Franck Liaigre, *Ainsi finissent les salauds: Séquestrations et exécutions clandestines dans Paris libéré* (Paris: Robert Laffont, 2012).

8 Marcel Jouhandeau, *Journal sous l'Occupation,* suivi de *La Courbe de nos angoisses* (Paris: Gallimard, 1980), 348.

9 Janet Flanner, *Paris Journal,* ed. William Shawn (New York: Atheneum, 1965), 25.

10 Duras, *The War,* 8.

11 Ibid., 32–33.

12 Ibid., 53–54.

13 Ibid., 8, 23.

Chapter Eleven: Is Paris Still Occupied?

1 Marguerite Duras, *The War: A Memoir,* trans. Barbara Bray (New York: The New Press, 1986), 47. Published in 1985 in France as *La Douleur.*

2 Olivier Wieviorka, *Divided Memory: French Recollections of World War II from the Liberation to the Present,* trans. George Holoch (Stanford, CA: Stanford University Press, 2012), 15. This is an excellent résumé of the adroit and clumsy attempts at reremembering made by politicians.

3 André Malraux, *Entre ici, Jean Moulin: Discours d'André Malraux, Ministre d'État chargé des affaires culturelles, lors du transfert des cendres de Jean Moulin au Panthéon, 19 décembre 1964* (Paris: Éditions Points, 2010), 12, 16.

4 Cited in Wieviorka, *Divided Memory,* 106.

5 Jacques Chirac, *Discours et messages de Jacques Chirac: en hommage aux Juifs de France victimes de la collaboration de l'État français de Vichy avec l'occupant allemand* (Paris: Fils et filles des déportés juifs de France, 1998), 7, 8.

6 Ibid., 21.

7 Ibid., 25.

8 François Hollande, "The 'Crime Committed in France, by France,'" *The New York Review of Books* 59, no. 14 (September 27, 2012), 40.

9 Cited in Jean-Marc Berlière et Franck Liagre, *L'Affaire Guy Môquet: Enquête sur une mystification officielle* (Paris: Larousse, 2009), 11.

10 Cited in Scott Sayare, "At New Holocaust Center, French Leader Confronts Past," *New York Times,* September 22, 2012, A8.

11 Jean-Paul Sartre, *The Aftermath of War (Situations III),* trans. Chris Turner (London: Seagull Books, 2008), 22.

12 Ibid., 21.

13 Ibid., 20.

14 Christophe Girard, cited in *Le Monde,* April 25, 2008.

15 Pierre Assouline, cited in *Le Monde,* July 4, 2008.

16 The term comes from Kevin Lynch, *The Image of the City* (Cambridge, MA: MIT Press, 1960), 119.

17 Italo Calvino, *Invisible Cities* (New York: Harcourt Brace Jovanovich, 1974), 10–11.

18 Ibid., 67.

Selected Bibliography

Any bibliography about the Occupation of France, or just the Occupation of Paris, must be perforce selective. The plethora of works—fiction, nonfiction, film, photography, catalogs, manuscripts, oral reminiscences, all in a half dozen major languages—can cause any writer initial despair. And they keep coming. The subject remains fascinating to successive generations, from those who lived through it to those just opening the record on this massive history.

The list below represents the works that are in my notes as well as those that informed much of the structure and content of the book. They themselves have extensive bibliographies that can send interested readers further afield. A Pulitzer Prize–winning biographer told me: "Just list the works you consulted at least twice." Even then, I had to cull in order to ensure that the list would not be longer than the book itself.

In the end, this bibliography represents the wide range of observations about the twentieth century's most calamitous period and can serve as a guide to both the curious and the learned reader.

Every effort has been made to identify sources of quotations and anecdotes. Where information is inadvertently missing or incorrect, I would appreciate being so informed. Corrections will be made in future editions.

Libraries and Collections
Archives nationales, Paris
Archives de la Préfecture de police, Paris
Bibliothèque Fondation de la Maison des sciences de l'homme, Paris
Bibliothèque historique de la ville de Paris
Bibliothèque de l'Hôtel de ville de Paris
Bibliothèque nationale de France, Paris
British Library, London

Centre de documentation juive contemporaine, Paris
Cinémathèque française, Paris
Imperial War Museum, London
Mount Holyoke College Library, South Hadley, MA
Musée de l'Armée, Paris
Musée du Général Leclerc de Hauteclocque et de la Libération de Paris/Musée Jean Moulin, Paris
Musée de la Résistance nationale et de la Déportation, Champigny-sur-Marne, France
New York Public Library, New York, NY
Robert Frost Library, Amherst College, Amherst, MA
Smith College Library, Northampton, MA
United States Holocaust Memorial Museum, Washington, DC
W. E. B. Du Bois Library, University of Massachusetts at Amherst
Widener Library, Harvard University, Cambridge, MA

Historical Sources

Abrami, Léon. *A l'Ombre de l'étoile: Souvenirs d'un enfant caché*. Paris: Harmattan, 2010.
Achard, Paul. *La Queue: Ce qui s'y disait, ce qu'on y pensait*. Paris: Mille et une nuits, 2011.
Ackerman, Diane. *The Zookeeper's Wife: A War Story*. New York: W. W. Norton, 1997.
Adler, Jacques. *The Jews of Paris and the Final Solution: Communal Response and Internal Conflicts, 1940–1944*. New York: Oxford University Press, 1987.
Aglan, Alya. *Le Temps de la Résistance*. Arles: Actes sud, 2008.
Alary, Eric. *Les Français au quotidien: 1939–1949*. Paris: Librairie Académique Perrin, 2009.
Ambrière, Francis, and Jacques Meyer. *Vie et mort des Français, 1939–1945*. Paris: Hachette, 1971.
Amouroux, Henri. *La Vie des Français sous l'Occupation*. Paris: A. Fayard, 1961.
Arendt, Hannah. *Eichmann in Jerusalem: A Report on the Banality of Evil*. New York: Viking Press, 1963.
Atack, Margaret. *Literature and the French Resistance: Cultural Politics and Narrative Forms, 1940–1950*. Manchester, UK: Manchester University Press, 1989.
———. "Secrets and Lies: Representing Everyday Life under the Occupation." Paper presented at the Society for French Studies Conference, University of Birmingham (UK), July 2–4. 2007. Abstract at http://www.frame.leeds.ac.uk/conferences.html.
———. "Sins, Crimes and Guilty Passions in France's Stories of War and Occupation." *Journal of War and Culture Studies* 1, no. 1 (2007): 79–90.
Atack, Margaret, and Christopher Lloyd. *Framing Narratives of the Second World War and Occupation in France, 1939–2009*. Manchester, UK: Manchester University Press, 2012.
Aubrac, Lucie. *La Résistance expliquée à mes petits-enfants*. Paris: Éditions du Seuil, 2000.
Audiat, Pierre. *Paris pendant la guerre, 1940–1945*. Paris: Hachette, 1946.
Augé, Marc. *In the Metro*. Trans. Tom Conley. Minneapolis: University of Minnesota Press, 2002.
Auroy, Berthe. *Jours de guerre: Ma vie sous l'Occupation*. Montrouge, France: Bayard, 2008.
Azéma, Jean-Pierre. *1940: L'Année noire*. Paris: Fayard, 2010.
———. "Les Débuts de la résistance dans la France occupée." In Wolfgang Drost et al., eds., *Paris sous l'Occupation (Paris unter deutscher Besatzung)*. Heidelberg: Universitätsverlag C. Winter, 1995.
———. *L'Occupation expliquée à mon petit-fils*. Paris: Éditions du Seuil, 2012.

———."Préface," in Barronet, Jean, ed. *Les Parisiens Sous l'Occupation: Photographies en couleur d' André Zucca*. Paris: Gallimard, 2008, 5–11.

Azéma, Jean-Pierre, and François Bédarida, eds. *La France des années noires*. Paris: Éditions du Seuil, 1993.

Azoulay, Floriane, and Annette Wieviorka. *Le Pillage des appartements et son indemnisation*. Paris: La Documentation Française, Mission d'études sur la spoliation des Juifs de France, 2000.

Bachelard, Gaston. *The Poetics of Space*. Trans. Maria Jolas. Boston: Beacon Press, 1994.

Badia, Gilbert. "Vivre à Paris (1939–1944): Impressions d'un témoin." In Wolfgang Drost et al., eds., *Paris sous l'Occupation (Paris unter deutscher Besatzung)*. Heidelberg: Universitätsverlag C. Winter, 1995.

Bandinelli, Ranuccio Bianchi. *Quelques jours avec Hitler et Mussolini*. Trans. Dominique Vittoz. Paris: Carnets Nord, 2011.

Banger, Hans, and Emmanuel Boudot-Lamotte. *Paris, Wanderung durch eine Stadt*. Paris: Verlag der Deutschen Arbeitsfront, 1942.

Bard, Mitchell Geoffrey. *48 Hours of Kristallnacht: Night of Destruction/Dawn of the Holocaust, An Oral History*. Guilford, CT: Lyons Press, 2008.

Bargatzky, Walter. *Hotel Majestic: Ein Deutscher im besetzten Frankreich*. Freiburg im Breisgau: Herder, 1987.

Barronet, Jean, ed. *Les Parisiens sous l'Occupation: Photographies en couleurs d'André Zucca*. Paris: Gallimard, 2008.

Barrot, Olivier, and Raymond Chirat. *La Vie culturelle dans la France occupée*. Paris: Gallimard, 2009.

Barry, Mrs. M. T. Private Papers of Miss R. T. Barry, catalog number 17656, Imperial War Museum, London. Unpublished manuscript, n.d.

Bartov, Omer. *Hitler's Army: Soldiers, Nazis, and War in the Third Reich*. New York: Oxford University Press, 1991.

Basse, Pierre-Louis. *Guy Môquet: Une enfance fusillée*. Paris: Stock, 2000.

———.*Hitler at My Side*. Houston, TX: Eichler Publishing Corporation, 1986.

Baur, Hans. *Hitler's Pilot*. Trans. Edward Fitzgerald. London: Frederick Muller Ltd., 1958.

Bayard, Pierre. *Aurais-je été résistant ou bourreau?* Paris: Minuit, 2013.

Bayliss, Mabel. Private papers of Miss M. Bayliss, catalog number 5527. Imperial War Museum, London, unpublished manuscript, n.d.

Beauvoir, Simone de. *Journal de guerre: Septembre 1939–janvier 1941*. Paris: Gallimard, 1990.

———.*Letters to Sartre*. Trans and ed. Quintin Hoare and Sylvie Le Bon de Beauvoir. New York: Arcade Publishing, 1992.

———.*The Prime of Life: The Autobiography of Simone de Beauvoir*. New York: Paragon House, 1992.

———.*Wartime Diary*. Ed. Margaret A. Simons and Sylvie Le Bon de Beauvoir. Trans. Anne Deing Cordero. Urbana and Chicago: University of Illinois Press, 2009.

Beevor, Antony. *D-Day: The Battle for Normandy*. New York: Viking, 2009.

———. *The Fall of Berlin, 1945*. New York: Viking, 2002.

———. *The Second World War*. New York: Little, Brown and Co., 2012.

Beevor, Antony, and Artemis Cooper. *Paris After the Liberation, 1944–1949*. New York: Doubleday, 1994.

Beisel, David R. "Paris, 1940: A Traumatized City and Postwar Political Reliving." Paper presented at the thirty-first annual meeting of The International Society of Political Psychology, Paris, June 9, 2008. Abstract at http://citation.allacademic.com/meta/p_mla_apa_research_citation/2/4/6/1/9/p246199_index.html?phpsessid=888aa3ed5c6187d23092db5e8bf4682c.

Bensimon, Doris, and Sergio Dellapergola. *La Population juive de France: Socio-démographie et identité*. Paris: Centre National de la Recherche Scientifique, 1986.

Benvenisti, Eyal. *The International Law of Occupation*. Princeton, NJ: Princeton University Press, 1993.

Berlière, Jean-Marc, and Laurent Chabrun. *Les Policiers français sous l'Occupation: D'après les archives inédites de l'épuration*. Paris: Librairie Académique Perrin, 2001.

Berlière, Jean-Marc, and François Le Goarant de Tromelin. *Liaisons dangereuses: Miliciens, truands, résistants: Paris, 1944*. Paris: Librairie Académique Perrin, 2013.

Berlière, Jean-Marc, and Franck Liaigre. *Ainsi finissent les salauds: Séquestrations et exécutions clandestines dans Paris libéré*. Paris: Robert Laffont, 2012.

———. *L'Affaire Guy Môquet: Enquête sur une mystification officielle*. Paris: Larousse, 2009.

———. *Le Sang des communistes: Les Bataillons de la Jeunesse dans la lutte armée, automne 1941*. Paris: Fayard, 2004.

Bernard, Jean-Pierre Arthur. *Le Goût de Paris*. Vol. 2, *L'Espace*. Paris: Mercure de France, 2004.

Berr, Hélène. *Journal: 1942–1944*. Paris: Tallandier, 2008.

———. *The Journal of Hélène Berr*. Trans. David Bellos. New York: Weinstein Books, 2008.

Bertin, Célia. *Femmes sous l'Occupation*. Paris: Stock, 1993.

Bertin-Maghit, Jean-Pierre. *Le Cinéma sous l'Occupation: Le Monde du cinéma français de 1940 à 1946*. Paris: Librairie Académique Perrin, 2002.

Betz, Albrecht, Stefan Martens, and Hans Manfred Bock. *Les Intellectuels et l'Occupation, 1940–1944: Collaborer, partir, résister*. Paris: Autrement, 2004.

Biélinky, Jacques. *Journal, 1940–1942: Un journaliste juif à Paris sous l'Occupation*. Paris: Cerf, 1992.

Blanc, Brigitte, Henry Rousso, and Chantal de Tourtier-Bonazzi. *La Seconde guerre mondiale: Guide des sources conservées en France, 1939–1945*. Paris: Archives nationales, 1994.

Bloch, Marc. *L'Étrange défaite: Témoignage écrit en 1940*, suivi de *Écrits clandestins 1942–1944*. Paris: Armand Colin, 1957.

Boal, David. *Journaux intimes sous l'Occupation*. Paris: Armand Colin, 1993.

Boissel, Xavier, and Didier Vivien. *Paris est un leurre (La véritable histoire du faux Paris)*. Paris: Inculte, 2012.

Bollnow, Otto Friedrich. *Human Space*. London: Hyphen, 2011.

Bood, Micheline. *Les Années doubles: Journal d'une lycéenne sous l'Occupation*. Paris: Robert Laffont, 1974.

Borgé, Jacques, and Nicolas Viasnoff. *Les Véhicules de l'Occupation*. Paris: Balland, 1975.

Bourderon, Roger. "Le Régime de Vichy était-il fasciste? Essai d'approche de la question." *Revue d'histoire de la Deuxième Guerre mondiale* 23, no. 91 (July 1973): 23–45.

Bourget, Pierre. *Histoires secrètes de l'Occupation de Paris (1940–1944)*. Vol. 1, *Le Joug*. Paris: Hachette, 1970.

Bourget, Pierre, and Charles Lacretelle. *Sur les murs de Paris, 1940–1944*. Paris: Hachette, 1959.

Braithwaite, Rodric. *Moscow 1941: A City and Its People at War.* New York: Knopf, 2006.

Brassaï. *Conversations with Picasso.* Trans. Jane Marie Todd. Chicago: University of Chicago Press, 1999.

Breker, Arno. *Paris, Hitler et moi.* Paris: Presses de la Cité, 1970.

Bretos, Lydia, ed. "Vivre en France sous l'Occupation." *Textes et Documents pour la Classe (TDC)* 852 (March 15, 2003). Paris: SCÉRÉN-CNDP, 2003.

Buchheim, Lothar-Günther. *Mein Paris: Eine Stadt vor dreißig Jahren.* Munich: Piper, 1977.

Buisson, Patrick. *1940–1945, Années érotiques.* Vol. 1, *Vichy, ou Les infortunes de la vertu.* Paris: Librairie générale française, 2011.

———. *1940–1945, Années érotiques.* Vol. 2, *De la grande prostituée à la revanche des mâles.* Paris: Librairie générale française, 2011.

Bullivant, Keith, ed. *Culture and Society in the Weimar Republic.* Manchester, UK: Manchester University Press, 1977.

Burrin, Philippe. *La France à l'heure allemande: 1940–1944.* Paris: Éditions du Seuil, 1995.

———. "Writing the History of Military Occupations." In Sarah Fishman, ed., *France at War: Vichy and the Historians.* Oxford: Berg, 2000.

Burton, Richard D. E. *Blood in the City: Violence and Revelation in Paris, 1789–1945.* Ithaca, NY: Cornell University Press, 2001.

Buruma, Ian. "Occupied Paris: The Sweet and the Cruel." *New York Review of Books* 56, no. 20 (December 17, 2009): 26–30.

———. "Une Belle opération de séduction." *Books: L'Actualité par les livres du monde* 23 (June 2011): 25–33.

———. *Year Zero: A History of 1945.* New York: Penguin Press, 2013.

Cabanes, Bruno, and Guillaume Piketty, eds. *Retour à l'intime au sortir de la guerre.* Paris: Tallandier, 2009.

Calvino, Italo. *Invisible Cities.* New York: Harcourt Brace Jovanovich, 1974.

Camus, Albert. *Lettres à un ami allemand.* Paris: Gallimard, 1991.

———. *Notebooks, 1935–1942.* Trans. and ed. Philip Thody. New York: Modern Library, 1965.

———. *Notebooks, 1942–1951.* Trans. and ed. Justin O'Brien. New York: Knopf, 1965.

Capuano, Christophe. "Le Régime de Vichy: Un fascisme à la française?" Paper presented at the Plan Académique de Formation, Académie de Bourgogne, November 18–19, 2004.

Carco, Francis. Preface to Colette's *Oeuvres*, vol. 4. Paris: Gallimard, 2004.

Carell, Paul. *Ils arrivent! Le Débarquement vécu du côté allemand.* Paris: Tallandier, 2011.

Carr, Godfrey. "'A Sudden and Passionate Revulsion Towards Germany': Friedrich Sieburg's Concept of Political Thought." In Keith Bullivant, ed., *Culture and Society in the Weimar Republic.* Manchester, UK: Manchester University Press, 1977.

Caspary, Gerard Ernest. "From the Edge of the Holocaust: Letters from My Mother and Grandmother." Unpublished typescript.

Certeau, Michel de. *The Practice of Everyday Life.* Berkeley: University of California Press, 1984.

Chambon, Albert. *Quand la France était occupée—1940–1945: Fin des mythes, légendes et tabous.* Paris: Éditions France-Empire, 1987.

Chambrun, Clara Longworth. *Sans jeter l'ancre (1873–1948).* Paris: Plon, 1953.

———. *Shadows Lengthen: The Story of My Life.* New York: Charles Scribner's Sons, 1949.

Chirac, Jacques. *Discours et messages de Jacques Chirac: En hommage aux Juifs de France victimes de la collaboration de l'État français de Vichy avec l'occupant allemand.* Paris, Fils et filles des déportés juifs de France, 1998.

Choltitz, Dietrich von. *De Sébastopol à Paris: Un soldat parmi des soldats.* Paris: Aubanel, 1964.

Christophe, Francine. *Une Pétite fille privilégiée: Une enfant dans le monde des camps 1942–1945.* Paris: Éditions L'Harmattan, 1996.

Cloonan, William J. *The Writing of War: French and German Fiction and World War II.* Gainesville: University Press of Florida, 1999.

Cobb, Matthew. *Eleven Days in August: The Liberation of Paris in 1944.* London and New York: Simon & Schuster, 2013.

———. *The Resistance: The French Fight against the Nazis.* London: Simon & Schuster, 2009.

Cobb, Richard. *French and Germans, Germans and French: A Personal Interpretation of France Under Occupations, 1914–1918/1940–1945.* Hanover, NH: University Press of New England, 1983.

Cocteau, Jean. *Journal, 1942–1945.* Paris: Gallimard, 1989.

Coetzee, J. M. "Irène Némirovsky: The Dogs and the Wolves." *The New York Review of Books* 55, no. 18 (November 20, 2008): 34–37.

Cointet, Jean-Paul. *Paris 40–44.* Paris: Librairie Académique Perrin, 2001.

Cointet, Michèle, and Jean-Paul Cointet. *Dictionnaire historique de la France sous l'Occupation.* Paris: Tallandier, 2000.

Colette. *Oeuvres.* Bibliothèque de la Pléiade. Paris: Gallimard, 1984.

Collingham, E. M. *The Taste of War: World War II and the Battle for Food.* New York: Penguin Press, 2012.

Collins, Larry, and Dominique Lapierre. *Is Paris Burning?* New York: Simon and Schuster, 1965.

Cone, Michèle C. "Il fallait bien vivre." *Books: L'Actualité par les livres du monde* 23 (June 2011): 39–42.

Conley, Tom. *Cartographic Cinema.* Minneapolis: University of Minnesota Press, 2007.

Connerton, Paul. *How Societies Remember.* New York: Cambridge University Press, 1989.

"Convention d'armistice." Available on the Digithèque de matériaux juridiques et politiques website: http://mjp.univ-perp.fr/france/1940armistice.htm.

Corcy-Debray, Stéphanie. *La Vie culturelle sous l'Occupation.* Paris: Librairie Académique Perrin, 2005.

Corday, Michel. *The Paris Front: An Unpublished Diary, 1914–1918.* London: Victor Gollancz Ltd., 1933.

Cornut-Gentille, Gilles, and Philippe Michel-Thiriet. *Florence Gould: Une Américaine à Paris.* Paris: Mercure de France, 1989.

Corpet, Olivier, and Claire Paulhan, eds. *Archives de la vie littéraire sous l'Occupation.* Paris: Éditions Tallandier/Éditions de l'IMEC, 2009.

Courtois, Stéphane, Denis Peschanski, and Adam Rayski. *Le Sang de l'étranger: Les Immigrés de la MOI dans la Résistance.* Paris: Fayard, 1989.

Cowan, Alexander, and Jill Steward. *The City and the Senses: Urban Culture Since 1500.* Burlington, VT: Ashgate, 2007.

Crémieux-Brilhac, Jean-Louis. *La France libre: De l'Appel du 18 juin à la Libération.* Paris: Gallimard, 1996.

————."L'Image de l'Allemagne dans l'opinion des Français de 1939–1940, ou de quelques facteurs psychologiques pendant la 'drôle de guerre.'" In Wolfgang Drost et al., eds., *Paris sous l'Occupation (Paris unter deutscher Besatzung)*. Heidelberg: Universitätsverlag C. Winter, 1995.

Cyrulnik, Boris. *Sauve-toi, la vie t'appelle*. Paris: O. Jacob, 2012.

Dagen, Philippe. "Que faisiez-vous pendant la guerre? Je peignais." *Le Monde*, October 14–15, 2012:19.

Damase, Jean. *Ici Paris*. Paris: Les Éditions de France, 1942.

Davies, Peter. *France and the Second World War: Occupation, Collaboration, and Resistance*. New York: Routledge, 2001.

Decq, René. "15 Décembre 1940: Le Retour des cendres du Roi de Rome, fils de Napoléon 1er." http://napoleon1er.perso.neuf.fr/Aiglon-Rene-Decq.html.

Delanoë, Bertrand, Hélène Font, et al. *Paris insurgé, Paris libéré*. Paris: Paris-Musées, 2006.

Demetz, Peter. *Prague in Danger: The Years of German Occupation, 1939–45 — Memories and History, Terror and Resistance, Theater and Jazz, Film and Poetry, Politics and War*. New York: Farrar, Straus and Giroux, 2008.

Desmarais, Julie. *Femmes tondues: France-Libération — Coupables, amoureuses, victimes*. Québec: Presses de l'Université Laval, 2010.

Desprairies, Cécile. *Paris dans la Collaboration*. Préface de Serge Klarsfeld. Paris: Éditions du Seuil, 2009.

————.*Ville lumière, années noires: Les Lieux du Paris de la Collaboration*. Paris: Denoël, 2008.

Diamond, Hanna. *Fleeing Hitler: France 1940*. New York: Oxford University Press, 2007.

Domarus, Max, ed. *Hitler: Speeches and Proclamations, 1932–1945 — The Chronicle of a Dictatorship*. Trans. Chris Wilcox and Mary Fran Gilbert. 4 vols. Wauconda, IL: Bolchazy-Carducci, 1997.

Dréano, Jean. "L'Internat en pharmacie de 1941 à 1945." In Dominique Meyniel, ed., *Tenon, l'hôpital de Ménilmontant*. Paris: Cherche-Midi, 2008.

Dreyfus, Jean-Marc, and Sarah Gensburger. *Nazi Labour Camps in Paris: Austerlitz, Lévitan, Bassano, July 1943–August 1944*. New York: Berghahn Books, 2011.

Drost, Wolfgang, Géraldi Leroy, Jacqueline Magnou, and Peter Seibert, eds. *Paris sous l'Occupation (Paris unter deutscher Besatzung)*. Actes du 3ième colloque des Universités d'Orléans et de Siegen. Heidelberg: Universitätsverlag C. Winter, 1995.

Dubois, Edmond. *Paris sans lumière, 1939–1945: Témoignages*. Lausanne: Payot, 1946.

Duras, Marguerite. *Le Bureau de poste de la rue Dupin, et autres entretiens*. Paris: Gallimard, 2005.

————.*La Douleur*. Paris: P.O.L., 1985.

————.*The War: A Memoir*. Trans. Barbara Bray. New York: New Press, 1986.

Eder, Cyril. *Les Comtesses de la Gestapo*. Paris: Grasset, 2006.

Edsel, Robert M. *Rescuing da Vinci*. Dallas, TX: Laurel Publishing, 2006.

Ehrenburg, Ilya. *The Fall of Paris*. Trans. Gerard Shelley. New York: Knopf, 1943.

Einaudi, Jean-Luc. *Traces: Des Adolescents en maisons de redressement sous l'Occupation*. Paris: Éditions du Sextant, 2006.

Einaudi, Jean-Luc, and Maurice Rajsfus. *Les Silences de la police: 16 Juillet 1942–17 Octobre 1961*. *L'Esprit Frappeur* no. 104. Paris: L'Esprit frappeur, 2001.

Eisenhower, Dwight D. *Crusade in Europe*. Garden City, NY: Doubleday, 1948.

Eismann, Gaël. *Hôtel Majestic: Ordre et sécurité en France occupée (1940–1944)*. Paris: Tallandier, 2010.

Elek, Hélène. *La Mémoire d'Hélène.* Paris: F. Maspero, 1977.

Elek, Thomas. Letter of good-bye to his friends. Available on the *L'Affiche rouge* blog: http://lafficherouge.skyrock.com/3.html.

———. Letter to Hélène Elek. February 21, 1944. Available on the *L'Affiche rouge* blog: http://lafficherouge.skyrock.com/3.html.

Éparvier, Jean. *À Paris sous les bottes des Nazis.* Paris: Aux Éditions Raymond Schall, 1944.

Epstein, Catherine. *Model Nazi: Arthur Greiser and the Occupation of Western Poland.* New York: Oxford University Press, 2010.

Fauxbras, César. *Le Théâtre de l'Occupation: Journal, 1939–1944.* Paris: Allia, 2012.

Feldman, Michèle. *Le Carnet noir: Un Notable "israélite" à Paris sous l'Occupation (1er novembre 1942–12 octobre 1943).* Paris: Harmattan, 2012.

Feliciano, Hector. *The Lost Museum: The Nazi Conspiracy to Steal the World's Greatest Works of Art.* New York: Basic Books, 1997.

Fest, Joachim C. *Albert Speer: Conversations with Hitler's Architect.* Malden, MA: Polity Press, 2007.

———. *Hitler.* New York: Harcourt Brace Jovanovich, 1974.

Fishman, Sarah. "'Gender': Vue de famille et retour des prisonniers de guerre français: une réevaluation." In Bruno Cabanes and Guillaume Piketty, eds., *Retour à l'intime au sortir de la guerre.* Paris: Tallandier, 2009.

Fishman, Sarah, Laura Lee Downs, Ioannis Sinanoglou, Leonard V. Smith, and Robert Zaretsky, eds. *France at War: Vichy and the Historians.* Trans. David Lake. Oxford: Berg, 2000.

Fiss, Karen. *Grand Illusion: The Third Reich, the Paris Exposition, and the Cultural Seduction of France.* Chicago: University of Chicago Press, 2009.

Flanner, Janet. *Paris Journal.* Ed. William Shawn. New York: Atheneum, 1965.

Fogg, Shannon Lee. *The Politics of Everyday Life in Vichy, France: Foreigners, Undesirables, and Strangers.* New York: Cambridge University Press, 2009.

Fonkenell, Guillaume, Sarah Gensburger, Catherine Granger, and Isabelle Le Masne de Chermont. *Le Louvre pendant la guerre. Regards photographiques, 1938–1947.* Paris: Musée de Louvre, 2009.

Foulon, Charles-Louis, Christine Levisse-Touzé, and Grégoire Kauffmann. *Les Résistants.* Vol. 1, *Jean Moulin et les soutiers de la gloire.* Paris: Société Éditrice du Monde, 2012.

———. *Les Résistants.* Vol. 2, *Lucie Aubrac et l'armée des ombres.* Paris: Société Éditrice du Monde, 2012.

Foville, Jean-Marc de. *L'Entrée des Allemands à Paris, 14 juin 1940.* Paris: Calmann- Lévy, 1965.

Franck, Dan. *Minuit.* Paris: Grasset, 2010.

Freeman, Kirrily. *Bronzes to Bullets: Vichy and the Destruction of French Public Statuary, 1941–1944.* Stanford, CA: Stanford University Press, 2009.

Friedländer, Saul. *Nazi Germany and the Jews.* New York: HarperCollins, 1997.

Fritzsche, Peter. *Germans into Nazis.* Cambridge, MA: Harvard University Press, 1998.

Galtier-Boissière, Jean. *Mon journal pendant l'Occupation.* Paris: La Jeune parque, 1944.

Gaucher, Roland. *Histoire secrète du Parti Communiste Français (1920–1974).* Paris: Albin Michel, 1974.

Gaulle, Charles de. *The Complete War Memoirs of Charles de Gaulle.* New York: Simon and Schuster, 1964.

————.*Mémoires de guerre.* Paris: Plon, 1954.

Gaussen-Salmon, Jacqueline. *Une Prière dans la nuit: Journal d'une femme peintre sous l'Occupation.* Éditions Frederic Gaussen. Paris: Payot, 1992.

Geiger, Wolfgang. "L'Image de la France dans l'Allemagne hitlérienne et pendant l'après-guerre immédiate." Doctoral thesis. Université de Nantes, Faculté des Sciences humaines, May 31, 1996.

Gensburger, Sarah. *C'étaient des enfants: Déportation et sauvetage des enfants juifs à Paris.* Paris: Skira-Flammarion, 2012.

Giasone, Claude. *Paris occupé: 14 juin 1940–24 août 1944.* Paris: Grancher, 1997.

Giesler, Hermann. *Ein anderer Hitler: Bericht seines Architekten Hermann Giesler; Erlebnisse, Gespräche, Reflexionen.* Leoni am Starnberger See: Druffel, 1978.

Gilbert, Martin. *The Day the War Ended: May 8, 1945— Victory in Europe.* New York: Henry Holt, 1995.

Gildea, Robert. *Marianne in Chains: Everyday Life in the French Heartland under the German Occupation.* New York: Metropolitan Books, 2003.

Gildea, Robert, Olivier Wieviorka, and Anette Warring. *Surviving Hitler and Mussolini: Daily Life in Occupied Europe.* Oxford: Berg, 2006.

Gillain, Anne. *Les 400 coups: François Truffaut.* France: Nathan, 1991.

Gilot, Françoise, and Carlton Lake. *Life with Picasso.* New York: McGraw-Hill, 1964.

Ginzburg, Lidiia. *Blockade Diary.* Intro. Alan Myers and Aleksandr Kushner. London: Harvill Press, 1995.

Girard, Bernard. "Journée Guy Môquet, ou Journée Sarkozy dans les lycées?" *Rue 89,* October 22, 2009. http://www.rue89.com/2009/10/22/journee-guy-moquet-ou -journee-sarkozy-dans-les-lycees-122669.

Glass, Charles. *Americans in Paris: Life and Death under Nazi Occupation.* New York: Penguin Press, 2010.

Goebbels, Joseph, and Fred Taylor. *The Goebbels Diaries, 1939–1941.* New York: Putnam, 1983.

Goglin, Jean Louis, and Pierre Roux. *Souffrance et liberté: Une géographie parisienne des années noires (1940–1944).* Paris: Paris Musées, 2004.

Goldhagen, Daniel Jonah. *Hitler's Willing Executioners: Ordinary Germans and the Holocaust.* New York: Knopf, 1996.

Golsan, Richard, and Jean-François Fourny, eds. "The Occupation in French Literature and Film, 1940–1992." *L'Esprit Créateur* 33, no. 1 (spring 1993).

Gopnik, Adam. "Finest Hours." *The New Yorker* 86, no. 25 (August 30, 2010): 74–81.

Gordon, Bertram M. *Collaborationism in France during the Second World War.* Ithaca, NY: Cornell University Press, 1980.

————. "'Ist Gott Französisch?' Germans, Tourism, and Occupied France, 1940–1944." *Modern and Contemporary France* 4, no. 3 (August 1996): 287–98.

————. "Warfare and Tourism: Paris in World War II." *Annals of Tourism Research* 25 (1998): 616–38.

Granet, Marie. *Ceux de la Résistance, 1940–1944.* Paris: Éditions de Minuit, 1964.

————. *Les Jeunes dans la Résistance: 20 ans en 1940.* Paris: Editions France-Empire, 1985.

Gray, Francine du Plessix. *Simone Weil.* New York: Viking, 2001.

Grayling, A. C. *Among the Dead Cities: The History and Moral Legacy of the World War II Bombing of Civilians in Germany and Japan.* New York: Walker & Co., 2006.

Greenberg, Clement. "Avant-Garde and Kitsch." *Partisan Review* 6, no. 5 (fall 1939), 34–49. Available at: http://www.sharecom.ca/greenberg/kitsch.html.

Gregor, Neil. *How to Read Hitler.* New York: W. W. Norton, 2005.

Griffiths, Richard. "A Certain Idea of France: Ernst Jünger's Paris Diaries 1941–44." *Journal of European Studies* 23, nos. 1 & 2 March 1993: 101–120.

Groult, Benoîte, and Flora Groult. *Diary in Duo.* New York: Appleton-Century, 1965.

———.*Journal à quatre mains.* Paris: Denoël, 1962.

Gruat, Cédric. *Hitler à Paris: June 1940.* Paris: Tirésias, 2010.

Gruat, Cédric, and Cécile Leblanc. *Amis des Juifs: Les Résistants aux étoiles.* Paris: Tirésias, 2005.

Grunberg, Albert. *Journal d'un coiffeur juif à Paris sous l'Occupation.* Paris: Éditions de l'Atelier/Éditions Ouvrières, 2001.

Guéhenno, Jean. *Journal des années noires, 1940–1944.* Paris: Gallimard, 1947.

Guéno, Jean-Pierre. *Paroles d'étoiles: Mémoire d'enfants cachés, 1939–1945.* Paris: Librio–Radio France, 2002.

Guéno, Jean-Pierre, and Jérôme Pecnard. *Paroles de l'ombre: Lettres et carnets des Français sous l'Occupation, 1939–1945.* Paris: Arènes, 2009.

Guerrin, Michel. "Comment a échoué une exposition critique des photos de Paris occupé." *Le Monde,* April 24, 2008. http://www.lemonde.fr/culture/article/2008/04/24/comment-a-echoue-une-exposition-critique-des-photos-de-paris occupe_1038025_3246.html.

Guitry, Sacha. *Quatre ans d'occupations.* Paris: l'Elan, 1947.

Gunthert, André. "André Zucca, la couleur rêvée." *Recherche en histoire visuelle,* May 18, 2008. http://www.arhv.lhivic.org/index.php/2008/05/18/713-andre-zucca-la-couleur-revee.

Halbwachs, Maurice. *On Collective Memory.* Ed., trans., and intro. Lewis A. Coser. Chicago: University of Chicago Press, 1992.

Hamann, Brigitte. *Hitler's Vienna: A Dictator's Apprenticeship.* New York: Oxford University Press, 1999.

Hammond, Bryan, and Patrick O'Connor. *Josephine Baker.* London: Jonathan Cape, 1988.

Harris, Frederick John. *Encounters with Darkness: French and German Writers on World War II.* New York: Oxford University Press, 1983.

Harris, Mark J., and Deborah Oppenheimer. *Into the Arms of Strangers: Stories of "Kindertransport."* London: Bloomsbury, 2000.

Hartlaub, Felix. *Paris 1941: Journal et correspondance (extraits).* Trans. Jean-Claude Rambach. Intro. Paul Nizon. Arles: Actes Sud, 1999.

Hastings, Max. *Armageddon: The Battle for Germany, 1944–45.* New York: Knopf, 2004.

———.*Inferno: the World at War, 1939–1945.* New York: Knopf, 2011.

———."The Most Terrible of Hitler's Creatures." *The New York Review of Books* 59, no. 2 (February 9, 2012): 38–39.

Hecht, Emmanuel. "1939–1945: La Mémoire vive." *L'Express,* December 24, 2009.

Heiber, Helmut, and David M. Glantz, eds. *Hitler and His Generals: Military Conferences 1942–1945.* New York: Enigma Books, 2003.

Heller, Gerhard. *Un Allemand à Paris: 1940–1944.* Trans. Jean Grand. Paris: Éditions du Seuil, 1981.

Hensbergen, Gijs van. *Guernica: The Biography of a Twentieth-Century Icon.* New York: Bloomsbury, 2004.

Selected Bibliography

Hewitt, Leah D. *Remembering the Occupation in French Film: National Identity in Postwar Europe*. New York: Palgrave Macmillan, 2008.

Histoire, L'. Les Collabos. Collection Pluriel. Paris: Arthème Fayard/Sophia Publications, 2011.

Hitler, Adolf. *Mein Kampf*. Trans. Ralph Manheim. Boston: Houghton Mifflin, 1943.

Hitler, Adolf, and H. R. Trevor-Roper. *Hitler's Table Talk, 1941–1944: His Private Conversations*. Trans. Norman Cameron and R. H. Stevens. New York: Enigma Books, 2000.

Hoffmann, Peter. *Hitler's Personal Security*. Cambridge, MA: MIT Press, 1979.

Hoffmann, Stanley. *Decline or Renewal? France Since the 1930s*. New York: Viking Press, 1974.

Hollande, François. "The 'Crime Committed in France, by France.'" *The New York Review of Books* 59, no. 14 (September 27, 2012): 40.

Humbert, Agnès. *Résistance: A Woman's Journal of Struggle and Defiance in Occupied France*. Trans. Barbara Mellor. New York: Bloomsbury, 2008.

Jackson, Julian. *France: The Dark Years, 1940–1944*. New York: Oxford University Press, 2001.

Jamet, Dominique. *Un petit Parisien, 1941–1945*. Paris: Flammarion, 2000.

Jamet, Fabienne. *One two two*. Paris: Presses pocket, 1979.

Janis, Harriet and Sidney. "Picasso's Studio." In Marilyn McCully, ed., *A Picasso Anthology: Documents, Criticisms, Reminiscences*. Princeton, NJ: Princeton University Press, 1982.

Jasper, Willi. *Hôtel Lutétia: Ein deutsches Exil in Paris*. Munich: Hanser, 1994.

———.*Hôtel Lutétia: Un Exil allemand à Paris*. Trans. Jacqueline Grenz, Françoise Toraille, and Nicole Bary. Paris: Michalon, 1995.

Joly, Laurent. *Vichy dans la "Solution finale": Histoire du Commissariat Général aux Questions Juives (1941–1944)*. Paris: Grasset, 2006.

Joly, Laurent, ed. *La Délation dans la France des années noires*. Paris: Librairie Académique Perrin, 2012.

Joseph, Gilbert. *Une si douce Occupation: Simone de Beauvoir, Jean-Paul Sartre, 1940–1944*. Paris: Albin Michel, 1991.

Josephs, Jeremy. *Swastika over Paris: The Fate of the French Jews*. London: Bloomsbury, 1989.

Jouhandeau, Marcel. *Journal sous l'Occupation*, suivi de *La Courbe de nos angoisses*. Paris: Gallimard, 1980.

Jucker, Ninetta. *Curfew in Paris: A Record of the German Occupation*. London: Hogarth, 1960.

Judt, Tony. *Postwar: A History of Europe since 1945*. New York: Penguin Press, 2005.

Jules-Rosette, Bennetta. *Josephine Baker in Art and Life: The Icon and the Image*. Urbana: University of Illinois Press, 2007.

Jünger, Ernst. *Journaux de guerre*. Vol. 2, *1939–1948*. Paris: Gallimard, 2008.

Kageneck, August von. *Examen de conscience: Nous étions vaincus, mais nous nous croyions innocents*. Paris: Librairie Académique Perrin, 1996.

———.*La France occupée*. Paris: Librairie Académique Perrin, 2012.

Kaplan, Alice. *The Collaborator: The Trial and Execution of Robert Brasillach*. Chicago: University of Chicago Press, 2000.

Katz, Ethan. "Did the Paris Mosque Save Jews? A Mystery and Its Memory." *Jewish Quarterly Review* 102 (2012): 256–87.

———."Jews as Muslims and Muslims as Jews: Shifting Dynamics of Power and Identity Under the Occupation," in "Jews and Muslims in the Shadow of Marianne:

Conflicting Identities and Republican Culture in France (1914–1975)." PhD dissertation. University of Wisconsin, Madison, 2009.

———."Memory at the Front: The Struggle over Revolutionary Commemoration in Occupied France, 1940–1944." *Journal of European Studies* 35, no. 2: 153–68.

Katz, Robert. *The Battle for Rome: The Germans, the Allies, the Partisans, and the Pope, September 1943–June 1944*. New York: Simon and Schuster, 2003.

Kaufmann, Dorothy. *Édith Thomas: A Passion for Resistance*. Ithaca, NY: Cornell University Press, 2004.

Kaufmann, Dorothy, ed. *Pages de journal, 1939–1944*; suivies de *Journal intime de Monsieur Célestin Costedet*. Paris: Viviane Hamy, 1995.

Kedward, H. R. *Occupied France: Collaboration and Resistance, 1940–1944*. New York: Blackwell, 1985.

Kedward, H. R., and Nancy Wood, eds. *The Liberation of France: Image and Event*. Oxford: Berg, 1995.

Keegan, John. *The Battle for History: Re-Fighting World War II*. New York: Vintage Books, 1996.

Kent, Victoria. *Quatre ans à Paris*. Paris: Éditions le Livre du Jour, 1947.

Kernan, Thomas Dickenson. *France on Berlin Time*. New York: J. B. Lippincott, 1941.

Kershaw, Ian. *The End: The Defiance and Destruction of Hitler's Germany, 1944–1945*. New York: Penguin Press, 2011.

———.*Hitler, 1889–1936: Hubris*. New York: W. W. Norton, 1999.

———.*Hitler, 1936–45: Nemesis*. New York: W. W. Norton, 2000.

Kirsch, Jonathan. *The Short, Strange Life of Herschel Grynszpan: A Boy Avenger, a Nazi Diplomat, and a Murder in Paris*. New York: Liveright, 2013.

Kitson, Simon. "The Police in the Liberation of Paris." In H. R. Kedward and Nancy Woods, eds., *The Liberation of France: Image and Event*. Oxford: Berg, 1995.

Klarsfeld, Serge. *Adieu les enfants (1942–1944)*. Paris: Mille et une Nuits, 2005.

———.*L'Étoile des Juifs: Témoignages et documents*. Paris: l'Archipel, 1992.

Knipping, Franz. "Die Deutsche Frankreichpolitik, 1940–1942." In Wolfgang Drost et al., eds., *Paris sous l'Occupation (Paris unter deutscher Besatzung)*. Heidelberg: Universitätsverlag C. Winter, 1995.

Kofman, Sarah. *Paroles suffoquées*. Paris: Galilée, 1987.

———.*Rue Ordener, rue Labat*. Paris: Galilée, 1994.

———.*Rue Ordener, Rue Labat*. Lincoln, NE: University of Nebraska Press, 1996.

Kracauer, Siegfried. *From Caligari to Hitler: A Psychological History of the German Film*. Princeton, NJ: Princeton University Press, 1947.

Krauss, Rosalind E. *The Picasso Papers*. New York: Farrar, Straus and Giroux, 1998.

Kristeva, Julia. "Adolescence, a Syndrome of Ideality." *Psychoanalytic Review* 94, no. 5 (October 2007): 715–25.

———."The Adolescent Novel." In John Fletcher and Andrew Benjamin, eds., *Abjection, Melancholia, and Love: The Work of Julia Kristeva*. New York: Routledge, 1990.

Krivopisco, Guy. *Les Fusillés de la Cascade du Bois de Boulogne, 16 août 1944*. Paris: Mairie de Paris, 2000.

Krob, Melanie Gordon. "Paris through Enemy Eyes: The Wehrmacht in Paris 1940–1944." *Journal of European Studies* 31, no. 121 (March 1, 2001): 3–28.

Kupferman, Fred. *Le Procès de Vichy: Pucheu, Pétain, Laval: 1944–1945.* Brussels: Éditions Complexe, 1980.

La Hire, Jean de. *Les Crimes de l'évacuation: Les Horreurs qu'on a vues.* Paris: Tallandier, 1940.

Laborie, Pierre. "1940–1944: Double-Think in France." In Sarah Fishman et al., eds., *France at War: Vichy and the Historians.* Oxford: Berg, 2000.

———.*Le Chagrin et le venin: La France sous l'Occupation, mémoire et idées reçues.* Montrouge, France: Bayard, 2011.

———.*Les Français des années troubles: De la Guerre d'Espagne à la Liberation.* Paris: Desclée de Brouwer, 2001.

———.*Les Mots de 39–45.* Toulouse: Presses universitaires du Mirail, 2006.

Lafarge, Catherine. "Souvenirs de Guerre: Paris 1940–1945." Personal diary. Unpublished typescript.

Lambauer, Barbara. "Otto Abetz, inspirateur et catalyseur de la collaboration culturelle." In Albrecht Betz and Stefan Martens, eds., *Les Intellectuels et l'Occupation, 1940–1944: Collaborer, partir, résister.* Collection Mémoires 106. Paris: Autrement, 2004.

Lambert, Raymond-Raoul, and Richard I. Cohen. *Carnet d'un témoin: 1940–1943.* Paris: Fayard, 1985.

Langeron, Roger. *Paris, juin 1940.* Paris: Flammarion, 1946.

Laqueur, Walter, and Judith Tydor Baumel-Schwartz, eds. *The Holocaust Encyclopedia.* New Haven, CT: Yale University Press, 2001.

Larson, Erik. *In the Garden of Beasts: Love, Terror, and an American Family in Hitler's Berlin.* New York: Crown, 2011.

Laub, Thomas Johnston. *After the Fall: German Policy in Occupied France, 1940–1944.* New York: Oxford University Press, 2010.

Laurens, Corran. "'La Femme au Turban': Les Femmes tondues." In H. R. Kedward and Nancy Wood, eds., *The Liberation of France: Image and Event.* Oxford: Berg, 1995.

Le Boterf, Hervé. *La Vie parisienne sous l'Occupation, 1940–1944.* 2 vols. Paris: Éditions France-Empire, 1975, 1978.

Le Maire, Maurice. "Cahier de Guerre, mai–juin 1940: Tome II." Personal diary. Unpublished manuscript.

Lean, E. Tangye. *Voices in the Darkness: The Story of the European Radio War.* London: Secker and Warburg, 1943.

Leleu, Jean-Luc, Françoise Passera, Jean Quellien, and Michel Daeffler. *La France pendant la Seconde Guerre mondiale: Atlas historique.* Paris: Fayard: Ministère de la Défense, 2010.

Lemire, Laurent, ed. *Où sortir á Paris: Le Guide du soldat allemand.* Trans. of *1940–1944 Der Deutsche Wegleiter.* Paris: Alma, 2013.

Levert, Jean-Pierre, Thomas Gomart, and Alexis Merville. *Paris, carrefour des résistances.* Paris: Éditions des Musées de Paris, 1994.

Levisse-Touzé, Christine, and Pierre Argaw with Mémorial du Général Leclerc de Hauteclocque et de la Libération de Paris and Musée Jean Moulin. *1940, l'Année de tous les destins.* Paris: Paris-Musées, 2000. Exhibition catalog.

Lévy, Claude, Paul Tillard, and Joseph Kessel. *La Grande rafle du Vél d'Hiv.* Paris: Tallandier, 2010.

Liddell Hart, Basil H. *The German Generals Talk.* New York: Morrow, 1948.

Liebling, A. J. *World War II Writings.* New York: Library of America, 2008.

Loiseau, Jean-Claude. *Les Zazous*. Paris: Le Sagittaire, 1977.

Lorenz, Karl. *Frankreich: Ein Erlebnis des deutschen Soldaten*. Paris: Ode Verlag, 1942.

———.*Soldaten fotografieren Frankreich: Ein Bilderbuch mit Erzählungen*. Paris: Wegleiter-Verlag, 1943.

Lottman, Herbert R. *The Fall of Paris: June 1940*. New York: HarperCollins, 1992.

———.*The People's Anger: Justice and Revenge in Post-Liberation France*. London: Hutchinson, 1986.

Lubrich, Oliver. *Travels in the Reich, 1933–1945: Foreign Authors Report from Germany*. Chicago: University of Chicago Press, 2010.

Ludewig, Joachim. *Rückzug: The German Retreat from France, 1944*. David T. Zabecki, ed. Lexington, KY: University Press of Kentucky, 2012.

Lukacs, John. *June 1941: Hitler and Stalin*. New Haven, CT: Yale University Press, 2006.

———.*The Legacy of the Second World War*. New Haven, CT: Yale University Press, 2010.

Luneau, Aurélie. *Radio Londres, 1940–1944: Les Voix de la liberté*. Paris: Librairie Académique Perrin, 2005.

Lusseyran, Jacques. *And There Was Light: Autobiography of Jacques Lusseyran, Blind Hero of the French Resistance*. Sandpoint, ID: Morning Light Press, 2006.

———.*Et la lumière fut*. Paris: Félin, 2008.

Lynch, Kevin. *The Image of the City*. Cambridge, MA: MIT Press, 1960.

MacCannell, Dean. *The Tourist: A New Theory of the Leisure Class*. New York: Schocken Books, 1976.

Maine, Paul. "L'Image de Paris et de la France occupée dans les actualités allemandes (*Deutsche Wochenschau*) de mai 1940 à novembre 1942." In Wolfgang Drost et al., eds., *Paris sous l'Occupation (Paris unter deutscher Besatzung)*. Heidelberg: Universitätsverlag C. Winter, 1995.

Malcolm, Janet. *Two Lives: Gertrude and Alice*. New Haven, CT: Yale University Press, 2004.

Malraux, André. *Entre ici, Jean Moulin: Discours d'André Malraux, Ministre d'état chargé des affaires culturelles, lors du transfert des cendres de Jean Moulin au Panthéon, 19 décembre 1964*. Paris: Éditions Points, 2010.

Marchand, Bernard. *Les Ennemis de Paris: La Haine de la grande ville des lumières à nos jours*. Presses universitaires de Rennes, 2009.

Marcus, Sharon. *Apartment Stories: City and Home in Nineteenth-Century Paris and London*. Berkeley: University of California Press, 1999.

Marrus, Michael Robert, and Robert O. Paxton. *Vichy France and the Jews*. New York: Basic Books, 1981.

Martin, Russell. *Picasso's War: The Destruction of Guernica and the Masterpiece that Changed the World*. New York: Dutton, 2002.

Martinez, Gilles, and Thierry Scotto di Covella. *La France de 1939 à 1945: Le Régime de Vichy, l'Occupation, la Libération*. Paris: Éditions du Seuil, 1997.

Marty, Alan T. "The Art of Walking in Paris: Pathways to the Sublime." Unpublished manuscript.

———."A Walking Guide to Occupied Paris: Germans and their Collaborators." Unpublished manuscript.

Mathot, René. *Au Ravin du loup: Hitler en Belgique et en France, mai–juin 1940*. Brussels: Racine, 2000.

Matot, Bertrand. *La Guerre des cancres: Un Lycée au coeur de la Résistance et de la collaboration*. Paris: Librairie Académique Perrin, 2010.

Maupassant, Guy de. *Boule de suif.* Paris: Albin Michel, 1957.

May, Ernest R. *Strange Victory: Hitler's Conquest of France.* New York: Hill and Wang, 2000.

Mayne, Judith. *Le Corbeau: Henri-Georges Clouzot, 1943.* London: Tauris, 2007.

Mazower, Mark. *Hitler's Empire: How the Nazis Ruled Europe.* New York: Penguin Press, 2008.

McDonough, Frank. *Opposition and Resistance in Nazi Germany.* New York: Cambridge University Press, 2001.

McKee, Alexander. *Wreck of the "Medusa": The Tragic Story of the Death Raft.* New York: Signet, 2000.

McLoughlin, Catherine Mary. *The Cambridge Companion to War Writing.* New York and Cambridge: Cambridge University Press, 2009.

Meinen, Insa. *Wehrmacht et prostitution sous l'Occupation (1940–1945).* Payot, 2006.

Meyers, Odette. *Doors to Madame Marie.* Seattle: University of Washington Press, 1997.

Michel, Henri. *Paris allemand.* Paris: Albin Michel, 1981.

Michot, Alexandra. "Rafle du Vél' d'Hiv': Les Archives s'ouvrent." *Le Figaro,* July 16, 2012. http://www.lefigaro.fr/actualite-france/2012/07/15/01016-20120715ARTFIG00143 -rafle-du-vel-d-hiv-les-archives-s-ouvrent.php.

Miles, Jonathan. *The Wreck of the "Medusa": The Most Famous Sea Disaster of the Nineteenth Century.* New York: Atlantic Monthly Press, 2007.

Miller, Henry W. *The Paris Gun: The Bombardment of Paris by the German Long Range Guns and the Great German Offensives of 1918.* New York: Jonathan Cape and Harrison Smith, 1930.

Misch, Rochus, and Nicolas Bourcier. *J'étais garde du corps d'Hitler: 1940–1945.* Paris: Cherche Midi, 2006.

Mitchell, Allan. *The Devil's Captain: Ernst Jünger in Nazi Paris, 1941–1944.* New York: Berghahn Books, 2006.

———.*Nazi Paris: The History of an Occupation, 1940–1944.* New York: Berghahn Books, 2008.

———. *A Stranger in Paris: Germany's Role in Republican France, 1870–1940.* New York: Berghahn Books, 2006.

Moati, Serge, and Laure Adler. *Mitterrand à Vichy: Le Choc d'une révélation.* La Tour d'Aigues, France: Éditions de l'Aube, 2008.

Moisson, Pascale. *Anecdotes . . . sous La Botte,* suivi de *"Dans les rues de Paris vers la Libération."* Paris: Harmattan, 1998.

Moorehead, Caroline. *A Train in Winter: An Extraordinary Story of Women, Friendship, and Resistance in Occupied France.* New York: HarperCollins, 2011.

Moorhouse, Roger. *Berlin at War.* New York: Basic Books, 2010.

Mornet, André. *Quatre ans à rayer de notre histoire.* Paris: Éditions Self, 1949.

Mosse, George L. *Nazi Culture: Intellectual, Cultural, and Social Life in the Third Reich.* Madison: University of Wisconsin Press, 2003.

Muracciole, Jean-François. *Histoire de la Résistance en France.* Paris: Presses universitaires de France, 1993.

Murphy, Robert. *Diplomat among Warriors.* Garden City, NY: Doubleday, 1964.

Musée de la Résistance. "Résistance." *Notre Musée* 1, no. 11. Champigny-sur-Marne, France: Musée de la Résistance, 2011.

Nagorski, Andrew. *Hitlerland: American Eyewitnesses to the Nazi Rise to Power.* New York: Simon and Schuster, 2012.

Naour, Ingrid, and Maurice Rajsfus. *L'Humour des Français sous l'Occupation*. Collection "Le Sens de l'humour." Paris: Le Cherche Midi, 1995.

Neaman, Elliot Yale. "Warrior or Esthete? Reflections on Jünger's Reception in France and Germany." *New German Critique* 59 (1993): 118.

Neiberg, Michael S. *The Blood of Free Men: The Liberation of Paris, 1944*. New York: Basic Books, 2012.

Neitzel, Sönke, and Harald Welzer. *Soldats: Combattre, tuer, mourir: Procès-verbaux de récits de soldats allemands*. Paris: Gallimard, 2013.

Némirovsky, Irène. *Suite française*. Préface de Myriam Annisimov. Paris: Denoël, 2004.

———. *Suite Française*. Trans. Sandra Smith. New York: Knopf, 2006.

Nettelbeck, Colin W. *War and Identity: The French and the Second World War: An Anthology of Texts*. London: Methuen Educational Ltd., 1987.

Newman, Victoria Beck. "*The Triumph of Pan*: Picasso and the Liberation." *Zeitschrift für Kunstgeschichte* 62 (1999): 106–22.

Nicholas, Lynn H. *The Rape of Europa: The Fate of Europe's Treasures in the Third Reich and the Second World War*. New York: Knopf, 1994.

Nordling, Raoul, with Victor Vinde and Fabrice Virgili. *Sauver Paris: Mémoires du consul de Suède (1905–1944)*. Fabrice Virgili, ed. Brussels: Éditions Complexe, 2002.

Ory, Pascal. *Villes sous l'Occupation: L'Histoire des Français au quotidien*. Paris: Éditions L'Express, 2012.

Ouana, Charles. *Joséphine Baker contre Hitler: La Star noire de la France libre*. Paris: Éditions Duboiris, 2006.

Ousby, Ian. *Occupation: The Ordeal of France, 1940–1944*. New York: Cooper Square Press, 2000.

Ouzoulias, Albert. *Les Bataillons de la Jeunesse*. Paris: Éditions Sociales, 1967.

Ovenden, Mark. *Paris Underground: The Maps, Stations, and Design of the Métro*. New York: Penguin Books, 2009.

Overy, R. J. *The Battle of Britain: The Myth and the Reality*. New York: W. W. Norton, 2001.

———. *Why the Allies Won*. New York: W. W. Norton, 1995.

Passera, Françoise. *Les Affiches de propagande: 1939–1945*. Caen, France: Mémorial de Caen, 2005.

Paul, Elliot. *The Last Time I Saw Paris*. London: Sickle Moon Books, 2003.

Paxton, Robert O. *The Anatomy of Fascism*. New York: Knopf, 2004.

———. "Les Arts dans la défaite." *Books: L'Actualité par les livres du monde* 23 (June 2011): 34–38.

———. "The Bottom of the Abyss." in Olivier Corpet and Claire Paulhan, eds., *Collaboration and Resistance: French Literary Life under the Nazi Occupation*. Trans. Jeffrey Mehlman. New York: Five Ties Publishing, 2009.

———. "Inside the Panic." *The New York Review of Books* 54, no. 18 (November 22, 2007): 49–50.

———. "The Jew Hater." *The New York Review of Books* 53, no. 18 (November 16, 2006): 26–29.

———. *Vichy France: Old Guard and New Order, 1940–1944*. New York: Knopf, 1972.

———. "Vichy Lives!—In a Way." *The New York Review of Books* 60, no. 7 (April 25, 2013): 21–23.

Perrault, Gilles, and Jean-Pierre Azéma. *Paris under the Occupation*. New York: Vendome Press: 1989.

Perrier, Jean-Louis. *L'Exil de la Joconde*. Versailles, France: Éditions Feryane, 2006.

Peschanski, Denis, and Lory Frankel, eds. *Collaboration and Resistance: Images of Life in Vichy France, 1940–1944*. New York: Harry N. Abrams, 2000.

Picaper, Jean-Paul. *Le Crime d'aimer: Les Enfants du STO*. Geneva: Éditions des Syrtes, 2005.

Picaper, Jean-Paul, and Ludwig Norz. *Enfants maudits: Ils sont 200,000; on les appelait les "enfants de Boches."* Paris: Syrtes, 2004.

Pleshakov, Konstantin. *Stalin's Folly: The Tragic First Ten Days of World War II on the Eastern Front*. Boston: Houghton Mifflin, 2005.

Poisson, Georges. *Le Retour des cendres de l'Aiglon*. Paris: Nouveau Monde, 2006.

Poliakov, Léon. *L'Étoile jaune*. Paris: Grancher, 1999.

Poznanski, Renée. *Jews in France during World War II*. Waltham, MA: Brandeis University Press in association with the United States Holocaust Memorial Museum, 2001.

Préfecture de Police de Paris. Service de la mémoire et des affaires culturelles. *La Rafle du Vélodrome d'Hiver: Les Archives de la Police, un regard policier sur Paris, sous l'Occupation*. Paris: Service des Archives de la Préfecture de Police, 2012.

Preston, Paul. *The Spanish Civil War, 1936–39*. New York: Grove Press, 1986.

Pritchard, Marietta. *Among Strangers: A Family Story*. Northampton, MA: Impress, 2010.

Pryce-Jones, David. *Paris in the Third Reich: A History of the German Occupation, 1940–1944*. New York: Holt, Rinehart and Winston, 1981.

Pugh, Anthony C., ed. *France 1940: Literary and Historical Reactions to Defeat*. Durham, UK: University of Durham, 1991.

Quenet, Marie. "'Pour nous, la rafle du Vél' d'Hiv, c'était ici.'" *Journal du Dimanche* (July 1, 2012): 14–15.

Rabinovitch, Gérard. *Questions sur la Shoah*. Toulouse, France: Éditions Milan, 2006.

Ragache, Gilles, and Jean-Robert Ragache. *La Vie quotidienne des écrivains et des artistes sous l'Occupation, 1940–1944*. Paris: Hachette, 1988.

Rajsfus, Maurice. *Opération Étoile jaune*, suivi de *Jeudi noir*. Paris: Cherche Midi, 2002.

———. *La Rafle du Vél d'Hiv*. Paris: Presses universitaires de France, 2002.

Rayski, Adam. *L'Affiche rouge: Une Victoire posthume*. Paris: Délégation à la Mémoire et à l'Information Historique, 1999.

Reid, Anna. *Leningrad: The Epic Siege of World War II, 1941–1944*. New York: Walker & Co., 2011.

Renaudeau, Pierre-Marc. *La Troisième République*. Paris: Éditions du Seuil, 1998.

Richard, Lionel. "Soixante ans de romans sur le nazisme d'Albert Camus à Jonathan Littell." *Magazine littéraire* 467 (September 2007): 28–61.

Riding, Alan. *And the Show Went On: Cultural Life in Nazi-Occupied Paris*. New York: Knopf, 2010.

Rioux, Jean-Pierre. "Everyday Culture in Occupied France." In Sarah Fishman et al., eds., *France at War: Vichy and the Historians*. Oxford: Berg, 2000.

Robb, Graham. *Parisians: An Adventure History of Paris*. New York: W. W. Norton, 2010.

Roberts, Andrew. *The Storm of War: A New History of the Second World War*. New York: HarperCollins, 2011.

Roberts, Marie Louise. "Photographier les G.I.: Érotisme et photojournalisme en France pendant la Seconde Guerre mondiale." In Bruno Cabanes and Guillaume Piketty, eds., *Retour à l'intime au sortir de la guerre*. Paris: Tallandier, 2009.

———. *What Soldiers Do: Sex and the American GI in World War II France*. Chicago: University of Chicago Press, 2013.

Roberts, Sophie B. "A Case for Dissidence in Occupied Paris: The Zazous, Youth Dissidence, and the Yellow Star Campaign in Occupied Paris (1942)." *French History* 24 (2010): 82–103.

Rosenberg, André. *Les Enfants dans la Shoah: La Déportation des enfants juifs et tsiganes de France*. Paris: Les Éditions de Paris Max Chaleil, 2013.

Rosnay, Tatiana de. *Sarah's Key*. New York: St. Martin's Press, 2007.

Roussel, Eric. *Le Naufrage: 16 juin 1940*. Paris: Gallimard, 2009.

Rousso, Henry. *Les Années noires: Vivre sous l'Occupation*. Paris: Gallimard, 1992.

———.*Juger Eichmann, Jérusalem, 1961*. Paris: Mémorial de la Shoah, 2011. Exhibition catalog.

———.*Le Syndrome de Vichy: De 1944 à nos jous* Paris: Éditions du Seuil, 1987.

———.*The Vichy Syndrome: History and Memory in France Since 1944*. Cambridge, MA: Harvard University Press, 1991.

Rousso, Henry, and Henri Michel. *Le Régime de Vichy*. Paris: Presses universitaires de France, 2007.

Roynette, Odile. "La Nostalgie du front." In Bruno Cabanes and Guillaume Piketty, eds., *Retour à l'intime au sortir de la guerre*. Paris: Tallandier, 2009.

Ruelle, Karen Gray, and Deborah Durland DeSaix. *The Grand Mosque of Paris: A Story of How Muslims Rescued Jews during the Holocaust*. New York: Holiday House, 2009.

Russell, Nicolas. "Collective Memory before and after Halbwachs." *The French Review* 79, no. 4 (March 1, 2006): 792–804.

Ryback, Timothy W. *Hitler's Private Library: The Books That Shaped His Life*. New York: Knopf, 2008.

Sabbagh, Antoine, ed. *Lettres de Drancy*. Paris: Tallandier, 2002.

Saint-Exupéry, Antoine de. *Pilote de guerre*. Paris: Gallimard, 1942.

Saint Marc, Hélie de, and August von Kageneck. *Notre histoire, 1922–1945: Conversations avec Étienne de Montety*. Paris: Arènes, 2002.

Salat-Baroux, Frédéric. *De Gaulle-Pétain: Le Destin, la blessure, la leçon*. Paris: Éditions Tallandier, 2013.

Sansot, Pierre. *Poétique de la ville*. Paris: Klincksieck, 1971.

Sartre, Jean-Paul. *The Aftermath of War (Situations III)*. Trans. Chris Turner. New York: Seagull Books, 2008.

Sayare, Scott. "At New Holocaust Center, French Leader Confronts Past." *The New York Times*, September 22, 2012.

Schall, Roger. *Paris au quotidien 1939–1945*. Préface de Pierre Miquel. Paris: Éditions du Cherche Midi, 2005.

Schiff, Stacy. *Saint-Exupéry: A Biography*. New York: Henry Holt, 2006.

Schneider, Michel. *Un Rêve de pierre: Le "Radeau de la Méduse," Géricault*. Paris: Gallimard, 1991.

Schroeder, Liliane. *Journal d'Occupation: Paris, 1940–1944: Chronique au jour le jour d'une époque oubliée*. Paris: Guibert, 2000.

Schwab, Thomas J. "Experiences of My French Jewish Family Under German Occupation, 1940–1944." Unpublished manuscript, 2002.

Schwarz, Daniel R. *Imagining the Holocaust*. New York: St. Martin's Press, 1999.

Sebald, W. G. *Austerlitz*. New York: Random House, 2001.

———.*On the Natural History of Destruction*. New York: Random House, 2003.

Seib, Philip M. *Broadcasts from the Blitz: How Edward R. Murrow Helped Lead America into War.* Washington, DC: Potomac Books, 2006.

Semelin, Jacques. *Persécutions et entraide dans la France occupée: Comment 75 percent des Juifs en France ont échappé à la mort.* Paris: Éditions du Seuil/Éditions des Arènes, 2013.

Serge, Victor. *Unforgiving Years.* Trans. and intro. Richard Greeman. New York: NYRB Classics, 2008.

Shirer, William L. *Berlin Diary: The Journal of a Foreign Correspondent, 1934–1941.* New York: Knopf, 1941.

———. *The Collapse of the Third Republic: An Inquiry into the Fall of France, June 1940.* New York: Simon and Schuster, 1969.

———. *"This Is Berlin": Radio Broadcasts from Nazi Germany.* Woodstock, NY: Overlook Press, 1999.

Siebers, Tobin. "Hitler and the Tyranny of the Aesthetic." *Philosophy and Literature* 24, no. 1 (April 1, 2000): 96–110.

Sieburg, Friedrich. *Dieu est-il français?* Traduit de l'allemand, et suivi d'une lettre de Bernard Grasset à Friedrich Sieburg. Paris: Bernard Grasset, 1930.

———. *Gott in Frankreich?: ein Versuch.* Frankfurt am Main: Societäts-Verlag, 1931.

———. *Who Are These French? A German Study of France in the Modern World.* Trans. Alan Harris. New York: Macmillan, 1938.

Siefridt, Françoise. *J'ai voulu porter l'étoile jaune: Journal de Françoise Siefridt, chrétienne et résistante.* Paris: Robert Laffont, 2010.

Sinclair, Anne. *21, rue La Boétie.* Paris: Bernard Grasset, 2012.

Sisk, John P. "The Tyranny of the Aesthetic." *American Scholar* 63, no. 1 (winter 1994): 119–22.

Slama, Alain-Gérard. "Vichy était-il fasciste?" *Vingtième Siècle: Revue d'histoire* 11, no. 1 (1986): 41–54.

Smith, Bonnie G. *Confessions of a Concierge: Madame Lucie's History of Twentieth-Century France.* New Haven, CT: Yale University Press, 1987.

Snell, John L., and Allan Mitchell. *The Nazi Revolution: Hitler's Dictatorship and the German Nation.* Lexington, MA: D. C. Heath and Company, 1973.

Snyder, Timothy. "What We Need to Know About the Holocaust." *New York Review of Books* 57, no. 14 (September 30, 2010): 76–81.

Sontag, Susan. *Regarding the Pain of Others.* New York: Farrar, Straus and Giroux, 2003.

Sowerwine, Charles. *France Since 1870: Culture, Politics, and Society.* New York: Palgrave Macmillan, 2001.

Speer, Albert. *Inside the Third Reich: Memoirs.* New York: Macmillan, 1970.

———. *Spandau: The Secret Diaries.* New York: Macmillan, 1976.

Spitz, Jacques, and Clément Pieyre. *La Situation culturelle en France pendant l'Occupation et depuis la Libération; Notes rédigées en 1945 pour la Section historique de l'Armée américaine.* Nantes, France: Éditions Joseph K., 2010.

Spotts, Frederic. *Hitler and the Power of Aesthetics.* New York: Overlook Press, 2002.

———. *The Shameful Peace: How French Artists and Intellectuals Survived the Nazi Occupation.* New Haven, CT: Yale University Press, 2008.

Steer, G. L. "Historic Basque Town Wiped Out; Rebel Fliers Machine-Gun Civilians." *The New York Times,* April 28, 1937.

Stein, Gertrude. *Wars I Have Seen.* London: Brilliance Books, 1984.

Steinberg, Lucien, and Jean Marie Fitère. *Les Allemands en France: 1940–1944*. Paris: Albin Michel, 1980.

Suleiman, Susan Rubin. *Crises of Memory and the Second World War*. Cambridge, MA: Harvard University Press, 2006.

———."Memory Troubles: Remembering the Occupation in Simone de Beauvoir's *Les Mandarins*." *French Politics, Culture & Society* 28 (2010): 4–17.

Sullerot, Évelyne, ed. *Nous avions quinze ans en 1940: Récits*. Paris: Fayard, 2010.

Sweeting, C. G. *Hitler's Personal Pilot: The Life and Times of Hans Baur*. London: Brassey's, 2002.

Tabouis, Geneviève R., and Albert Mousset. *Quand Paris résiste: L'Occupation romaine, Paris sous les Anglais, l'occupation espagnole, l'occupation des "Alliés", les Prussiens en 1871*. Paris: Seimrha, 1951.

Taft, Hessy Levinsons. "Perfect Aryan." In Gertrude Schneider, ed., *Muted Voices: Jewish Survivors of Latvia Remember*. New York: Philosophical Library, 1987.

Taieb, Karen, and Tatiana de Rosnay. *Je vous écris du Vél' d'Hiv: Les lettres retrouvées*. Paris: Robert Laffont, 2011.

Tank, Kurt Lothar. *Pariser Tagebuch, 1938, 1939, 1940*. Berlin: S. Fischer Verlag, 1941.

Teissier du Cros, Janet. *Divided Loyalties*. New York: Knopf, 1964.

Texcier, Jean. "Conseils à l'occupé." July 1941. Musée Virtuel de la Résistance. Available at http//:www.museedelaresistanceenligne.org/doc/flash/texte/2616.pdf.

———.*Propos de l'occupé*. Paris: Kellar, 1941.

Thomas, Edith. *La Libération de Paris*. Paris: Mellottée, 1945.

———.*Pages de Journal, 1939–1944*; suivies de *Journal intime de Monsieur Célestin Costedet*. Dorothy Kaufmann, ed. Paris: Viviane Hamy, 1995.

Thoraval, Anne. *Des Résistants à Paris: Chemins d'histoire dans la capitale occupée, 14 juin 1940–19 août 1944*. Paris: SPE-Barthélemy, 2001.

Todd, Olivier. *Albert Camus: A Life*. New York: Knopf, 1997.

Todorov, Tzvetan. *Une Tragédie française, été 44: Scènes de guerre civile*, suivi de *Souvenirs d'un maire* par René Sadrin. Paris: Éditions du Seuil, 1994.

Toklas, Alice B. *What Is Remembered*. New York: Holt, Rinehart and Winston, 1963.

Toll, Seymour I. "Liebling Covers Paris, Hemingway Liberates It." *Sewanee Review* 112, no. 1 (2004): 35–55.

Tombs, Robert, and Isabelle Tombs, eds. *Voices from Wartime France 1939–1945: Clandestine Resistance and Vichy Newspapers* (from British Library Newspaper Library). Woodbridge, CT: Primary Source Microfilm, 2002 (http://gdc.gale.com/archivesunbound/).

Torgovnick, Marianna. *The War Complex: World War II in Our Time*. Chicago: University of Chicago Press, 2005.

Trevisan, Carine. "'On ne sait pas à quoi on appartient': Le roman du retour." In Bruno Cabanes and Guillaume Perketty, eds., *Retour à l'intime au sortir de la guerre*. Paris: Tallandier, 2009.

Triolet, Elsa. *Quatre récits de l'Occupation*. Brussels: Société des amis de Louis Aragon et Elsa Triolet/Aden, 2010.

Tuan, Yi-fu. *Topophilia: A Study of Environmental Perception, Attitudes, and Values*. Englewood Cliffs, NJ: Prentice-Hall, 1974.

Tucker, Erica L. *Remembering Occupied Warsaw: Polish Narratives of World War II*. DeKalb, IL: Northern Illinois University Press, 2011.

United Nations Information Office. "Ten Conquered Allies: Belgium, Czechoslovakia, France, Greece, Luxembourg, the Netherlands, Norway, the Philippines, Poland, Yugoslavia." New York: United Nations, 1943.

United States Army. *Instructions for American Servicemen in France during World War II.* With a new introduction by Rick Atkinson. Chicago: University of Chicago Press, 2008.

Urry, John. *The Tourist Gaze.* Thousand Oaks, CA: Sage Publications, 2002.

Urwand, Ben. *The Collaboration: Hollywood's Pact with Hitler.* Cambridge, MA: Harvard University Press, 2013.

Vaïsse, Maurice. *Mai–juin 1940.* Paris: Éditions Autrement, 2000.

Vale, Lawrence J., and Thomas J. Campanella. *The Resilient City: How Modern Cities Recover from Disaster.* New York: Oxford University Press, 2005.

Valland, Rose. *Le Front de l'art: Défense des collections françaises.* Paris: Plon, 1961.

Vaughan, Hal. *Doctor to the Resistance: The Heroic True Story of an American Surgeon and His Family in Occupied Paris.* Washington, DC: Brassey's, 2004.

Vegh, Claudine. *Je ne lui ai pas dit au revoir: Des Enfants de déportés parlent.* Postface de Bruno Bettelheim. Paris: Gallimard, 1979.

Veil, Simone. *Une Jeunesse au temps de la Shoah: Extraits d'une vie.* Paris: Librairie générale française, 2010.

Veillon, Dominique. *Fashion under the Occupation.* Oxford: Berg, 2002.

———."1940–1944: Le Front de La Mode." *l'Histoire* 235 (September 2009): 78–81.

Vercors. *Le Silence de la mer, et autres récits.* Paris: Albin Michel, 1951.

Vercors, *The Silence of the Sea.* Ed. James W. Brown and Lawrence D. Stokes. Oxford: Bloomsbury Academic, 1991.

Verny, Françoise. *Serons-nous vivantes le 2 janvier 1950?* Paris: Grasset, 2005.

Vidler, Anthony. *The Architectural Uncanny: Essays in the Modern Unhomely.* Cambridge, MA: MIT Press, 1992.

———.*Warped Space: Art, Architecture, and Anxiety in Modern Culture.* Cambridge, MA: MIT Press, 2000.

Vincenot, Alain. *Les Larmes de la rue des Rosiers.* Paris: Éditions des Syrtes, 2010.

Vinen, Richard. *The Unfree French: Life Under the Occupation.* New Haven: Yale University Press, 2006.

Virgili, Fabrice. *Shorn Women: Gender and Punishment in Liberation France.* Oxford: Berg,, 2002.

Wagner, Margaret E., et al. *The Library of Congress World War II Companion.* New York: Simon and Schuster, 2007.

Wakeman, Rosemary. *The Heroic City: Paris, 1945–1958.* Chicago: University of Chicago Press, 2009.

———."Street Noises: Celebrating the Liberation of Paris in Music and Dance." In Alexander Cowan and Jill Steward, *The City and the Senses: Urban Culture Since 1500.* Burlington, VT: Ashgate, 2007.

Walter, Gérard. *Paris under the Occupation.* Trans. Tony White. New York: Orion Press, 1960.

Wardhaugh, Jessica. *In Pursuit of the People: Political Culture in France, 1934–39.* New York: Palgrave Macmillan, 2009.

Warner, Philip. *Battle for France.* London: Cassell, 2001.

Weil, Simone. "The *Iliad*, or the Poem of Force," in Simone Weil and Rachel Bespaloff, *War and the Iliad*. New York: New York Review Books, 2005.

Welzer, Harald, Sabine Moller, and Karoline Tschuggnall. *"Grand-père n'était pas un nazi": National-socialisme et Shoah dans la mémoire familiale*. Trans. Olivier Mannoni. Paris: Gallimard, 2013.

Werth, Alexander. *The Last Days of Paris: A Journalist's Diary*. London: Hamish Hamilton, 1940.

Wescott, Glenway. *Apartment in Athens*. London: Harper & Bros., 1945.

Weyr, Thomas. *The Setting of the Pearl: Vienna Under Hitler*. New York: Oxford University Press, 2005.

Wieviorka, Annette. *Auschwitz expliqué à ma fille*. Paris: Éditions du Seuil, 1999.

Wieviorka, Olivier. *Divided Memory: French Recollections of World War II from the Liberation to the Present*. Trans. George Holoch. Stanford, CA: Stanford University Press, 2012.

———.*Histoire de La Résistance: 1940–1945*. Paris: Librairie Académique Perrin, 2013

———.*La Mémoire désunie: Le Souvenir politique des années sombres, de la Libération à nos jours*. Paris: Éditions du Seuil, 2010.

Will, Barbara. *Unlikely Collaboration: Gertrude Stein, Bernard Faÿ, and the Vichy Dilemma*. New York: Columbia University Press, 2011.

Wirth, Louis. "Urbanism as a Way of Life." *American Journal of Sociology* 44, no. 1 (July 1, 1938): 1–24.

Wood, Nancy. "Memory by Analogy: *Hiroshima, Mon Amour*." In H. R. Kedward and Nancy Wood, eds., *The Liberation of France: Image and Event*. Oxford: Berg, 1995.

Yonnet, Jacques. *Paris Noir: The Secret History of a City*. Trans. Christine Donougher. Sawtry, UK: Dedalus, 2006.

———.*Rue des Maléfices: Chronique secrète d'une ville*. Paris: Phébus, 1987.

Zaidman, Annette. *Mémoire d'une enfance volée (1938–1948): Récit*. Paris: Ramsay, 2002.

Zaloga, Steve. *Liberation of Paris 1944: Patton's Race for the Seine*. New York: Osprey, 2008.

Fiction and Poetry

Assouline, Pierre. *La Cliente*. Paris: Gallimard, 1998.

———.*Lutétia*. Paris: Gallimard, 2006.

Aymé, Marcel. *Le Chemin des écoliers*. Paris: Gallimard, 1946.

———.*Le Passe-muraille: Nouvelles*. Paris: Gallimard, 1943.

———.*Le Vin de Paris: Nouvelles*. Paris: Gallimard, 1947.

Bernardi, Mathias. *La Ville sans regard: Roman*. Paris: J. C. Lattès, 2008.

Binet, Laurent. *HHhH*. Trans. Sam Taylor. New York: Farrar, Straus and Giroux, 2012.

Blottière, Alain. *Le Tombeau de Tommy*. Paris: Gallimard, 2011.

Bober, Robert. *Quoi de neuf sur la guerre? Roman*. Paris: P.O.L., 1993.

Boussinot, Roger. *Les Guichets du Louvre*. Paris: Denoël, 1960.

Camus, Albert. *La Peste*. Paris: Gallimard, 1947.

———.*The Plague*. Trans. Stuart Gilbert. New York: Modern Library, 1948.

Catonné, Jean-Marie. *Portraits volés*. Paris: Plon, 2003.

Cauvin, Patrick. *Venge-moi*. Paris: Albin Michel, 2007.

Céline, Louis-Ferdinand. *Castle to Castle*. New York: Delacorte Press, 1968.

———.*D'un château l' autre*. Paris: Gallimard, 1957.

Dean, Debra. *The Madonnas of Leningrad*. New York: William Morrow, 2006.

Deforges, Régine. *La Bicyclette bleue.* Paris: Librairie générale française, 1995.

————. *101, Avenue Henri-Martin.* Paris: Ramsay, 1983.

Dutourd, Jean. *Au bon beurre; ou, Dix ans de la vie d'un crémier: Roman.* Paris: Gallimard, 1952. (Published later as *Au bon beurre: Scènes de la vie sous l'Occupation.* Paris: Gallimard, 1972.)

Éluard, Paul. *Au Rendez-vous allemand.* Poems. Paris: Éditions de Minuit, 1945.

Everett, Peter. *Matisse's War.* London: Jonathan Cape, 1996.

Fallada, Hans. *Every Man Dies Alone.* Trans. Michael Hofmann. Brooklyn, NY: Melville House, 2009.

————. *Seul dans Berlin.* Trans. Alain Virelle and André Vandevoorde. Paris: Gallimard, 2004.

Furst, Alan. *The Foreign Correspondent: A Novel.* New York: Random House, 2006.

————. *Mission to Paris: A Novel.* New York: Random House, 2012.

————. *Red Gold: A Novel.* New York: Random House, 1999.

————. *The World at Night: A Novel.* New York: Random House, 1996.

Grimbert, Philippe. *Un Secret: Roman.* Paris: Grasset, 2006.

————. *Un Traître: Roman.* Paris: Flammarion, 2008.

Kerr, Philip. *Hitler's Peace: A Novel of the Second World War.* New York: G. P. Putnam's Sons, 2005.

Kessel, Joseph. *L'Armée des ombres.* Paris: Plon, 1990.

Littell, Jonathan. *Les Bienveillantes: Roman.* Paris: Gallimard, 2006.

Modiano, Patrick. *Les Boulevards de ceinture.* Paris: Gallimard, 1972.

————. *La Place de l'Étoile.* Paris: Gallimard, 1968.

————. *La Ronde de nuit.* Paris: Gallimard, 1969.

Piercy, Marge. *Gone to Soldiers: A Novel.* New York: Summit Books, 1987.

Saint-Exupéry, Antoine de. *Pilote de guerre.* Paris: Gallimard, 1942.

Semprun, Jorge. *Adieu, vive clarté . . .* Paris: Gallimard, 1998.

Slocombe, Romain. *Monsieur le Commandant.* Paris: Pocket, 2011.

Soazig, Aaron. *Le Non de Klara.* Paris: Maurice Nadeau, 2002.

Vailland, Roger. *Drôle de jeu: Roman.* Paris: Phébus, 2009.

Films, Filmstrips, and Music

Autant-Lara, Claude, dir. *La Traversée de Paris* (Crossing Paris). Neuilly-sur-Seine, France: Gaumont Video, 2009. DVD.

Bard, Nicole and Barak, dirs. *Ich bin Jude! Ich bin Jude! Jewish Youth Movements' Resistance in Occupied France.* Tel Aviv, Israel: J.M.T. Films, 2005. DVD.

Batty, Peter, dir. *The Battle for Warsaw: The Nazi Annihilation of Poland's Historic Capital.* Newton, NJ: Shanachie Entertainment Corp., 2004. DVD.

Bosch, Roselyne, dir. *La Rafle.* Québec, Canada: Séville Pictures, 2010. DVD.

Carasso, Jean-Gabriel, Boris Cyrulnik, et al. *Nous étions des enfants: Dix-huit témoignages d'enfants rescapés des rafles et des camps de la Seconde Guerre Mondial.* Paris: L'Oizeau rare, 2011. DVD.

Chabrol, Claude, dir. *The Eye of Vichy (L'Oeil de Vichy).* New York: First Run Features Home Video, 1993. DVD.

Clarke, Isabelle, and Daniel Costelle, dirs. *L'Occupation intime.* Issy-les-Moulineaux, France: TF1 Vidéo, 2011. DVD.

Clément, René, dir. *La Bataille du rail* (The Battle of the Rails). Chicago: Faces Multimedia, 2006. DVD.

————.*Is Paris Burning?* Hollywood, CA: Paramount Home Entertainment, 2003. DVD.

Clouzot, Henri-Georges, dir. *Le Corbeau.* New York: Criterion Collection, 2004. DVD.

Cohen, Peter, dir. *The Architecture of Doom.* New York: First Run Features, 1995. DVD.

Cozarinsky, Edgardo, dir. *La Guerre d'un seul homme, d'après les "Journaux parisiens" d'Ernst Jünger.* Paris: Marion's Films et INA (Institut National de l'Audiovisuel), 1981. DVD.

Curtiz, Michael, dir. *Casablanca.* Burbank, CA: Warner Home Video, 2003. DVD.

Drach, Michel, dir. *Les Violons du bal.* Santa Monica, CA: Connoisseur Video Collection, 1993. VHS.

Frankenheimer, John, dir. *The Train.* Santa Monica, CA: MGM Home Entertainment, 2005. DVD.

Guédiguian, Robert, dir. *L'Armée du crime.* London: StudioCanal, 2010. DVD.

Halimi, André, dir. *Délation sous l'Occupation/Chantons sous l'Occupation.* Paris: Editions Montparnasse, 2009. DVD.

Isaacs, Jeremy, prod. *The World at War.* New York: A&E Home Video, 2004.

Jeuland, Yves, dir. *Being Jewish in France* (Comme un juif en France). Waltham, MA: National Center for Jewish Film, 2007. DVD.

Kern, Jerome, with Oscar Hammerstein. "The Last Time I Saw Paris." New York: Chappell, 1940.

Lanzmann, Claude. *Shoah.* Irvington, NY: Criterion Collection, 2013. DVD.

Losey, Joseph, dir. *Monsieur Klein.* Home Vision Entertainment, 2004. DVD.

Madsen, Ole Christian, dir. *Flame and Citron.* Toronto, Canada: Mongrel Media, 2009. DVD.

Malle, Louis, dir. *Au revoir les enfants.* Irvington, NY: Criterion Collection, 2006. DVD.

————.*Lacombe Lucien.* Irvington, NY: Criterion Collection, 2006. DVD.

McLeod, Norman Z., dir. *Lady Be Good.* Culver City, CA: MGM/UA Home Video, 1991. DVD.

Melville, Jean-Pierre, dir. *L'Armée des ombres* (Army of Shadows). Irvington, NY: Criterion Collection, 2007. DVD.

————.*Le Silence de la mer.* MKS Video: Distributed by Water Bearer Films, 1997. DVD.

Mitrani, Michel, dir. *Les Guichets du Louvre* (Gateways to the Louvre). Paris: Les Films de Parnasse, 2007. DVD.

Ophüls, Marcel, dir. *Le Chagrin et la pitié: Chronique d'une ville française sous l'Occupation* (The Sorrow and the Pity: Chronicle of a French City Under the Occupation). Neuilly-sur-Seine, France: Gaumont Video, 2011. DVD.

Paquet-Brenner, Gilles, dir. *Elle s'appelait Sarah* (Sarah's Key). Issy-les-Moulineaux, France: TF1 Video, 2011. DVD.

Resnais, Alain, dir. *Hiroshima mon amour.* Irvington, NY: Criterion Collection, 2003. DVD.

————.*Nuit et brouillard* (Night and Fog). Irvington, NY: Criterion Collection, 2003. DVD.

Ronce, Philippe, dir. *Archives de guerre 1940–1945: Ce que les Français ont vu dans les salles de cinéma.* Paris: INA (Institut National de l'Audiovisuel), 2004. DVD.

Rossellini, Roberto, dir. *Germany, Year Zero.* Irvington, NY: Criterion Collection, 2010. DVD.

————.*Roma, città aperta.* Irvington, NY: Criterion Collection, 2010. DVD.

Selected Bibliography

Schuler, Hannes, dir. *Hitler's Museum: The Secret History of Art Theft During World War II.* West Long Branch, NJ: Kultur, 2009. DVD.

Spielberg, Steven, dir. *Schindler's List.* Universal City, CA: Universal Studios Home Entertainment, 2004. DVD.

Tarantino, Quentin, dir. *Inglourious Basterds.* Universal City, CA: Universal Studios Home Entertainment, 2009. DVD.

Truffaut, François, dir. *Le Dernier métro* (The Last Metro). Irvington, NY: Criterion Collection, 2009. DVD.

Viseur, Reinhardt, ed. *Jazz sous l'Occupation.* Paris: Universal Music/Gitanes Jazz Productions, 2002. CD.

Waren, Mark. *Dancing Lessons: A Documentary Film.* New York: Dramatic Risks, Inc., 2010. DVD.

Index

Note: *Italic* page numbers refer to illustrations.

About the Author

Ronald C. Rosbottom was born in New Orleans and raised in the American South. He was educated at Tulane University and Princeton University, and he taught at the University of Pennsylvania and the Ohio State University. For the past two and a half decades he has been a professor at Amherst College in Massachusetts, where he is the holder of an endowed chair, the Winifred Arms Professsorship in the Arts and the Humanities. He has published extensively, editing or authoring five books and dozens of articles and reviews on French and English narrative literature. For many years, he was the executive secretary and a member of the executive board of the Amercian Society for Eighteenth-Century Studies. At Amherst, he has taught courses on the history of Paris, the legends of Napolean, and on how World War II has been represented in film and literature. A frequent visitor to Paris and France, Rosbottom is married to cookbook author Betty Rosbottom and lives in Massachusetts.